The Writing Teacher as Researcher

THE WRITING TEACHER AS RESEARCHER

Essays in the Theory and
Practice of Class-Based Research

Edited by

Donald A. Daiker

and

Max Morenberg

Both of Miami University

BOYNTON/COOK PUBLISHERS
HEINEMANN
Portsmouth, NH

BOYNTON/COOK PUBLISHERS
A division of
HEINEMANN EDUCATIONAL BOOKS, INC.
70 Court Street, Portsmouth, NH 03801
Offices and agents throughout the world

The publishers and the authors wish to thank the students and teachers whose words and writings are quoted here for permission to reproduce them, and to the following for permission to quote from previously published works:

Pages 48–50: From R. Gebhardt and D. Rodrigues, *Writing: Processes and Intentions* (Lexington, MA: D.C. Heath, 1989), pp. 15, 17–18, 19, 21. Reprinted by permission of the publisher.

Page 74: From Jerome Bruner, *Actual Minds, Possible Worlds* (Cambridge: Harvard University Press, 1986), pp. 9–10. Copyright © 1986 by the President and Fellows of Harvard College. Reprinted by permission.

Every effort has been made to contact the copyright holders and the students and their parents for permission to reprint borrowed material. We regret any oversights that may have occurred and would be happy to rectify them in future printings of this work.

Library of Congress Cataloging-in-Publication Data

The Writing teacher as researcher: essays in the theory and practice
   of class-based research / edited by Donald A. Daiker and Max
   Morenberg.
      p.   cm.
   Includes bibliographical references.
   ISBN 0-86709-255-6
   1. English language—Composition and exercises—Evaluation.
   2. Education—Research—Methodology.   I. Daiker, Donald A., 1938-
   . II. Morenberg, Max, 1940-
   LB1576.W75 1990
   370'.7'8—dc20   89-36957
                                                                   CIP

Printed in the United States of America.

90 91 92 93 94 9 8 7 6 5 4 3 2 1

for
ANDREW KEREK
Scholar, Colleague, Friend

Contents

Preface

The twenty-five essays that appear in this volume were originally presented at the Third Miami University Conference on the Teaching of Writing in October 1988. The conference was titled "The Writing Teacher as Researcher: Learning from Our Students." It focused on studies in which students play an important and conscious role in research and in which teachers become learners within their own classrooms in order to be educated by their students.

The three-day conference, which attracted more than five hundred students and teachers, consisted of sixteen featured addresses, eight half-day workshops, and over eighty other presentations during concurrent sessions.

For help both in organizing the conference and in creating this volume of essays, we are indebted to a number of our colleagues. The Program Committee, responsible for reading and evaluating more than 200 proposals, consisted of Sara Farris, Mary Fuller, Nedra Grogan, John Heyda, Susan C. Jarratt, Naton Leslie, Diane Rawlings, and Jeffrey Sommers, all of Miami University; DJ Hammond of Madeira High School; Mary Johnson of Kramer Elementary School; Andrew Kerek of Bowling Green State University; and Chester H. Laine and Lucille M. Schultz of the University of Cincinnati. Conference Coordinators were Sara Farris, Nedra Grogan, Brian Kennedy, Naton Leslie, Corinne Miller, Diane Rawlings, Karen Slaper, and Gregg Wentzell.

The conference was made possible by a generous grant from the Exxon Education Foundation. Other support came from the Ohio Writing Project (Mary Fuller, Max Morenberg, and Janet Ziegler, Co-Directors), from the Miami University Center for the Study of Writing (Jeffrey Sommers, Director), and from the Miami University Department of English (C. Barry Chabot, Chair). Co-sponsors included the National Council of Teachers of English and its state affiliate, the Ohio Council of Teachers of English Language Arts.

The publication of this volume is supported by funds provided by the Exxon Education Foundation, for which we are grateful to the Foundation and its Research Director, Richard R. Johnson. We also thank our friend and editor, Peter R. Stillman, for his help and encouragement.

Donald A. Daiker
Max Morenberg

THE
THEORY
OF TEACHER
RESEARCH

1

The Teacher as Researcher: Democracy, Dialogue, and Power

James A. Berlin

One of the most important discussions of the teacher as researcher is a collection of essays assembled by Dixie Goswami and Peter Stillman. Its title is particularly telling: *Reclaiming the Classroom: Teacher Research as an Agency for Change*. The militancy of the formulation and its placement within a conflictive context are unmistakable. One obvious thesis of this collection is that teachers have been deprived of the power to control their pedagogical activities; another is just as obviously the positing of a new conception of the classroom teacher, defined in terms of a particular notion of research, as an agent for effecting change. It is curious to note, however, that despite the unmistakably political and polemical quality of its title, the volume offers little discussion of larger economic, social, and cultural conditions in addressing the issues at hand. Instead, the conflict is seen in terms of competing research paradigms—quantitative against qualitative—and different levels of the educational hierarchy—college teachers against teachers in the grades. I offer this observation, however, not to disparage this collection of essays and the phenomenon it examines. I would instead like to use this omission as an occasion for addressing this absence, situating the teacher-as-researcher development within the larger social and political context. One of my major concerns will be an examination of the ways it is an inevitable and appropriate response to the assault on education that has taken place during the last twenty years or so. I will in addition explore those elements of the development that I find most important given this larger context of antagonism. My thesis is that the teacher-as-researcher concept contains the seeds of a new model for the teaching profession—a model described elsewhere by such observers as Paulo Freire, Ira Shor, and Stanley Aronowitz and Henry Giroux as the "transformative teacher." Since I also readily admit that these seeds are as yet scattered and only partially nurtured in the formulations put forth by the materials in Goswami and Stillman, this chapter will also attempt to point to suggestions for future developments in the ongoing discussion.

No one reading this volume needs to be told that public education and those most directly involved in it have been under attack for at least twenty years. This has been adequately documented in Joel Spring's history of U.S. schools, in Shor's *Culture Wars: School and Society in the Conservative Restoration 1969–1984*, and in Aronowitz and Giroux's *Education under Siege*. Here I would like to examine briefly the form this assault has taken in recent years.

The political strategy adopted by the Reagan administration was an unabashedly combative one, aggressively charging the schools with failing to meet the needs of our nation. Significantly, these needs were defined in explicitly economic terms. For example, after an interview with outgoing Secretary of Education William J. Bennett, Edward B. Fiske of the *New York Times* explained that, for the Reagan administration, "the overriding educational issue of the day" has been "how to improve the quality of public schools so that the United States could remain economically competitive with the rest of the developed world" (*Council-Grams*, May 1988, p. 1). Schools were made directly accountable for the success or failure of the American economy, with such mammoth concerns as gross national product, balance of trade payments, and unemployment rates placed at the doorstep of the neighborhood school. The remarkable feature of this development is that if this argument is followed to its logical conclusion, the schools ought now to be enjoying showers of praise for having achieved a resounding success. As George Bush continually reminded us during his presidential campaign, our nation is undergoing a period of exceptional economic prosperity: employment is up, taxes are down, and inflation has remained under control. Economic conditions, he repeatedly assured us, have rarely been rosier. Given the blame that schools have shouldered for the economic downturn of the 1970s and early 1980s, one would think, now that the economy according to Reagan and Bush has become robust, that the schools would at last be given their fair share of applause.

Kudos for our nation's schools have, however, not been forthcoming, and the reason is not difficult to discern. While economic conditions were used to designate the schools a failure, the measure applied to them, now that the economy has been declared a success, has been removed from the economic arena altogether. Suddenly student scores on the ubiquitous nationally normed standardized tests are hauled to center stage to continue the villification of education. As William Bennett charged in a final blast at the schools before leaving his cabinet post, the follow-up study of *A Nation at Risk* (1983) has shown a modest improvement in our schools, but one still "unacceptably low." For Bennett, "our students know too little, and their command of essential skills is too slight." He went on to focus on the real villains in this whole affair: teachers' unions and other educational groups have done little to address these failures, instead pursuing a "narrow, self-interested exercise of political power" to preserve the status quo, while engaging in "extortion" by demanding more federal spending for our schools (*Council-Grams*, September 1988, p. 3). (This "extortion," I should add, was obviously not successful since, as *Time* for 12 September 1988 reported, federal spending for elementary and secondary education during the Reagan years was reduced by 20 percent in inflation-adjusted dollars, while defense spending was up 37 percent.) This duplicitous strategy enabled the Reagan administration to take credit for those who profited from its economic policy, and to blame the schools for those who were victimized by it—for example, the 1 million adults and one hundred thousand children who sleep in the streets every night, the 31 million people without health insurance, and the holders of the 8 million new poverty-level jobs.

Here I want to consider in some detail the reliance on test scores to evaluate the schools, since it is these that are among the strongest forces taking the classroom away from the teacher and making schools the hapless instruments of a mechanistic and limited notion of education. Teachers, it should be first emphasized, have responded strongly to the calls for better test scores. A congressional budget office request for 1986 reported that "scores have been going up nationwide for more than a decade in the lower grades and nearly a decade at the senior high level" (Koretz, p. 13). The ability of teachers to meet the demands of standardized tests, then, is not really at issue. A number of other grave matters, however, are.

Not the least of the complaints against standardized tests is that they encourage practices among school administrators that are highly questionable on ethical grounds. When standardized tests are given great weight in judging a district's performance, there is strong motivation to choose a test that will make a district look especially successful. This strategy can take a number of forms. Since national norms for standardized tests are not determined yearly, the administration of a school district may decide to select a test that has not recently been recalibrated. At a time of rising test scores, such as the late 1980s, this means that a school district can register very impressive gains by selecting a test that relies on an old norm. This phenomenon is partly behind the so-called "Lake Woebegon" effect. It is possible for a disproportionate number of students to be above average in a community if a test based on an out-of-date norm is used. Another strategy for inflating a district's test scores is to choose a test that closely matches a district's curriculum. This in itself is not problematic. It does, however, distort the results of making comparisons since some school districts—say those with innovative curricula—will not be able to locate nationally standardized tests that match their practices. More to the point, certain tests may begin to determine the kind of curricula adopted by schools—in effect, destroying innovation. Notice, furthermore, that outright cheating is not being discussed here—giving students test items in advance, for example—but practices that are legal and impossible to prevent, although located on the margins of the ethical in their effects on scores.

Of course, one of the most dangerous results of standardized tests is that they encourage (and sometimes require) teachers to teach to the tests. This is the most devastating of the effects of these tests on the quality of our schools. As RAND Corporation testing expert Daniel Koretz points out, teaching to the test can narrow the curriculum, excluding nontested items from the classroom—art, music, and even science and writing, for example, the heart of the liberal arts' emphasis on creative and critical thinking. Standardized tests, furthermore, are virtually without items not couched in the multiple-choice format. While this kind of test can evaluate some learning effectively— mechanical skills such as recognizing misspelled words or nonprivileged grammars and usages—it does not provide the ability to generate correctly spelled words and the authorized version of grammer and usage. In other words, these devices test the passive recognition of error rather than the active generation of thoughtful discourse. There is also evidence, furthermore, that most multiple-choice tests do not assess what are called "higher-order skills." Thus, while factual recall is tested, the ability to reason in a way appropriate to solving problems is not. Teaching to standardized tests results in encouraging certain lower-level skills needed for higher-level skills, but discourages the teaching of the higher-level skills themselves. There is even evidence that the twenty-five-year decline in SAT scores may be the result of teaching for standardized tests. (I realize these test scores have gone up slightly since 1980, but experts still describe them as in decline.) In a recent Gannett News Service interview, Herbert C. Riedman, education professor at Michigan State University and coauthor of the SAT, explained that the "youngsters contributing most to test score decline are the highest achieving students, not the lowest ones" ("Tests Becoming the End"). While students in the bottom 25 percent of the population taking the test have shown slow, modest gains, the higher range of scores have steadily declined. Such a result could indeed be hypothesized of an education in which there was a focus on lower-level skills to the neglect of higher-level skills.

It is clear that not much can be said in favor of using standardized tests as the sole instrument for assessing achievement, especially for purposes of accountability. Practices ranging from the downright unethical to the morally marginal have been encouraged, and the curriculum across the nation as a whole has suffered an appreciable loss. Besides, the results of these tests are almost always predictable. As Christopher Jencks has demonstrated, tests reflect class, race, ethnic, and gender inequities in our society. This means that if we figure out a way to improve, for example, working class math scores or Hispanic verbal scores, the same devices will be used immediately in the more privileged sectors of the schools. The relative ranking will thus remain the same. Furthermore, as Bowles and Gintis have shown, neither the relative distribution of wealth nor the relative distribution of education has changed much in the last twenty-five years. More schooling, for example, has not meant more wealth for most: it has simply resulted in an increase in the years of education required for most jobs. Young people now need more education than their parents had simply to keep even with their parents' standard of living. The problem with a meritocracy is that there are always more skilled workers than there are slots for them to fill (Wallerstein). As a result, the educational ante for good jobs keeps getting stiffer and stiffer. Standardized tests, then, simply legitimate the status quo, providing "objective" evidence for the inevitability of class, race, ethnic, and gender inequities in our system, while supporting these inequities, as we have seen, by the kinds of schooling they encourage.

The immediate response of teachers to these tests ought to be formal and informal efforts to make both the public and school officials aware of their dangers. This should take the form of letters and calls to local school board members and school administrators. Information pointing to the pitfalls of testing should also be sent to these officials so that their decisions can be better informed. Professional organizations at all levels must likewise make an effort to resist the uses of standardized tests that contribute to poor teaching and poor learning. We probably cannot soon get rid of standardized tests, but at least we can get school administrators to use them appropriately—as devices that provide information helpful in evaluating a given school's performance (helpful, however, only in connection with other evidence). Such efforts have already begun to have their effects, and this leads me to the second part of my argument.

A number of articles have appeared in newspapers lately reporting the results of teacher resistance to curricular decisions based exclusively on improving test performance. This of course has been long in coming, and the effects of its delay have been devastating. Two recent polls of teachers have revealed the depth of dissatisfaction experienced by teachers nationwide. A survey by the Carnegie Foundation for the Advancement of Teaching discovered that only 63 percent of teachers nationally felt they had any voice in shaping the curriculum, and in some states the figure was as low as 40 percent. Fewer than 10 percent felt they had any effect on teacher evaluation and on selecting new teachers and administrators. Ernest L. Boyer, president of the surveying group, eloquently summarized the meaning of the survey: "During the past five years, academic requirements have been tightened, standards have been raised, but most of the mandates for reform have been imposed top-down, and we're beginning to discover that outside regulation has its limits" ("Teachers Feel They Lack Influence"). These "limits" have diminished teacher morale, leading many to question their decision to enter the profession. After all, most of us enter education not for money, but out of a desire to serve our communities while maintaining a measure of creativity and control in our lives. What too many have recently found instead is a heavy reliance on cut-and-dried workbooks and other "teacher-proof" materials, and narrow prescriptions from above on the activities to be permitted in the classroom. Teachers are being proletarianized, their jobs reduced to mechanical techniques requiring little or no creative and critical thinking. As Mary Hatwood Futrell, president of the National Education Association, commented: "The [Carnegie] report endorses what I have often said—that teachers are treated like very tall children instead of professionals" ("Teachers Feel They Lack Influence").

These conditions, however, *are* at last being challenged, and teachers are leading this effort. A fifty-state survey by reporters from the Associated Press recently concluded: "After spending five years and billions of tax dollars raising classroom standards and teacher salaries, some states and school districts are turning to the teachers themselves to lead the next leg of the journey to better schools" ("School Reform Takes Another Twist"). (Teachers may be forgiven an ironic smile at their being consulted in desperation, only after all other measures have failed.) The top-down reforms of the mid-1980s are being replaced by teacher-initiated programs in a number of states. In Rochester, New York, for example, the school system has coupled a substantial pay raise (the top salary for classroom teachers has been set at $70,000) with "school-based planning teams in which teachers and administrators will plan how to run their schools relatively free of school board interference." A similar school-based curricular design plan is being implemented in Miami, Florida. And the state of Washington is taking this concept even further by implementing in twenty-one school districts a program in which teachers are being paid additional stipends to reorganize curricula and classrooms to meet the special needs of their district's students ("School Reform Takes Another Twist").

Of course, perhaps the most important effect of this effort to reinstate the teacher's role in the shaping of the English curriculum and classroom has been the notion of the "teacher as researcher." Critics of standardized testing who point to the higher-order skills that are not addressed in the multiple-choice format invariably advise, in the words of one, that teachers "must be encouraged to rely routinely on measures such as essays, term papers, experiments, and debates, far beyond the limited extent to which such measures are standardized for accountability" (Koretz, p. 12). In other words, they are calling for the development of those abilities that use language effectively in reading, writing, and speaking—the particular province of the English teacher. Therefore, if teachers as a group are to regain control of their classrooms to enhance learning, English studies must be at the center of the effort. After all, English remains in most states the only subject required of students during each year of schooling. In addition, recent developments in the study of language in philosophy, sociology, psychology, as well as linguistics, literature, and composition have all underscored the central place of language in all human activity. Language, we are now beginning to see, does not simply record our experience, it actually shapes it, structuring it in a way that determines what we see and do not see, what we know and do not know, who we are and who we are not. The lesson of the linguistic turn in the human sciences is clear: language is determinative in the very formation of self and society. Figures as diverse as French poststructuralists and American neopragmatists (the latter followers of John Dewey) underscore this theme.

The teacher-as-researcher model is located at the intersection of all of these developments, representing a direct response to the social, political, and cultural moment. It is first of all important to point out that the potential of the model for bringing about worthwhile change resides in its regarding *all* teachers as researchers. In other words, each and every teacher is to be considered responsible for researching her students, and doing so in order to improve the quality of student learning, not purely for purposes of publication. Publication of some research findings is inevitable and desirable, but to emphasize publication over pedagogy is to encourage the inequitable top-heavy hierarchy of power in the teaching community that already exists, a distribution of power that the teacher-as-researcher movement is openly designed to challenge. The aim of this research then is not primarily to publish but to enable the teacher to understand her students by using research methods that will identify their characteristics as learners. The phenomenon in the United States has been strongly influenced by the methods of ethnographic studies in anthropology, especially as demonstrated in Shirley Brice Heath's work. But it has also profited from the experimental studies of Janet Emig, Donald Graves, Lucy Calkins, Nancie Atwell, Dixie Goswami, Lee Odell, and others. One strength of the methods developed from this research is that it does not require a tight pre- and posttreatment experimental design, instead relying on a context-dependent, nonstatistical model. An additional important strength is that inscribed in its method is a notion of the political and ideological nature of learning and teaching that denies the claims to objectivity forwarded in other kinds of educational research, especially of a quantitative nature. This last feature deserves closer examination.

The teacher-as-researcher program in writing emphasizes the study of the unique language practices of students in their particular social setting. It includes, as in the work of Shirley Brice Health and Gail Martin, for example, a consideration of the relation between class and learning *and* race and learning. Significantly, rather than relying on the research of distant university experts to determine classroom and curriculum decisions, the writing teacher is encouraged to conduct her own research, to investigate the conditions of her own social setting in determining instructional content and strategies. It is important, furthermore, to note the democratic character of the program. Teachers are engaged in challenging the hierarchical power structures of the schools, as they make their own decisions about instruction and use their own expertise to analyze their own situations. Sometimes this takes the form of a collaborative effort by teachers to rewrite an entire curriculum, as Nancie Atwell reports. Sometimes it simply means replacing prescribed teacher-centered classroom activities with original student-centered activities devised by the teachers themselves. This democratization of authority, however, also extends to students. They too are empowered in this classroom since their language patterns in all their cultural uniqueness are privileged, are indeed called upon as the basis for learning effective language use. Rather than imposing language practices, replacing the students' mode with the institution's, this method builds on the students' socially determined disposition in language use as the source of growth in complexity and competence. The result of such a classroom is that teacher and students are both learners, sharing the discovery process in a community that often includes a democratic sharing of authority.

The teacher-as-researcher concept displays the potential to become a revolutionary force in schooling. It is changing the consciousness of teachers, making them aware of a democratic and empowering response to their victimization by social, political, and cultural forces. As I noted earlier, this development bears the seeds of genuine change, making our schools more democratic and just, and our society more responsive to its members. My main reservation about the teacher-as-researcher plan as it is manifested in the United States—particularly in the discussion in Goswami and Stillman's excellent collection—is that it is not emphasizing and problematizing its own political agenda. It seems to me that the sort of ethnographic method it recommends makes inevitable a confrontation with the inescapably value-inscribed quality of all schooling. As is suggested in the theoretical statements of Garth Boomer, Ann E. Berthoff, Mina Shaughnessy, and Heath, and in the research of Atwell and Martin, schools are places where ideological and political battles are enacted, with sharp conflicts among classes, races, and genders about the distribution of wealth and privilege. But in all of their various essays this theme is only suggested, not placed front and center. The teacher-as-researcher program in U.S. English studies—unlike its counterpart abroad, called "action research"—has thus far avoided addressing this matter directly. It must do so eventually if it is to survive, and I wish to suggest that guidelines for this effort can be found in the work of Ira Shor and Stanley Aronowitz and Henry Giroux. The three are staunch critics of American education, Shor as a teacher in English studies at Staten Island College, City University of New York, Giroux as a professor in the education department at Miami University, and Aronowitz as a sociologist at City University of New York. They all call extensively on the Frankfurt School and Paolo Freire, with Giroux and Aronowitz also invoking Antonio Gramsci. And all three have themselves forwarded the notion of teacher as researcher, much along the lines found in the various voices assembled in Goswami and Stillman. The important difference is that they have explicitly problematized the political and ideological in promoting their notion of teacher as researcher, a figure they refer to as the "transformative teacher" or the "transformative intellectual."

Like the supporters of the teacher-as-researcher program, these observers encourage democratic relations in the school as a preparation for participation in a democratic society, and they are dedicated to schools as places for individual and social empowerment. The important difference is that they see the school as the site of intense ideological conflict, a place, as Aronowitz and Giroux explain, "of struggle over what forms of authority, orders of representation, forms of moral regulation, and versions of the past should be legitimated, passed on, and debated" (p. 32). The political nature of education is thus openly acknowledged, and the teacher is made responsible for formulating a conscious political position. This means recognizing and resisting the inequities in our society, the economic, social, and political injustices inscribed in class, race, ethnic, and gender relations—relations that privilege the few and discriminate against the many. Furthermore, the teacher must not only note the differences in language and learning patterns in her students, but she must also relate these to their economic, social, and cultural causes and effects. The teacher must act as a critic of her discoveries as a researcher, not merely a recorder. Teachers in the schools, in addition, are especially well situated to act as "organic" intellectuals (to use Gramsci's term), sharing and representing the interests of their students. Teachers are, after all, themselves marginalized, discriminated against in salary and working conditions, made responsible for the victimization of their students as well as themselves, and ignored by those in power (often, one suspects, because so many teachers are women). At the same time, teachers have mastered the register of the dominant discourse, enabling them to articulate the injustices they encounter in school and society in this language, exerting their power as trained intellectuals.

The transformative intellectual provides a classroom that likewise resembles the model for the teacher as researcher, and Ira Shor's description of it is particularly useful for readers of this volume since he is himself a writing teacher. Classroom activities are of course grounded in the teacher's own study of her students. Citing the research strategies of Heath as well as Noelle Bisseret and Richard Hoggart, Shor argues that the teacher must situate learning "inside the languages, themes, and cognitive levels of the students" ("Educating the Educators," p. 24), and that this can be done only by studying the students themselves. The teacher must then familiarize students with cross-cultural communication—language that cuts across race, class, ethnic, and gender lines—an activity as important to the advantaged as to the disadvantaged. This of course requires dialogue in the classroom, interchanges that make learning participatory. This dialogue, furthermore, will invoke problem-posing, what Shor calls "desocializing students," making them aware of the concealed contradictions in their experience and encouraging them to talk and write about them. It is important here that the teacher respond appropriately to the language habits of her students, taking care not to overwhelm them with her verbal dexterity as a member of the educated. This dexterity also makes possible, however, a bidialectalism for teacher and student.

This dialogic classroom is intended to encourage students to be critical of their experience, making them transformative intellectuals in their own right. Shor explains: "Critical literacy invites teachers and students to *problematize* all subjects of study, that is, to understand existing knowledge as historical products deeply invested with the values of those who developed such knowledge." For this teacher, all learning is based in values, and reading, writing, and talking in the classroom must challenge the "dominant myths" in society, going "beneath the surface to understand the origin, structure, and consequences of any body of knowledge, technical process, or object under study." Students then research their own language, their own society, their own learning, just as the teacher does, examining the values inscribed in their experience. Learning for students and teachers, furthermore, also becomes a form "of research and experimentation, testing hypotheses, examining items, questioning what we know" ("Educating the Educators," p. 24). This means that the way schools are run, the way the classroom is conducted, the way the students relate to each other, are all subject to questioning and examination, locating conflicts and problems and addressing them. Such a classroom is thus situated in the student's own experience as it takes students from the role of passive objects to the role of active subjects of their experience—doing not what they are told, but learning to decide for themselves what to do to recognize, understand, and change their own environments. It is not enough, for example, simply to record the language practices and histories of one's family. It is also necessary to understand how this history and language came to be. This of course often involves coming face to face with inequality and injustice, and considering ways to create change. Students in this kind of classroom in fact become authorized to make changes in their own school environment as preparation for actively affecting larger social structures later on. A classroom and school environment that is open to student and teacher intervention, furthermore, is important for all students, regardless of race, gender, and social class. All students in a democracy need school experiences that are participatory, critical, values-oriented, multicultured, student-centered, and research-minded. Anything less denies the promises of our nation's constitutional guarantees.

Transformative teachers must also work outside the school to make possible the conditions of the critical classroom. They must join with other transformative teachers as well as with established teacher associations, undertaking projects that, in the words of Aronowitz and Giroux, "interrogate existing school curricula, the hidden curricula, policy formation at the local and state levels, the form and content of school texts, and the working conditions under which teachers operate" (p. 41). Teachers must become involved in school board elections, in local school councils, and in parent-teacher groups, articulating their democratic and liberating notions of schooling. They must also support alone and collectively political candidates, as well as form alliances with other groups working for emancipation—with ecologists, feminists, peace groups, trade unions, and neighborhood groups. In other words, the transformative teacher-researcher is engaged in the community, serving as an example for her students of political agency, in the classroom and outside of it. It is through these means that teachers can improve their working conditions—again, collectively as well as alone—implementing the kind of institutional support and services called for by the workers in Goswami and Stillman, and echoed by Shor, Aronowitz, and Giroux: "conditions that will allow them to reflect, read, share their work with others, produce curriculum materials, publish their achievements for teachers and others outside of their local schools, etc." (Aronowitz and Giroux, p. 42). The aim, furthermore, will be more democratic and just schools for a more democratic and just society.

In closing I would like to reiterate that my intention here has been not to deny but to offer a focused and expanded version of what I take to be the tacit politics of *Reclaiming the Classroom: Teacher Research as an Agency for Change*. I realize I am open to the criticism leveled at me by Janet Emig at the 1988 New Hampshire Conference on Writing: "If Berlin wants to know my politics, why doesn't he just ask?" My answer is the poststructuralist assertion that language speaks us as much as we speak language (as Donald Murray in another chapter in the present collection seems to be saying). In other words, political and ideological positions are often voiced in indirect and unconscious ways. I should also say, however, that virtually every feature of the transformative teacher described by Shor and Aronowitz and Giroux can be located in isolation in one or another of the voices in *Reclaiming the Classroom*. My real fear about the attenuated politics of the U.S. version of "action research" is finally that its democratic, egalitarian, and contestatory qualities will be lost through appropriation by the very forces it opposes. It is not difficult for me to imagine state-mandated versions of the teacher-as-researcher model that locate in students the confirmation of the eternal truths of competitive individualism, economic exploitation, patriarchy, racism, and class division—complete with a fill-in-the-blank workbook provided by a major publisher. Teachers must emphasize the oppositional nature of their work as researchers, questioning the forces that would make them technicians in the reproduction of an exploitational social order. It is gratifying to report that this new collection of essays gives us every reason to have faith that resistance and rebuilding have begun in earnest. The long revolution continues its inexorable course.

2
Teaching, Reflecting, Researching

GEORGE HILLOCKS, JR.

Teaching, reflecting, researching: generally, we regard these terms as representing distinct activities. We think of *teaching* as what we do in front of a classroom. *Reflecting* is a term usually associated with an armchair—a philosophical activity. *Researching* carries the connotations of scientific method. On the other hand, they have something in common. In a very important sense, effective teaching must involve both reflecting and researching. In teaching we involve students in certain activities in the hope that they will learn something. In research we undertake a series of actions in the hope of discovering something. Both research and teaching have goals, involve observation, and predict results. We can use the language of research to describe teaching. The teacher hypothesizes that an activity will help students learn, engages students in the activity, observes the process, and evaluates the results.

Let me provide a simple example. I have a tape recording of my receiving a bagpipe lesson from an expert Scots piper, trying to teach me to play pibroch, a classical Scottish Highlands bagpipe music, which, like a fugue, develops from a simple melodic line setting the mood and rhythmic pattern for everything that follows. I am learning to play one phrase of three notes. To begin with, he hears me play it and is dissatisfied with the way I render the second note. He plays the phrase for me and asks that I try it again. I do. "No," he says, "make the note thin." He plays it again, says "Just make it thin." I try once more, and fail. He says, "Well, glide off it; make it thin and glide off it." He plays it again. I try again. He says, "You're getting it, but don't bring your finger off so fast, just glide off it gently. It's a gentle note. It's a thin, gentle note. You ken what I mean?" I try it again, and this time he is satisfied. He says, "You've got it. Now try it again." I try it again and fail. "No," he says. He goes through the metaphors again and adds, "Don't jerk your finger up." I try it again. "You've got it now. Just do it again." I do it

This research was supported in part by a grant from the Benton Center for Curriculum and Instruction.

several times, and finally he is satisfied that I have learned to play one note of a massive composition.

Here this teacher has a very specific goal. His first hypothesis is that I will be able to imitate what he plays. He collects data and finds that it was an incorrect assumption. I have not been able to play it simply by imitation. He develops a new hypothesis: that a metaphor will help me. And he tests that one. Failing again, he tries two metaphors. Finally, he ends by trying to put all his metaphors together, demonstrating one more time, and finally I play the note as he had hoped I would. In the process of doing all this, he has also collected certain data concerning the perspicacity and coordination of his student. Those observations suggest yet another hypothesis, namely, that the student will require several repetitions of this very brief phrase to "get it."

A final parallel between teaching and researching is that we learn something from both. In research we set out to learn something—to teach ourselves something, as it were. In teaching we set out to help someone else learn, but if we are astute we also learn something on the way. My bagpipe teacher may have learned more about the abilities of his student than anything else. On the other hand, he may have learned a new metaphor that he can use in the future. In teaching English our goals are far more complex than the goal in this example. We ask that our students learn to construe and create meaning for themselves. That demands far more complex kinds of learning than the relatively simple imitation involved in the bagpipe lesson. When the goals of teaching are so complex, it is imperative that we learn from what we do.

What makes it possible to learn from our teaching? The answer, I think, is reflection. Reflection in teaching involves observation, assessment, and speculation about alternatives. My piping teacher had to listen to what I played, assess it, and think of alternative ways to instruct me. The number of times he had to instruct me suggests that reflection also involves the patience to play with ideas perhaps, restructure our thinking, and try again. Clearly, reflection is involved in both research and teaching.

However, the nature of reflection in these two activities discriminates sharply between them. A researcher has the leisure to examine other relevant research, consider alternatives, restructure or redesign the problem, and retest it. A teacher, on the other hand, must perceive problems in action and exercise what Donald Schon calls reflection-in-action. When teachers are reflective during practice, they must make almost instantaneous assessments of conditions in terms of the goals they have, their knowledge of the field and related research, and the accumulated wisdom of practice. They must frame problems and consider alternatives very quickly, intuitively, without the leisure of the researcher.

At the same time, however, teachers must also have the kind of reflective nature that philosophers have. Teachers need to question their goals, their planning, their practice, and their methods of assessment. Only in part can these be examined empirically. For example, no amount of research will tell us what are the most appropriate goals for a group of students.

Unfortunately, not all teachers are reflective. Take the example of Ms. A. (The following analysis is based on data collected by Ann Goethals.) Ms. A teaches at an integrated high school in a large city system. About 33 percent of its students are Afro-American, 33 percent Hispanic, and 33 percent white ethnic. Ms. A is regarded as a crackerjack teacher. She teaches all the advanced placement senior classes. In addition, she teaches average tenth grade students. She regards her tenth grade students as having extremely limited backgrounds. Of them she says, "They need to develop a sense of history, and many kids don't have that. They have very much a sense of tunnel vision. They don't understand anything about the world around them except what's right there in front of them." When she teaches poetry, she first reads a poem aloud and then takes students through it line by line, or perhaps "section by section." She asks questions that get at what she calls "basic comprehension of what's going on." Then she takes them back "to look at various parts of the poem: What does this say to you? How do you feel about it? What does the poet think about here?" She admits, however, that with the exception of her advanced placement students she usually tells students what "the deeper meanings" are. She says that "most of the time the students do not have enough depth to find many meanings."

Let us turn to one class. As it opens, Ms. A reminds students that they have an assignment due on Friday, an original sonnet. When Teresa states she missed the class in which the assignment was made, Ms. A summarizes the requirements of a sonnet as follows: "Ultimately, what you have to have [she writes *iambic feet* on the board] are ten syllables in the line. If you think of one word with ten syllables, that would follow this pattern, OK? [Laughter.] Otherwise you would have words that fit the unaccented, accented pattern. That's five iambic feet in each line. You have fourteen lines. Lines one and three rhyme together, and lines two and four, and so on. It has this rhyme scheme: ABAB CDCD EFEF GG. The lines that have the same letters rhyme with each other, so one and three, two and four, five and seven, six and eight, like that. Those rhyme. Any topic. Iambic pentameter, five iambic feet per line. That's due this Friday."

Teresa asks, "If it's less than five iambic feet?" Ms. A responds, "Then you don't really have a true sonnet." But Teresa persists, "Well, can you do it though?" Ms. A responds, "Not if you wish to have a true sonnet. In other words, if you do it, fine. You will turn it in that way. But it won't be a true sonnet, which is what I'm looking for." Rosemary states with some astuteness, "Which your grade will be based on." Ms. A confirms it: "Which your grade will be counted on."

Ms. A teaches in the sense that she conveys information to students who must write it down. And she does this masterfully. Her presentations flow smoothly without any of the syntactic convolutions so common to normal conversation. She orchestrates the classroom discourse with students adding words at certain points. Fourteen of twenty-six students respond at least once. Her talk occasions a good deal of laughter.

At the same time, however, 67 percent of all student responses consist of three or fewer words. Three students account for 61 percent of all the responses. The instruction in a 42-minute period is divided among the sonnet assignment, three poems by different writers, two minilectures on Emily Dickinson, and two brief discussions of worksheet questions related to other poems. Most of these episodes result in students' filling in the blank following a question on a worksheet (e.g., *Q*: What were two major influences on Dickinson's poetry? *A*: Transcendentalism and Puritanism). The students are only incidentally involved in making the class meanings. Their central task is to record (and remember?) certain details that Ms. A regards as important. But none of the episodes seem designed to empower students to read poetry on their own.

The more I think about the lack of reflection exhibited by Ms. A and many others, the more I believe it must be linked to the very common assumption that the bulk of our students cannot learn more than a modicum of what we hope to teach our brightest students. If we assume that most of our students can learn no more than very basic information and skills, or if we assume, with Ms. A and E. D. Hirsch, that teaching such terms as *sonnet*, *Puritanism*, and *transcendentalism* will provide students with the tools for cultural literacy, then there is no need to wonder how we might teach students to construe or create meaning for themselves. However, if we assume with Benjamin S. Bloom that most (95 percent) of our students, given appropriate teaching and time, can learn as much as students receiving A's do with conventional methods, then we must become reflective about all dimensions of teaching.

What is involved in being reflective? To illustrate, let me describe briefly the experience of some prospective teachers that appears to help them become reflective. The students are five young people in the University of Chicago's Master of Arts in Teaching English program. One major goal of the program is attitudinal. M.A.T.'s should assume that most of their students want to learn and are capable of learning. The second major goal of the program is to help

M.A.T.'s learn to teach so that they advance their own students toward independence in reading and writing, as makers of meaning. To do that, they need to learn how to be reflective about their students, goals, planning, practice, and assessments. Judgments and decisions about each of these are indeterminate and vary from class to class and from day to day. They cannot be made mechanically, but must be the product of reflection about specific circumstances based on knowledge of theory, research, and practice.

Early in their program, the M.A.T.'s teach writing to what the Chicago public school near us calls the "low-level language arts class" of seventh graders. The group works out the general plans for the "workshop" together, laying out the general goals for the four weeks as well as the specific daily goals and activities. The M.A.T. in charge of a particular day, however, plans the specific details of the lesson and presents it to the group for discussion and revision. When the M.A.T. students are not teaching, they act as observers along with me and the doctoral student involved as part of a practicum on teacher training. This combination of planning together, teaching, and observing insures a very high degree of coherence from day to day.

Each day our observational data permit us to examine how particular students respond to activities, what their levels of attention are, and how they have handled particular writing tasks. We consider how lessons might or should have changed and how we might have responded to individual students. When did we begin to lose student attention? When might an activity have been halted? When signs appear that students have failed to understand, how might the lesson structure have been changed or even aborted in order to deal with the problem? Thus, we can encourage the M.A.T. students to adapt lesson structures, materials, and even time frames to the responses of the students. In short, we can coach reflection-in-action. Our reflections have focused upon students, goals, plans, teaching, assessments, and the interrelationships among these. Let me examine each of these in turn.

STUDENTS

The recent 1988 class is taught by a talented teacher who is a specialist in mathematics. He appreciates our coming in to teach language arts for four weeks. The class includes twenty-two Afro-Americans, three Asians, and a Tanzanian. Two cousins from Cambodia have limited English skills. One speaks pretty well and is eager to talk, but the other is very shy. The Vietnamese girl carries an English-Vietnamese dictionary, and from time to time she surreptitiously slips it from her desk to check words. The student from Tanzania has been in the United States for only a year. She also has very limited English, but works hard and wishes to speak English and to be successful in this American school.

Two weeks before the workshop began, the regular teacher had asked the students to write a composition that we could use as a pretest: "Write about an experience that is important to you for some reason. Write about it so specifically that another person reading your composition will be able to see what you saw and feel what you felt." The same topic would be used at the end of the workshop under nearly the same conditions, although administered by the M.A.T. teachers.

We studied the writing to determine its characteristics. These students have judged an experience as "important" if it is out of the ordinary. (So it is that year after year we find compositions about vacations—clearly a favorite, which may explain the old clichéd assignment, "What I Did on My Summer Vacation"—or trips to sporting events or amusement parks, or parties.) Generally, the class compositions meandered as though the writers were using what Bereiter and Scardamalia call the "what next strategy" of writing. Details were few and far between. When they did occur, their appearance was often irrelevant to any rhetorical purpose. Details seemed to appear because the writer happened to remember them at a particular juncture in the writing. The papers typically told virtually nothing of the writer's specific response to the experience. If any response appeared, it was stated in the broadest terms (e.g., "It was great!"). Metaphor was nonexistent. Very few students used dialogue or direct quotation. In fact, few used even indirect quotation. Finally, errors in spelling, punctuation, and usage were legion. A survey of the class papers revealed to us that one of the most common errors had to do with punctuating main clauses. All the students made run-on errors, with or without commas. Nearly all students tied main clauses together without using a comma.

A look at one composition will illustrate these problems. We judged the following paper, by Ranakea, to be one of the two best in the class.

The Night I Went to Wisconsin Dells

This summer 1988 on Friday night at 9:30 p.m. my parents decided to go on a trip to Wisconsin Dells. We packed our bags and loaded the car. We headed out to the highway and the first time my father paid the toll was $1.20 and the next toll was 40 cents. My father drove for 3 hours, but we didn't make it to Wisconsin Dells because my father made a wrong turn and we were heading our way back to Chicago! So my father turned around and said "we'll go to lake Geneva because it was a shorter ride. I fell asleep and my mother did to, finally I woke up and we were at a Motel.

It was $60.00 for one night and all it was was a little cottage and all of us couldn't sleep in one bed so father slept on a cott me and my mother slept in the bed. I was so excited because my Grandfather work down in lake Geneva he owned a barbecue pit called Gino's. He sold ribs, chicken, fish, bread pudding, salad, and all the drinks you want. We went there for a little while then I went shopping with my mother to be some biking shorts, Gym Shoes, and a T-Shirt.

Then we kept riding and went to Wisconsin dells. We found a hotel at Wisconsin dells 6:00 a.m. in the morning. So then we all took showers put on our new clothes and headed out to explore Wisconsin. We got on the boat ride call the upper dells at 2:00 p.m. and I saw a lot interesting that God made and nature did together it was beautiful! I rock formation trees that were growing out of the rocks it was a extrodinary. Then after all that we had a 17 year old captain it was fun. Then it was time to go back home to Chicago and we made it home at 12:00 p.m.

Ranakea's paper is fairly typical of compositions about vacations. She is more specific than most students about certain features of the trip: the time of departure, the cost of tolls, the price of the motel room, her grandfather's menu, and so forth. Such details give the essay a kind of credibility but do not evoke empathy in the reader or add to the rhetorical effect. Ranakea's sentences about the wrong turn and her father's decision to go to Lake Geneva instead of the Dells, with its use of an exclamation point, seems to be an attempt to evoke a response in the reader, probably laughter. She passes over an opportunity for evoking excitement about her grandfather's barbecue pit with a list of a few items on the menu. She also passes over other opportunities for development: the shopping trip with a list of purchases; the scenery on the boat trip, with the generalized statement that "It was extrodinary"; and the seventeen-year-old captain, with the bland statement that "it was fun." Ranakea has written six run-ons and has joined main clauses without commas seven times, but for this class Ranakea's punctuation is quite good.

GOALS

Given these competencies, what should we do in the four weeks available? What should be the focus of our instruction? If we were to respond traditionally to the writing of the students, we might wish to begin with lessons on parts of speech leading to the analysis of simple sentences in order to promote better punctuation. We could teach paragraph structure and development: by detail, by illustration, by comparison, by contrast, and so forth. We could focus on spelling or usage. Beginning with any one of these, however, would mean asking students to learn certain abstract rules about discourse in order to write about something later. Available research on the teaching of composition indicates that focusing on either grammar or on model compositions is ineffective. The same research, however, indicates that focusing on something concrete—what we might call a data set—and learning strategies to write about that data set in the process of discussion or writing result in better writing (Hillocks, *Research on Written Composition*).

We should begin with the concrete, but what specific concrete things we should begin with is not so clear. Research does not tell us. One M.A.T. suggests that we should have students write about their own experiences, at least in part. M.A.T.'s agree that that would allow students to have fun and gain confidence as writers. We agree that gaining confidence and enjoying writing will be two of our major goals. Well and good, but that gets us no closer to deciding what to teach on Monday.

I ask what features we expect in good writing about personal experience. We begin to list characteristics: (1) sharp focus, (2) concrete detail, (3) metaphor, (4) dialogue that moves the story forward or reveals something about the characters, (5) personal reactions to experiences. We would like the students' writing to exhibit these characteristics by the end of our four weeks. That brings us to specific plans.

PLANS

Someone suggests that we begin with some of the activities we developed and studied during the summer. We decide we will have students work on describing seashells, textures, sounds, street scenes, and physical sensations. One lesson may involve writing about an animal in a picture, then using that description in a story in which the student imagines encountering the animal and being chased by it. We decide we should do something with describing people, developing conflicts, and writing and punctuating dialogue. Another option is writing fables. All of our lessons will build toward writing about a personal experience as the final writing assignment. In addition, we are aware that we need to deal with punctuating sentences.

We will help students use the writing process. Prewriting and writing will be important parts of nearly every lesson. However, students will not revise everything. We decide that not all assignments are worth revising. But the major ones probably are. We want students to realize that writers take time to think about what they are writing, write a draft, think about what they have written and perhaps receive comments from others, then revise and edit.

In developing specific lessons we bear in mind the guidelines we worked with during the course on teaching writing during the summer.

1. Each lesson should be worthwhile, in itself, as a writing lesson. At the same time, each lesson should move students toward the larger goal of writing effectively about personal experience.
2. Each should be interesting and enjoyable for students. We will be looking for signs of inattentiveness, boredom, and frustration.
3. Each lesson will reflect an analysis of the task involved.
4. Early episodes in lessons should provide a high level of support for new writing tasks, while subsequent episodes should move the students toward eventual independence.
5. Lessons should be organized so that one episode supports the next.
6. Each lesson should provide ample opportunities to observe students' responses, gauge their understanding and proficiency, and coach them in the use of the procedures being taught *before* we receive final writing.

We begin to plan the first lesson together. The question is, what should we do first? Probably we should let the students know that we are going to be working on personal writing. The problem is, they may not know what we mean by personal writing. We decide that it would be a good idea to use a sample, to distribute a piece of writing that we regard as a good one. We examine several back issues of *Merlyn's Pen: The National Magazine of Student Writing* for a personal experience piece by a seventh, eighth, or ninth grader, suitable for using with our students. We decide most of the pieces are either too long or culturally too removed from the students in our class. One of the M.A.T.'s suggests using a piece that we had examined during the summer, a piece by a student in a previous workshop about the writer's first day at the school. We review Verita's composition (see Smith and Hillocks for this piece) and decide that it will do. It has all the features that we hope will be present in the writing of our seventh graders: dialogue, sensory detail, metaphor, conflict, personal reactions.

I suggest that we use next a lesson that we refer to as the shell game (Hillocks, *Observing and Writing*). The writing activities of the "shell game" ask students to describe a seashell that is shown to them—one of two somewhat similar univalves provided when the students are working in groups, one of thirty shells when they are writing independently. They are to write so carefully that another student reading what they have written will be able to identify the particular shell described.

We examine a couple of alternatives but decide on the shell game. Why should we use this lesson? We consider the following: (1) students in the past have always seemed to respond positively to it; they enjoy looking at the shells and writing about them, (2) it involves students immediately in a rhetorical situation, (3) it always evokes metaphor from the majority of students, (4) it prompts a very high level of specificity in writing, and (5) it will provide an opportunity for asking students to work collaboratively in groups, an activity that we hope to use often during our four weeks.

We decide to begin with the simpler activity, which asks students working in groups of four or five to write about one of two shells as a group and then to pass their two shells and composition to a second group. The second group reads the composition, identifies the shell described, and underlines details that were helpful to them in identifying the shell. This group activity has several advantages: (1) it provides the teacher with access to the thinking of students as they struggle to describe a shell, (2) the teacher can coach by making suggestions, providing encouragement, and asking questions, and (3) the students can help each other.

Although my students and I have been using these shell activities for many years, and although it is clear that the group shell activity helps prepare students for the individual writing about a shell, the group activity itself remains difficult because students have no way of knowing what kinds of language to use, which details to focus upon, or perhaps even how to think about the problem of writing about a shell. After fifteen years of using this approach, it suddenly dawns on me that it would be a good idea to have a teacher-led discussion of one or two sample shells to illustrate the kinds of things that might be said about a seashell, about its color, its shape, and possible comparisons.

Even with the broad outlines of the lesson laid out, we continue planning in detail. For example, because the M.A.T. students have never taught, we spend considerable time planning for grouping. How many groups should we set up? (We decide on six so that we have no more than five students per group.) Should students be allowed to choose their own groups? (We decide against that, at least until we know the students better.) What will be the basis of assigning students to groups? (We decide to assign a known strong writer to each group and to spread the weaker writers among all groups. At the same time, we try to balance boys and girls among all groups.) Finally, we plan the directions for the group work.

TEACHING

Because the M.A.T.'s have no experience, I teach the first day. After introductions, I distribute copies of Verita's composition, read it aloud, then ask what details the students liked. One student responds that she liked the way the writer talked about her reactions. I ask for a specific reference in the text. The girl points to a simile ("my heart was pounding like a volcano about to erupt"). I ask for another detail that people liked. There is a long, long pause. I wait. Then I say, in an attempt to be encouraging, "You can look at the piece of writing and see what there is." Another long pause ensues. "Yes?" Another long pause. Out of the corner of my eye I can see the M.A.T.'s beginning to fidget in their seats. I wait longer. Finally, I decide to go through the piece a few lines at a time, and I begin, "Let's take a look at—" when a student raises a hand. This student refers to the details about entering the auditorium and seeing all the strange students present. Then another hand is up. I get five responses in succession, each to a detail the student thinks is effective. Soon, twelve students have responded. My impression is they have gained some idea of effective detail.

Noting that we are behind schedule, I pull a large seashell out of a paper bag and explain that I'm going to ask them to describe a seashell as specifically as they can. I begin to walk around the room with the large shell, allowing students to touch and hold it momentarily.

I ask, "How would you describe it if you had to describe this shell in language, in words, so that somebody else could picture it without seeing it? What would you say about it?" As I hold it by the bottom tip, one boy states, "The shell looks sort of like a trophy cup." Another boy says very softly that it has different kinds of colors, tan, white, a pinky color. Another says that it looks like an ear. I am surprised: "All right, if you look at this part, it does look like an ear. That's very good." I shift the shell about. Another student says, "When you hold it that way, it looks like a mouth with teeth." Eventually there are other similes; it's like a beehive, a little cap with a slightly twisted top, a tepee, or it's "rough and scaly like an old person's skin."

I decide the students have gotten the idea of describing the shell and set up the six groups, each with two shells, and begin to visit the groups. During the initial visit I ask if someone has been selected to write and if the students have picked a shell. I urge each student to contribute to the description. Observer notes indicate that during the first fifteen minutes, I make eighteen visits to the groups, asking questions, making suggestions, and giving praise. Despite these relatively frequent visits, two groups offer problems. One observer notices that in Group Two a boy and a girl have a disagreement about the foot space available under the desks and engage in some under-the-desk kicking. Another observer is watching an even more obstreperous group. In that group LaTonya volunteers to be secretary and asks the students to describe the shell. A boy opens up, saying, "I don't know. It's ugly." LaTonya responds, "You want me to write that down? It's ugly? What makes it ugly?" LaTonya complains that the boy isn't doing what he's supposed to be doing. IDris begins to draw. Kiva, a tall, aggressive girl, snatches IDris's paper from his desk. He snatches it back. The observer notes, "They snatch back and forth."

After about eighteen minutes of group work, when four groups are finished, I collect the group compositions and distribute the proofreading tests to those groups that have completed the composition. The students, relatively quiet now, work away on their punctuation tests. When all groups have completed their writing about a shell, I redistribute shells and compositions. Each group is asked to read over the composition and identify the shell described. In addition they are to underline the most helpful details. Completing this task and the punctuation inventory takes the class to the end of the hour.

Our "postmortem" begins almost as soon as we reach the stairwell. The first question from the M.A.T.'s is, "What did you think when nobody answered?" I admit I was beginning to think perhaps no one would answer and was just getting ready to be more direct when someone did speak up. I emphasize the necessity of waiting while students collect their ideas or identify things that do interest them. We talk about that. The M.A.T.'s spend a few minutes commenting excitedly on what they saw. Out of all their commentary, the main concern obviously is that the groups did not appear to be as productive as the M.A.T.'s had expected. We talk about why that might be. The seventh graders are not used to us. They seem not to be used to true collaborative work in groups. I note a colleague's finding that group work in elementary school often means sitting in a small group but working independently. We have asked the students to work together to develop a piece of writing. We consider the possibility of moving students in or out of the unruly groups, but decide against it. We will give the students clearer directions about collaboration and encourage them to be responsible for working together. (These discussions continue over the next few days. By the fifth day, after changing some of the group members around, the groups function well. One observer writes, "The changes work." But there will be relapses.)

We go through the lesson step by step, examining problems along the way. We examine the compositions developed by the groups. Four groups have written the kind of composition we expected, a unified piece incorporating descriptive phrases and comparisons. One group wrote two paragraphs, one about each shell. Clearly, they misunderstood the directions and the teacher's visits did not pick up this problem. Each paragraph, however, contains some strong detail. The weakest effort appears to have come from our most troublesome group. Rather than write a unified paragraph, LaTonya has recorded separate sentences for each student, such as the following from IDris: "It's ugly, badge [beige] is a ugly color. The brown design is ugly." We decide, however, that the students are generally prepared to write on a shell independently. That will be the first part of the next day's lesson, which an M.A.T. has volunteered to teach.

ASSESSMENTS

Clearly, we must make assessments from moment to moment, as students work in groups and individually, as they show evidence of learning and frustration, as they gain understanding and develop their own questions. These assessments are based on our knowledge of where students are, what the demands of effective reading and writing are, our expectations for our instruction, and our conceptions of the learning tasks. The function of assessment is to provide insight into how the instruction may be improved. Such reflection involves keeping a range of possibilities in mind. Difficulties may arise anywhere from our conception of the subject matter to the physical arrangements of the classroom. For example, if our groups are not working, we must consider a number of possibilities: (1) the task is too difficult or ambiguous, (2) the directions are unclear, (3) the task has no interest, (4) students have brought animosities from elsewhere into their group work, (5) students may not be used to working collaboratively, (6) the coaching of the teacher is inadequate in some respect.

At the same time, our assessments must consider the cumulative effects of instruction. We can look at changes in the use of detail, metaphor, dialogue, and the portrayal of personal, physical, and emotional response to experience. We can ask if students are making their personal experience come to life more fully on paper. But we also look at other things. We want to know if students are enjoying writing, putting more effort into it, using the full process of writing instead of trying to produce a single correct draft. Every year we see a significant change in the quality of student writing. This year we assessed change using a holistic scoring procedure with at least three raters for each paper, and the students made fairly impressive gains.

But we can see the improvement in the writing of individuals without formal scoring. On the posttest, for example, Ranakea writes two stories, each one longer than her pretest story.

Her writing has sharpened in a number of ways. First, her focus in both new stories is much tighter than in her pretest. In the first, she looks at her personal turmoil over an invitation her mother will not allow her to accept. She dramatizes the story by incorporating dialogue and by including her own internal dialogue. Ranakea also uses two metaphors effectively as she despairs over her mother's refusal. The metaphor of being "stuck" in "a dark alley all alone" emphasizes her isolation at being shut out of the party. Her second metaphor ("My mind tore to pieces") indicates her own divided feelings about the party. On the one hand, she wants to be with the kids she regards as "cool." On the other, as she tells us, there will be things about the party she will not like: "There will be boys kissing on the girls. Yuck!" Then, when she makes her decision to pass up the party, she returns to the same metaphors, changing them to show her feelings of relief and wholeness. Finally, she has reduced the frequency of sentence punctuation errors from about four in ten T-units to two in ten T-units.

We might expect improvement from Ranakea, one of the strongest writers on the pretest sample, but the weak writers show improvement too. Maurice, on the pretest, presented a flat chronicle of a day, without detail or emotion: "Last night when I left school I went home and talked on the phone for about one hour and then I went out front and talked to freinds and then came back upstairs and talked on the phone again." He wrote 135 words, the word *and* making up 12 percent of the total—a telling fact. He included no punctuation, not even at the end. On his posttest, however, a long account of a trip to Detroit, Maurice writes 605 words and includes periods at 35 percent of the accepted locations, doubles the frequency of subordinate clauses, uses dialogue and simile, and reveals his feelings in a variety of ways. We judge the piece to be somewhat stronger than Ranakea's pretest.

Another sign of progress is that the students no longer regard a first draft as a final product. They are no longer content to make revisions that consist merely of cosmetic changes with whiteout. When given the opportunity to revise, most students go well beyond sentence-level revisions by adding or deleting chunks of several sentences. With the encouragement of teacher comments, several students now show a willingness to rethink their ideas and develop them in a new way, while maintaining the central idea of the first draft. In general, we believe that most revisions are improvements.

Although we can be fairly confident about the improvement of writing in these nineteen days of teaching, we need to ask if the improvement has been adequate. How might we make our instruction more effective in the future? How can we insure that all students make gains? Such questions take us back to our initial reflections upon goals. We need to ask, are our goals and expectations adequate?

The process of reflecting on our teaching is necessarily recursive. Thinking about results necessarily takes us back to thinking about conceptions of what we hoped to accomplish. Even reflection in the action of teaching is recursive, moving forward at once to goals and backwards to our conceptions of the subject. This consciousness of assumptions and goals during action makes possible productive changes in directions and new conceptions.

REFLECTING AND RESEARCHING

The kind of reflecting under consideration here, of course, leads directly to researching. The kinds of questions asked in considering students' goals, plans, teaching, and assessments are indicative of the kinds of questions asked in research. The main difference is that the research question is posited and treated more formally. During teaching we will ask ourselves how Maurice is doing in a particular lesson. To do research, we need to stipulate what we mean by "how Maurice is doing," to marshal evidence formally, and to consider the relevant data carefully enough to explain hypotheses and deal with competing explanations.

The M.A.T. students will use the data generated for research: lesson plans, several sets of observer notes for each class, writing samples and a few tests from students, and audio recordings of several classes. One M.A.T. student, for example, will explore changes in the seventh graders' use of metaphor. Another may focus on four or five students, tracking changes in their writing through all writing assignments and taking advantage of observer notes to consider the level of student involvement in particular lessons. Another may focus on changes in sentence punctuation. These projects are a formal extension of workshop reflections. The more careful and systematic reflecting becomes, the more it becomes like researching.

3

The Writing Teacher as Historian

EDWARD P. J. CORBETT

We are all familiar with the cliché "Those who ignore history are condemned to repeat it." Despite the warning, many of us may already have done our share of ignoring history. And some of us may have been a member of that school-age generation during the 1970s that studiously avoided taking any history courses if we could elect our own academic program. The irony of that disposition is that all of us, simply because we are alive, are part of the history of our own time, and every day we make some contribution to that history. Although we may succeed at ignoring history, history does not ignore us. We are all part and parcel of the March of Time.

More ironic than usual is the situation in which teachers, of all professionals in our society, think that by an act of will they can ignore history. According to the prevailing folklore, teaching is not the oldest of the professions, but it may very well be the oldest of the respectable professions that are recognized today. There is a rather shadowy figure of a medical doctor in Homer's *Iliad*, but we would need the fingers of both hands to count up the number of characters in that same epic who could be regarded as teachers. And if we went to an even older literature, the Hebrew Bible, we would have a hard time of it deciding who was *not* a teacher in that document.

If we were to consider what we teachers teach, we would have an even more difficult time escaping the ubiquity of history. Most of the literature we teach is rooted in the distant past. The language we speak every day is as contemporary as this morning's headline, but for all of its newness, we know that it evolved from forms that now strike us as being foreign or at least quaint. When we enunciate a pentameter line like "Whan that April with his shoures soote," we experience a shiver of oddness about that succession of sounds, but we all recognize that we have just heard an earlier version of the English language. And when we consider another of our pedagogical provinces, reading and writing, we know that we are right at the heart of the matter. As John Gerber once reminded us, we are fundamentally teachers of reading and writing.

Back in 1974, Paul T. Bryant published an article entitled "A Brand New World Every Morning," in which he made the point that we teachers of writing often "behave as if there is no continuity in the teaching of composition, as if the subject has just been invented and every idea for teaching it is new at the moment. We fail to draw on the experience of our colleagues." Lest we fall into the delusion that every morning presents us with a brand new world, I want to point out in this chapter how we teachers and our students can maintain our contact with history, how we can record the history we are making in our classrooms, how we can pass on our heritage to subsequent generations of teachers and students.

One of the situations that complicate our performing as historians is the fact that, traditionally, teaching is the most private of the professions. Doctors, lawyers, engineers may deliberate in private, but ultimately they have to go public with their activities. An engineer, for instance, ultimately builds a bridge, and if he or she has not calculated shrewdly and correctly, tomorrow's headlines will scream that twenty-seven automobiles, with their load of morning commuters, plunged into the bay when the bridge collapsed. In a case like that, the engineering profession is exposed to public scrutiny as blatantly as the college football coach is every Saturday afternoon. But once a teacher closes the door of the classroom, only God and the captive students know what goes on within those four walls.

Just reflect for a moment on how rare are the published accounts of what actually goes on in the typical classroom. Occasionally, teachers will publish accounts in the professional journals of what they did in the classroom on Monday morning. But those accounts are likely to be edited versions of what actually went on in that Monday morning class. Occasionally, students are required to keep a daily journal of what goes on in a classroom. It would be great if we could get a peek into those journals, but they are reserved for the perusal of the teacher, and rarely do they get published. (Wouldn't you love to have a detailed account of what transpired during an eight-hour day in the Tudor grammar school that had a wimpy student named William Shakespeare sitting in the back row of the classroom?) Maybe someday, when the rights to privacy have been nullified by the statutes of limitations, we will have access to tape recordings or even to videotapings by a director of Freshman English of some quivering teaching-assistant's conduct of a composition class.

Those of us who are interested in what went on in the Greek and Roman schools of the classical period have to settle for Werner Jaeger's masterful but secondary reconstruction in his book *Paideia: The Ideals of Greek Culture* or for H. I. Marrou's *A History of Education in Antiquity*. Even when we look at some of the texts that have survived, we can only speculate whether they reflect what actually went on in the classroom. Do the Platonic dialogues indicate the way that Socrates taught philosophy to the young men who came to him for enlightenment? Aristotle's *Rhetoric* is said to be a set of lecture notes that reflect what he taught to interested students in the afternoon. But what did the students actually *do* in Aristotle's rhetoric class? Did they just sit and listen to the lectures? Did they take notes? Did they ask questions of the teacher? What did they have to do for homework in that class? Did they have to write anything for that class? If so, what did they write on and with? Who evaluated the writing, if any was done—the teacher or the students?

When we look at the *progymnasmata* of such people as Theon and Aphthonius, that series of elementary exercises in composition in the Greek and Roman schools, these theme assignments at least make it easier for us to imagine the kind of instructions and exercises that the schoolboys were exposed to. The authors of the *progymnasmata* sometimes provided the pupils with examples of the kind of themes that they were asked to write. But wouldn't it be wonderful if some of the elementary themes that the Greek and Roman schoolboys wrote survived today so that we could see some representative examples of what they were required to write and what they were capable of writing? If they were representative examples, would we find the writing better or worse than the writing of the ordinary freshman student today? What judgments could we make about the value of the sequential series of writing exercises that constituted the *progymnasmata*? What could we adopt from that system that would be helpful to the students in our own writing courses?

These are all intriguing questions, which we may never be able to answer satisfactorily. We might get some answers if there had been some self-appointed historians among the teachers or the pupils to record what went on from day to day in those Greek and Roman classrooms. One can imagine that there was a lot of drill and recitation—and a lot of caning of lazy or unruly or recalcitrant or erring pupils. But these impressions are conjured up by our imaginations, and our imaginations may be disposed to conjure up what we *think* went on in the classical schoolrooms. It would be nice if some contemporary had described what actually went on in those schoolrooms.

We do in fact have two very useful accounts, by contemporaries, of what went on in the Tudor grammar schools. John Brinsley in his *Ludus Literarius: or, The Grammar Schoole* (1612) and Charles Hoole in *A New Discovery of the Old Art of Teaching Schoole* (c. 1637, published 1660) give detailed information about classroom practices in the English grammar schools of the Tudor period.

These accounts, both reissued early in this century, have been supplemented by two secondary works published in the 1940s: T. W. Baldwin, *William Shakespere's Small Latine & Lesse Greeke*, and Donald Lemen Clark, *John Milton at St. Paul's School: A Study of Ancient Rhetoric in English Renaissance Education*. Even if we are horrified by the accounts of what went on in those classrooms, we can at least be guided in shaping our own classroom practices by those historical records of particular pedagogies.

What we need more of from our own times are accounts written by students or by former students of the classroom behaviors, methodologies, and strategies of effective teachers. (I was tempted to say "of popular teachers," but popular teachers are not always or necessarily effective teachers. We sometimes get more showmanship than substance from popular teachers. Nevertheless, it needs to be said that *effective* teachers can also be—and often are—*popular* teachers.)

I once read an impressive account by a Harvard student of his first encounter with the noted Swiss-born marine zoologist Louis Agassiz. The student came to Agassiz and said that he would like to take a course in marine biology from the great teacher. To test the student, Agassiz handed him a bucket with a fish in it and told him to go home and study the fish very carefully and then come back and describe the fish in great detail. Well, as the story goes, the student was sent away two or three times to study the fish more intensely because he could not answer a number of even superficial questions about the specimen. *There* was a story of an effective teacher, a teacher who wanted to impress that student with the need for keen observation if he wanted to become a scientist.

I recall reading a few years ago in the *New Yorker* a fascinating account by a woman who had once taken a class in comparative literature from Vladimir Nabokov when he was teaching at Wellesley College in Massachusetts. Not only did we get descriptions of his typical attire and of his striding across the quad on a winter day, but we also got detailed accounts of his classroom demeanor, of the kinds of questions he asked of the students, of his astute commentaries on a particular author or a particular work of literature. After reading that account of an effective and popular teacher, one wonders how much of Nabokov is in Pnin, the committed but sometimes eccentric university teacher who is the focal character in Nabokov's novel of the same name. Fortunately, we now have printed collections of Nabokov's classroom lectures at Cornell on some of the great authors of world literature.

Virtually everyone who ever had the privilege of going to school has fond memories of a favorite teacher—very often of a teacher who changed the direction of one's life. And virtually everyone has at one time or another listened to or read somebody's account of a favorite teacher. Wouldn't it be wonderful if there were some magazine or journal that printed accounts by former students of effective teachers? What a school of education such a journal would be! Prospective teachers could read a number of these historical accounts, pick out those teachers who exemplified a style and a philosophy of pedagogy that they admired, and model themselves on those teachers.

Most English teachers on the college and university level have rarely had a formal, credit-bearing course in how to teach their subject. The closest they have probably come to a course in pedagogy is the practicum they took from the director of Freshman English in their first year as a graduate TA. Now a number of graduate programs in English are beginning to offer credit-bearing courses in how to teach composition, how to teach literature, how to teach business and technical writing. What most of us did who went to graduate school before such courses in pedagogy were offered was model our own teaching on that of some teacher or teachers we admired. A collection of historical accounts of the classroom practices of some of the great teachers of the past would give prospective teachers a much wider range of exemplary models upon which they could base their own teaching.

As teachers of English, we could do more about engaging our students in the writing of history. I would hesitate to recommend that we require our students to write and to submit to us papers or journals that describe in great detail what went on in our classroom during a particular week or during an entire quarter or semester. Such written records could be valuable for future reference if they could be stored in the archives of the school where we teach, but if they were submitted as an assignment to be evaluated and graded by us, those records could be seriously inhibited and therefore something less than truthful. With that caution, however, I would urge you to engage your students in the recovery and the recording of history.

In a sense, we English teachers have regularly engaged our students in the recovery and recording of history. In our writing classes, for instance, we often require our students to write personal narratives and autobiographical sketches. The much maligned theme topic "What I Did on My Summer Vacation" is a quintessential instance of a personal historical narrative. Very often the topics that our students choose or that we set for our students for their term papers involve the students in the process of retrieving historical data. On the graduate level, whenever we ask our students to trace out the evolution of an extant literary text, we are engaging them in historical research. Although our students often gripe about such assignments, they do ultimately profit from such excursions into history.

I want to encourage teachers to think up some uncommon kinds of assignments for our students in researching and reporting history. As a member of a large clan of Corbetts that has staged five huge family reunions in various cities of the United States in the last twelve years, I have become increasingly aware of the importance of constructing genealogies, of recording the reminiscences of older members of the family, and of preserving for the family archives records of births, deaths, weddings, graduations and also detailed written accounts of family reunions. There are twenty-six distinct families among the members of my generation, and I am trying to encourage some son or daughter within each of those twenty-six families to record and preserve such vital statistics about his or her family. We regret now that we did not interview members of my father's generation of siblings and get precious information from them for future generations of Corbetts. With the death in 1987 of the last member of my father's generation, we have forever lost the opportunity to get firsthand testimony about the members of that generation.

I did not intend to spend so much time talking about the Corbett clan; what I intended to do was suggest to you teachers that you consider engaging the students in your writing classes in recovering and writing up some piece of history about their families. Because of the many sociological changes that have taken place in family life in the United States in the last fifty years or so, it may be more difficult for young people today than it was earlier to establish contact with relatives. Frequently, the brothers and sisters of a family live in different cities, and the parents and the grandparents often live in a town or city remote from any of the brothers and sisters. Then there is the situation of the families that have been broken up by death or divorce. So if a teacher were to ask the students in his or her class to gather information about a family member or an event connected with the family (for instance, the fortunes of the family during the first five years after they immigrated to America), some students would have a more difficult time complying with such an assignment than other students would. But even in single-parent families, every student would be able to gather some piece of family history from talking with the parent that resides in the household.

Such an assignment falls within the capabilities of every student; it is an assignment that most students would become vitally interested in once they got involved in it; and it is an assignment that could produce a document that would be valued and preserved by the family. Besides, such an assignment can teach students important lessons about the value of history and the difficulties that attend the gathering and the dissemination of historical information.

Another form of historical research is the case study. Students in the social sciences are accustomed to gathering and writing up information about living individuals or groups of living people. But until Janet Emig introduced us to this kind of research with her case studies of a number of Chicago-area high school students, English teachers were not acquainted with this kind of re-search. But now some of our graduate students are doing case studies as part of their dissertation, and even some teachers in undergraduate classes are introducing their students to case studies and are assigning them to do case studies, on a more modest scale, of an individual or a group of individuals.

On a more advanced level, some English teachers are now engaging their students in the kind of ethnographic study that Shirley Brice Heath did among families in the Piedmont area of the eastern part of the United States for her prize-winning book *Ways with Words*. I mention the "more advanced level" because such studies need to be done over a long period of time. Teachers cannot assign their students to do a piece of ethnographic research on Monday morning and expect the report to be handed in two weeks later. For that reason, it is graduate students, for the most part, who have been engaged in such ethnographic studies. To do an adequate study of this sort, researchers need to spend at least six months and often two years or longer as participant-observers in some kind of community. For that reason, it is mainly graduate students preparing to write a master's thesis or a doctoral dissertation that English teachers have engaged in such studies.

But there are less ambitious kinds of ethnographic research that English teachers can engage their students in. There are the kinds of projects that teachers of folklore assign to their students or the kinds of investigative projects that Eliot Wigginton set for his high school students in Rabun Gap, Georgia, and that were written up by the students and later published in at least nine issues of *Foxfire* in the 1970s. Eliot Wigginton got his students to interview parents, relatives, friends, and residents of the region about ordinary customs, crafts, and activities of the local culture and to write up their findings. The subjects listed in the subtitles of some of the *Foxfire* collections give us a good idea of the kinds of things the students investigated—from *Foxfire 2*: ghost stories, wild plant foods, spinning and weaving, midwifing, burial customs, corn shuckin's, wagon making, and so on; from *Foxfire 3*: animal care, banjos and dulcimers, hide tanning, summer and fall wild plant foods, butter churns, ginseng, etc. The young people of Rabun Gap may not have had a natural interest in some of these subjects when they started, but there is ample evidence that they became wildly enthusiastic about the subjects once they started interviewing people. And you can imagine how proud they were when they saw the fruits of their efforts printed in a book that was distributed on a national scale. Many folklore books also had their beginnings in classroom assignments.

Once teachers set their minds to the task, they can come up with other investigative projects that can stimulate students' interest, can acquaint students with the fascination and difficulties of historical research, and can ultimately make students and their families proud of their efforts and their writing.

I may have given you the impression that I am interested in history for its own sake, but I am really interested in the pursuit of history for what it can do for one's personal enlightenment and liberal education. For that pursuit, we teachers have a gold mine in our classrooms and in our students. If we can refrain from exploiting our riches, we may help our students to eventually reach the pot of gold at the end of the rainbow.

4

Introspection and Observation for Insight and Instruction in the Processes of Writing

RICHARD C. GEBHARDT

Composition teachers can turn to many sources of information about the writing process—everything from the testimony of published authors, to observational studies of writers at work, to analyses of the changes in successive drafts of papers, to protocol examinations of the tape-recorded running commentaries writers make as they work. But as teachers read anecdotes by established authors or reports of research on anonymous experimental subjects, they should not overlook some of the most accessible sources of information about writing—their *own* writing processes and activities, and those of their students.

After all, the most carefully conducted and clearly reported research about twelfth-grade writers is about twelfth-grade writers, and any research project will be based on certain assumptions about the nature of writing and about the proper methods to use to study writing. And then the teacher enters the picture, perhaps reading an article in *Written Communication* or *Research in the Teaching of English*. This teacher is not a twelfth-grade student; most likely, this teacher is not teaching twelfth grade students in *just* the sort of social and curricular environment described in the article; quite possibly, this teacher has an imperfect sense of the underlying research assumptions and methodologies in the report. So what is our hypothetical teacher going to do when she or he reads our hypothetical research report?

On the one hand, should she accept as true the conclusions of every research report? That would be a frustrating (even a schizophrenia-producing) approach. The teacher, for instance, would need to reconcile what Carol Berkenkotter found about the role of audience as a touchstone against which writers test rhetorical, organizational, and stylistic decisions as they draft with Duane Roen and R. J. Wiley's finding that audience consideration has less impact during drafting than it does during revising. Then the teacher could try to accept as equally true Sharon Pianko's research showing that pausing to reread and reflect is critical to effective writing and Sheridan Blau's conclusion that some people write better if they can't even see their developing texts while they draft.

It would be frustrating, even silly, for writing teachers to try to accept every research study as fully accurate, or as providing equally useful answers to our instructional dilemmas. Writing research, George Hillocks, Jr., feels, has answered some questions and promises to answer more; and yet, he writes, "[p]erhaps all the research on composing in the last two decades raises more questions than it answers" (p. 61). On the other hand, should teachers dismiss all research-based articles because of apparent contradictions, or because they are "too theoretical" or "not practical enough" to help in the classroom? That, of course, is exactly what many teachers do. And while the current situation is not as bad as the one Richard VanDeWeghe described in 1979, his words still have a ring of truth: "despite nearly a century of empirical research in composition, most writing teachers . . . either ignore the findings or do not even know they exist. Teachers continue to teach . . . with little or no attention given to the wealth of information readily available in composition research" (p. 28).

Neither uncritical acceptance of every research study nor skeptical resistance to all composition research is a defensible approach for today's writing teacher. A far more reasonable approach—the one I'll argue here—is for teachers to take composition research seriously, but to test it against their own writing behaviors and those they observe in their students. Professional writing teachers should read research-based articles. They should not be passively predetermined to *believe* or cynically motivated to *doubt* but constructively inclined to *wonder*—to wonder, as they read a given research study, how (or *if*) its conclusions might extrapolate to their teaching.

Extrapolations "from the research to classroom contexts," Arthur Applebee has written, is the most productive way composition research can affect teaching, and "a necessary part of the overall process of improving teaching." This process, of course, does not involve a simple or a straight-line extrapolation from research to classroom. Instead, it works through what Applebee calls a "long process of interpretation and debate"—a "reflection of a healthy exploration of what particular research results mean in the complex context of classrooms that differ in student populations, in goals, and in conditions of instruction" (pp. 222–23).

In such an exploration, most writing teachers are not going to be as systematic as a researcher developing a controlled experiment to test the potential applicability of an earlier study. But we can take at least as objective a posture toward writing research as we do when we try to sort out the truth of advertising claims or political campaign promises. We can check new data against what we know firsthand from our own experience—including our firsthand experiences with our own writing practices and the writing behaviors we see in our classrooms.

We can, in other words, use informed introspection and classroom observation as tools to help validate research studies we read and to help weave abstract or theoretical articles into personally felt perspectives on writing. Then, having used introspection and observation to expand and sharpen our understanding of composition, we can help our students develop their own personally felt perspectives on writing by using introspection and observation as teaching strategies.

INTROSPECTION AND OBSERVATION AS INFORMAL TESTS OF RESEARCH

The utility of introspection and classroom observation as sources of teacher insight into composing can best be seen, perhaps, in the context I discussed earlier: the fact that research may provide more questions than answers and that classroom teachers may be confused or alienated by apparent contradictions in research studies. Let's manufacture a hypothetical high school or college writing teacher who has learned from Linda Flower and John Hayes that dynamic, evolving plans are central to the recursive process of writing, and from Mike Rose that rigid plans contribute to writer's block. Now this teacher confronts Glenn Broadhead and Richard Freed's *The Variables of Composition* and reads that very effective writing can come from rigid plans and linear writing strategies. A composition researcher would not be troubled: differences in underlying research would be apparent (for instance, Rose's use of freshman writers and Broadhead and Freed's focus on professional technical writers). The teacher, though, may read only for the conclusions of research studies or may miss the significance of experimental variables. To this teacher, the writer's claim to authority and the fact of publication (matters of ethos, really) may be the key tests of research. From their authors' notes, Linda Flower and John Hayes, Mike Rose, and Glenn Broadhead and Richard Freed all appear to be authorities, with their research published by scholarly journals and university presses—and yet their findings seem to disagree. For our hypothetical teacher, who assumes a sort of face validity for each article, the apparent contradictions will create some confusion. Worse, the contradictions may prompt outright rejection of one or another of the research findings, or they may feed the teacher's growing skepticism about composition research in general.

These negative reactions to research—confusion, rejection, alienation—are less likely when readers test each research study against something other than the writer's authority and the fact of credible publication. Composition researchers would test apparently contradictory findings against such things as the experimental designs, the subjects under study, and the hypotheses explored in the studies. Many high school and college writing teachers cannot apply such tests, or are uninterested in doing so, and a lot of teacher skepticism about the usefulness of research stems, I think, from these causes. But even if most teachers can't apply rigorous "scientific" methods to help them test and understand research articles, they can sort through apparent contradictions in research and work toward a fuller understanding of writing if they test research studies against their own practices as writers and the writing behaviors they observe in their classes.

INFORMED INTROSPECTION

I recommend introspection because it is a source of information so very accessible to teachers and because I know from personal experience how one's own writing processes and practices can help a person understand composition research and put it into a personally meaningful perspective. Recall our hypothetical teacher confused about plans and linearity in writing. In a sense, I am that teacher. For twenty years I have wondered about the relative power of initial plans and spontaneous composition, and I have used my own practices as a writer to help me understand and sort through research bearing on such related issues as recursiveness vs. linearity and behavioral vs. thought-comes-first writing. The research has been informative, often enlightening. But if I had not also thought about my own writing practices, the research would not have had as much impact on my understanding of writing and my approaches in the classroom.

I'd like to give a couple of examples to illustrate what I mean and, maybe, to inspire introspection in a few readers. The first is an experience that took place in 1981 while I was working on a draft of what eventually became a *College English* article called "Initial Plans and Spontaneous Composition." Early in the first draft I analyzed two fairly contradictory quotations; I personally agreed with one of the passages, for the most part, and I planned to use the other as a foil to argue for composition as a spontaneous, nonlinear act. This is what I wrote at one point in that draft:

> So it seems clear that King's linear theory of composing cannot encompass the issues Mandel raises. It does not, that is, account for diversity in the

phenomena of writing; it does not weave into its theoretical fabric the practices of people who know that they do not move through a conscious preproduction period of thinking, planning, organizing, and incubating.

When I returned to the draft later, a funny thing happened to my original plan for the essay. I had just started retyping that part of the draft when I suddenly saw different words coming out of my typewriter: "So it seems clear that *neither* King's linear description of the writing process, *nor* . . ." I sensed immediately that my argument was changing direction, and I realized I would have to revise my original plans for the article when, a few seconds later, I saw a period marking definite closure replaced by a semicolon, thus opening the way to more balanced criticism:

> King's linear explanation . . . does not weave into its theoretical fabric the practices of people who know that they do not move through a conscious preproduction period of thinking, planning, organizing, and incubating; Mandel's nonlinear view excludes the writing practices of those who know they *do*.

By that point in the draft, my original and limited plan—to argue for recursiveness and behavioral writing—was beginning to change into a grander one: to outline a theory of writing process broad enough to include linearity *and* recursiveness, thought-comes-first *and* behavioral writing. It was an outrageous plan, one that probably would not have survived a moment's reflection. But when I first saw my thesis changing on the paper as I drafted, my mind encouraged the new idea by recalling an earlier experience.

In 1975, I was working on a brief review of Michael Brownstein's novel, *Country Cousins*. As I read, I noticed similarities to fiction by William Faulkner, Kurt Vonnegut, Jr., and Henry Miller, and I wondered, "What if those authors could have collaborated on a novel?" Later, when I settled down at my typewriter to write, that thought was so powerful—as a thesis, an implicit organization, and a principle by which to select illustrative details— that it took only about twenty minutes to write the first draft of this review:

> If William Faulkner, Henry Miller, and Kurt Vonnegut could collaborate on a book today, it might resemble this bizarre first novel. . . . Faulkner might contribute the small town/rural aura; the slightly insane main character, Martin Kilbanky, with his dream of building a lasting edifice on the family farm; and the sycophantic Bill and Marge Parsons who exploit Martin and his mother. Miller might add the outrageous sexual exploits of Marge and Martin—including 54 hours of uninterrupted sex in the kitchen, on the stairs, on the porch. Vonnegut might add the simultaneous and parallel

planes of existence that Martin dimly perceives; the plus-sign and minus-sign creatures who visit Martin in a peanut-sized spacecraft; and Martin's final dream of being a hunted deer or bear or beaver in a bulky animal suit. And Vonnegut might also add the matter-of-fact flatness of explanations and descriptions, the uncontrolled exposition, and the unexpected and slightly askew language . . . that contribute so much to the style and texture of the novel." (*Choice*, March 1975, p. 68)

I mention these two experiences—a time my thesis changed before my eyes and a review that wrote itself—because they suggest how my awareness of my own writing processes have contributed to my developing understanding of the writing process. I began on my *College English* article by reading contradictory sources, presentations of linear and nonlinear theory, and I ended up trying for the audacious synthesis signaled by the eventual subtitle: "Toward a Comprehensive Theory of the Writing Process." The synthesis I achieved did not come only (or perhaps even primarily) from the sources I was reading. Introspection into my own processes as a writer showed me that initial plans *and* spontaneous composition really do work together. Introspection helped me understand what I was reading and contributed significantly to the understanding of the writing process I achieved.

And so I recommend informed introspection as one framework within which to understand composition research. For the act of writing creates data against which teachers can test and clarify composition theory and research.

To use this data requires little more than an introspective attitude and a notebook in which to jot occasional thoughts during drafting. When you sense that your writing is beginning to change direction, you can ask yourself "why?" and jot down an answer. When you find yourself stuck or wandering far afield, you can ask yourself "why?" and jot down some possible answers. You could imagine how you *look* sitting at your computer—especially how your eyes flit over what you are writing and how your fingers pause while you scan and think—and jot down some observations. The habit of self-observation may sensitize you to your own writing processes, and the information you discover through it may help you better understand the research you do and the problems you see in the writing practices of your students.

OBSERVATION OF STUDENTS WRITING

The behavior of students at work writing is a second source of data against which teachers can test and clarify composition research. Like one's own writing, this is a source of data very close at hand—living, breathing authors whose drafts we can see and discuss in conferences, and whose writing practices we can observe during in-class drafting sessions.

Such observation can be rigorous and systematic, or occasional and casual, or something in between. Most teachers aren't going to take the first course, and the second one isn't likely to bring much insight. But most teachers could find out a lot about the processes of writing—and about their own students— by simply watching and taking notes during in-class writing sessions. They could focus and systematize their observations by developing observation guides that incorporate ideas about the writing process they have learned from earlier introspection and background reading.

Figure 4–1, "Observing Writing Activities," is a little guide I developed this way in 1982. I had been thinking about my own writing practices, and

Figure 4–1
Observing Writing Activities

Physiological Behaviors During Writing

R— Rituals	Adjusting chair, shuffling papers, tapping pencil, crumpling paper in disgust, sharpening pencils, organizing the writing area, meditating, etc.
M— Movements of the Face and Body	Nonverbal cues to attitude, involvement/boredom, frustration/success, nervousness, sweating, etc.
V— Verbal Expressions	Talking to self, forming words with lips, muttering, significant sighs.
RU— Resource Use	Using reference works, talking to others present, etc.

Scribal Behaviors During Writing

D— Doodling	
L— Listing	Putting down isolated words and phrases—not sustained, margin-to-margin production of writing.
S— Sustained Production of Writing	More continuous, fluid, margin-to-margin production of sentences. Note: There may well be interruptions for "Changing" and for "Mental Behaviors."
C— Changing	Making changes *in* a draft by crossing out, adding, and changing words and phrases. Note: It may be significant whether a person does this "as he goes" or whether a person finishes a draft and then goes back to make her changes "from the beginning." Changing is not "Re-Drafting."
RD— Re-Drafting	Working with clean paper to do over an earlier draft or a significant section. Note differences from "Changing."

(continued)

those of my students, and working with the spate of writing-process research that was going on in the late 1970s and early 1980s—articles such as Janet Emig's "Hand, Eye, Brain," Sondra Perl's "Understanding Composing," Sharon Pianko's "Reflection," and Nancy Sommers' "Revision Strategies of Student Writers and Experienced Adult Writers."

From such reading, I tried to distill an approach to classroom observation that would not be too complicated to use even though it acknowledged the complexity I was reading about and reflecting on in my own writing:

- Interconnections of cognitive and physical processes in drafting
- The centrality of change to writing and the blurred borders separating what textbooks often called "drafting" and "revising"
- The impact that reviewing an already-produced text can have on the production of more text

(continued)

Mental Behaviors During Writing

G—	Glancing	A quick interruption in "Scribal Behavior" to scan words or phrases.
P—	Perusing	A longer interruption in "Scribal Behavior" to read or re-read larger segments of a draft.
?—	Pausing	Neither "Scribal Behavior" nor reading is going on. Apparently, the writer is thinking about the project, daydreaming, procrastinating, waiting for "inspiration," being preoccupied by other thoughts, etc.

Summary Questions about Writing Activities

1. What does the writer do to get started writing?
2. What percent of the time goes to Physiological, Scribal, Mental activities?
3. When the writer "runs out of steam" Drafting, does he or she Pause or Peruse and then launch again into businesslike Drafting?
4. Does the writer Peruse or Pause before making changes?
5. Does the writer Glance in the midst of Drafting—with fingers still moving or with only momentary interruptions?
6. When the writer makes Changes, do they involve words, punctuation, phrases, sentences?
   Does the writer Change by adding, deleting, modifying?
   Does the writer Re-Draft whole paragraphs or longer sections?
7. During which writing activities does the writer seem the most efficient? The least?

True to the spirit of writing-as-a-way-of-learning, creating that observation guide crystalized my understanding of writing; it helped me see connections between writing-process research and the more concrete reality of my own writing and my students' writing; and it helped me understand my students and their writing strategies.

With my observation guide and a note pad close by, I have watched hundreds of students at work, their eyes shifting back to read an earlier section, hands moving or pausing, their speed dropping to a frustrated crawl and then shifting into an efficient gallop. And I've talked with dozens of students about what they felt was happening when the drafting was going well or was blocked, and especially about what they thought was occurring during pauses and rescanning. From observing my students, I've learned such things as this:

- Different people write differently.
- Some writers seem to leap at a single bound from assignment to sustained writing, while others fidget, doodle, and outline their way toward sentence-to-sentence drafting.
- Once started, some writers enjoy long stretches of sustained writing during which their eyes glance back, as if they are working mentally to connect where they are going to where they have been. Others work in shorter stretches of sustained production, with pauses in which they look around the room or reread long passages.
- Some writers clearly seem to be helped along by words on the page. Their sustained writing slows, as if they are getting confused or running out of ideas; their eyes glance back and seem to spot something on the page; then the pace of their drafting immediately picks up.
- Some writers get similar help from the notes or outlines they scribbled earlier. They seem to work along, referring periodically to notes on separate paper.
- One person may seem to write quite differently at different times depending on the assignment and many other variables.

I know these aren't particularly stunning discoveries, but they do corroborate things I've learned from reading research by people too numerous to mention. I also know that the observations that have led me to such conclusions were not "real" research. But arriving at such conclusions on the basis of my *own* observations has confirmed the research and helped me to understand it better. I believe the observation of students writing would bring these same benefits to most college and high school writing teachers who are trying to keep up on developments in composition.

INTROSPECTION AND OBSERVATION AS
TEACHING STRATEGIES

Up to this point, I have been concerned with *teachers* and how we can use informed introspection and classroom observation to expand and sharpen our understanding of composition. For the remainder of this chapter I want to shift the focus to our *students* and how we can use introspection and observation as teaching strategies.

Just a few sentences ago I said that observing *for myself* student writing behaviors I'd read about in other people's research made insights from those articles clearer and more significant to me. The principle at work here is a commonplace of educational psychology: that understanding is enhanced when people have personal connections with material. Composition research is often difficult material—dense, theoretical. On the other hand, introspection into one's own writing practices is quite personally connected. Observation of real human beings in your class is personally connected too. And the firsthand, connected quality of introspection and observation can help teachers understand research more fully.

This same psychology, of course, can work the same way for writing students who are dealing with textbooks, course handouts, teacher presentations, comments on papers, and the like. Process-oriented courses ask students to cope with material that may seem fairly abstract (for instance, how hands, eyes, and brain coordinate powerfully during writing) and rather challenging (for example, learning to adjust established writing habits to try new approaches). As I've tried to help students understand the complexity of writing and to expand their repertoires of writing techniques, I've found that classroom activities and writing assignments involving introspection and observation are very effective teaching strategies.

It would be possible to lecture, in good current-traditional fashion, about the processes of writing—thoughts, emotions, muscular activity, rereading and reflection during pauses, etc.—and to expect students to be so convinced that their writing practices become more productive. Of course it would also be futile. A good deal more success can come from activities and assignments through which students make their *own* discoveries about the processes of writing and about effective writing strategies.

A key to this kind of teaching about the processes of writing is classroom observation—one student keeping notes as another writes, and then a switch of roles. Just as the teacher benefits from an observation guide, students can use a guide to help them recognize and keep track of the writing behaviors they observe. By developing an observation guide and orienting students to it, teachers provide students with writing-process information that is organized, simplified, and contexted for understanding. For instance, the somewhat cryptic notes in the teachers' observation guide in figure 4–1 became fuller and were more closely interwoven with instructions for the students as these were incorporated into the textbook *Writing: Processes and Intentions*.

> *Sustained Production*: Fairly continuous production of sentence after sentence. If you are observing someone who alternates between writing by hand and writing directly at the computer screen, try to note when the writer changes from one method of production to the other. In either case, the *flow* of writing will be interrupted occasionally by the next several kinds of behaviors.
>
> *Glancing*: Quick movement of the eyes to scan words or phrases. It might happen while the hand continues to draft, or during momentary pauses in sentence-after-sentence writing. With computer writers, notice how often the writer uses the arrow keys to "scroll" through the text.
>
> *Studying*: Eyes seem to pay more careful attention to words and sentences during longer pauses in sustained writing.
>
> *Changing*: Modifying a draft by adding and changing words, crossing things out, drawing arrows to indicate a changed order, etc. The changes are made *on* a draft, not by starting over on clean paper or in a new file. They may seem to be part of the ongoing writing, and may occur in brief pauses within the sustained production of sentences. Computer writers will probably make some changes as they write, but at some point they will get a printed copy of their writing. Note whether they begin making major changes at the computer or whether they may make only minimal changes on the computer screen and then get a printed copy of their writing. (Gebhardt and Rodrigues, pp. 17–18)

Because writing-process information presented with the help of an observation guide is background for a task to be performed—observing classmates writing—and not just abstract information, students may experience this information as something concrete and useful. And by giving information about how to use the observation guide, teachers can increase the usefulness of the approach for students. As an example, consider this passage from the same textbook:

> As you observe, pay special attention to the behaviors we called Sustained Production, Glancing, Studying, and Changing. Keep these questions in mind as you observe:
>
> a. What does the writer do to get started writing?
> b. How does Glancing seem to fit into the writer's behaviors? For instance, you might note that your partner writes sentence after sentence for several minutes, then seems to run out of steam, glances back to see how things are fitting together, and then picks up speed again.

    c. Is there a relationship between Glancing and Studying and the Changes the writer makes during writing? For instance, do the eyes seem to be active just before the hand makes changes?

    d. When the writer makes Changes, do they involve words, phrases, whole sentences, or punctuation? Are they changes of elimination, addition, or substitution? (In other words, does the writer delete words in some places, add words in other places, or does the writer delete a few words and substitute other words?)

Try to find one or two points in your partner's writing that you can talk about later. Look for combinations of behaviors: Glances just before Changes; eye movements that seem to trigger hand movements; periods of slow, labored writing giving way to more fluid writing. Do you see points in your partner's drafting that make you wonder whether something significant was going on in the writer's head? If so, remember the place on the paper; later ask your partner to talk about what was going on at that point in the writing.

Summarize what you have observed—the writing behaviors you have noticed. While you are writing your summary, your partner should write down what he or she thinks went on. Are there any discrepancies? Have a debriefing session with your partner, a session in which you read one another's summaries and then talk about your observations. Encourage your partner to talk about the session. What did you learn about your partner's writing behaviors? What did your partner learn about his or her writing behaviors? What processes did your partner engage in that were not observable? (p. 19)

The directions in the first half of this excerpt emphasize two things that are especially significant in writing-process instruction—the hand–eye–brain relationship that shows in "glancing" and "studying" pauses; and the kinds of changes made during drafting. The middle paragraph suggests that students look, during observation sessions, for one or two points where significant things seem to be "going on in the writer's head" (places to talk about in a debriefing session). And the final paragraph asks students to prepare for debriefing sessions by summarizing their observations in written reports to the writers they have observed.

These summary writings can be detailed and fairly formal reports or short precludes to discussion, such as these reports through which two students learned that writers and observers can have very different perceptions of the same writing activities:

    Marilyn: It was interesting to watch you write, Kelly. You obviously are a well-organized person and self-disciplined. You spent the first few seconds thinking about the assignment, then picked up the pen and began writing rapidly. The speed amazed me as did your infrequent pauses for reflection. It looked like you knew what you wanted to say and how to say it. I was surprised to hear you say that you really weren't sure where your thoughts were headed. Anyway, you were self-disciplined, and it showed in your tight posture, your attitude, the way you gripped the pen, and the few body movements I was able to observe.

Kelly: The first thing I noticed about the way you did the assignment, Marilyn, was that you had some "rituals" it looked like you had to go through before you could start writing. You folded your notebook over very businesslike and moved around in the chair like you had to get some feeling or beginning. Instead of writing right from the start, you moved down the page a couple of lines. A second thing I noticed was that you did a lot of glancing. I thought I saw you looking back a couple of words to keep your train of thought. And you had a look on your face as if you were deep in thought. I was amazed to hear you tell me that you were daydreaming! (Gebhardt and Rodrigues, p. 21)

From observation sessions and observation reports written for others, the approach I am suggesting moves to more introspective writing, perhaps journal entries or brief how-I-write sketches like these:

Gregoria: When I write, I like to sit somewhere comfortable and have thoughts run through my mind. I see pictures in my mind. This helps me know what it is that I'm trying to write. I always take a few moments to pause and then go back to my writing. When I pause, sometimes my mind will drift far away but other times it dwells on what I'm writing about. I think many sentences through carefully, sifting words out to make the sentence "sound" just right to me as I put them down. After I have written words, often I will reread them out loud to myself. If it sounds OK, I will leave it but other times I will change words to make them sound better.

Becky: When I write with a computer in the Apple Lab, my thoughts flow quickly. With pen and paper, it takes me longer to write down what I'm thinking and I sometimes lose an idea before it goes down in words, or because of a silly problem like running out of ink. With a word processor I never worry about this because I always save my work on a disk and I can always wait to print it later if the ribbon is bad. If I get stuck on an idea, I sort through my text and find what is causing my problem. Sometimes I move a paragraph to a different point in my text to see if that helps me get going again, and I especially like to be able to stick new ideas right into the middle of sentences when I get a new idea. When I find mistakes, I can correct them right away (with the delete key) but what I like to do is just keep going until later and then go back to work with spelling errors and typing mistakes. (Gebhardt and Rodrigues, p. 15)

Such writing helps students better understand their own writing processes and practices. And when students read and discuss a number of their classmates' introspective pieces, they can learn valuable lessons about the diversity of writing processes and strategies.

Obviously, the past few pages offer only a rough sketch of an instructional approach. This approach grounds writing-process information in firsthand observation, and it encourages students to make personal connections to the information. The approach also involves a lot of writing—in-class drafting sessions, observation reports, introspective journal entries, possibly papers blending insights discovered through observation and introspection with information presented by teacher and textbook. This approach fosters active thinking about writing and about one's own writing processes, and it shows students that people use many different strategies as they write.

All this, of course, is quite supportive of instruction in a process-oriented writing course. So, just as I began this essay by recommending introspection and observation as ways for the teacher to gain insights into the processes of writing, I end it by recommending introspection and observation as ways to help students learn about the writing process.

5

The Case for Collaboration—in Theory, Research, and Practice

ANDREA A. LUNSFORD

It is the central argument of this chapter that all teaching involves research, that all teachers are researchers, and that all research implicates theory and is by nature collaborative. It therefore follows, in a kind of syllogistic goose-step, that all teaching implicates theory and collaboration.

Rather than present a traditional argument in support of this thesis, however, I want to *demonstrate* it through the telling of three representative stories or anecdotes, hoping that they will strike a metonymic note in you and carry the burden of proof.

A STORY ABOUT THEORY

Let me begin with a brief story about how I and my frequent coauthor Lisa Ede first became interested in collaborative writing. In 1982 we decided to write an article together, and in the course of that exercise we became increasingly intrigued by a series of theoretical questions: Who exactly was the *author* of this piece? Where did our concept of authorship come from? Extensive research turned up very few discussions of these questions and led us to set out an agenda by which we could study this odd phenomenon, collaborative writing. Five years later, we know from our own and our students' research that collaborative writing is the norm in most on-the-job writing. Our book, *Singular Texts/Plural Authors*, traces our attempt to understand the origin of the *construct* of authorship as singular and originary in Western culture and reports on research of collaborative writers on the job. Hence this "story" attempts to show how a theoretical question leads to collaboration among theory, research, and practice—and among teacher and students, for Lisa and I very quickly involved our students in these practical and theoretical questions and out of those efforts there eventually evolved a research design. As an example of that research, let me share the report of one of our on-site visits, this time to a group of collaborative writers in the West.

Technical Writers in a Construction Equipment Firm

"Correct," said Allan Warrior when we asked if we had interpreted a printout accurately. "Not 'right.'" "Correct." "We do not use 'right,'" explains Warrior, "unless it is the opposite of 'left.' Everything else is 'correct.'"

Defined exclusively as "the opposite of left," "right" is part of a carefully constructed 2,000-word controlled vocabulary developed especially for the international construction equipment manufacturing firm that employs Warrior as a technical writer. This prescriptively rigid style guide acts as a primary constraint on the technical writers who use it at the same time that it allows them to establish international collaboration. Naturally, it and the writers who use it fascinated us.

Having a style guide is, as Warrior notes, far from unique: "Every technical writing group has to come up with a certain style guide. . . . Some of them are more formal than others but [even] if you go to a newspaper, they inevitably have a style guide." But the specificity and formality of this guide is unusual. As is most often the case, this particular style guide grew out of very practical concerns. Faced with the need to produce operating and service manuals that could be used to assemble and maintain equipment in many non-English-speaking countries, the firm turned to machine translation and to loose translation produced by people in the target country. The result was "pretty sterile." And, occasionally, pretty funny as well. One such occasion featured a "feeler gauge":

> There is a gauge we use in checking clearances, a machine gauge. It is a feeler gauge. Every mechanic in the U.S. knows what a feeler gauge is. But then it came back translated into French. The only word [the translator could find] for feelers were the little things on the end of a butterfly's antenna. This came back as "Go catch a butterfly . . ." The use of strictly controlled vocabulary helped solve such problems.

"The key element" in the language, notes Warrior, is that "one word can only have one meaning. Take, for instance, 'switch'":

> We had a lot of trouble with "switch." It is quite common for us to say turn on the switch or turn off the switch. Most switches don't turn. You see, we used to have oil lamps—you turned the light up, you turned the light down. Then the first electrical switches were rotary. But if you are in a country now where you have only had a wall switch that flips, try to tell them to turn the switch on—they wonder "What does that mean?" So [now] we [say] move the switch to the on position or . . . to the off position. . . . Another

interesting point is that "switch" can be a noun or a verb in our language. We just throw it around and don't even pay attention to it. We are very careful about that. We just tell them it is a noun.

This vocabulary and "Max," the text editor program that checks the use of the vocabulary and several dozen other factors (no sentences longer than seventeen words; no more than two descriptors plus a noun; all negatives within four words of the verb; noun and verb close together; no inversion of word order; no use of should, would, or could; no passive verbs; and so on), are very much partners in the collaborative writing Warrior and his colleagues do. According to this team of writers, using the controlled vocabulary well "is kind of an art form. If we can write text so that the person reading it doesn't realize that it is in a controlled language, I think I have done my job."

The job cannot be done alone, however, as Warrior and his colleagues stressed again and again. Any piece of technical discourse they produce results from a complex and highly collaborative process, which typically begins when the company decides to come out with a new product. In such cases, Harold Jones, head of the five-person writing division, assigns the project:

> And then we go through and see what material has to be created. We make up a list. Then it is up to us to go to find out what engineering has done. A lot of times at that stage they are not complete yet, but we get involved as much as we can so we can learn about it. Start pulling out all the drawings and go through and interpret what there is. Look for similarities to what else we have produced.

Eventually, engineering provides the writers with a "new product advance information guide," a set of preliminary drawings and statement of aims, which the team studies for additional information. As soon as a prototype and a rough draft of a manual to accompany it are developed, the writers "verify" or "try it out" by completely disassembling the product and checking to see if they can follow their own directions. In this stage of their work, they call not only on their own training (all have degrees in science and engineering as well as "mechanical experience") but on the team engineers and team mechanics. "Afterwards," says Warrior, "we usually rewrite."

The rewrite then goes back to the engineers: "We take what they give out and put it in our [language] and we feed it back through them. They mark it up again. And it is good because then we rewrite and it comes out better."

Throughout this process, the text editor program monitors the language and syntax of the manual, and the writers work with illustrators to create and label graphics. The draft copy is then "routed again to engineering, marketing, legal." The entire process, which takes "maybe six months," usually works smoothly: the team is small and comfortable with each other. Harold Jones, the leader, "looks at the overall picture," "sets the priorities," and "does the choreography." In spite of the highly constrained nature of the writing that they do and the many levels of review to which their work is subjected, these writers find their collaborative experience "satisfying" and "challenging." Though each started out in some area of engineering, they moved into technical writing out of choice, not necessity. As one team member said, "As an engineer, I always have to write . . . and all my life, words and language have been important. I enjoy words."

These writers also stressed the satisfaction that comes from the broadest form of collaboration their work calls for: establishing direct ties with one primary audience—those people around the world who operate and maintain their equipment. Ironically, they are able to establish this collaborative bond through the constraints imposed by their highly controlled language. Through it they create a text that readers in, say, Nepal can use in constructing meaning:

> We put things in our manuals that other people do not . . . but we do it because people need it, not only those people who will write the marketing information, but the people in the field—who need to understand how it is supposed to work and how to fix it. We concentrate on writing for the end user.

Thus in the work of this collaborative team do reading and writing, readers and writers, interanimate one another. (Ede and Lunsford, *Singular Texts/ Plural Authors* (Carbondale, Ill.: Southern Illinois University Press, 1990).

Let me point out what is perhaps already completely obvious: Lisa and I as teacher-researchers interviewed technical writers who are themselves teacher-researchers. They and we worked collaboratively—in each case and together. We might also note that Warrior and his colleagues' practice strongly implies a theory of language and learning, one I will interrogate later in this paper. To go one step further, let me say that my students are also identifying writers to interview and study, that they are trying to corroborate or disprove the findings that will appear in our book, and that they are thus *also* teacher-researchers and collaborators—with me and with each other. May the circle, as we say in Tennessee, be unbroken.

A STORY ABOUT RESEARCH

A second story I wish to offer as evidence for my claim that research, theory, and collaboration are always implicated in one another began some five years ago, when Bob Connors and I got interested in error patterns in student writing as a result of historical investigations we had been conducting separately. I had found Scottish professors of the nineteenth century marking sentences as "loose and runny"—Bob had found an error called "stringy syntax"—and we both were amused by a 1901 account stating that the major problem Harvard writers displayed was the inability to use *shall* and *will* correctly. We also noted that the first edition of Harbrace (1941) was based on a study of 20,000 student essays—so we decided to collaborate on studying error patterns in an equally large sample of student writing. This research-collaboration involved hundreds of teachers who sent us marked essays written by over 21,000 college students, many more teachers who helped us analyze a stratified sample of 3,000 papers, and many, many more teachers and students who collaborated with us to produce our textbook.

Briefly, here are some of the most significant findings of this large and lengthy collaborative research process. (For the most complete discussion, see "Frequency of Formal Error Patterns in Current College Writing: Ma and Pa Kettle Do Research," *CCC* [December 1988]: 395–409.)

1. Not surprisingly—and here comes the theory part of the story—*error* is a construct just as is authorship, and is very much time and place bound. Conventions are socially constructed and shift across time, place, culture. We must never forget this lesson—*shall* and *will* and "loose and runny" have given way to our own perceived patterns and conventions of usage.

2. Teachers' ideas about what constitutes a serious, markable error vary widely. As most of us may have expected, some teachers pounce on every "very unique" as a pet peeve, some rail at "Every student . . . their . . . ." The most prevalent "error," failure to place a comma after an introductory word or phrase, was a *bête noire* for some teachers but was ignored by many more. Papers marked by the same teacher might at different times evince different patterns of formal marking. Teachers' reasons for marking specific errors and patterns of error in their students' papers are complex, and in many cases they no doubt are guided by the perceived needs of the student writing the paper and by the stage of the composing process the paper has achieved.

3. Teachers do not seem to mark as many errors as we often think they do. On average, college English teachers mark only 43 percent of the most serious errors in the papers they evaluate. In contrast to the popular picture of English teachers mad to mark up every error, our results show that even the most-often-marked errors are only marked two-thirds of the time. The less-marked patterns (and remember, these are the Top Twenty error patterns overall) are marked only once for every four

times they appear. The number of errors found compared to the number of errors marked suggests a fascinating possibility for future research: detailed observation of teacher marking, accompanied by talk-aloud protocols. Such research seems to us a natural follow-up to the findings presented here.

4. The reasons teachers mark any given error seem to result from a complex formula that takes into account at least two factors—how serious or annoying the error is perceived to be at a given time for both teacher and student, and how difficult it is to mark or explain. Some of the lesser-marked errors we studied are clearly felt to be more stylistic than substantive. Certain of the comma errors seem simply not to bother teachers very much. Others, like wrong words or missing inflection errors, are much more frequently marked, and might be said to have a high "response quotient" for teachers. In addition our study suggests that in most cases errors go unmarked not because a teacher failed to see them, but because they were not germane to the lessons at hand. A teacher working very hard to help a student master subject-verb agreement with third-person-singular nouns, for instance, might well ignore most other errors in a given paper.

   Teachers' perceptions of the seriousness of a given error pattern seem, however, to be only part of the reason for marking an error. The sheer difficulty of explanation presented by some error patterns is another factor. Jotting "WW" in the margin to tip a student off to a diction problem is one thing; explaining a subtle shift in point of view in that same marginal space is quite another. Sentence fragments, comma splices, and wrong tenses, to name three classic "serious" errors, are all marked less often than possessive apostrophes. This is, we think, not due to teachers' perception that apostrophe errors are worse than sentence-boundary or tense problems, but to their quickness and ease of indication. The its/it's error and the possessive apostrophe, the two highest-marked patterns, are also two of the easiest errors to mark. This is, of course, not laziness; many composition teachers are so chronically overworked that we should not wonder that the errors most marked are those most quickly indicated.

5. Error patterns in student writing are shifting in certain ways, at least partially as a result of changing media trends within the culture. Conclusions must be especially tentative here, because the time-bound nature of studies of error makes comparisons difficult, and definitions of errors counted in earlier research are hard to correlate. Our research turned up several earlier lists of serious errors in freshman composition, however, whose order is distinctly different from the order we discovered.

In general our list shows a proliferation of error patterns that seem to suggest declining familiarity with the visual look of a written page. Most strikingly, spelling errors outnumber all others on our list by a factor of 300 percent! Spelling is the most obvious example of this lack of visual memory of printed pages seen, but the growth of other error patterns supports it as well.

Some of the error patterns that seem to suggest this visual-memory problem were not found or listed in earlier studies but have come to light in ours. The many wrong-word errors, the missing inflected endings, the wrong prepositions, missing or misspelled apostrophes, even the its/it's errors—all suggest that students today may be less familiar with the visible aspects of written forms. These findings confirm the contrastive analysis between 2,000 papers from the 1950s and 2,000 papers from the 1970s that was carried out by Gary Sloan in 1979. Sloan determined that many elements of formal writing convention broke down severely between the fifties and the seventies, including spelling, homophones, sentence structure elements, inflected endings, and others (pp. 157–159). Sloan notes that the effects of an oral—and we would stress, an *electronic*—culture on literacy skills are subversive. Students who do not read the "texts" of our culture will continue to come to school without the tacit visual knowledge of written conventions that "text-wise" writers carry with them effortlessly. Such changes in literate behavior have and will continue to affect us in multiple ways, including the ways we perceive, categorize, and judge "errors."

Finally, our study points up some good news. One very telling fact emerging from our research is the realization that college students are *not* making more formal errors in writing than they used to. The numbers of errors made by students in earlier studies and the numbers we found in the 1980s agree remarkably. Our findings chart out as follows:

Study	Year	Average Paper Length	Errors per Paper	Errors per 100 Words
Johnson	1917	162 words	3.42 errors	2.11
Witty & Green	1930	231 words	5.18 errors	2.24
Ma & Pa	1986	422 words	9.52 errors	2.26

The consistency of these numbers seems to us extraordinary. It suggests that although the length of the average paper demanded in freshman composition has been steadily rising, the formal skills of students have not declined precipitously.

In the light of the "Johnny Can't Write" furor of the 1970s and the sometimes hysterical claims of educational decline often heard today, these results are striking—and heartening. They suggest that in some ways we *are* doing a better job than we might have known. The number of errors has not gone down, but neither has it risen in the past five decades. In spite of open admissions, in spite of radical shifts in the demographics of those attending college, in spite of the huge escalation in the population percentage as well as in sheer numbers of people attending American colleges, freshmen are still committing approximately the same number of formal errors per one hundred words that they were before World War I. In this case, not losing means that we are winning.

My point in telling this particular story of research findings is twofold— first, to demonstrate the ways in which theory, practice, and research animate one another, and second, to note the intensely collaborative nature of all three. Let me also say that, in this case, student teacher-researchers have been and are right now at work, examining error patterns in their own and other students' writing and building their own theories to account for these phenomena.

A STORY ABOUT PRACTICE

My last story grows not out of my theoretical work or my research, but out of my practical concerns in teaching one particular course at Ohio State— English 302, an introduction to the English major course on critical writing. Last year my colleague Louis Ulman and I decided to "work up" this course collaboratively, and that collaboration led us to theoretical and research-related questions—and to extensive collaboration with our students. We decided to focus on the concept of intertextuality, and to ask our students to join us in an intertextual exploration that could lead us to an understanding and practice of critical writing. We began to plan the course as teacher-researchers by choosing a central text (Mary Shelley's *Frankenstein*) and auxiliary texts (*Textbook* and *Preface to Critical Reading*), and by doing some preliminary research to get together a Kinko packet to start our intertextual conversation. This packet included the "Prometheus" and "Pandora" stories from Bullfinch, Adam's speech in *Paradise Lost*, Byron's "Prometheus," Hawthorne's "Rappaccini's Daughter," Oppenheimer's speech after World War II, and a number of other pieces as well. But as soon as the students arrived, we asked them to take it from there. The result was more information on allusions and references to *Frankenstein* than I could have imagined possible—ranging from a whole series of Far Side cartoons to studies in psychotheraphy on multiple personality disorders. Throughout, the students were directly involved in orchestrating this intertextual conversation; they were themselves teacher-researchers who worked collaboratively to answer what came to seem more and more profound questions: "Why has the Prometheus/Frankenstein myth or story so captivated the Western mind?" "How do we all 'create' our best and our monster selves—and our best and monster others?"

Grappling with such questions brought students out of their traditional roles, revealed the intimate link between theory, research, and practice, and turned them into committed collaborators. The class ended with a joint collaboration, awards to the most effective final essays (judged by the class), and repeated performances of a collaboratively produced hit for guitar and harmonica, "The Frankenstein Blues."

In a way, the three stories I have insisted on telling seem perhaps to be unrelated. But in ways that are increasingly important to me, they are closely related—are, in fact, the same story. To me, all three suggest that teacher-researchers are at their best when they become *student*-teacher-researchers, working in close collaboration with other teachers—whether in the academy or in other workplaces—and always with students. A very wise teacher once remarked that where learning occurs, teaching *may* follow. That, I believe, is why we are teacher-researchers—learners who aspire also to be teachers—in the strongest and best sense of the term.

6
Learning from Teachers

KEN KANTOR

Some years ago I had a slightly disgruntled graduate student say to me: "You need to have more of the kind of situation that we as high school teachers have, so that you'll be more realistic in your teaching of curriculum and methods." Reactively, I responded that he perhaps ought to have more of what I as a university professor had, particularly in terms of the time to reflect on and exchange ideas about teaching. In a sense I think now that we were both wrong (in our defensiveness) and right: educational researchers and theorists need to have a greater awareness of what happens in classrooms and schools (and what it *feels* like to teach in those situations), while teachers need greater opportunities to read, write, talk, and think about teaching.

I've been thinking quite a lot lately about relationships between university researchers and classroom teachers, and how those relationships might be redefined to allow for greater collaboration and understanding. Something helpful to me in this regard has been to look back at my own writings and assess how my views have changed and evolved in recent years. In this chapter I'd like to evaluate critically four pieces of mine that were published between 1981 and 1985, and then to discuss how my current views represent both an extension of and a divergence from the ideas presented in these writings. To a great extent, this assessment confirms what Courtney Cazden has said about language development: "What one sees depends on how one looks" (p. 435).

The first of these writings was an article that appeared in the February 1981 issue of the *English Journal* with the somewhat condescending title "Research in Composition: What It Means for Teachers." In this article I summarized various studies done in the areas of discourse analysis, composing processes, naturalistic inquiry, evaluation and assessment, and curriculum, instruction, and teacher education, with brief discussions of implications for teaching. I did stress the point that I saw little direct connection between research findings and specific classroom practices, but also argued that looking at research studies could inform teachers' understanding and perhaps guide their practice.

I received two extreme responses to this article. The first came from a high school English department chair active in NCTE who thanked me for the contribution to his knowledge; he said he was planning to use the article as a basis for in-service sessions with his department members. The second was from a teacher who wrote a lengthy negative critique of the article to the journal editor (who subsequently sent it on to me). In this critique he assailed my writing as being jargon-ridden and my ideas as remote from the concerns of most English teachers. The one positive note in this diatribe was his agreement with my proposal that teachers should write and share their writing with their students. Initially I felt wounded by his attack, but also noted that at several points he cited as his hero Richard Mitchell, the elitist "underground grammarian." I observed too that the writer knew little about the work of James Britton and others on writing development which I had cited in the article. So it became easier to dismiss his argument as self-serving and unfairly biased.

At the same time I sensed that there was some grain of truth in his criticism. As I reread my piece I could see that I had unintentionally implied that researchers possessed a higher theoretical knowledge which it was their job to pass on to more practical-minded teachers. And the language in which I had presented my summaries was indeed marked by jargon and removed from the discourse with which we might normally communicate.

Later that year, in the December 1981 issue of *Research in the Teaching of English*, I coauthored with Dan Kirby and Judith Goetz (then colleagues at the University of Georgia) a longer bibliographic essay titled "Research in Context: Ethnographic Studies in English Education." In this article we distinguished between naturalistic and experimental forms of inquiry, and described five major features of ethnography: hypothesis-generating, contextuality, thick description, participant-observation, and meaning-making. We tried to avoid being unnecessarily polemical, at the same time suggesting that ethnographic approaches were compatible with many of the current emphases in English education. We also cited a number of studies in composition, literature, and language that employed ethnographic techniques, and pointed out several problems in conducting such research.

Again, we received both praise and criticism for this effort. Many of our colleagues expressed their appreciation for what they thought was a useful discussion. Others were less charitable, as with one researcher who wrote a letter claiming that we were calling for opposition to any kind of experimental studies. (One colleague with whom I shared this letter commented wryly that, as proponents of response-based theory might say, readers do indeed create their own texts.)

A more reasoned critique was later provided by Stephen North in *The Making of Knowledge in Composition*. North suggested that we were sending mixed messages, promoting ethnography on the one hand while trying too hard on the other to reconcile it with experimental research. Though I object to North's pigeonholing us as among "the Ethnographers," I agree that the statement was perhaps too conciliatory, using terms like "reliability" and "validity" and citing a number of studies that were only partly ethnographic in order not to have ethnography seem too different from traditional experimental or quantitative studies. At the same time, I think the article should be viewed in its historical context. It appeared at a time when naturalistic studies of English teaching were beginning to emerge; a more strident advocacy might have alienated a greater number of readers. More to the point, I think that we were just beginning to define the place of ethnographic research in our field; a certain amount of uncertainty and cautiousness was to be expected.

To gain a clearer perspective on ethnography during this time, I conducted a naturalistic study of a creative writing class in a nearby high school. This study was eventually published as a chapter in Beach and Bridwell's *New Directions in Composition Research* and titled "Classroom Contexts and the Development of Writing Intuitions: An Ethnographic Case Study." As a participant-observer in this class for several months, I generated a number of insights regarding students' composing processes and written products. I also described the approach of a skillful teacher-writer, as he helped students grow in their writing ability through their interactions with others in a classroom community.

The responses to this chapter were not as extreme as those in reaction to the articles previously discussed, but they nonetheless reflected a range of opinion. Some, likely Shirley Koeller, praised the study for its contextual richness; others contended that it was not truly ethnographic. Lucy Calkins provided perhaps the most helpful critique, as she referred to the relatively brief time I had spent in this setting, and the lack of a theoretical perspective related to methodology. She also proposed a classification of naturalistic studies, including descriptive, ethnographically oriented, and teaching case studies. Her essay goes far in clarifying differences among types of naturalistic research, toward the goal of developing stronger communities among researchers.

If I were writing these pieces today, I would, like Calkins, make a clearer distinction between ethnography and other kinds of naturalistic or observational studies. As Harry Wolcott argues, length of time spent, use of ethnographic techniques, good description, and rapport with participants are necessary but not sufficient traits. What distinguishes ethnography, according to Wolcott, is its *intent*, specifically "to describe and interpret cultural behavior" (p. 43). While I did look in my study at the interactions and meanings created within a particular classroom, I did not relate those to a larger cultural context or theory. So I would now refrain from calling my study, or any similar to it, an ethnography (though Calkins' term, "ethnographically oriented," may be all right). At the same time, I would defend the study in terms of what it says about teaching and learning. Essentially it is the story of an excellent writing teacher engaging his students in creative processes through establishing and maintaining an interactive community. A number of teachers have told me that the report touched chords in their own experience or suggested possibilities they hadn't considered; that is perhaps the best compliment I might receive. As Kirby, Goetz, and I contended in the *RTE* article, naturalistic research potentially shapes itself to the contours of teaching in actual settings, and the findings thus carry meaning for teachers who work in those settings.

Finally, in an article published in the *English Journal* of October 1985, I dealt with the issue of teacher as researcher. Citing a number of informal studies conducted by teachers in a graduate class, I pointed out how they reflected various kinds of experimental, survey, observational, and historical research. While I recognized the importance of teachers conducting their own inquiries, I still characterized this effort as a kind of junior version of "professional research." I have since come to reject this view, seeking now to recognize and define various kinds of research, whether conducted by classroom teachers or college professors (or both), in terms of their own uniqueness and integrity. In particular, I am exploring the values of collaborative inquiry, in which hierarchical power relationships are broken down, and coresearchers bring their own perspectives and strengths to bear on their studies, and build, where possible, a shared vision.

Given the traditional state of things, however, that is no easy task. Great misunderstandings still exist among teachers, teacher educators, and researchers. I am especially concerned about certain attitudes expressed toward the teacher-researcher movement. On the one hand, some show an uncritical acceptance of almost anything teachers do in the name of research. They might agree with Woody Allen (as I sometimes do) that "98 percent of life is showing up." More detrimental, however, is an intolerance for teacher-conducted inquiries, characterized by a demand that studies must follow established rules of design and methodology in order to be justifiably classified as "research." This dogmatic attitude (often subtly disguised) only serves to reinforce the separation of theory and practice, and of university professors from classroom teachers.

To move, then, to a greater sense of collaboration, we must first ask the questions, "What knowledge is privileged?" and "To whom does it belong?" The researcher and teacher educator need to diminish their roles as "experts"—transmitters of prestige knowledge or welfare worker/missionaries—and begin to take on the roles of colearner and coparticipant with teachers. I am influenced here by feminist and critical theory, which challenge elitism and inequity and emphasize empowerment, caring, and social justice. I am also moved by Peter Elbow's eloquent statement about the importance of uncertainty and vulnerability in our teaching:

> Rather than trying to be perfectly fair and perfectly in command of what we teach—as good examiners ought to be—we should reveal our own position, particularly our doubts, ambivalences, and biases. We should show we are still learning, still willing to look at things in new ways, still sometimes uncertain or even stuck, still willing to ask naive questions, still engaged in the interminable process of working out the relationship between what we teach and the rest of our lives. Even though we are not wholly peer with our students, we can still be peer in this crucial sense of also being engaged in learning, seeking, and being incomplete. Significant learning requires change, inner readjustments, willingness to let go. We can increase the chances of our students being willing to undergo the necessary anxiety involved in change if they see we are also willing to undergo it. (pp. 332–33)

The collaborative view also requires us to look carefully at the contexts in which the researcher and the teacher work, and how forces in those cultural environments perpetuate the divisions between them. For better or worse, university research tends to be "theory-driven," while classroom teaching tends to be "practice-driven." In the teaching of writing particularly, there is a strong tension between theoretical emphases on personal growth, discovery processes, and meaning-making, and practical concerns with efficiency, standards, and management of social situations. Teachers and researchers need time and opportunities to work together to develop a more common frame of reference; otherwise they continue to be like the proverbial ships passing in the night.

A first step toward broadening that frame of reference is the recognition of teachers' practical knowledge, or what has variously been referred to as "practical wisdom" (Shulman), "practice-as-inquiry" (North), "situational decision-making" (Bolster), "reflective practice" (Schön), and "dilemma management" (Lampert). Experienced teachers in particular have developed an awareness that is in certain ways qualitatively different from, but not inferior to, the knowledge that is held by researchers and theorists. Moreover, this kind of knowing often requires a form of discourse that differs from the analytic, expository mode associated with "good research." Specifically, as Connelly and Clandinin point out, the narrative genre represents for many teachers a central mode of inquiry, and deserves recognition as such. Some theorists, like Gordon Pradl in the field of English education, have also been calling our attention to the significance of narrative understanding, "the sharing and testing of stories" (p. 133), to our growth as teachers.

Essentially, I am arguing here for a greater concern with "praxis," or the dialectic between theory and practice. This middle ground is, like the real world, complex and messy, requiring the university researcher to consider things more in terms of the teacher's experiences and perceptions, and the classroom teacher to view things more in light of educational issues and theories. Mostly it compels us to challenge assumptions, especially about who has what to say to whom. As I recently asked a doctoral student at her dissertation orals, "What do you feel your case studies of the teaching of revision might reveal to researchers and theorists as well as to teachers?"

Ultimately, I think, all of us should first define ourselves not as teachers or researchers but as *persons* who teach, read, write, discuss, and research (among other things), and learn from each other in the processes of doing so. Consequently we enter more easily into an interactive and interpretive learning community. Julie Jensen makes the point nicely:

> First, I wish we could encourage a redefinition of the word *researcher*. To the ranks of thesis and dissertation writers, assistant professors seeking tenure, and the small crowd that we represent, let's recruit anyone who has a question and a disciplined approach to finding an answer. . . . Membership in the club of reading/writing researchers needs to be broad enough to encompass those who read, who write, who know children, and who know classrooms. (pp. 57–58)

I'm beginning to see this inclusionary process unfold in a current project on writing across the curriculum with middle grade teachers in the Baker Demonstration School at National College of Education. In a more conventional sense I am observing in classrooms and interviewing the teachers, but we are also sharing journal entries, responding to students' writing, and discussing problems and possibilities in teaching writing. Later in the school year I plan to do some team-teaching with them. The project involves research, yes, but also teacher education, curriculum development, and above all collaborative inquiry. It is compelling me to redefine my relationships with my colleagues, and to reevaluate and broaden my conceptions of research.

As part of this discovery process, I am also collecting entries from the journals of teachers in my graduate writing and linguistics courses, looking especially for places at which theoretical and practical knowledge intersect (or where they conflict). This journal writing represents a way to bring teachers' voices into the conversation about language teaching and learning, and a means to develop jointly a more grounded theory of writing instruction. I'll close this chapter by sharing three such excerpts. The first was written by Mary, a prospective teacher in an M.A.T. program in elementary education, in response to sections of Lucy Calkins' *The Art of Teaching Writing* and Donald Graves's *Writing: Teachers and Children at Work*:

As I read Calkins and Graves I wonder whether, realistically, what they describe about the Writer's Workshop and what they are asking writing teachers to do isn't a fantasy that is a bit farfetched. Certainly many aspects of the workshop are common sense, practical, and wonderful. But it seems too difficult, too complicated, too unstructured, that it is a bit scary and unrealistic. I can't picture the first and second graders I work with in the types of scenarios the authors describe. It is scary to me because of the fear of losing classroom management and control, but I realize that like anything else, you have to adapt it to your own style in order to make it work for you and your classroom. It is also scary because the way they present the kinds of questions a teacher should ask, etc., is in such a way that makes me feel, as a reader, fearful I won't teach the RIGHT way. Sometimes it's a GOOD fear, in that it's gotten me thinking that in my own education, teachers have looked at my writing as well as other students' writing, and have made changes to the extent that it became their writing and not ours, the students. I feel it is wrong to instill your own values and preferences into the writings of your students. It is so important for the child to feel that he is in control of his own writing, and believe he has ownership of his work. . . . As a prospective teacher, I am most comfortable in the highly structured situations and methods of teaching that I experienced as a student. I am beginning to question these methods and also starting to think back to my own experiences as a student. Did my teachers do some of the things the authors say we often do (although we shouldn't) and do I do those things too because of my upbringing and out of habit?

What is striking here is the struggle with uncertainty, as Mary encounters new knowledge that challenges previous assumptions and at the same time suggests positive directions. She is willing to think reflectively about these issues, recognizing both her levels of comfort and the need to take risks. She is also relating these difficult questions to her own personal history (which further suggests the importance of autobiography in research and teacher education). Even as a novice, Mary is more thoughtful than many experienced teachers and researchers who believe that they have ultimate answers to difficult problems.

The second entry comes from Danielle, a language arts resource teacher:

The hallowed "time distribution sheet" glares down from its revered position on the classroom wall. It is there to remind the teacher not to deviate from the prescribed schedule. It is her ever-present guide and watchdog. Reading will take place from 10:35 to 11:50. There will be exactly 645 minutes per week devoted to Language Arts in the fourth grade and no more than 120 for Science. There are 35 units to be covered in the basal reader, nearly 100 skills and subskills to be taught and tested, and reading scores must be improved. The children and their teachers scurry in and out of classrooms on their way to reading groups, the reading lab, to the T.E.S.L. class, to a classroom down the hall where Social Studies is taught to one group while the others regroup for Math. It is widely held . . . that the more efficiently students are grouped, the more effectively their teachers can perform.

All of this in-and-out and to-and-fro makes the head spin. It's no wonder that the teachers feel they have no time. It is also understandable that when a "Language Arts teacher" is assigned to them they feel relieved of the responsibility of teaching that "subject."

This is not to say that some teachers have not found effective and creative ways to incorporate language arts skills into other content areas. One teacher reads daily to her children, thus giving them an opportunity to hear really fine literature read in a fluent manner. She breaks into the sacred time allotment devoted to the basal reader, but will defend this deviation most eloquently. Another teacher of Social Studies, after teaching a unit on the colonization of the States, assigns a written project. The children are to assume the role of a Pilgrim child and tell of their feelings and experiences coming over on the Mayflower.

These teachers are valuable resources. They haven't found more time in the school day. They haven't eliminated the teaching of one subject in favor of another. They have simply (or not so simply) been able to view their subjects another way and see that language arts skills can be used to enhance rather than replace. They have altered their focus on a subject to expand the learning potential of their students. We need these teachers to show others what they have done. Through poems, books, written assignments, group projects, and oral reports, these teachers have brought their subjects to life and made them more real to their students. They have encouraged their students to use a variety of avenues to explore a concept.

Danielle skillfully articulates dilemmas and pressures that teachers face. At the same time, she recognizes the efforts of teachers who use language as an integrating force in their teaching of content across the curriculum. It is this kind of practical knowledge that complements and gives concreteness to abstract theoretical perspectives.

Finally, Peg, an experienced teacher in an independent school, describes a problem she encountered in helping students get started in their writing:

Several interesting things have happened this week as a result of sharing with my students the list of journal story starters. The approach has differed from many in the past because I typically have allowed my students to write about ANYTHING which interested them, or to respond in writing to specific questions in their journals. Although there was a lot of success with certain assignments, and many of the students relished the opportunity to write without the limitations of topics imposed from the outside, many of the students wrote in a limited fashion. I was pleasantly surprised to see what happened this week. Interestingly enough, one of the girls who was new to my class last year and had a real problem facing the empty page got wonderfully motivated and excited by the format presented this week. She could write when given a choice of topics, but she couldn't choose one from thin air. . . . Needless to say, she was excited about the choices presented to her and wrote with much more voice and style than I've heard from her before. Her writings, and those of some other students, proved to be the catalyst that the other students needed. As one student wrote on one of the topics, other students would get an idea and share their thoughts the next day. For me my interest was heightened because I had tried some of the assignments myself and was therefore, just as the students were, more interested to hear how others responded to the ideas provided.

It was also very interesting for me that one of my students who has always enjoyed writing his own stories, stood up on the first day of sharing and stated VERY plainly that his story was one that was totally made up by him. Furthermore, he thought that list of story starters was stupid and useless. It was instructive for me to realize that this was an actual example of what Graves warned about where he stated, "Teachers should never assign what children choose to do when they find their own voice." As more of my students gain their voice, and feel confident about writing, I'm sure that more of them will abandon such sorts of selection lists as well.

Through perceptive observation Peg discovered that she had more than an either-or choice between using story starters and encouraging students to generate their own topics. She realized instead that different students needed different kinds of initial motivation. At the same time, she concurred with Graves that when students find their own voice they will more naturally pursue their own directions. She is a wise practitioner indeed.

Some researchers may regard these reflections of teachers as quaint, or less than scholarly and intellectual. To the contrary, I see them as profound, in their revelations of a tolerance for ambiguity, a search to understand better the complex relationships between theory and practice, and above all a great sensitivity to the interests and needs of students.

Inspired, then, by what represents for me a new and better way of looking at the world of teaching and research, I'll conclude by offering a kind of manifesto: If Research (with a capital R) requires a hierarchy of preferred and less-preferred modes, with university-sponsored investigations published in "prestige" journals considered as superior to studies conducted by classroom teachers, then I must seriously question the value of Research. If, on the other hand, research is regarded as a quintessential human endeavor, with people of all ages, backgrounds, occupations, interests, and talents collaborating in processes of inquiry and constructing meaning, then I say "Hurray for research, and let's get on with it."

7

Small Is Beautiful: Case Study as Appropriate Methodology for Teacher Research

GLENDA L. BISSEX

My title is taken from E. F. Schumacher's *Small Is Beautiful: Economics as if People Mattered*. "Small is beautiful": we live in a society where bigger is seen as better not only for business but often for research as well. (Is there a connection?) The larger the number of subjects, the more reliable the results. Numbers generate truth—or do they? "Economics as if people mattered": why not research as if people mattered—as if students and teachers mattered more than externally imposed programs, as if classrooms were centers of humane activity rather than production lines?

"Appropriate methodology" echoes the concept of "appropriate technology"—tools compatible with their contexts. For a teacher to teach one class by an approach he believes in and another class by an approach he is at least less convinced about, in order to have a control and an experimental group, is inappropriate methodology. For a teacher to observe and inquire into and reflect on the events and persons in his classroom is to use methodology in keeping with his role as an educator—methodology that does not alienate him or intrude on his teaching.

I am not asserting that case studies are appropriate solely and exclusively for teacher research as a sort of small-scale version of "real" research. Case study has a long tradition as a major way of knowing and of teaching in a number of disciplines and professions. Nor am I suggesting that case studies are the ONLY route to knowledge, for teachers or for anyone else.

A *case* can be a single individual in her environment, or several such individuals, or an interactive group such as a writing conference group, or a special project as viewed through a close observation of responses from the individuals involved in it. A *case study* I see as a reflective story of the unfolding, over time, of a series of events involving particular individuals. The persons studied are regarded as full human beings, having intentions and making meanings, not merely "behaving." The researcher includes these intentions and meanings in the meaning that she makes of the story and, as interpreter if not also actor, is herself a character in it.

What can we learn from a single case?

What can we learn from Frost's "The Death of the Hired Man?" Or from Conrad's *Lord Jim?*

Why is the study of individual cases an essential part of the training of lawyers, physicians, psychotherapists, social workers, and business managers?

What do we learn from reading a biography or an autobiography—from one life? Or from studying an historical case like the French Revolution?

Consider the expression "getting down to cases," meaning getting down to the specifics that really matter in a situation.

"And what does that prove?" one faculty member challenged me during an interview for my first full-time college teaching position. I had just finished telling him about my dissertation, a case study of my young son's writing and reading development over five years. Nobody on my dissertion committee had asked me that question, nor had I asked it of myself during the years I collected and poured through data, searching for patterns. "And what does that prove?" I was confronted with an alien view from which, I too keenly grasped, my research appeared worthless. I see now that the question was as inappropriate as asking what "The Death of the Hired Man" proved. The relevant question would have been, "And what did you *learn* from that?" Or "What can *I* learn from that?" A case study is a way of learning, not a method for proving.

A faculty member at another college, on hearing about this same study of mine, responded: "Oh, just like Piaget and Freud." Clearly she had a context for understanding and valuing case study.

Donald Schön in *The Reflective Practitioner*, a set of case studies of professionals reflecting in action, speaks of cases as "exemplars" (a term he borrowed from Thomas Kuhn). An exemplar is a situation or experience seen as similar to a subsequent one and thereby instructive about it; or an example of a way of thinking about something that is applicable in another situation. Professionals learn to see new problems as similar to ones they've already encountered. As they build a repertoire of exemplars, they become more knowledgeable, resourceful, and successful. Schön's comments suggest the value of case studies as exemplars not only for the researcher herself but for others: teachers, teachers in training, and other researchers.

Science has accustomed us to looking for cause and effect relationships in order to predict and control behavior. As psychologist Robert White observed about the individual lives he studied, "Many forces operate at once on a given personality, producing an elaborate lattice of interconnected events rather than a simple model of cause and effect" (p. 329). Looking closely at an individual, we see that lattice. The end of a case study should be insight, not control—an understanding of others and of ourselves that helps us to be educators, not manipulators.

As educators we teach individuals in the context of groups. In the statement preceding my case study, *GNYS AT WRK: A Child Learns to Write and Read*, I stressed the importance to education of the individual and his context:

> Except in the form of an individual person's reading a particular text or writing a particular message in a specific situation, reading and writing do not exist. "Reading" and "writing" are abstractions, convenient abbreviations enabling us to *refer* to certain kinds of human activities. These terms can also lead us to believe that what they refer to has a concrete existence. For example, we are told the "reading" level of various groups of children, although *groups* do not read. We are not told what these individuals have been asked to read or under what conditions, nor are we reminded that "reading" tests can only indirectly measure "reading." Unless we keep reminding ourselves that "reading" and "writing" are abstractions and abbreviations, we may come to believe—or, just as dangerously, to act as though we believe—in their disembodied existence.
>
> Furthermore, someone reads or writes something *for some purpose*. We do not read for the sake of reading, nor write for the sake of writing. Consider why you are reading this now. "Reading" and "writing" are meaningless as well as disembodied if they are regarded as ends in themselves, not as means of learning, imagining, communicating, thinking, remembering, and understanding.
>
> We cannot always specify who is reading or writing what under what conditions and for what purpose—but we sometimes must, to bring us back to the only concrete reality there is. Grade levels, test scores, and statistical analyses of "reading" and "writing" are very abstract—are abstractions about abstractions—although they may appear reassuringly tangible. Only individuals read and write particular messages, under particular conditions. (p. xiv)

Traditional, empirical science has accustomed us to seeking meanings in similarities, in generalizations. It is of no relevance to the laws of gravity whether the falling apple happens to be a Red Delicious or a Granny Smith.

But in the understanding of human beings, differences do make a difference. So Peter Johnston, leading us to understand reading disability through three case studies, explains: "Case studies were used on the assumption that there can be substantial individual differences in experience and in important dimensions of behavior (both overt and covert) which are as critical as the commonalities between individuals" (p. 155). Statistical studies cause differences to appear as one-dimensional, as differences in degree, blurring the qualitative differences among individuals which teachers confront daily in their classrooms. There is reason to believe diversity should not be viewed as an inconvenience or an anachronism but, as in biology, as conferring survival and evolutionary benefits, which we dismiss and disguise at our peril. If our students were all alike, wouldn't we be bored to death?

Harold Rosen has observed another value of case studies:

> Intellectual life is more and more haunted by a dilemma. On the one hand, it produces powerful propositions, abstractions and principles which offer the seductive possibility of making sense of a chaos of evidence. On the other hand, such a formidable armoury often leaves a sense of dissatisfaction. The sense of the actual, the particular, the idiosyncratic, the taste of direct experience seems to get lost or buried or made to appear irrelevant. This is particularly true when we ourselves are the object of our study. The demand for "case studies" arises from that powerful feeling that there is more to life than generalizations can encompass. We are always greedy for accounts of "actual" experience which give off that special aroma of the authentic. Such accounts are neither atheoretical nor anti-theoretical, for always, however implicit, there are principles and assumptions at work. So it is with all narratives of personal experience, including narratives of teaching experience. (pp. 171–72)

Case studies can only disprove the universality of generalizations; they cannot generalize from one case to many. Conversely, we cannot presume to know an individual in terms of generalizations drawn from groups. Marjorie Kinnan Rawlings in *Cross Creek* put it this way: "Thoreau went off to live in the woods alone, to find out what the world was like. Now a man may learn a good deal of the general from studying the specific, whereas it is impossible to know the specific by studying the general" (p. 359).

Those of us who love and teach literature know that. We appreciate what can be learned from a single case—from "The Death of the Hired Man" or from *Lord Jim*.

"The more particular, the more specific you are, the more universal you are," Nancy Hale is quoted as saying (Murray, p. 15). A similar sense of the illuminating quality of the particular led William James to claim that to study religion one should study the most religious man at his most religious moment.

Movement from the particular to the *general*—the way of science—is a different mode of thought than movement from the particular to the *universal*: "Instead of a movement of mental abstraction from the particular to the general, there is a perception of the universal reflected in the particular. . . . The universal is the unity of the intuitive mind. The general is the unity of the intellectual mind" (Bortoft, p. 43). By disciplining and trusting the intuitive mind, as well as the logical and linear mind, we approach a more holistic research.

Jerome Bruner, in *Actual Minds, Possible Worlds*, speaks of two modes of thought:

> I discovered that there were two styles of approaching narrative, a discovery pressed upon me while I was teaching concurrently two seminars on narrative. One of them, at the New School for Social Research, was dominated by psychologists. The other, at the New York Institute for the Humanities, was made up of playwrights, poets, novelists, critics, editors. Both seminars were interested in literary questions. Both were interested in readers and in writers. Both were interested in texts. But one group, the psychologists, was dedicated to working "top-down," the other to working "bottom-up." . . .
>
> Top-down partisans take off from a theory about story, about mind, about writers, about readers. The theory may be anchored wherever: in psychoanalysis, in structural linguistics, in a theory of memory, in the philosophy of history. Armed with an hypothesis, the top-down partisan swoops on this text and that, searching for instances (and less often counter-instances) of what he hopes will be a right "explanation." In skilled and dispassionate hands, it is a powerful way to work. It is the way of the linguist, the social scientist, and of science generally, but it instills habits of work that always risk producing results that are insensitive to the contexts in which they were dug up. . . .
>
> Bottom-up partisans march to a very different tune. Their approach is focused on a particular piece of work: a story, a novel, a poem, even a line. They take it as their morsel of reality and explore it to reconstruct or deconstruct it. They are in search of the implicit theory in Conrad's construction of *Heart of Darkness* or in the worlds that Flaubert constructs. . . . The effort is to *read* a text for its meanings, and by doing so to elucidate the art of its author. They do not forswear the guidance of psychoanalytic theory or of Jakobsonian poetics or even of the philosophy of language in pursuing their quest. But their quest is not to prove or disprove a theory, but to explore the world of a particular literary work.
>
> Partisans of the top-down approach bewail the particularity of those who proceed bottom-up. The latter deplore the abstract nonwriterliness of the former. The two do not, alas, talk much to each other. (pp. 9–10)

Because there are different modes of thinking, of knowing, of understanding, there are different modes of researching. Since these different modes of thought coexist in the human mind, let us hope they can also coexist in the research community. Case study is a genre of research—most effective, I believe, for understanding (not controlling) human beings; most suitable for studying the human acts of composing and of interpreting literature; and most appropriate for teachers of English, whose commitment to and education in literature and writing, and whose personal engagement with students would seem to create an appreciation of case study. It seems altogether fitting, then, that teachers who know the ways of interpretation should interpret the texts of their own classrooms, and that teachers who understand the value of story should see and tell the stories of themselves and of their students. If any mode of inquiry speaks from and to the heart and soul and mind of our profession, it is surely case study.

8
How the Text Instructs: Writing Teaches Writing

Donald M. Murray

Every morning I go to school to learn to write—and the teacher is the text. The faculty is my evolving drafts. I do not learn from outside the text but from within. If I am able to achieve appropriate dumbness (and I do), if I am receptive, if I listen well enough, the text will teach me how to write it.

When the writing goes badly, when the deadline moves close, I have learned, on instruction from my teachers, not to press, not to grow tense, not to work hard, but to relax, listen, wait, to let the text instruct.

THE TEXT AND ITS WRITER

As Eudora Welty says, "Everything I write teaches me how to do it as I go." Most writers feel a more detached relationship to their text than readers—and English teachers—expect.

Margaret Atwood: "You don't make a decision to write poetry, *it* makes a decision to be written." Ann Beattie: "If I get to page three or four and the material hasn't shown me the way, I don't revise, I throw it out." Marvin Bell: "I did teach myself to write mostly by abandoning myself to the language, seeing what it wanted to say to me." Saul Bellow: "A character has his own logic" (or her own, I might add). Thomas Berger: "He's my friend and he talks to me. When I'm writing him, I can't wait to get to the typewriter and find out what he's going to say" (his friends are only men).

Is this an alphabetical list? Yes. Am I going to have to go all the way to composer Ellen Zwilich?: "You've got to be prepared, once you're well into a new work, to let it take you somewhere you've never been before." Not unless you read the quotations of writers, painters, and composers I've appended to this chapter. I have included that appendix because I find their testimony overwhelming and because it contradicts the relationship of student to text usually demanded in an academic setting.

Of course all writers do not agree with this. Dr. Barbara Tomlinson has done important work, far more scholarly than mine, with writers' testimony. She points out in "Characters Are Coauthors" that John Cheever said, "The legend that characters run away from their authors—taking up drugs, having sex operations and becoming president—implies that the writer is a fool with no knowledge or mastery of his craft." (I point out that he also said, "I never know where my characters come from or where they are going.")

Dr. Tomlinson quotes John Barth as saying, "[the idea of characters taking charge is] a lot of baloney. You hear respectable writers, sensible people like Katherine Anne Porter, say the characters just take over. I'm not going to let those scoundrels take over."

Yet Barth also said, "But one's loyalty, as William Gass says, is finally neither to oneself as Author nor to one's readers. One's loyalty is to the object—the project in the womb, excuse the metaphor. Some objects want to be terse little stories: I've written one ten words long! Some want to be novellas, that delicious, unmarketable narrative space, too long to sell to a magazine, too short to sell to a book publisher. Some want to be lean, Flaubertian novels. And some demand to be whole countries, like *Gargantua and Pantagruel*, or Burton's *Anatomy of Melancholy*, or the other Burton's *1001 Nights* with its crazy notes. Or Richardson's *Clarissa*, with its 537 letters compared to my meager 88."

The work, if not the characters, has an identity of its own. It stands apart, even from Barth, and dictates its own making. Of course there are writers who see their work in different ways, but there is remarkable consistency among writers in their relationship to their work, and if we are to understand the writing process and the teaching of writing process, then, I believe, we must take into account the evidence of, dare I say the dirty word, practitioners.

WHAT DOES THE PRACTITIONER KNOW?

Recently I was attacked at a conference, as I have been in print, for only being a practitioner. I write, therefore I know nothing about writing. Scholars distrust the retroactive accounts of writers, as they should, but then they ignore all that writers say about their writing and close a door on a valuable and insightful resource.

Many academics do not respect the metaphors writers use to describe their craft, although Barbara Tomlinson and a few others have found value in metaphors examined with appropriate intellectual rigor. Many authorities on the composing act, however, seem to want their marriage manuals written by nuns, who indeed have a purity of vision and clarity of belief about the marriage act that may appear superior to those of us who thrash about in a tangle of sheets.

As a thrasher, I don't claim to know everything about writing, even about my own writing, but I have been at the writing desk for more than fifty years and I know something of one person's experience of writing. And when writers get together, they understand each other's life in writing. They know, better than anyone, that writing is a complex activity that always offers the writer the gift of contradiction. Still they find common territory in which to visit and share the experience of writing.

They accept the fact that the process of writing changes with the individual, with the task, with the experience with the task, but there *are* consistencies and when those consistencies are supported by the testimony of hundreds of other practitioners we must pay attention and aim at least a few of our research howitzers in the direction of "practitioner speculation"—or we evaporate in a haze of irrelevant cocktail party theorizing where talk chases the tail of talk. Count the metaphors in that sentence!

I am not concerned here with whether the writer dictates the characters—or the ideas—or whether they are in control of the writer, but with how the writer perceives this relationship of writer and evolving text, how and what the writer learns from this single aspect of a complex issue, and what some of the implications may be for research and teaching.

I'd like to share something of how texts instruct me. There is no one text, one process of instruction. I go from text to text as the student goes from subject to subject, teacher to teacher. Some texts are martinets, making their needs clear and absolute; others are evasive, drawing me on, making me go more than half the way.

IN THE CLASSROOM OF THE TEXT

There is continual variety on my personal faculty, as I move from newspaper column to academic article, textbook to novel, poem to newsletter. There is no single style for any genre or topic. The variety of my faculty seems almost infinite and their ever-changing dissonance brings me to school each morning with youthful anticipation.

I think in metaphors, with metaphors, delight in metaphors, in part because they are slippery, saying one thing and *not quite* meaning another, nudging the truth, giving the listener room to make a personal meaning.

As I prepare to write, the text is the smell of baking bread from a neighbor's kitchen; a cloud, a ship, no, an island at the edge of the ocean horizon; a conversation in an office down the hall, heard but not yet made out.

All the metaphors have a similar implication. *IT* is there, the text is complete, not yet written, revealed, understood, but in existence. The text is not to be created by me, but to be received if I make myself skilled at the patient act of receptivity.

In my Daybook I play with the fragments of information and language as a child constructs towers of blocks to teeter totter and fall down. I twist the dial of the shortwave radio listening for the crackles of sound that promise a message if tuned in. I make doodles, sketches, lines that are erased, crossed out, drawn over until the pen has a plan.

Eventually, in its own time, in its own way, the text becomes a presence. It appears in the draft, beckoning, pulling me on—into the river at flood, off the ridge and down the ski slope, making me follow the white flash of the deer gone from the meadow and into the wood.

I write faster and faster—a mad weaver, a furious rubbing over the stone on the colonial grave, the potter's hands holding the shape of the pitcher not yet seen. The text comes full and clear, usually heard before it is seen, arriving as music, then form, then line, at last, meaning—its meaning, not mine.

I sit back to read this stranger text, asking what it needs. If I read well it will tell me: more evidence here, please; make this line of reasoning stronger, rub that out; build up my case in this section, define and describe; slow me down about now so they'll have a chance to think about what I'm saying; hey, speed it up, they'll go to sleep if you let me drone on; what's this sound, a little tuning please, I want to sing; I'm a little smooth here, rough it up, make it appear spontaneous; what's the word, you know, not this one, the right one; I need some verbs, a jolt of verbs.

The text tells me how the text must be read, how the music must be played, how the meaning will come clear. If I listen, if I don't force, the writing will come. It always does; it wants to make itself heard, seen, understood.

HOW TO LEARN FROM THE TEXT

The Text School practices a very different pedagogy from what is taught in regular school. If I am to learn from the text, I must come to that not-yet-appearing text in ignorance. If not ignorance, innocence: I must achieve a sort of retroactive virginity, not come to class with my head full of knowledge but to lay an appropriate emptiness before the work.

I must put aside knowledge, especially truth, traditions, and other preconceptions. I must be prepared for the opposite of the famous Charles Addams cartoon, for the nurse may *not* bring out a baby to the monster parents.

I must be comfortable with chaos or at least used to the discomfort of chaos. In fact I must seek disorder to find the place where order is needed and then I must wait, observe, study until I see the order arising from that particular disorder.

I must welcome the unexpected—disquiet, contradiction, doubt, question, putting aside what I have learned, what I have become good at, knowing that there is no degree at the end of this schooling, not certification but the greater gift of uncertainty, of more texts from which I will learn what I do not expect to learn and texts beyond those in which what I have just learned will be of no value.

WHAT ARE THE SKILLS TAUGHT BY THE TEXT?

Sitting. The student of the text has to learn, first of all, to sit. Writers grow to look like pears. No accident. We sit where the text may come, with notebook on our knee or lapdesk, before typewriter or word processor, waiting—without anxiety or as little anxiety as possible, reminding ourselves that writing will come as it has before, at the moment of terror and essential emptiness. As Alice Walker says, "I strip myself bare."

Play. We are untaught to play in school, but the text instructs through play, recess is more important than study hall for the text appears through play. We must learn again productive idleness, toying with ideas, constructing tottering blocks of fragments, engaging in wordplay, being silly, especially being silly. My playgrounds lie between my ears and in the Daybook open on my lap.

Receivingness. The world rewards the seeking game. We are taught to struggle, to achieve, to compete. Our parents and our society say to be outgoing, but if we are to write we must be ingoing. Action is praised by the world, but passivity and the great art of receptivity are what is taught by the instructing text.

Ignorance. Most teachers want their students to come to them full of information, bursting with facts, shiny with brightness. The text wants ignorance, or at least innocence, a necessary naiveté which makes the ordinary extraordinary. The text often lies in the area of the unknown. "Writing is a process of dealing with not-knowing," Donald Barthelme reminds us.

It is not easy to achieve true ignorance. In writing we discover what we know that we did not know that we knew, and what we now know we know may interfere with the reception of the next text. The danger is that the writing of the text makes us feel full of knowing, and it may be difficult to develop the skill of retroactive ignorance.

Irresponsibility. The text knows of tradition and convention and expectedness, but the best texts instruct against these. Inconsistency is what is rewarded. We need to learn the skill of not doing what we have done well before. Instead of building upon our skills we must learn to build down from them, work at what can't yet be said in a way that we haven't yet been able to say it.

Seeing the Unseen. The text rarely appears whole and complete. We have to see in fragments of language, or less, the shaping fog that may become a text. We deal with implication and possibility, what will be said often exists between words. The meaning is just beyond the phrase in our head. The music is but a feeling of the music that we may begin to hear if we have the courage to write in dumbness, allowing a text to appear. (Study Chapter 2—"Seeing"—in Annie Dillard's *Pilgrim at Tinker Creek*.)

Causing Accidents. The greatest problem is that we may write too well. In glibness, talent, and fluency we may not allow the best text to appear. The text instructs by accident. There may be a whole theology in a typo. We must seek the wrong word, the collapsing sentence, the running-on line, the exploding paragraph. The text tells us that we will discover the text in the unexpected; to paraphrase Frost, to mean one thing and write another. And to accept it, to allow the accident to appear and be cultivated. As John Fowles tells us: "Follow the accident, fear the fixed plan—that is the rule."

Wasting Time. The text instructs delay, the fine art of procrastination. Texts arrive in their own time, and we must prepare ourselves to be ready for the text, to engage in play and passivity and waiting. Most bad writing is premature; it is not ready to arrive. And so we must learn to waste time, to go on errands, to stare out the window, *not* to write.

Fastwriting. And then to pounce. Once we hear the text or the hint of a text then we must learn to let it flow through us as fast as possible. Speed encourages accident and insight. It allows the text to escape from tradition and preconception, from the censorship that lurks in all our minds. Yes, go with the flow, the flowing text, the clumsy fluency of the draft.

Making Mistakes. We must discover, our texts tell us, to make mistakes, to treasure error, to court failure. It is in these territories which conventional schools so fear that discoveries lie. Winning may, in writing, be losing.

Listening. We must train our ears to hear the not-yet-written text, and then to hear the coming clear text. It would seem that writing is read with the eye, but writing's magic lies in the creation of speech. The meaning is carried by the music of the text, and we must learn to train and trust our ears so that we may receive the text and make it heard to readers.

Inattention. The text classroom does not look like a conventional school. There are windows on all sides, a sunroof, windows in the floor that look down on the streams running underneath the classroom. The chairs are turned away from each other, and the students are not listening to a teacher, but to their own teachers, learning to concentrate on what may appear on the word-screen in the brain or on the individual page, paying no attention to editors, readers past or future, colleagues. They are learning the talent of inattention.

Stubbornness. The text demands stubbornness. The mule is the school mascot.

Insubordination. Graham Greene wrote: "Isn't disloyalty the writer's virtue as loyalty is the soldier's?" Advanced students have learned to achieve insubordination.

Submission. And, at last, the contradictory skill of submission, obedience to the text that is as unexpected and impolite as this one. This is the writer's challenge, to accept a text with which the writer can argue, even disagree, knowing that it does not contain all of the truth, but hoping that it has a worthwhile wisdom—or at least a question worth asking—and a good deal more truth than could be expected when the writer first heard it rustling in the woods outside the writing room.

All these skills and more are taught by the texts I do not expect, often do not welcome, but must accept. They confuse and contradict, unsettle, disturb, lead me where I do not want to go. And in old age, keep me young, always a freshman on this campus.

Yesterday I thought this text was finished. And then in the seminar I was teaching this week at Miami University, the text told me to invite the students to write a short poem that says everything the entire essay had said. And on my own Daybook page, the first version of the following piece of scholarly evidence of the power of the text to command appeared, unbidden but received, and later, on its own instruction, developed into this poem:

Morning

It is always October.
I trudge to school,
kick a stone, leap the crack
that goes to China,
take my seat in the back row, jam
my knees under the desk,
avoiding chewing gum, waiting
for recess. The substitute
teacher hesitates
by the door. The bell
rings. She commands
attention to the text.
I cannot find my place.
There is no meaning
in the words. Nearsighted,
I squint at the blackboard:
the tails of dogs, a banana,
a winding river, a diving
hawk. I am in the wrong grade,
in a foreign school, another
century. I stare out the window,
learn how a robin drives a squirrel
from her nest, imagine
a fear of wings. Teacher
calls my name. I speak,
as surprised as if a bee
flew from my mouth.

There is no graduation from the School of the Text, no proud moment of certified knowing, no hood trimmed with imitation fur that descends on the writer's shoulders. Each new text reminds the writer that new lessons are to be learned and then discarded.

In every classroom of this school a statement by Eudora Welty is framed and hung over the blackboard:

The writer himself studies intensely how to do it while he is in the thick of doing it; then when the particular novel or story is done, he is likely to forget how; he does well to. Each work is new. Mercifully, the question of *how* abides less in the abstract, and less in the past, than in the specific, in the work at hand.

Others who speak of their relationship with their text

AMADO, JORGE

I just follow where the characters lead me.

AMIS, MARTIN

Writing a novel always feels to me like starting off in a very wide tunnel—in fact it doesn't look like a tunnel at all, since it's marvellously airy and free at the beginning, when you are assigning life to various propositions—but finishing off by crawling down a really cramped tunnel, because the novel has set up so many demands on you. There is so little room for manoeuvre by the end that you are actually a complete prisoner of the book, and it is formal demands that cause all those constrictions: the shape gets very tight by the end, and there are no choices any more.

ASTURIAS, MIGUEL ANGEL

The novelist has to become a slave to his novel; it's sort of mental bureaucracy.

BLUME, JUDY

The characters don't really live in my head; they come alive as I start to write about them; then I am never sure what is going to happen. I'm always surprised.

BOWLES, PAUL

I don't feel that I wrote these books. I feel as though they had been written by my arm, by my brain, my organism, but that they're not necessarily mine.

BROOKS, JAMES

I put the first brush stroke on the canvas. After that, it is up to the canvas to do at least half the work.

BRONTE, CHARLOTTE

The writer who possesses the creative gift owns something of which he is not always the master.

BROWN, ROSELLEN

I often feel myself following a step or two behind my characters, full of curiosity about what they're going to do next.

BURROUGHS, WILLIAM

I felt reborn and was content to spend long hours at the typewriter, transcribing the images and characters of the novel, who took shape as though of their own volition.

CALDWELL, ERSKINE

I have no influence over them. I'm only an observer, recording. The story is always being told by the characters themselves.

CALISHER, HORTENSE

The real surprise is afterward. When I see that the book has made its own rules. Each one in the end makes its own form.

CARSON, RACHEL

The discipline of the writer is to learn to be still and listen to what his subject has to tell him.

CORTÁZAR, JULIO

It's the characters who direct me.

DIDION, JOAN

I don't have a very clear idea of who the characters are until they start talking.
Nota bene:
   It tells you.
   You don't tell it.

DOCTOROW, E. L.

There are always characters in the books who do the writing. I like to create the artist and let the artist do the work.

ERDRICH, LOUISE

It's almost like the story is all done, and we have to live long enough to be receptive to it.

FAULKNER, WILLIAM

It begins with a character, usually, and once he stands up on his feet and begins to move, all I do is trot along behind him with a paper and pencil trying to keep up long enough to put down what he says and does.

FLAUBERT, GUSTAVE

One is not free to write this or that. One does not choose one's subject. That is what the public and the critics do not understand.

FRANKENTHALER, HELEN

You tell the painting what you want; then it tells you.

GIDE, ANDRÉ

The bad novelist constructs his characters; he directs them and makes them speak. The true novelist listens to them and watches them act; he hears their voices even before he knows them.

GILCHRIST, ELLEN

I have a character named Nora Jane Whittington who lives in Berkeley, California, and who has so much free will that I can't even find out from her whether the twin baby girls she is carrying belong to her old boyfriend, Sandy, or her new boyfriend, Freddy Harwood. I can't finish my new book of stories until Nora Jane agrees to an amniocentesis. She is afraid the needle will penetrate the placenta and frighten the babies.

I created Nora Jane but I have to wait on her to make up her mind before I can finish the title story of my new book. This is a fiction writer's life.

GREENBERG, JOANNE

Your writing is trying to tell you something. Just lend an ear.

GREENE, GRAHAM

When I construct a scene, I don't describe the hundredth part of what I see; I see the characters scratching their noses, walking about, tilting back in their chairs—even after I've finished writing—so much so that after a while I feel a weariness which does not derive all that much from my effort of imagination but is more like a visual fatigue: My eyes are tired from watching my characters.

HELLER, JOSEPH

With me there's very little that I do actively in choosing the subject or choosing the person or point of view. The novel comes to me as it's written. I did not sit down to write a book about World War II, and I didn't decide to put it in the third person rather than the first person. The same thing is true of all my books. The idea occurs to me as a novel, rather than as a subject, and the novel already encompasses a point of view, a tempo, a voice.

HIGGINS, GEORGE V.

I had to learn to listen to the characters and not to push them around.

HINTON, S. E.

My characters always take shape first; they wander around my mind looking for something to do.

HOBAN, RUSSELL

I'm at the service of the material that enters me. It takes me where it wants to go.

KING, STEPHEN

I let the fiction, I let the book, boss itself.

KUNITZ, STANLEY

A poem has secrets that the poet knows nothing of. It takes on a life and a will of its own.

L'ENGLE, MADELEINE

I have to go where the book wants to.

LEONARD, ELMORE

The characters audition in their opening scene—I listen to them, see how they sound. The plots develop on their own.

L'HEUREUX, JOHN

Every story has its own rules. If it's not held together by its own bloodstream, it's just self-indulgence.

MAXWELL, WILLIAM

I didn't so much write them as do my best to keep out of the way of their writing themselves. I would sit with my head bent over the typewriter waiting to see what was going to come out of it. The first sentence was usually a surprise to me. From the first sentence everything else followed. A person I didn't know anything about and had never known in real life—a man who had no enemies, a girl who doesn't know whether to listen to her heart or her mind, a woman who never draws breath except to complain, an old man afraid of falling—stepped from the wings and began to act out something I must not interrupt or interfere with, but only be a witness to: a life, with the fleeting illuminations that anybody's life offers, written in sand with a pointed stick and erased by the next high tide. In sequence the tales seem to complement one another. There are recurring themes. But I did not plan it that way. I have sometimes believed that it was all merely the result of the initial waiting with an empty mind.

MICHELANGELO

The sculptor has to see within the marble the form it already holds.

MILLER, ARTHUR

I have written as my character dictated, not to some style, and I think that's true of anybody who takes the art with some seriousness.

MOWAT, FARLEY

I can't program what I want to write. There's a wall between my conscious and subconscious, and I have to wait until a little trapdoor opens. What comes out is something over which I have no control. I can use it, manipulate and shape it, but I can't consciously control it.

MURDOCH, IRIS

Good writing is full of surprises and novelties, moving in a direction you don't expect.

OATES, JOYCE CAROL

My characters really dictate themselves to me. I am not free of them, really, and I can't force them into situations they haven't themselves willed. They have the autonomy of characters in a dream.

OZICK, CYNTHIA

The art of fiction is freedom of will for your characters.

PALEY, GRACE

If it turns out to be a novel, then I will have wanted to write a novel. But if it turns out to be stories, it'll turn out that that's what I wanted to do.

PARINI, JAY

[F]ictional characters, for me, soon take on a life of their own. They run with the bit between the teeth.

PICASSO, PABLO

To know what you want to draw, you have to begin drawing. If it turns out be a man, I draw a man. If it turns out to be a woman, I draw a woman.

PINTER, HAROLD

The thing germinated and bred itself. It proceeded according to its own logic. What did I do? I followed the indications, I kept a sharp eye on the clues I found myself dropping. The writing arranged itself with no trouble into dramatic terms. The characters sounded in my ears—it was apparent to me what one would say and what would be the other's response, at any given point. It was apparent to me what they would not, could not, ever, say, whatever one might wish . . . the play was now its own world.

PIRANDELLO, LUIGI

[They] went on living on their own, choosing certain moments of the day to reappear before me in the solitude of my study and coming—now one, now the other, now two together—to tempt me, to propose that I present or describe this scene or that, to explain the effects that could be secured with them, the new interest which a certain situation could provide, and so forth. . . . [It]became gradually harder and harder for me to go back and free myself from them. . . . They are detached from me; live on their own; have acquired voice and movement; have by themselves—in this struggle for existence that they have had to wage with me—become dramatic characters, characters that move and talk on their own initiative; already see themselves as such; have learned to defend themselves against me.

PORTER, KATHERINE ANNE

I don't choose my stories, they choose me. Things come to my mind. Sometimes it takes years and years for them to coalesce—it's like iron filings collecting on a magnet.

POWELL, ANTHONY

You establish a character; then the character follows his own logic, and what the character does, that's his doing.

RENARD, JULES

The impulse of the pen. Left alone, thought goes at its will. As it follows the pen, it loses its freedom. It wants to go one way, the pen another. It is like a blind man led astray by his cane, and what I came to write is no longer what I wished to write.

ROSSNER, JUDITH

I went to sleep one night and when I woke up, this girl, Dawn, had entered the room. I called myself Ouija board. I sit down and stuff just passes through my hands.

SIMPSON, LOUIS

A poet begins by losing control; he does not choose his thoughts, they seem to be choosing him.

SINGER, ISAAC BASHEVIS

[W]hen I sit down to write, I don't say to myself, "I am trying to show this." I don't really know what I'm going to try; I let the story work for itself.

SPANIDOU, IRINI

Writing the novel the characters took over and began to have their own say.

STAFFORD, WILLIAM

For me an artist is someone who lets the material talk back. A relationship with the material is the distinction an artist has.

STONE, ROBERT

You construct characters and set them going in their own interior landscape, and what they find to talk about and what confronts them are, of course, things that concern you most.

TATE, JAMES

The poem is in control. The poem, not what I'm imposing on the poem, makes the demand.

THEROUX, PAUL

It may sound pompous to say so, but I feel as if what I'm writing is inevitable. I'm not so much creating a character as discovering the character that already exists. I can't make him a certain way. He is what he is.

WARREN, ROBERT PENN

You don't choose a story, it chooses you. You get together with that story somehow . . . you're stuck with it.

WILKINSON, SYLVIA

When you create a character like Miss Liz, you suddenly find out she never does anything she doesn't want to. You, as a writer, have no control over her once she's established. And suddenly no man could come into that novel because of Miss Liz's presence.

WILLIAMS, TENNESSEE

My characters make my play. I always start with them. They take spirit and body in my mind. Nothing that they say or do is arbitrary or invented. They build the play about them like spiders weaving their webs.

WILLIAMS, TOM

You learn what the characters are if you pay attention. They do things valid for what they are, not for what you thought they would be.

THE
PRACTICE
OF TEACHER
RESEARCH

THE WRITING TEACHER
IN THE ELEMENTARY
AND SECONDARY SCHOOL

9
Children's Choices: The Topics of Young Writers

JOAN E. ALOFS AND JANET GRAY-MCKENNIS

What do children write? Figures 9–1 through 9–4 give some examples. These are voices from two of the open classrooms at Ancona School, a progressive private school located in an integrated, middle-class neighborhood on Chicago's south side. In the preprimary class, teachers schedule no special writing time. Writing is one of the activities children can always choose. In the primary class, teachers encourage children to write in the context of many academic areas (science, history, etc.) in addition to holding writing workshops four mornings a week. We ask that children write in their journals on the fifth morning, though the children may write in them at other times if they choose. In both classes, children may share each day's work.

When the Ancona faculty began an intense study of the writing process three years ago, we began gathering the most interesting writing done by the children in our preprimary and primary classrooms. Last year we began a thorough collection of our children's writing. We wanted to learn what three- to eight-year-old children write when they have complete control over topic choice. We began by defining twelve genres that we saw in our children's work. After classifying the material according to these genres, we tabulated the genres by age and sex. We also listed those factors that we found recurring in many children's writing.

Our preliminary findings show that children's first writings are usually in one of three genres: captions, fiction, and/or fictional reporting.

Young children write captions as a way of explaining their drawings, but captions are not limited to very young writers. Older children who enjoy drawing or draw well will also caption. However, their drawings limit their writing to descriptive sentences which often begin with "This is—"

All of our children also write fiction. One characteristic of this genre is an introductory sentence using "once upon a time" or other formulaic phrases.

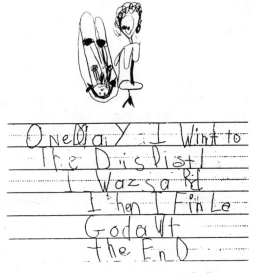

ⁱⁱMᶤˢ ᴵM ᶜRLS
ᶜAT ᶜM ᵀHE
ᴿAWᴹD ᵗHEᴹ U
ˢTEMᴿOLᴿ RAᴹ
ᴼVR
ᵀHEᴹ ᵀHE GRLˢₚₙ
WR FᴬT ₚₙ
ᵗᴼ GAᴺᴹᴰ

NICK

(Once upon a time some girls sat on the ground. Then a steamroller ran over them. The girls were flat into the ground.)

Figure 9–1
Nick, Age 4

OⁿeᴰaY I Wiⁿᵗ ᵗo
The DᵘⁱˢᵖⁱˢˡI
WazˢoⁱRᵈ
I ʰeⁿ I Fⁱⁿ Le
Godⁱᵘᵗ
ᵗheₙ Enᴰ

(One day I went to the dentist! I was afraid. Then I finally got out. The end.)

Figure 9–2
Leila, Age 5

95

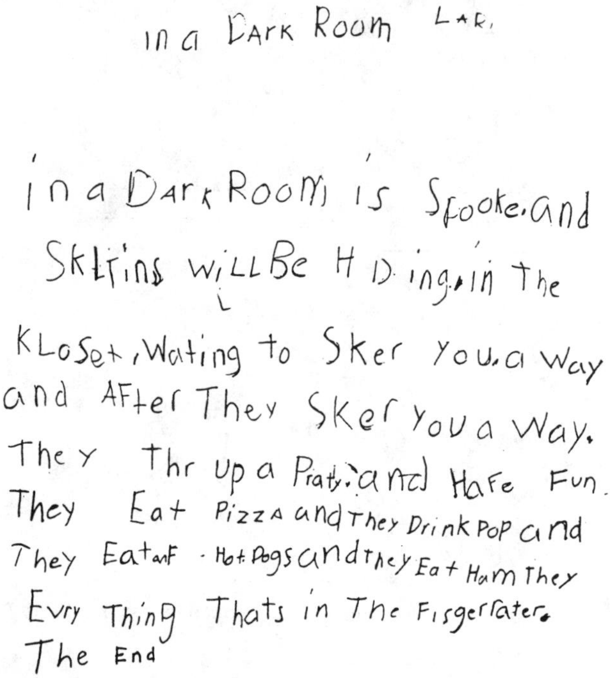

In a Dark Room L*R.

in a Dark Room is Spooke.and
Skltins will Be H D.ing.in The
KLoSet,Wating to Sker You.a way
and After They Sker You a Way.
They thr up a Praty.and Hafe Fun.
They Eat Pizza andThey Drink PoP and
They Eat.F · Hot Pogs andThey Eat Ham They
Evry Thing Thats in The Fisgerfater.
The End

(In a dark room is spooky. And skeletons will be hanging in the closet waiting to scare you away. And after they scare you away they throw up a party and have fun. They eat pizza and they drink pop and they eat and eat hot dogs and they eat ham. They [eat] everything that's in the refrigerator. The end.)

Figure 9–3
Larissa, Age 6

Another identifying trait is the use of the past rather than the present tense. These first stories are often incomplete by adult standards. Five-year-old Dennis's story is an example of an early fiction piece (See Figure 9–5).

The first addition to the formula is frequently the ending. This may be merely the words, "The End." "Once upon a time there was a killer whale. The end," writes six-year-old Jordan (Figure 9–6).

The story is complete when children add a body, as five-year-old Akia does when he writes the story shown in Figure 9–7: "Once upon a time there was a war. The good guys won. The bad guys lost. The end."

Among the four- and five-year-olds, we find that boys are the most frequent practitioners of this genre. They often choose superheroes or transformers as their topics, while four- and five-year-old girls are more apt to write about

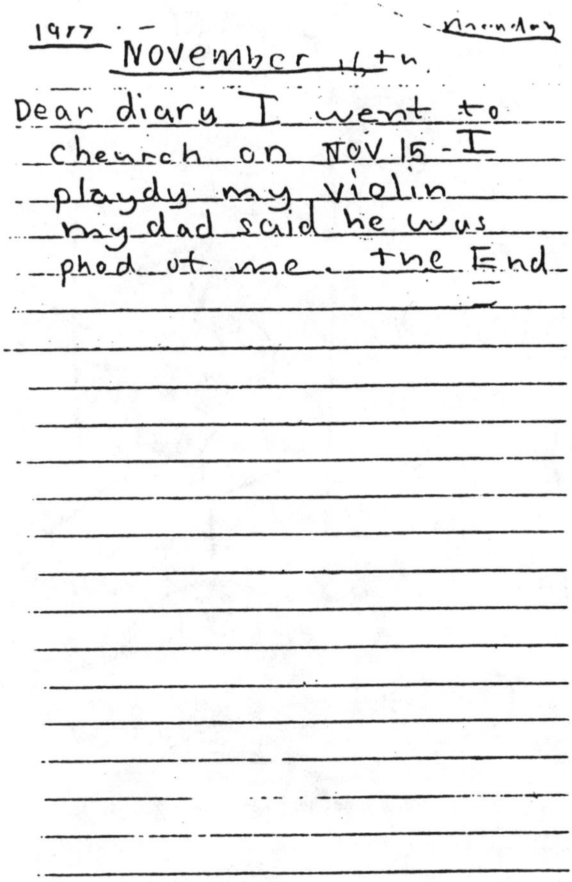

1977

November 1th

Dear diary I went to
Cherch on Nov 15 - I
playdy my violin
my dad said he was
phod of me the End

(Dear diary, I went to church on Nov. 15. I played my violin. My dad said he was proud of me. The end.)

Figure 9–4
Stanley, Age 7

family or friends. No matter what topic children choose, the use of formulaic elements and the past tense remain hallmarks of early fiction.

We find a third genre in the work of our less mature writers which we call fictional reporting. When elements of fact and fiction appear within the same piece, the child is engaging in fictional reporting. Four- and five-year-old girls dominate this genre. These stories are always formulaic and frequently show the writers' occupation with autonomy. Three-year-old Lindsey writes.

(Once upon a time there was a little butterfly.)

Figure 9–5
Dennis, Age 5

"Once upon a time there lived a little girl named me. And my boy friend and me went out on a date tonight."

At the beginning of second grade, both fiction and fictional reporting can evolve into chapter books. Chapter books are also dominated by the theme of independence, which is worked out as the characters struggle through a series of adventures or romantic episodes. Typically, dialogue between teenage or animal protagonists moves the stories along.

In stories of this category, adults are either hostile or absent, as in seven-year-old Karen's story (Figure 9–8).

Three Steps at a Time

Once there was two girls. They were sisters. Everyone liked them. Except their mother and father. Their names were Shara and Cathy. Since their

(Once upon a time there was a killer whale. The end.)

Figure 9–6
Jordan, Age 6

(Once upon a time there was a war. The good guys won. The bad guys lost. The end.)

Figure 9–7
Akia, Age 5

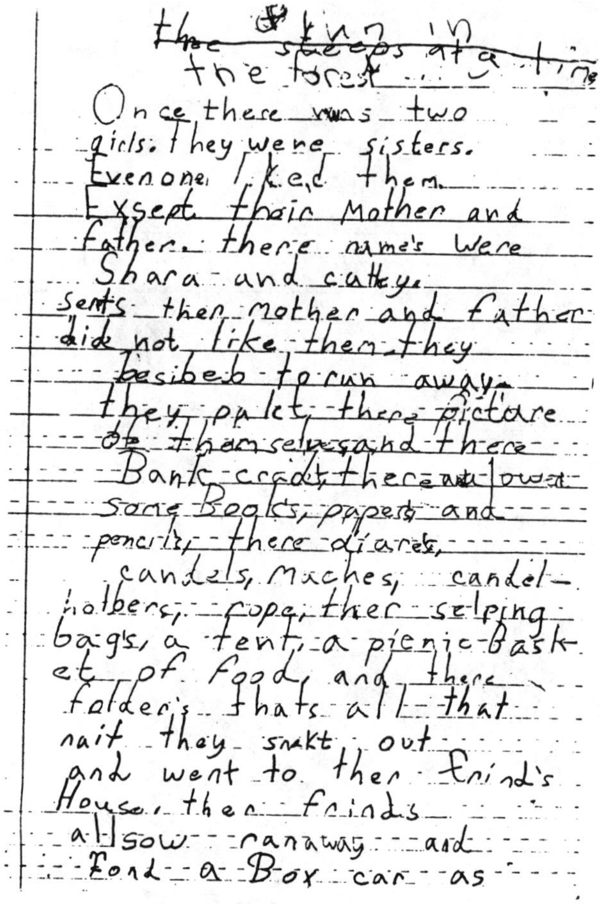
~~the steeps at a time~~ Fun in
the forest
Once there was two
girls. They were sisters.
Evenone liked them.
Exsept their Mother and
father. there name's Were
Shara and catty.
Sents then mother and father
did not like them they
besibeb to run away.
they paket there picture
of themselves and there
Bank cradt there allowen
some Books, papers and
pencils, there diares,
candels, maches, candel-
holbers, rope, ther selping
bag's, a tent, a picnic Bask
et of food, and there
folder's thats all that
nait they snakt out
and went to ther frind's
House. then frinds
allsow ranaway and
fond a Box car as

(Once there was two girls. They were sisters. Everyone liked them. Except their mother and father. Their names were Shara and Cathy. Since their mother and father did not like them they decided to run away. They packed their picture of themselves, and their bank cards, their allowance, some books, papers and pencils, their diaries, candles, matches, candleholders, rope, their sleeping bags, a tent, a picnic basket of food and their folders. That's all. That night they sneaked out and went to their friends' house. Their friends also ran away and found a box car as a house. So they. . .)

Figure 9–8
Karen, Age 7: "Three Steps at a Time"

mother and father did not like them they decided to run away. They packed their picture of themselves, and their bank cards, their allowance, some books, papers and pencils, their diaries, candles, matches, candleholders, rope, their sleeping bags, a tent, a picnic basket of food and their folders. That's all. That night they sneaked out and went to their friends' house. Their friends also ran away and found a box car as a house. So they . . .

Nonfictional reporting is characterized by brief, declarative sentences in the past tense. This fifth genre first appears in the work of our four-year-olds. "We went out on Halloween," writes four-year-old Ken (Figure 9–9).

When children anticipate future events or add reflections to their statements about past events, they are no longer merely doing nonfictional reporting, but are making diary-like observations. In our classes, this begins in girls as young as four and is common in the work of both boys and girls by age six. Our girls remain the most frequent practitioners of this form but many boys enjoy it also.

About a year after children begin keeping diaries, they start to write formal letters. These letters consist of a greeting, a body that talks of more than one subject, and a closing. They evolve from the note-writing genre (which appears about age four).

This progression can be seen in one child's letters written to Santa over a three-year period. At age five, Karen's letter is really just a note—a reminder, addressed to no one in particular: "For Christmas I would like a cabbage patch kid and a pink tower and brown stair." A year later she writes:

Figure 9–9
Ken, Age 4

Dear Santa,
   I would like a Skipper doll for Barbie
   some charmkins
   and a Barbie house
   get-in-shape girl
   walkie-talkie
   my little pony baby hospital
   stickerbook

At age seven, she applies revising and editing skills to produce the well-crafted piece in Figure 9–10.

Spontaneous signs appear first in our primary classes at age six or seven. In our preprimary class, children use signs only after they've been prompted by a more sophisticated writer.

About age seven, our children also begin to make functional lists. Younger children add reminders to others' lists, but do not make spontaneous lists for themselves in our classes.

Humor is an element in children's writing at all ages. Our children enjoy writing and sharing stories whose entire purpose is to entertain. About age six, humor also emerges as a genre. Some children construct mazes, codes, and

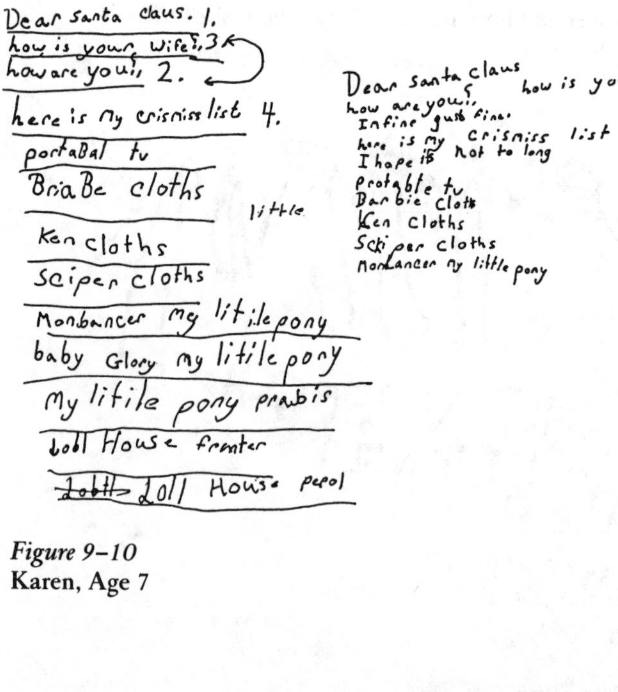

Figure 9–10
Karen, Age 7

activity sheets to amuse themselves and their readers. Children may write down jokes and riddles they have heard or read and compile them into books. Frequently six-year-olds do not fully recall or understand the jokes. Their garbled jokes are rehearsals for the successful, polished joke books of seven-year-olds.

In our classes, while some very young children retold nursery rhymes and slightly older children wrote poetically, we saw no poetry written until it had been formally introduced. These first poems in Figures 9–11 and 9–12 were written after the authors had studied several poems, including Nikki Giovanni's "mommies" and "daddies."

While we were classifying these twelve genres in our children's writing, we noticed several factors that affected their work repeatedly. As with adults, everything children experience is a potential source of inspiration. While we can't begin to identify all the factors that affect their writing, we have identified five major influences. In our classes, the children are most influenced by our curriculum, by popular culture, by their peers, by literature, and by our dual role as teacher and researcher.

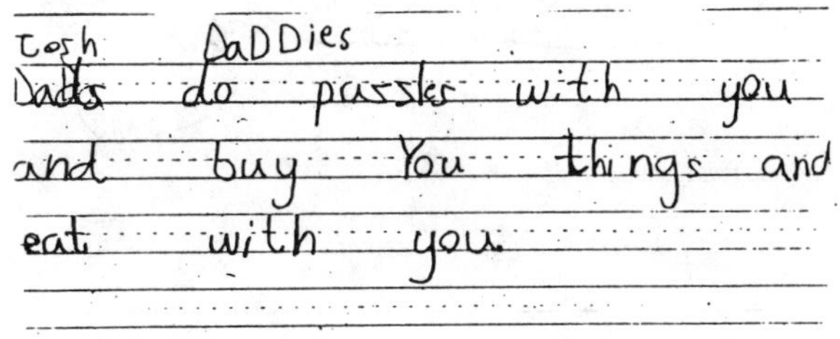

Figure 9–11
Josh, Age 6

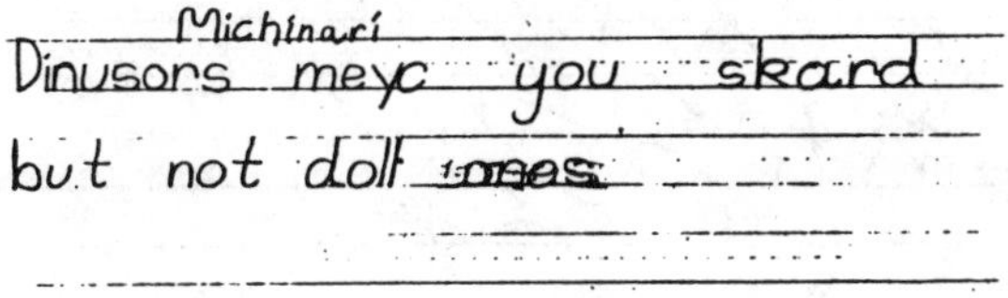

(Dinosaurs make you scared but not doll ones.)

Figure 9–12
Michinari, Age 7

We find that a strong curriculum encourages children to write. For example, our school devotes six weeks in January and February to the study of an "All School Theme." Last year's theme was "The Deep." It proved so inspirational that we were still getting "deep stories" in June. Three-year-old Lindsey used the genre of fiction to write the piece in Figure 9–13. Seven-year-old Stanley made the web in Figure 9–14 in preparation for an oral nonfiction report.

We find that the influence of curriculum is strongest in younger children's writing. Curricular influences appear in 39 percent of the three-year-old girls' stories and 25 percent of the four-year-old boys' stories that we collected. In the primary class, the influence diminishes but remains stable; about 15 percent of six-, seven-, and eight-year-olds' writing stems from the curriculum.

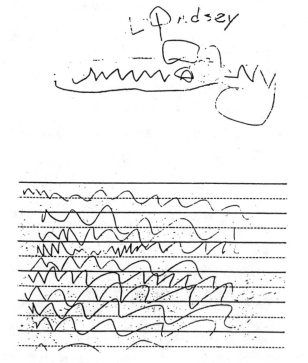

(Once there was a shark with a mosquito bite. He ranned away.)

Figure 9–13
Lindsey, Age 3

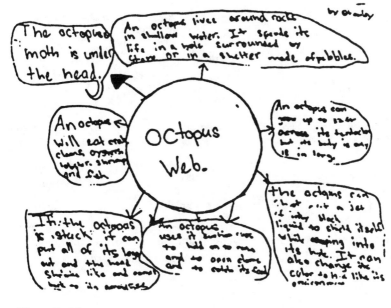

Figure 9–14
Stanley, Age 7

Popular culture is another important influence we find reflected in our children's writing. By popular culture we mean holidays and cult figures, as well as the characters that fill the TV screen and stock the shelves of toy stores. As we noted earlier, boys are particularly fascinated by superheroes. These characters influence 40 percent of the stories written by our four-year-old boys, and 51 percent of those by our five-year-old boys. However, at age four, our girls' writing also begins to show the influence of popular culture.

In her book *Wally's Stories*, Vivian Paley laments the abundance of these dead-end stories. While we agree that formulaic fiction is a limited and limiting form, we feel that we must accept and indeed celebrate the endless barrage of superhero and transformer stories. We are encouraged to see that the children eventually will move on to other subjects when they are ready.

About 5 to 7 percent of the work of six-, seven-, and eight-year-olds is influenced by popular culture. Eight-year-old Gwen writes:

> Once there was six girls. Their names were Lisa Lisa and Sheila E., Janet Jackson and Vanity and Manka. And they were real rich and you should know because they are singers. . . . (Figure 9–15)

Oineo Thar Was 6 girs Thar Names
were lisa lisu And Shelde Janet Jackson
And Vantiy ': And Manka . And Thar
Were Rell Rich And You shod No becasc
Thar Are Singers. A palwnq Allways

(Once there was six girls. Their names were Lisa Lisa and Sheila E., Janet Jackson and Vanity and Manka. And they were real rich and you should know because they are singers. . . .)

Figure 9–15
Gwen, Age 8

The next story, by three-and-a-half-year-old David, shows both the influence of popular culture and the influence of his peers. He writes: "Once upon a time there were transformers. Batman and Superman beat the transformers up" (Figure 9–16). This is his version of stories he has heard the five-year-olds share throughout the year.

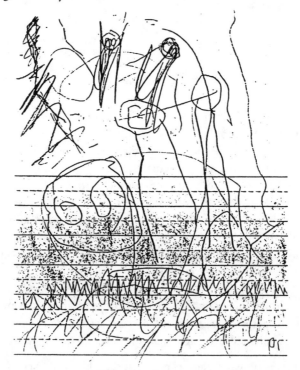

(Once upon a time there were transformers. Batman and Superman beat the transformers up.)

Figure 9–16
David, Age 3½

Children often try on someone else's ideas. They recognize when the writing style fits and they wear it. When it doesn't suit them, they discard it, often abandoning a piece of work just as they would reject an outfit of the wrong size.

As with adult writers, children who base their writing on another's learn from their model, even when the resulting work is derivative. Peer models help some children to find their voices. Five-year-old Dennis wrote the original piece in Figure 9–17 after watching his seven-year-old friend Michinari at work during writing workshop (see Figure 9–18).

(*Godzilla*. Once there was a cave. There was a monster in there. His name was Godzilla. One day people wanted to look in the cave, so people went in the cave.)

Figure 9–17
Dennis, Age 5

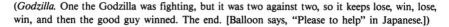

(*Godzilla.* One the Godzilla was fighting, but it was two against two, so it keeps lose, win, lose, win, and then the good guy winned. The end. [Balloon says, "Please to help" in Japanese.])

Figure 9–18
Michinari, Age 7

Literature also provides children with an opportunity for trying on different writing styles. Very young or immature children sometimes retell nursery rhymes or pattern books before they have a sense of their own voices.

After hearing a second retelling of "Little Miss Muffet," another child asked three-year-old Angie why she always wrote the same story. Angie replied, "It's the only story I know." Continuing to listen to literature and her peers will help Angie to write the stories only she knows.

In our school we never use story-starters, but six-year-old Larissa devised her own. For the first eight weeks of school she sat in the book corner during writing workshop, picking her topics from among the dust jackets stapled to the wall. The stories were entirely hers, despite such titles as *Where the Wild Things Are, Black Gold,* and the one in Figure 9–19, *A Chair for My Mother.*

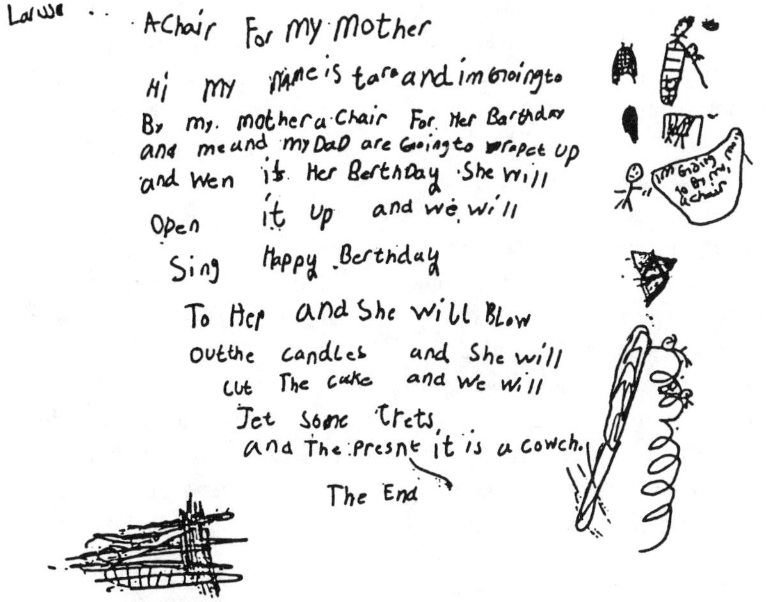

(*A Chair For My Mother.* Hi, my name is Tara and I'm going to buy my mother a chair for her birthday and me and my dad are going to wrap it up and when it's her birthday she will open it up and we will sing Happy Birthday to her and she will blow out the candles and she will cut the cake and we will get some treats and the present it is a couch.)

Figure 9–19
Larissa, Age 6: "A Chair for My Mother"

A Chair for My Mother

Hi, my name is Tara and I'm going to buy my mother a chair for her birthday and me and my dad are going to wrap it up and when it's her birthday she will open it up and we will sing Happy Birthday to her and she will blow out the candles and she will cut the cake and we will get some treats and the present it is a couch.

As you can see, the chair has become a couch by the story's end. Always prolific, Larissa soon abandoned the dust jackets and by late January was working on a chapter book with two male protagonists.

When we began our research, we hoped that it would inform our teaching. Throughout the year, we were alternately horrified and delighted by its effects on our classrooms. Our influence as teacher-researchers has been both direct and indirect. The successful teacher-researcher is almost invisible; positive influence is correspondingly indirect. Negative influence of the teacher-researcher is more easily traced, and the lessons learned are unforgettable.

When his teacher read six-year-old Nathaniel's narrative over his shoulder during writing workshop, he incorporated a message to her into his work, then shifted into a new subject before stopping altogether: "Today I looked at a box in our reading group. It was really strange. I don't know why they named it a dumb name. Why are you reading this? The end. Another story. I know you want to hear a little story a man said. The kid was really mad. Then a magic bunny rabbit. . . . I don't know about you but I'm done for now." She knew that she had intruded.

As teacher-researchers, we have been more careful than before to collect and preserve our students' writing. We feel this contributes to the voluminous writing done by our preprimary children. We also see its effects in the primary classroom. First-grader Garrett wrote the following letter to a classmate who had moved to Texas in midyear (see Figure 9–20):

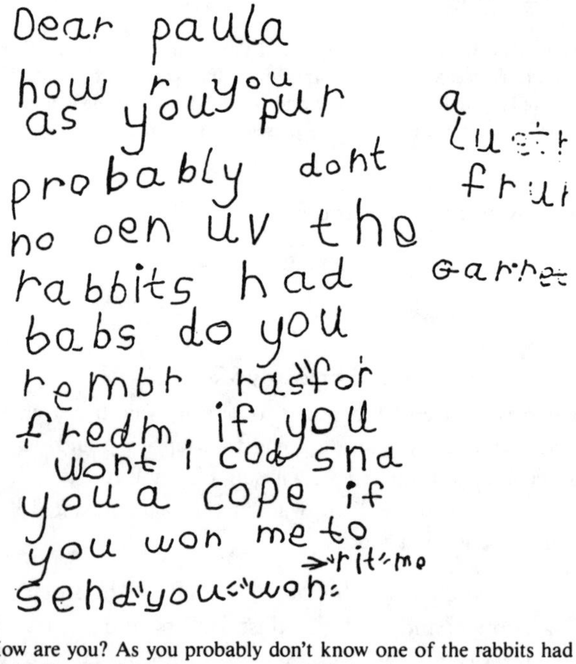

(Dear Paula, How are you? As you probably don't know one of the rabbits had babies. Do you remember *Race for Freedom*? If you want, I could send you a copy. If you want me to send you one write me. A letter from Garrett)

Figure 9–20
Garrett, Grade 1

Dear Paula, How are you? As you probably don't know one of the rabbits had babies. Do you remember *Race for Freedom?* If you want, I could send you a copy. If you want me to send you one write me. A letter from Garrett

Garrett thinks of himself as a writer and knows that his friend will share that view—and his values about writing. Our research and our teaching have contributed indirectly to these perceptions.

One of seven-year-old Karen's early chapter books (Figure 9–8) shows the influence of literature and the values of the teacher-researcher that have become hers. Five of the fifteen essential items that the runaways take with them have to do with writing. In addition to being the oldest daughter of one of the authors, Karen was a student of the other. For Karen there was no escape from the influence of the writing teacher as researcher.

Our teaching has also been influenced by our research. Continuous questioning has replaced periodic self-evaluation of our teaching practices and their effects in our classrooms. The answers that we're finding inform our teaching. We now feel that we can begin to identify some patterns in our students' topic choices.

Figure 9–21 summarizes our children's topic selection by genre. A rough chronology appears on the left, showing the approximate age when each genre first appears in our children's writing. The arrows show how the genres evolve as the children's writing matures. While our figures are not statistically

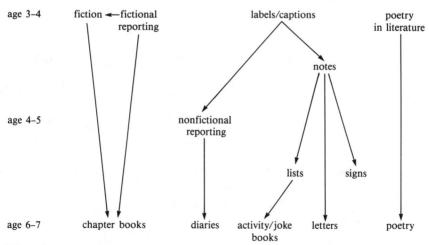

Figure 9–21
Children's Topic Selection by Genre

significant, when we tabulate genre usage by age and sex, some interesting trends emerge. Among the most striking is the fact that fiction accounts for 73 percent of our four-year-old boys' work and 88 percent of our five-year-old boys' writing. But only 8 percent of our five-year-old girls' work is pure fiction. Instead, the girls of this age did fictional reporting in 40 percent of their writing.

We don't yet know whether these and other differences are effects of gender or whether they are merely the reflections of the personalities of our students last year.

As we begin our second year of data collection for this naturalistic research project, we are excited by how much the children have taught us. We know that if we can remain patient observers, there is much we can continue to learn.

10

A Researcher in My Classroom for a Whole Year? You've Got to Be Kidding!

SHARON HAMILTON-WIELER

"Why can't my students spell better?" "Kids these days have no idea of basic grammar!" "If Donna could write a decent essay, she might have passed her history exam." "What do you English teachers teach your students nowadays?" Almost every English teacher has encountered such questions and accusations, from parents and politicians, and even from colleagues in other disciplines. As chair of the English department in a suburban secondary school in Winnipeg, Canada, I was assailed not only with the questions and accusations I have mentioned, but also with requests ranging from the French department's wanting us to teach parts of speech and verb tenses more explicitly in order to clarify French-English comparisons to the science department's wanting us to teach the finer aspects of scientific report writing. It was clear, in other words, that the English department was assumed to be responsible for the writing of students in all subject areas, or for writing across the curriculum. Frustrated with the assumptions about language and learning that impelled these sorts of questions and requests—and wanting to learn more about the role of language, particularly written language, in different subject areas—I embarked, during a three-year stay in England, upon an investigation of the writing of students in their final year of secondary schooling in six subject areas. Consequently, although I now speak as the researcher in these remarks, I was responding with the eyes and ears and concerns of a writing teacher as I observed and interpreted the language environments created in each of the six classrooms involved in the study.

This dual role has made me aware of one of the most challenging yet least discussed dimensions of classroom-based research: building relationships among teachers, students, and investigators. Besides policies protecting rights of confidentiality and basic safety, there are no guidelines to enable those involved in classroom-based research to know what to expect from each other. Each research project differs in its expectations of the participants, and the negotiating of each group's needs, even when initiated well before the beginning of the study, becomes an ongoing process that often continues after the project has left the classroom. This chapter looks at the dynamics of establishing and building relationships in this classroom-based study in London. My intention in telling you the story of this project is to suggest some moves for both teachers and researchers that might encourage deeper levels of collaboration. A second intention is to describe some of the unexpected, unanticipated interactions and the surprises that continually subverted my "best laid plans," in hope that others in similar situations might anticipate the unpredictability of interrelationships in classroom-based research.

OPENING MOVES

The story of a research project is similar to all stories that appear to have a beginning, a middle, and an end from the perspective of the storyteller, but not necessarily from the perspective of the participants. A researcher enters a classroom somewhat as Alice tumbles into Wonderland, confronted by bustling agendas established long before, and which will continue long after the completion of the project.

My relationship with Crown Woods School in south London, where the study was conducted, began with a letter of request for permission to conduct research in the school. As a Canadian "colonial" and thus a stranger in the imperial center, I had no automatic entry to schools and had to rely on the goodwill of others. To my dismay, my initial letter went unanswered for over six weeks. I faced a major dilemma. The school was so well suited to the needs of my study: it was a large inner-city school, with a wide range of course offerings for its diverse population of senior students; and it had already established research associations with the University of London Institute of Education. Bearing in mind that the English do not appreciate what they consider to be the pushiness of North Americans, I had to decide whether to try again or to seek out another school, assuming that Crown Woods did not want to participate in the research. Fortunately, I decided to try again, for shortly after my second letter, I received an apologetic reply, explaining about an administrative mix-up and welcoming me to the school.

Unfortunately, the delay of nearly two months forced an adjustment of my research plans. Whereas I had wanted to take advantage of the spring term to become familiar with the courses and routines of the school, as well as with the teachers and students who would be involved in the study, it was close to the end of term by the time I arrived at the school. I had already sent a description of the study, and of my research requirements, which were considerable: a full year of daily attendance, with cassette recorder, in the classes of the teachers involved; regular interviews with teachers and students; and access to all of the students' written work during the year. Ethnographic research in schools was still relatively new, and most teachers were more familiar with the traditional shorter and intermittent models of in-class research. Nonetheless, eight teachers greeted my discussion of the proposed study enthusiastically, wanting to be involved in the project. However, because of timetable problems, I had to reduce the number of participating teachers to six.

Right from the first group meeting, our widely varying agendas signaled an immediate need for negotiation and compromise. Although interested in writing across the curriculum and in my related research question ("How does writing emerge from the classroom context?"), each teacher had vastly differing expectations of what my presence in his or her classroom would entail. The biology teacher, Nick Potts, expressed a hope that my presence might encourage his students to spell better, to write grammatically correctly, and to use more precise scientific terminology. Pat Tweedie, the history teacher, wanted me to tell her how to enable her students to write analyses rather than chronological narratives of historical events. At the same time, she expressed the fear that I might be bored by lengthy lectures, and so limited me to attending every second class. The history of art teacher, Robin Sutton (the only teacher who would not allow me to tape his class sessions), was concerned that I would make judgments about him and his teaching based on his students' writing. At the same time, he was openly enthusiastic in his hope that my presence might stimulate better writing from his students. Peter McLeod, the geography teacher, was primarily concerned that I might be bored by his lengthy three-hour class, yet spoke eagerly of anticipated opportunities to talk about the problems his students encountered grappling with the discourse and traditions of geographical concepts. Ron Mannix, the sociology teacher, and Jane Ogborn, the English teacher and also my appointed liaison with the school, both expressed a desire that I would participate in class discussions, especially when they involved writing, at the same time expressing their concern that I might find the extensive examination-oriented written assignments too limiting. The need for clarification of expectations was obviously and immediately apparent.

My reaction to this first meeting was to position the expressed concerns and expectations of the six teachers in relation to features of ethnographic research, thereby laying the foundation upon which to base our collaborative efforts to learn more about student writing in the classroom context. This foundation comprised the following operational principles:[1]

1. That ethnographic research assumes the layering of multiple realities in perceived phenomena and seeks out relationships among these multiple realities. Each participant's version of perceived reality is therefore equally valid and subject to exploration rather than to judgment.

2. That the roles of participant- and nonparticipant-observer have flexible parameters and are highly context-dependent. Therefore, my role in each class would be dependent upon the teacher's normal structuring of the class. For example, if teachers primarily lectured to their students, I would sit and take notes as one of the students; when teachers held discussions, I would participate in those discussions. At the same time, as an observer, I would not be teaching in any formal, presentational sense.

3. That field notes of each teacher's classroom procedures and of each teacher's interviews would be kept confidential during my stay at the school.

4. That the integrity of each teacher's pedagogy should not be influenced by the presence of an observer. Nor should the teachers involved try to change or adapt their normal teaching procedures just because they were part of the research project.

However, as I would discover from time to time throughout the year, clarifying these operational principles at the outset, although essential, was not sufficient. Constant reinforcement and renegotiation, as I shall illustrate shortly, was necessary. But first I need to introduce the third major component of the research, the students.

Although all the students of these six teachers would be influenced by the study to the extent that they would have a "stranger" in their midst for a whole year, those students who were enrolled in the classes of two or more of the six teachers would be subject to more in-depth scrutiny, in order to develop a more comprehensive understanding of how writing emerges from particular classroom contexts. I arranged to meet with each of the twelve students who were taught by two or more of the teachers, in order to explain the purpose of my research and the extra requirements their involvement would entail, and to ask whether they were interested in participating. All twelve students appeared eager to participate in the study, most of them expressing the hope that the increased consciousness of their writing might improve their writing abilities. At this time, we agreed upon certain expectations, such as attending monthly interviews, sometimes singly, sometimes as a group; keeping a weekly journal of their writing (often in response to questions I would be asking); and giving me access to all their writing, including notes, tests, and essays. Although there was an occasional missed interview, and an occasional late journal, for the most part these twelve students conscientiously fulfilled their agreements.

The above arrangements were concluded at the end of the school year preceding the year I would be conducting the research. I should add, however, that the teachers requested that I not begin my study until the third week of the term, so as to allow them time to establish and begin to build their own relationships with their students. Although I very much wanted to observe the initial shaping of the language environments in each teacher's classroom, I of course agreed to the compromise, which seemed essential to the teachers' territorial needs and was a fair price for all that the research project was asking of them.

COLLABORATIVE MOVES AND SURPRISES

Although much of what occurred during the year of actual observation evolved on the basis of the above agreements coupled with regular informal chats and more formal interviews, several surprises throughout the year necessitated renegotiation and some redirection. Many of these were isolated events and seemed almost trivial at the time, yet each one was potentially a serious liability to the project. An example of one of these minor surprises occurred the day Pat Tweedie, the history teacher, arrived uncustomarily late to class, behaving very coolly, almost resentfully, towards me. She later told me that halfway to school she realized she had forgotten her lecture notes, and whereas under normal circumstances she would have talked through the information with her class, my presence in her class made her drive back home a considerable distance for her prepared lecture. I was shocked to have been the cause of such inconvenience. I suddenly realized that no matter how unobtrusive I was trying to be, my presence was continually influencing the behavior of the teachers involved in the research. Such minor but frequent episodes as these reminded me of the inevitable obtrusiveness of classroom observation, and of the continual need to reinforce and renegotiate the operational principles previously established.

The first surprise of major significance occurred during my second week in the school. Jane Ogborn relayed the message that Robin Sutton, the art teacher (and the one who had not wanted to be audiotaped), was "all in a fluster" because it seemed to him that I made copious notes whenever his comments were anti-Thatcher, antigovernment, or pro-Marxist. He wanted me to call a meeting to clarify what kind of data I was collecting, what was going to be done with it, and who was going to be reading it. After speaking with Sutton beforehand, in order to deal with his specific concern on an individual basis, I arranged for the requested meeting. That meeting became a significant learning opportunity for both the teachers and me.

During the course of this meeting, I was plunged pell-mell into the ideological issues confronting education in England, and particularly in inner-city London. I learned of the declining morale resulting from severe economic cutbacks coupled with entrenched attitudes among politicians who set educational policies, particularly with regard to curriculum and systems of external assessment. I learned also of the compromises these teachers had negotiated with themselves, sometimes comfortably, sometimes awkwardly, to solve the dilemma of preparing students to do well on final examinations while also encouraging them to engage enthusiastically with the bodies of knowledge that comprise their respective disciplines. As a consequence of this meeting, I was able to construct a much fuller picture of the different classroom contexts and of the wider social, cultural, and political contexts in which these classrooms were situated.

I responded to their concerns by explaining in greater depth some of the axioms of ethnographic research, acknowledging that although all inquiry is value-laden, I was not trying to force time-bound and context-bound working hypotheses into simple cause-effect relationships. I further explained that a flurry of field-note writing in class usually indicated my attempt to capture the full flavor of a particular instructional moment, and that I would most likely be wanting to talk to them, and their students, about many of these "moments" in order to gain a deeper sense of their relationship to writing and learning in the respective disciplines. The teachers appreciated knowing more about the theoretical values that informed my research, and they expressed the desire to be kept informed of developing hypotheses and questions. I was relieved that a potentially dodgy situation had instead enriched the understanding of all of us, and had opened doors for further related conversations.

My second major surprise, neither ideological nor theoretical in nature, is worthy of note primarily because, as researchers, we can become so caught up in our investigations that we often forget that we are also ambassadors from other institutions, and as such are responsible for developing and maintaining good relations between the different institutions. Although some of the teachers had commented on the regularity and punctuality of my attendance in their classes, the significance of their remarks did not take shape until the morning after the five-day midterm recess. Arriving at my usual time, I encountered astonished greetings from most of the teachers in the study, who had apparently assumed that I would extend the recess another week. When I questioned their astonishment, I learned that many of the staff had been involved with researchers prior to my study in the school, researchers who either had not made their schedules clear, or who had been consistently late or irregular with the schedules they had established. I thought back to these teachers' initial cool courtesy, which I had mistakenly interpreted as part of the British reserve, and now realized that it was instead forged upon an experience-based skepticism. As researchers, we sometimes forget to take into account attitudes that have resulted from teachers' former experiences with researchers, experiences that can easily inhibit the establishment of good working relationships in subsequent research projects.

Another misreading of British reserve was, in part, a dimension of my third surprise, which involved the students more than the teachers. Their contributions to class discussions could best be described as "safe," being most often an articulate synthesis of what had gone before, and only occasionally a comment or observation that went just a bit beyond mere synthesis. Yet, in conversations with these students, and from reading their written assignments, I learned that they often held quite divergent and much more original opinions than those they had articulated in class. I also learned, during this set of interviews, that, unlike my Canadian students, they rarely talked over or read each other's papers before handing them in. Juliet's answer to my questions about this dissonance between what they said in class and what they were really thinking raises some interesting issues:

> I'm not sure why I didn't say that in class. Perhaps it's because I'm selfish, because I don't want others to latch onto my ideas without having to do the thinking. . . . I think that also might be why we don't share our essays with each other, or talk about our own ideas in them before handing them in, although I would like to. . . . I would be interested in hearing what some of the others think. . . . I wonder if it's because in a way we're all competing on the examination for a university spot, but, of course, we're not really competing with each other. I don't know. I think more sharing would be good, but we just don't do it.

Juliet's almost serendipitous juxtaposition of the sanctity of her individual thinking with the competitive nature of individual performance on final examinations further illuminated my growing understanding of the contextual dynamics in these students' classrooms. Even more interesting, soon after this set of interviews with the twelve students in the study, I learned that five of them—who happened to be in the same English class as Juliet—began sharing their ideas and their writing out of class as well as in class. This newly developed collegiality offers an example of the power of indirect influence a researcher can unintentionally exert on participants in research.

Final examinations played an even stronger role in the next surprise. Without exception, all six teachers in the study became very edgy about halfway through the final term, and, for the first time, I began to feel like an intruder in their classrooms. One week, Jane Ogborn, my liaison with the school (and the teacher with whom I had established the strongest rapport), avoided our customary after-class talks. The source of the problem, as I found out later, was the annual heightened preparation for the approaching final examinations. Throughout the year, as we talked about the writing in their classrooms, these teachers had been articulating their previously tacit and implicit compromises between preparing students to write examinations and stimulating them to engage enthusiastically in writing with the concepts and constructs of their respective subjects. This emergent consciousness of negoti-ated compromises exacerbated the discomfort they always felt near the end of the year when they spent increasing amounts of class time coaching their students to write for examinations. Strategies such as sacrificing pithy conclu-sions and points involving lengthy explanations to the exigencies of time, and avoiding open-ended, challenging questions in favor of straightforward, information-bound questions where points could be ticked off most efficiently were sound advice for passing examinations, but were also at odds with their pedagogical beliefs about teaching and learning. My presence in their class-rooms heightened their consciousness of this dissonance, and therefore their discomfort, even more.

Going back to the axioms of ethnographic research with which we began the study slightly ameliorated the situation, but I slowly began to realize that the discomfort was less with me than with their own pedagogical compro-mises. This realization motivated the closing moves of the research project.

CLOSING MOVES

Two group meetings—one with the students and one with the teachers—brought the in-school portion of the research project to a close. The most repeated comment during the student meeting involved their growing appre-ciation for talking with each other about their ideas and their writing, both during the process of writing and after completion of the written text. Comments during the teachers' meeting embraced three major topics: (1) a growing interest in the writing problems students encountered in different disciplines, and the pedagogical strategies each teacher employed while ad-dressing these problems; (2) a growing appreciation of their own tacit (and now more explicit) views of language in relation to learning, and how their own views related to other teachers' views; and (3) a growing appreciation of how, within the rigid contextualizing constraints of a central external assessment system, they were nonetheless enabling their students to use writing to stimulate as well as to demonstrate learning. These topics emerged directly from a brief discussion paper I had prepared in response to the discomfort they had expressed during the final weeks, a paper designed to position their pedagogical concerns and achievements within larger cultural and political contexts. When I overheard such remarks as "I hope we continue to meet and talk about our students' writing next year" and "I would like to hear more about the kind of writing your students do, and how you help them write better," I realized that my discussion paper had accomplished its purpose.

Although written analysis of the data necessitated phone calls and subsequent meetings on an individual basis, for verification or clarification of details, the collaborative basis of the research project ended with that meeting. James Britton, writing of the extent of the collaboration during the project, surprised me with his phrase, "no easy achievement *for an outsider on temporary attachment to a busy school.*"[2] Caught up in the day-to-day exigencies of the study, I had rarely felt either temporary or an outsider. Britton's phrase sent me back to my memories, and back to my field notes. Only then did I realize how critical were those surprises I have described, and how easily an inappropriate response to the eloquent signals of the teachers and the students might have sabotaged our shared involvement in the project.

I agree with Margaret Spencer at the University of London Institute of Education that "the enterprise as a whole must be highly valued for the response it inspired in the school in which it took place: an unusual degree of cooperation, joint enquiry and collaboration between teachers and students."[3] That cooperation, joint inquiry, and collaboration can be attributed to a fortuitous combination of several factors, many of which were beyond my control. However, the deliberate moves a classroom-based researcher can make to build and maintain a communicative atmosphere sensitive to the needs of both the research project and the teachers comprise one very significant factor over which we can, and must, take control. At the same time, the unexpected—the surprises that arise from unanticipated reactions to our presence—will suggest more eloquently than any previously established checklist how to move from researcher as intruder to researcher as collaborating partner.

NOTES

1. The operational principles of ethnographic research that I adapted for this project were drawn from the following discussions of case study research: H. Simons, ed.,

Towards a Science of the Singular: Essays about Case Study in Educational Research and Evaluation, CARE Occasional Paper No. 10 (Norwich: University of East Anglia, 1980); and R. K. Yin, *Case Study Research: Design and Methods* (Beverly Hills, CA: Sage Publications, 1984).

2. This comment was part of James Britton's written evaluation, as external examiner, of the doctoral dissertation that presented this study: Sharon Hamilton-Wieler, "A Context-Based Study of the Writing of Eighteen-Year-Olds, with Special Reference to A-Level Biology, English, Geography, History, History of Art, and Sociology" (Ph.D. diss., University of London, 1986).

3. This comment was part of Margaret Spencer's written evaluation, as internal examiner, of the author's doctoral dissertation.

11

The Multigenre Research Paper: Melding Fact, Interpretation, and Imagination

TOM ROMANO

Perception is all. Ways of seeing. Ways of knowing. Ways of learning.

Sometimes I see the world through poetry: a bit of cadenced language, a striking image, a metaphor with extensions following close behind.

Sometimes I see the world through prose: a description that clarifies a vivid moment, a pointed narrative, a monologue marshaling all the points I should have brought up during an argument.

Sometimes I see the world through dramatic encounters: before a student arrives for a conference, I play the dialogue that might occur between us; I have talked with my father (dead now for twenty-five years) of things that were and things that might have been.

Each genre offers me ways of seeing and understanding that the others do not. I perceive the world through multigenres. They define me.

In Stratford, Ontario, at the Shakespeare festival, between "Good night, sweet Prince" and the hurly-burly of the "dead butcher and his fiendlike Queen," I visited a wonderful house-of-a-bookstore called Fanfare Books. In the jam-packed poetry room, my head tilted to scan the book spines, I saw a title I just had to pull from the shelf: *The Collected Works of Billy the Kid*.

Canadian writer Michael Ondaatje has created a treasure in this story of the last few years of outlaw Billy the Kid's life. Although Ondaatje takes his material from a real person and true events, his book (winner of the prestigious Governor-General's Award) is far from conventional biography. In fact, the subtitle Ondaatje provided in the original Coach House Press edition was *Left Handed Poems*. The Library of Congress catalog entry lists the book as

123

both poetry *and* fiction. At the same time, *The Collected Works of Billy the Kid* is loaded with fact.

Ondaatje thoroughly researched the vengeful, bloody life of William H. Bonney—alias Billy the Kid. Out of his *learning*, Ondaatje created a complex, multilayered, multivoiced blend of literary genres. In his learning-journal, my former student Jon wrote a good description of Ondaatje's book:

> Ondaatje is uncompromising. He shows us characters from every angle. He switches smoothly between personas—from Billy to Pat Garrett to Sally Chisum . . . and sometimes he steps back and writes simply as "the author."
>
> Blending stream of consciousness, narrative, verse, monologue, even newspaper style dialogue, he leaves nary a stone unturned. —And it all is effective.
>
> While sometimes author techniques run dry by book's end, Ondaatje builds on you. The more I read, the more I understood.

In addition to the genres Jon mentions, Ondaatje also included songs, thumbnail character sketches, imaginative creations of moments that could have occurred, even photographs and drawings from the era, and an authentic comic-book legend from The Five Cent Wide Awake Library.

Each genre reveals a facet of Billy the Kid or of the characters who moved in and out of his life. Each piece is self-contained, making a point of its own, and is not connected to any of the others by conventional transitional devices. The reader enters this different kind of book and drifts and puzzles and makes sense. Reading it is like listening to jazz: the reader feels something satisfying and meaningful, but may not be able to articulate what it is right away. The multiple genres, the nonchronological order, the language rhythms, the condensed imagery—all these the reader adjusts to and works with. Intellectual and emotional understandings mount. As Jon says, "The more I read, the more I understood."

I wondered if my class of high school junior and senior writing students could write in this style. Enrolled in an elective class named Advanced Writing, these students represented a wide range of writing ability, experience in English classes, and reasons for taking the course. Although ability and motivation varied greatly among the students, none were members of the academically alienated. The majority were bound for some kind of college work the following year. I wondered if Michael Ondaatje could become their "distant teacher," as Vera John-Steiner calls those who teach unknowingly from afar (p. 37). Could my students pick interesting people, research them, and then report on that research—*not* in traditional, expository research papers, but rather by employing Ondaatje's multigenre mode of writing?

I also wondered if my students and their audience would perceive and feel more deeply through the multiple ways of seeing and knowing that the various genres offered. *Sometimes I see the world through poetry, sometimes* . . . In *Writing and Learning Across the Curriculum, 11–16,* Nancy Martin contends that students deepen and extend their understanding if they engage their imaginations in learning (p. 86). I wanted my students to do this.

We spent a week and a half with Billy the Kid. Ondaatje's book is so complex that we first took two days to read and discuss biographical information on the Kid gathered from *Webster's American Biographies* (Springfield, MA: G. & C. Merriam Co., 1975); the *Dictionary of American Biography (Vol. 1); The Gunfighters* (Alexandria, VA: Time-Life Books, 1974); and *The Book of the American West* (New York: Julian Messner, Inc., 1963). Next, we explored *The Collected Works of Billy the Kid,* creating meaning and discussing the genres and language experimentation Ondaatje had employed.

Because Ondaatje's book is complex and takes liberties with the facts of William Bonney's life (and because I hadn't been intellectually hamstrung by a cursed teacher's guide), our study was necessarily collaborative. We groped for meaning. We spurred and enriched each other's interpretation. Meanings were up for grabs. No one had a lock on one right answer. Most of the students had never before read that way in a class. Nor had I. The communal reading experience was fulfilling and sometimes exhilarating. As we read and talked and wrote, our working code was this: to respect individual perception and to be willing to revise and extend interpretation. We had a good start for the work ahead.

For the next six weeks the classroom turned into a workshop, with these twenty-six southwestern Ohio students reading, writing, researching, and conferring about Elvis Presley, Marilyn Monroe, Ken Kesey, Maya Angelou, Charles Manson, John Lennon, Bob Dylan, Jimi Hendrix, G. Gordon Liddy, Jim Thorpe, Tom Seaver, Willie Mays, Bette Davis, Betty Grable, Carol Burnett, Nancy Wilson (of the old Supremes), Alan Alda, Helen Keller, undercover-FBI-man–mafioso-investigator Danny Brosco, Amelia Earhart, Tennessee Williams, and (in the spirit of nascent feminism and with a mother's cautious approval) Linda Lovelace.

The students kept learning-journals. Each week I asked them to write at least a thousand words about their research. Instead of trying to keep in their heads all the incoming information, ideas, and perceptions, I wanted them to use their journals—their personal language—as a tool to "audit" their learning (Berthoff, p. 11). I knew that such auditing would not only organize information, but also uncover findings and provoke new thinking.

Here's Amy rummaging around in her research:

> Went to the library today and found a couple of magazine articles on Carol Burnett. Nothing spectacular, just an article on her chin surgery in '83 and another article about the movie "Between Friends" that she'd played in a

few years ago. I found some interesting pictures that compare what Carol's chin looked like before, and after her surgery. You can certainly see a difference. The surgeon added 4 millimeters to it. I don't figure I should write much about it though, it's not really all that significant to the part of her life that I'm focusing on. But it's evident that to her it is in fact a "big deal." So I don't know whether I should or not, (what do you think). I did note one important pt. In the article, at the end, Carol comments that the best thing she likes about "getting a chin" was that when it rained now, she could feel it on her chin. And I thought that was neat because I was watching videotapes that Brian loaned me on Oprah & Donahue and she made the same comment. The article was written about 5 yrs ago and the video's were taped a year (or less ago). I guess it was the way she said she could finally feel rain on it, that got me, all through her book she mentions rain here and there. She's got some sort of fascination with it. She says rain puts her in a good mood. And brings her good luck. So I'm going to use rain here and there in my piece. I'm thinking about titling the whole thing

"Carol Burnett: The inspiration reigns on."

The bulk of the writing in the learning-journals was like this. James Britton has called it "expressive writing" (p. 8)—informal, personal, and unpressured prose with students seeking to recover information, to make connections, and to generate thinking with their close-to-speaking-voice language—the best learning tool available to them. Because of the nature of our multigenre project, however, I also wanted students to turn their expressive writing to the creation of various genres. I wanted them to experiment in their journals, to play with possibilities, to try genres *as* their research was in progress. I pushed them to do this.

Wendy dived deeply and quickly into David Henderson's *The Life of Jimi Hendrix: 'Scuse Me While I Kiss the Sky*. In her learning-journal she works out this poem about Hendrix's early career and a key person in his life:

Fayne, Jim Hendrix, And His Girl

The first time you heard
        Jimi Hendrix play
you could have been sitting in the cramped New York
                        night club
            dangling a cigarette between red,
                        chipped fingernails
            leaning back in your chair
            soaking in the music.
You may have been wearing a blue cotton dress
            sleek black shoes
            and cheap pearl costume jewelry

Maybe you wanted to get up
　　　out of that stiff chair
and dance
　　　　wildly to the beat
　　　　　　surging into your feet
　　　　　　pounding into your mind
But the world wasn't ready for you yet.
And I know you realized Jimi's talent
　　　eating up conservative ways
　　　paving roads for
　　　　free music
You felt all of Jimi's pain
　　　in each whining note
　　　　of his girl.
No doubt you were rapped up
　　　in the sounds
　　　　of the frantic guitar
No doubt you felt free.
And I know at the end of Jimi's gig,
　　　　you nodded your head yes
　　to the
　　　　crazy music
　　　　　you'd never heard
　　before.
But the world wasn't ready for Jimi yet.
So you, the girl from Harlem
　　　　with the foxy smile,
stood up for Jimi and his girl
　　　to the audiences
　　　and Big names.
You understood him
always laughing to forget those who
　　　　　　didn't understand.
Laughing about silly things like
how short poor Jimi looked in the white trousers he
　　　　　bought for his gig.

In Amy's earlier journal entry, she discussed the importance of rain in Carol Burnett's life. In the following journal excerpt, she fashions a draft of a poem with the rain imagery prominent and a new word tried on for size:

Rain (Chap 25 p. 217)
Ranging gusts of wind scream
outside the fragile windows.

Huge drops of rain swoosh in all
directions as if a giant invisible broom sweeps
them to a fanatical dance in the air.
The storm rages on
Unexpected explosions of thunder follow
close behind the blinding flashes of lightning.
There is tension all around me.
Nervousness results from the storm.
Yet I,
sit here calmly. No fright, no worry, no tension.
My mind at ease, I soak here
embellished in the eye of the storm.

Lucy Calkins defines a minilesson as a brief, pointed presentation that provides students with a helpful tip or strategy (p. 168). The journal entries here turned into instructive minilessons. I made transparencies of these genre experiments and, at the beginning of class, placed them on the overhead so that everyone shared the bright moments of the classroom's creative current (Romano, p. 171). After a week, I took Nancie Atwell's lead. When the students were willing (and most of these juniors and seniors were), I let *them* conduct the minilessons with their own writing (p. 122). The student pre-senter gave a good reading of her writing, then revealed the genesis of the idea. From each other we learned what Donald Murray calls "the geography of possibility" (1985, p. 88).

I sought to lead students to create drafts of their multigenre papers *during* their research. This paper was a major project, not one to attempt writing a night or two before a draft was due. I also believed that if we shared frequently along the way, this ongoing multigenre draft creation would spark ideas in the classroom community of writers.

Even though I urged and pushed and cajoled students to use their journals to try genres, I was not successful in all cases. Mary Beth's final paper was a sensitive, spare, and poetic examination of Marilyn Monroe. In her written evaluation of the project, Mary Beth acknowledged the usefulness of her learning-journal for discussing and discovering what she had learned. But she admitted that she hadn't used the journal for experimenting with genres.

"I really didn't try different genres in my journal, but maybe once," wrote Mary Beth, "because when I write, I just write with no 'pre' to it. I know this eats you up, but that's just me. In my journal, I wrote about considering a poem, but I never wrote anything until I wrote my poem. (Rough draft,— only draft)."

Mary Beth's process of writing was not my process. It wasn't what I was trying to teach her. And it did "eat me up," a little. But Mary Beth achieved quality results with her "no-'pre'-to-it" process of composition. Here is an excerpt from her paper, "The Simple Life":

SomedaySomemonthSomeyear
walked on the beach for hours watching the
water come and go just as i do with Marilyn
and Norma Jeane but who am i really i
know i'm not Marilyn because i wasn't
born Marilyn but i'm not Norma Jeane
because i wasn't born well i was born her
but i wasn't her once i got my "big break"
my big break that broke me in two or three
or however many i am who in the hell
am i i'm a flower a moth a spider a
bird a well i guess i'm everything everywhere
everyone i'm a sex symbol sex is strange
but it's all mine it's all i have to give
i haven't slept my way to the top i've
slept my way to your heart you love
me for my sex and why you like it i don't
know i hate it it's not for me it's not
me it's your pleasure not mine but that's
all i'm for is your pleasure
a trademark a fool
a lonely lonely
fool who wants
to die

When the students were nearing the end of their research, we spent a day working with mapping as a strategy for gaining an overview of their learning and discovering topics to write about. I showed the students an example of mapping from Donald Murray's *Write to Learn* (p. 26). Next, we tried a collaborative mapping activity. I placed a transparency on the overhead, in the center of it wrote and circled *President Reagan*, then asked students to brainstorm facts from his life. They knew him well. In minutes I had filled the transparency with Reagan facts (some, no doubt, that he'd rather forget).

Next, we speculated. Suppose we were going to write a multigenre research paper that would illuminate the character of President Reagan. What genres would be appropriate for writing about some of the crucial facts and events we had mapped on the overhead?

Todd suggested a simple list poem of the names of important figures in Reagan's life.

Jon thought an interview would be revealing, one between Nancy Reagan and Jane Wyman.

A thumbnail sketch of Reagan's would-be assassin, John Hinckley.

A stream-of-consciousness passage from Reagan's point of view in the moments when he was shot, pushed into a car, and hustled away.

And [if you spend time with teenagers, you soon learn that many of them are just a nudge away from broad, indelicate satire] a tabloid piece à la the *National Enquirer*, accompanied by a photograph of Reagan's one-time cancer-blighted nose.

The students then took ten minutes and let fly without self-censorship, rapidly mapping crucial facts, people, and events from their own characters' lives. Figure 11–1 is Traci's mapping of Charles Manson.

As their research neared an end, the students wanted to know what the multigenre papers should look like. What should be in them? How should they begin? And, yes, how long should they be? I had no answers. This was new territory. None of my previous students had ever done multigenre research papers. Neither had I. So I wrote the students a memo:

To: Advanced Writing Students
From: Romano
Date: 3/10/88
Re: Your research and final pieces of writing

First of all, what is it you should create based upon all the research, reading, sharing, and writing you have done? Fact is, I don't know what it should look like or how many words it should contain.

I do know that I want it to be deeply textured (Ondaatje showed us that), interesting, vivid, specific, insightful, diverse with many genres (we have worked very hard on that), intelligent, bold, experimental (I want to see your imagination and intellect turned loose), and comprehensible. When I finish reading, I want to really know your person through your perceptions. I want to be gasping for air from the excitement of reading you.

I want a lot. But I think you can do it if you're willing to risk and work (writing always involves both).

And I want to help you as you craft your writing, your vision.

It took the students about a week to assemble, create, and write drafts of their papers. I read them and conferred with the writers; the writers conferred with each other. I collected their final versions about a week later. I had never read anything like these papers. Although four or five were disappointing, showing little depth, breadth, or commitment, the rest were good, genuinely

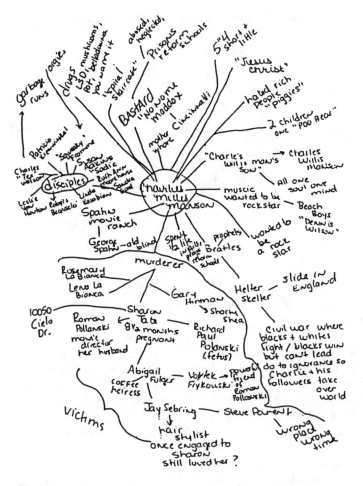

Figure 11-1
Traci's Mapping of Charles Manson

interesting in style and content, with seven or eight papers astonishingly superior. The visions were complex, the writing versatile.

Here is one of the papers. When it was published in *Menagerie*, Edgewood High School's creative arts anthology, author Brian McKnight agreed to alter the way the piece appeared on the page in order to save space. Here we have restored the original form with this exception: in the original version Brian assembled the piece following Michael Ondaatje's example of placing each part, or genre, however brief, on a page by itself. Brian intends the parts to work individually as well as collectively.

The Long and Wonderful Odyssey of the Walrus—A Heart Play

Unfinished Music #1—John

> He hit the pavement
> ass-first
> Yoko raised
> his
> head.
> He wanted to embrace her
> but
> a hundred people
> were
> standing on
> his arms.
>   Oh God, Yoko, I've been shot.

The Death of John Beatle

Outside the Indica Gallery, the world still oppressed ideas, fought wars, and censored news.

Inside, however, it was like nothing he had ever seen. It had only been 8 years since he had graduated from Liverpool Art College. He hadn't been in an art gallery since. And he had never been in one like this. White nails half driven in a white block of wood, white vases with white flowers sitting on a white table in a white corner. He saw a white, half-eaten apple on a white pedestal. (When he was a kid and had had a bad day, his aunt Mimi always gave him an apple. "There now, don't you feel better, then, John? Of course you do, now give your aunt Mimi a kiss.") The apple felt as smooth as glass in his hand—so white and smooth and pure.

"Don't touch anything, please." She stood menacingly in the doorway. "The show doesn't open until tomorrow, so you better not mess anything up."

"Yoko, this is John Lennon. The Beatle."

Lost in the Gallery, John had forgotten Tony was there. He took John by the arm and led him to the dark figure in the doorway.

"John, this is Yoko Ono."

"John stood there like a prize being awarded to someone who wishes he hadn't won in the first place.

Yoko didn't move. Her all-black outfit and long black hair contradicted the all-white gallery. The artist herself. She looked deep into John. Past his round-rimmed granny glasses, past John Beatle and into John Lennon. "Well, whoever you are don't touch anything."

Whoever you are?

But surely, he thought, everyone's heard of John Lennon, the Beatle. This Jap was daft! Didn't she know who she had in her gallery?

"I just wanted to look around, all right?"

She nodded and pulled her long hair away from her perfect, pristine, Oriental face. John made his way past Yoko and into the other room. He stopped at a white ladder leaning against the white wall. Suddenly she was at his side, holding a magnifying glass.

"Here," she said, "climb up and look."

He pushed his spectacles back on the bridge of his nose. Now she thinks I am bleedin' Sherlock Holmes.

When he arrived at the top, he raised the spyglass gently to the ceiling.

And he looked down at her.

And then the magnified word: YES, it said.

He smiled.

Two Virgins

A New Age
awoke
with the
Two Virgins.
Confusion and ignorance
were wiped away
with
the sleep in their
eyes.

Dressed all in
white
they paraded their
love
for the world to
see.

The Two Virgins
were wed
March 20, 1969
on the
Rock of Gibraltar.
The world was invited
to their bed-in
for the consummation.

From a maharishi
to
primal screaming
to
heroin
to
NEW YORK

The Two Virgins
arrived in
New York
to be welcomed
home
by a
family
they'd never
seen.

The Rotting Apple

"This is it. I want a divorce."

Paul was stunned. He looked across the table to see himself, mouth open wide, in John's spectacles.

"What do you mean?"

"Just that. I want a divorce. I don't want to be a Beatle anymore. I just want to be with Yoko. I'm tired of the pressures and the people and all the bullshit. Your bullshit, Paul."

"John, come on, Man. Don't do this. Listen, fine, if *you* want to be with Yoko, that's okay, but don't say anything to the press. It'll look bad . . ."

"I don't give a bleeding damn about how it looks!" Apple Corp had become a pain in the ass. He ran his ragged fingers through his long, unkempt hair and beard. He straightened his white jacket and fixed his white turtleneck. "Fine. I'm gone, but I won't say nuthin to the press. You deal with 'em. You're better at that shit anyway."

It took him a while, but 4 months later the news hit the stands:

PAUL McCARTNEY QUITS THE BEATLES

SOLO LP DUE OUT SOON

Beatles Break-up; McCartney, Ono To Blame

LONDON—A High Court ruled today that singer-songwriter-musician-Beatle Paul McCartney and screamer-songwriter-artist-Beatle-lover Yoko Ono were jointly responsible for the destruction of the greatest band in the history of music.

"Well, she's a bitch," replied Judge Len N. Fann, when asked about his decision. "She took John away from good music and turned him into something sick and perverted."

Paul McCartney, meanwhile, has been hiding out at his Scottish retreat, changing diapers, breast feeding, etc.

"It wasn't my fault," he said in a statement to the press. "We [the Beatles] just didn't get along anymore. They got real rebellious. They wouldn't play their instruments the way I told them to. But don't worry, I'll have another number one single out in no time."

Ms. Ono was unavailable for comment.

No. 9   No. 9   No. 9   No. 9   No. 9   No. 9   No. 9   No. 9

Born on the 9th He
NO. 9 Dreamed of the 9th Revolution beginning
on the 9th
Recorded on the 9th: Love Me Do: Parlophone R4949
All We Are Saying Is Give Peace A Chance
His son was born on the 9th to John Lennon
Who was born on the 9th who met
Sean's mother on the 9th
One after 909.

No. 9   No. 9   No. 9   No. 9   No. 9   No. 9   No. 9   No. 9

Unfinished Music #2—Yoko

She kissed him hard on the mouth.
She could already
taste
the blood
the blood
The blood
was thick and
made her sweater
heavy as
she held him
close
   Hold on, John, please hold on.

New York

Like a rose
New York City
opened its bud to
JohnandYoko.

Each crimson petal offered a
new opportunity to
live and love and grow.

Their home at the
Dakota Building
was the magical epicentre
of an ever extending
sea of possibilities.
Each ripple grew
larger and larger
picking up
ideas.

New York
pulsated and breathed just for
JohnandYoko.
It was the heart that
kept their spirits alive.
It was the safe place
that protected them
from
the rest of the world.

America

"Hey, John, how's the new album?"
"Yo, John, —where's Yoko?"
He was
free
in New York.
No hassles, man.
Sign the occasional
autograph
and move on.

Unfinished Music #3—The Reaction

The ambulance
barreled around
W. 72nd St.
Oh John
she screamed
Move out of the way ma'am.
Where are you taking him?

Roosevelt Hospital,
9th Ave.
They loaded his
heaving, dripping
body
into the ambulance.
Holy Shit, man. This is John Lennon.

The Coda

Flashbulbs
popped off a
morbid papparazzi
as
Dr. Lynn
spoke.
"John Lennon . . .
John Lennon
was
brought to
the emergency room of
Roosevelt Hospital
shortly before
11 pm.
He was
dead
on arrival."

"And in the end—the love you take is equal to the love you make."
        —John Lennon/Paul McCartney

References

Brown, Peter. *The Love You Make.* New York: McGraw Hill, 1982.
Coleman, Ray. *Lennon.* New York: McGraw Hill, 1985.
Lennon, John. *Skywriting by Word of Mouth.* New York: McGraw Hill, 1986.
Polskin, Howard. "How TV Reported the John Lennon Tragedy." *TV Guide* 29 (November 21, 1981): 2–8.
Wenner, Jann. "The John Lennon Interview." *Rolling Stone Magazine* 1970.

One of my original research questions was "How will the students decide which genres are appropriate for their multigenre papers?" We had emphasized genre; the students knew they were expected to write in a variety of them, but I hadn't mandated that any certain number of genres or any one in particular be used.

A few of the students described systematic processes for choosing genres—what I thought I'd find across the board, since we had been so systematic in identifying the many genres in *The Collected Works of Billy the Kid*.

Some students mentioned the appropriateness of subject matter for certain genres. "I picked genres that I thought would fit the piece," wrote Susan. "For example: When Maya was considering suicide, I thought a stream of consciousness would be best because all kinds of crazy thoughts were going through her mind."

Brian worked in a similar way: "First I would pick an event in John Lennon's life, like the Big Beatle Break-up. Then I would decide poem or prose or what? In this case I thought that since the world read about it in the news that I'd write a short news story."

Brian and Susan came closest to how I *thought* the kids would work and write in selecting genres. But most of them didn't work and write that way. Most of them worked in a manner reflected by the comments of Tari: "To be honest, there wasn't any specific way that I decided on which genres I used. The material that I read [Ken Kesey] was so powerful that certain things just grabbed me and I had to write about it, my genres were almost picked for me."

The students traveled deeply into their research. As I followed the twenty-six trails by reading learning-journals and holding individual and small-group conferences, I must admit I became less interested in how they chose genres. What seized my interest was the magnitude of the students' work. "I got so caught up in books," wrote Mary Beth. "It was amazing to feel that adventurous, to be there in the pages, to hear the words, and see, and feel the people and emotions."

It was amazing for me, too. Most of the students read and wrote more during these weeks than they had in any other comparable time period. They used language as utilitarian learning tool and as deft artistic instrument. They speculated and sparred with language; they created and refined with language.

I asked the students to write about the benefits and drawbacks of creating multigenre research papers. Nearly all the students believed that composing them was far more difficult than any writing they had done before. This was true for students who remained close to the ground during their research as well as for those who stretched and discovered wingspans that took them to places they'd never been. "The only drawback that I can think of," wrote Bobby, "would be that it makes you think a lot harder and it is a lot easier to write a standard research paper."

In most of the students' minds "standard research papers" were linked with boredom, perfunctory reading, and a kind of writing that offered little opportunity for surprise, individuality, and inventiveness. "I've done plenty of research papers with the old encyclopedia," noted Tari. "They're boring to write, read, and hear."

"A term paper or your basic social studies report would have been easy," wrote Holly, "because it requires no creativity."

There's the rub. No creativity. I find it heartbreaking that in the minds of most students, reporting on research through writing is divorced from creativity. I'm not talking about an airy-headed, ooo-wee-ain't-we-creative creativity. I'm talking about the real thing—when intellect, emotion, and imagination merge; when writers, painters, sculptors, dancers, composers, physicists, ecologists take that which is outside them and bring it inside, intimately; and when they give it back then, with form and imagination and meaning. Their own personal meaning stamped upon it.

That's the way we must live. We perceive through our minds and spirits. And we keep them growing. Our past comes into play, our self-awareness, our dreams—however grand or humble—and then we live our lives, putting our personal stamp upon them. Yet many students believe they are expected to feign some pure objectivity when writing reports. And facts become ashes in their mouths, often choking their voices. Listen to Amy:

> I can relate to this question very easily. In another class, we are having to do a research paper on anything we choose concerning the subject matter we've learned about. However, we're not free to write and explore, or discover through what we've written. Because we were instructed to make a basic outline of whatever it is we're doing our paper over then turn it in. (It's due today as a matter of fact). Anyway our grades will be determined by how closely we follow our outlines.
>
> I am not enjoying the assignment to say the least. I feel bound, prisoned, and dull. As if the wings of my mind and pen have been clipped. And that stupid outline is like some kind of merciless slave driver constantly breathing down my neck when I try to write.
>
> I would love to do a multigenre for my research paper. I'm sure I could get a point across a lot more.
>
> I wish I could burn that stupid outline.
>
> I don't believe there are any draw backs of a multigenre research paper (unless you're the type of person that doesn't like to, or feel comfortable writing.)

How can we create educational settings that will enable the Amys to escape wing-clipping so they may dazzle us with their flight? I saw Amy write for a year. She would have done something marvelous, something poignant and painfully truthful with a multigenre examination of her topic. She would have grounded herself in fact. And I know she would have reported her findings compellingly, surprisingly, and convincingly through the powerful medium of her mind and imagination, with language as her artistic tool. Her readers would have been moved intellectually and emotionally. I just know it.

The right kind of education, I believe, can sensitize teachers to the damage done by intentional and unintentional wing-clipping. Teachers and would-be teachers need experience in an education of *doing* and *diversity*. They need to engage often in the diverse and exhilarating possibilities that writing offers for learning, thinking, and creating.

And they need to participate in this *doing* in classrooms led by teacher-writers who value individuality. If teachers' individual diversity is valued, there is a better chance that they will encourage and value their students' individuality, not neglect it, crush it, or clip it. When individuality is valued, the modus operandi in classrooms becomes risk-taking, a priceless straying from the beaten path—the way Albert Eistein did and Thomas Edison and Margaret Mead and Henry Thoreau (that consummate researcher of the countryside of the soul). With much positive experience in *doing* and an ongoing, developing respect for *diversity*, teachers will begin to feel comfortable writing, will become open to its possibilities for perception.

There are many ways of seeing the world, of showing others what we see. Shakespeare saw the world through plays and poetry and poetry amid plays. I'm grateful that his spirit was indomitable, that no one had the power to compel him to forget those ways of seeing, and, instead, to write only prose chronicles in *reporting* what he had learned about the Scot and the Dane.

My students taught me much about writing, reading, and community learning. Jon, I think, articulated the discovery that applied to all the students and the writing they produced during this seven-week project. And what he wrote relates to something I said spontaneously during the first week of our research and, subsequently, had inscribed on a sign and hung at the head of the classroom: *Students' grades will be determined by the degree of fanatical madness they generate for their learning*.

Overloaded secondary school curricula and superficial attempts at coverage leave little room for an education of doing and diversity. And the pursuit of fine fanatical madnesses? You will find that happening outside school. You will also find that happening in the classrooms of teachers who pursue their own fanatical madnesses. Such teachers often write their own curriculum guides. But if they are stuck with impractical, suffocating curriculum guides, such teachers do not hesitate to employ them as mere part-time help. As teachers grow more confident in making their own way, as they become more aware of the exciting possibilities of the territory, they don't need guides to help them lead students to their own learning.

We must always leave room in our classrooms for Jon's deep understanding: "It is not a very earth-shattering discovery," he wrote, "but I was convinced that the words are more passionate and therefore, interesting if the author is immersed, not dabbling."

12

Searching for "Sloppy Trees": How Research Shapes Teaching

ROBERT P. YAGELSKI

The assignment I give to my high school juniors asks them to choose a story from Hemingway's *The Snows of Kilimanjaro and Other Stories* and write an essay of at least five hundred words that "presents your reading of the story to your classmates as effectively as you can." Andy submits the following essay.

> A man named Nick Adam's drove thu the rural area wich he grew up in. It brought back memories of shooting quail with his father. Nicks father was a large man with great vision, who was a very adept hunter and fisherman. Nick daydreams to the times when he was a youngman growing up with his father and sister Dorothy. He spent lots of time hunting in the hemlock woods behind the Indian Camp. Nick played with Nick and Trudy who were Objibawy Indians during the sumer.
>
> I believe this story is about youth, someday you have to grow up and be responsible, get a job and work. When your young you should not worry but just play and have fun because you can't be twelve forever.
>
> Nick has a son know, who is just under twelve, and his son asks him when he will be able to have a gun. Nick tells him when he is twelve, if he is worthy of it. He then realizes that he will only alow his son three shells per day, this was a bad rule, or so he thought back then. Nick relized his fathers wisdom in retrospect and knows he is a grown up responsible man.
>
> But when Nick was yonger, he thought it was a dumb rule he didn't realize that his father did for his own good so he would improve his shooting. Nick looked back upon his father in a different light than he had ever seen him before. He just then knew that his father was looking out for him.

I know Andy has worked hard on this essay; still, I am frustrated. It is April of his junior year, and we have been working together since September. Despite serious problems with his writing, Andy has written better essays than this one. As I look over his essay, though, I realize that his "better" essays are never the critical essays I assign. Why, I wonder, does Andy's progress as a writer seem to slow—or stop—when he writes about literature? Why, indeed, do most of my students seem to regress as writers when they write essays of literary analysis?

Most teachers of high school or college-level introductory literature courses have, I suspect, asked similar questions. My attempts to answer these questions led me, first, to the professional literature on writing and cognitive development, and second, to informal, classroom-based investigations of the writing my students were submitting to me. That is, to try to answer questions I had as a teacher, I became a researcher. My research has prompted me to rethink my understanding of "error" in student writing and has ultimately changed the way I teach literature.

This chapter tells the story of how research has shaped my teaching. I will describe my informal study of my students' writing and propose a way to classify the "errors" we typically find in students' essays about literature, arguing that these "errors" are related to students' intellectual development. I will also suggest ways to "use" these "errors" in order to help students write better critical essays and practice the critical skills that writing about literature can foster.[1] The research I describe here is neither systematic nor formally empirical; nevertheless, implicit in this article is the argument that teaching and classroom-based research are recursive activities, each of which continually informs the other.

The story of my research begins well before Andy turned in his essay on Hemingway. Andy wrote his essay as part of an exercise called Short Story Workshop, which I had used in my junior and senior English classes for two years.[2] In this exercise, each student in a class chooses a story from the assigned collection and writes a critical essay about that story. Before submitting the final version of the essay to me, the student reads his or her essay in a classroom workshop. The purpose of the workshop is twofold—to critique an early draft of each student's essay and give the writer ideas for revising the essay; and to initiate class discussion of the story itself. In addition, the class discussion could help the writer come to a richer interpretation of the story. After the workshop, the writer has several days in which to revise the essay and submit it for a grade.

I considered this exercise to be an effective blend of process-oriented writing instruction and the study of literature. I took as models for this exercise the work of other teachers who were making connections between writing and literature (Batker and Moran; Lindberg; Newkirk). Like these teachers, I was interested in helping students see that reading literature, as well as writing essays, is a recursive, often messy process. As a result, I hoped, my students would develop fuller understandings of the literature we were reading and write more effective essays about that literature.

As Andy's essay suggests, however, the short story workshops, although they were often lively and interesting, didn't result in better critical essays. The problems that mar Andy's essay were extreme but by no means uncommon. Even those of my students who routinely wrote effective narratives or arguments (about the drinking age, for example) submitted poor essays of literary analysis. These essays seemed to have more surface errors than their other essays, were often poorly organized, lacked coherence and cohesion, and reflected apparently superficial analysis. Writing essays of literary analysis simply seemed harder for my students than other writing assignments I gave them. Something in the task itself, I reasoned, was inhibiting my students' ability to write effectively in this form. But what?

I turned to the work of several composition theorists for a tentative answer to that question. Drawing on the work of cognitive psychologists such as Lev S. Vygotsky, Janet Emig argues that "writing serves learning uniquely" in part because "higher cognitive functions, such as analysis and synthesis, seem to develop most fully only with the support of verbal language—particularly, it seems, of written language" (p. 123). Andrea Lunsford posits that so-called basic writers are "often unable to practice analysis and synthesis" because they "have not attained that level of cognitive development that would allow them to form abstractions or conceptions" (p. 257). A review of the literature revealed a consensus among scholars (despite disagreements on specific points) that writing ability is related to a student's cognitive development. In addition, some research suggested that the way students respond to literature is also related to their cognitive development (e.g., Beach and Wendler).

My reading of the professional literature led me to see some of the problems in my students' critical essays as "developmental errors," in Mina Shaughnessy's sense of the term (p. 5), which occur for logical reasons based on a student's ability, experience with language, and level of cognitive development. The task of writing literary analysis required them not only to read critically the assigned works (a demanding and unfamiliar enough task for many of them), but also to "practice analysis and synthesis," as Lunsford puts it, as they tried to put their interpretations in writing. In addition, the students still had to contend with the demands of writing effective prose, a task that is difficult at best for most of them—even when they have a solid grasp of their subject.

Looking at this issue from a developmental perspective also gave me insight into why my students' comments in class discussions seemed to reflect a better understanding of the literature than did their essays. In *Thought and Language* Vygotsky describes in the adolescent "a striking discrepancy between his ability to form concepts and his ability to define them" (p. 79). Vygotsky goes on to say that even when an adolescent can grasp and use a concept, he "will find it strangely difficult to express that concept in words, and the verbal definition will, in most cases, be much narrower than might have been expected from the way he used the concept" (p. 79). Vygotsky found in his experiments that the "adolescent who had solved the problem of concept formation correctly very often descended to a more primitive level of thought in giving a verbal definition of the concept" (p. 80). Vygotsky suggested, as I had suspected, that my students understood the stories in much richer ways than their essays revealed. He also suggested that their ability to apply certain concepts—in this case, concepts of literary analysis (thematic development, for example)—might not be reflected in their writing.

With this rudimentary understanding of the cognitive demands that writing literary analysis placed on my students, I began to see the problems in their essays as rough maps to their thinking. Suddenly, the increased number of surface errors and incoherent paragraphs made sense. Patterns began to emerge. What I had previously regarded as frustratingly simplistic analyses in my students' essays I have come to call "sloppy trees."

I borrow the term *sloppy trees* from my son, Adam, who at age four coined it to describe weeping willows, which looked "sloppier" to him than "straight" trees. Here, *sloppy trees* refers to statements or ideas in students' critical essays which upon first glance seem to reflect a lack of understanding or a misunderstanding of a literary text but which in fact may describe in unfamiliar and problematic ways some aspect of the text (theme, motif, and so on) that can lead to a coherent and rich interpretation of that text. In other words, sloppy trees reflect the conceptual patterns that students bring to their readings of the story (or poem or novel).[3]

I've identified six kinds of sloppy trees. My description of these categories includes discussion of what I perceive to be the thinking—the conceptual patterns—behind each sloppy tree. Throughout, I am suggesting that teachers can use these patterns as a way to help their students become more astute readers and more successful writers of critical essays.

1. *The Affective Response.* This response is essentially a simple statement of how the story made the student feel. Here is a passage from the first paragraph of Taryn's essay on Hemingway's story "A Day's Wait":

> When he heard the doctor tell his temperature Schatz started to hold on tight. He didn't know what death was. Would it hurt? Should he cry?, the thoughts probably going through his head. No one knows how death feels. It is something everybody deals with sometime, but never knows how to feel. To think that you are going to die is the hardest thing ever, to Schatz, to anyone.

Teachers often dismiss this type of response, because it seems to reflect little thought on the part of the student. In this case, Taryn, a high school junior, superimposes on the character (Schatz) his own (Taryn's) feelings about fear of death. Nowhere in the story does the narrator say explicitly that Schatz is thinking the thoughts that Taryn describes here. All we know for sure is that Schatz is acting strangely. But Taryn isn't just putting himself in Schatz's shoes; within his personal reaction to Schatz's situation is an attempt to explain Schatz's strange behavior: "the thoughts *probably* going through his head." Taryn is trying to account for the character's actions. At the same time, Taryn moves quickly—too quickly—to a more general level of discussion: "No one knows how death feels." Although he needs to draw out in his essay the connection between his abstract idea and the incidents in the story itself, he has already begun to see the story in terms of theme. Once Taryn explores this theme more fully, he can perhaps build his essay around it. In this early draft, however, his personal feelings, his attempts to explain a character's behavior, and his sense of the larger issues implicit in the story are jumbled. With the teacher's help, Taryn may be able to sort these ideas out.

2. *The Plot Summary.* Every English teacher is familiar with the essay that simply restates a plot or parts of it. Dave's essay on Hemingway's "Fifty Grand" is typical:

> "Well, Jack says, "I'm going to need a lot of luck with the boy." (Hemingway, Ernest Fifty p. 95) Jack knew in his mind right from the beginning that he was going to lose. Jack even showed his disbelief in himself in front of others.
>
> Jack has many things that are going through his mind. "I miss the wife." (p. 99) Jack has been a champion, seen the sights, but now he relizes there are things that are more important to him. Throughout the story he talks about how he can't do anything against this guy. He doesn't think he can win. "How can I beat him?" Jack says." (p. 107).
>
> Jack later puts money against himself. He figures that if he's going to lose why not make some money off it. Jack's problems is that he has lost confidence in himself. He could have a chance at Walcott. He gets his mind set that he is going to lose and that brings him down.
>
> When the fight finally comes Jack is sort of wanting the fight. It's almost as if he wants to win now. This is where the conflict of whether he wants to win or lose comes into the story. Does Jack want to win or lose? That's the question.

Jack shows some want late in the fight, but then is hit below the belt. This gets Jack going and he throws a flurry of punches. Jack retaliates and throws a punch below the belt of Walcott.

The fight is called and Walcott wins by a penalty. I think Jack wanted it at the end. He wanted to be champion but by the time he started to realize it, it was too late. Jack beat himself.

· Dave offers in his essay a cursory and selective summary of Hemingway's story. But what Dave leaves out of his summary and how he describes what he does include reflect the beginning of an interpretation. Notice that Dave focuses on Jack's concerns about the fight. He mentions nothing about the training session or the attempts to fix the fight, which Hemingway describes in some detail. For Dave, Jack's indecision about winning the fight seems to be the most interesting aspect of the story. Moreover, Dave begins to explain this indecision: "Jack's problems is that he has lost confidence in himself." And in the fourth paragraph Dave states what he sees as the central issue of the story: "Does Jack want to win or lose? That's the question." Dave answers that question in the final paragraph ("I think Jack wanted it at the end"), but the essay is weak in part because Dave doesn't offer support for these statements. Nevertheless, he has the bare bones of an interpretation here.

It's significant that Dave states "the question" approximately three-quarters of the way through his essay. Up to that point he has been groping for a way to explain Jack's behavior. Now that he has identified the issue, however, he needs to return to it and go from there. This draft of his essay is an exploratory draft, one that helped him identify some key points in the story. His plot summary is the first step toward an interpretation.

3. *The Aesop's Fable Response.* In this response, the student makes a simple statement of what the story means, usually (but not always) tacked onto the end of a plot summary. (I would include Andy's essay in this category.) In the following essay on Ray Bradbury's "Kaleidoscope," for instance, Mike sums up in the final paragraph what he sees as the meaning of the story:

> What will space travel be like in the future?
>
> In Ray Bradbury's story "Kaleidoscope" the astronauts of a ship are in the middle of an asteroid field when their ship blows up.
>
> All the men in the crew are blown away from the explosion in different directions.
>
> I think the story was written to show that men cannot conquer space. Things may go well for a long time but eventually something

will go wrong and the men will die. "Even the captain was quiet, for there was no command or plan he knew that could put things back togther again." The men were hopeless. They knew there was nothing they could do except wait for their death.

The men did have a time of reckoning. One of the men yelled at the captain for past injustices. Many of the men thought about how long it has been since they had seen their wives and children.

After the ship exploded the men were on their own. They had no one to turn to except for God and I think many of them did. Most of the astronauts prayed and hoped that they would have a quick death.

I think that the purpose of this story was to demonstrate how the men could deal with the reality of facing death. Most of them accepted and got ready to wait for it. I think a question that Bradbury creates is how would you react?

What stands out about this essay is the way it shifts from one simple explanation to another. At the outset Mike asks a question that suggests a focus for his essay. Only three sentences later, however, Mike has another idea about the story: "I think the story was written to show that men cannot conquer space" (this might also be seen as a "satisficing response"; see below). And in his final paragraph, Mike offers yet another idea about the story: "I think that the purpose of this story was to demonstrate how men could deal with the reality of facing death." This last is perhaps his fullest statement of what the story "means" to him, and, I would argue, potentially the richest idea on which to focus his interpretation.

The important point here is that Mike is struggling to make meaning out of this story. The act of writing the essay seems to have helped him explore his thoughts about the story. That he continually tries to boil the story down into a simple statement—like one of Aesop's morals—may reflect both his lack of sophistication as a reader of literature and his tendency to see the world in terms of absolutes, which William Perry found was typical of some adolescents. Despite these difficulties, though, Mike has several good ideas (formulated, significantly, by the act of writing this draft) around which to build a more coherent reading of the story. As Mike's teacher, I want to help him develop these potentially rich ideas so that he might begin to see literary works not as embodiments of simple "morals" but as explorations of complex themes.

4. *The "Satisficing" Response.* I borrow this term from Tom Newkirk, who uses it to describe a strategy that students sometimes employ when they come upon an unfamiliar word or phrase in a poem. Newkirk suggests that students overcome the obstacle by "assigning a generally plausible

meaning to the word and going on" (p. 151). Students seem to employ the same strategy on the level of "meaning" in their reading of short stories, as Aaron demonstrates in this excerpt from his essay on Eudora Welty's "The Worn Path":

> Eudora Welty lived most of her life in the South, where she got the idea to write about black people. Her first job was during the depression, she was a "Junior Publicity Agent." Doing this job she travelled all over the state of Mississippi taking photographs, writing newspaper copies, and interviewing people.
>
> When Eudora Welty travelled she used to carry heavy luggage bags for a long period of time. In her first short story, "the worn path" she describes a black old lady walking a very long path to the hospital in town for her grandson who needs medicine for his throat.

The rest of Aaron's essay was almost exclusively plot summary. Clearly, Aaron had trouble "finding meaning" in this story. The information he offers in the first paragraph he found in the biographical blurb about Welty that accompanied her story in our anthology. For Aaron, the story seemed to hold little more "meaning" than what it literally describes, so he searched outside the story for a way to make sense of what happens in the story. His essay reflects his difficulty in moving from the specific to the general, from the concrete to the abstract. Nowhere in his essay does Aaron attempt to connect the plot of the story with abstract ideas about responsibility, purpose, determination, love. Part of the problem is that Aaron seems to have no clear sense of key literary concepts like theme and plot, but in addition he seems unable to conceptualize the story in terms of such abstractions as responsibility or love, a cognitive task he must accomplish in order to write an effective critical analysis. At this point, the best approach might be to begin with questions about the motives of characters, as Taryn and Dave seem to do above, which is a cognitive task that might be within his reach.

5. *The Symbolic Response.* In this category, students attempt to make sense of the story through the use of symbolism and metaphor. In his essay on Welty's "The Worn Path," for instance, Jim sees the old woman's journey to town and back as a metaphor for the journey through life:

> The story is very basic on the outside but if you use your imagination as you read it you may find there is more to it. The journey of the woman that Welty describes is very long and descriptive about this path she is taking. The path seems to be the journey of her life, for example, she has things to help her along her journey like

her cane. Then she gets to an obstacle the thorny bush that never want to let folks pass," representing a hard time in life. The big scene in the journey that coresponds to life is the corn field she comes upon and she says "through the maze now," crresponding to a time of decision in her life. The first half of the story just continues to parallel to life.

Like Mike's essay above, this excerpt from Jim's reflects a desire to fit the story into a neat framework, which tends to reduce it and exclude some of the complex themes at work in the story; at times, Jim obviously struggles to make particular events in the story fit. Nevertheless, it would be a mistake to dismiss Jim's essay as flawed on these grounds, for it also reflects a rather sophisticated ability to conceive of the story on an abstract level. Jim clearly understands the concept of metaphor and he uses that understanding to construct an interpretation of the story that works well for him—and for me as his teacher. The next step is to work with Jim so that he can explain his interpretation in a more effective fashion, keeping in mind that the difficulty of conceptualizing the story in terms of metaphor has resulted in some problems with the writing. For instance, Jim tends to repeat (and misspell) "correspond"; and there is the redundant use of "describe" and "descriptive." But these are problems that can be cleared up once Jim has worked out his ideas more fully.

The examples I cited above reflect my students' cognitive struggles to understand a literary work in ways that we as English teachers believe to be valuable and to present that understanding in an effective critical essay. Once we as teachers begin to appreciate these struggles, the surface errors, the incoherent paragraphs, and the underdeveloped ideas that show up in their essays about literature seem understandable. More important, they become manageable.

A better understanding of our students' cognitive struggles with literary essays may require a reevaluation of our approach to the teaching of literature. My investigation into the "errors" my students made in their essays led me to make four changes in my short-story exercise:

1. The first draft of the essay became an exploratory draft rather than a more formal attempt to advance an interpretation of the story. Instead of simply asking students to submit a draft for workshop, I assigned several brief writing exercises that encouraged them to explore the story before writing their essays. In doing so, I attempted (somewhat artificially) to separate the act of interpreting the story from the act of writing a finished essay that presents that interpretation.

2. I began to focus the workshops on the ideas the students expressed in their essays rather than on the writing itself. I wanted to prompt discussion of the stories in terms of the writers' ideas about the stories. Accordingly, each workshop included a handout on which members of the class wrote responses to the essays; these responses were given to the writers at the end of each workshop. At this point in the exercise, the writers are still formulating their interpretations of their stories.

3. I worked into the exercise conferences and a third draft especially to deal with the problems of writing the essay itself. Presumably, at this point the students have formulated their readings of their stories. My purpose at this stage is to help them produce better final drafts; the focus is the writing itself rather than the interpretation of the story.

4. Finally, I began looking for sloppy trees as a means to helping students understand their stories better. Instead of pointing out flaws in their early drafts, I began to look for the thinking behind those flaws and to build on the students' own ideas about the story, keeping in mind the cognitive hurdles that I was asking them to leap.

In the workshop I conducted at the Third Miami University Conference on the Teaching of Writing, I asked the audience what they would have done with Andy's essay if he had submitted it to them. The first person to respond said unequivocally that she would take a red pen to it. My impulse when Andy gave me his essay was to do the same (sans red pen); that is, I wanted to point out what was wrong with the essay and to suggest ways to improve it. But that impulse is based on the assumptions that Andy thinks about literature as I do and that he can simply "correct" the problems in his essay. My research indicates that both these assumptions, under which I think many teachers of literature operate, are not always valid. In effect, my research changed the way I teach because it challenged my assumptions about how my students learn. Challenging our assumptions and enriching our understanding of how our students learn so that we might be more effective teachers is, in the end, the purpose of teacher-research.

NOTES

1. I am passing over the question of whether or not we should require essays of literary analysis of our students. There are significant problems with the ways we use literary analysis in our English curricula, and I think we place too much emphasis on requiring our students to emulate a dry, critical style, as Tom Romano has argued in *Clearing The Way* (p. 149). Nevertheless, this kind of essay continues to be a mainstay

of the English curricula in this country, and having students write in this form does, I think, have benefits. My purpose here is to present teachers with ideas that might help them use the form more effectively in their own classes.

2. I am indebted to the late Gary Lindberg of the University of New Hampshire for the idea for this exercise. In his graduate seminars at UNH, Gary used an exercise very similar to the one I describe in this article, although he didn't call it "Short Story Workshop."

3. I am arguing here that problems in students' texts reflect certain conceptual patterns that the students bring to their attempts to understand literature and write about literature. I see these patterns as manifestations of certain cognitive functions. Where these patterns come from, however, is another matter, which I have taken up in subsequent research. As I try to show in this chapter, many of the difficulties our students have in writing literary analysis have cognitive roots. However, the way students think about literature and the way they go about writing literary analysis are not simply cognitive issues. The patterns I describe here, I think, are influenced (perhaps even created) by the students' literary, linguistic, and sociocultural experience and knowledge. How those kinds of experience and knowledge affect the way students read and write about literature is an important issue that is only recently being investigated.

13

On the Move in Pittsburgh: When Students and Teacher Share Research

Jeffrey Schwartz

Last year I taught a course that focused more on questions than answers. That was sometimes an uncomfortable position to be in—not to have *complete* control over the direction and subject matter of my course. But it was also part of the fun. "Once the teacher moves out of the traditional position of being the giver of questions and the receiver of right or wrong answers," Nancy Martin says, "there is no more certainty" (p. 24). In the course I describe below, the ground rules suddenly shifted. My students and I shared a process of inquiry. We raised questions together and we learned, sometimes by surprise, inside and outside the classroom. Students participated even more fully than they had in my previous courses in which they designed their own writing projects or were in charge of their writing workshops. In writing-process classrooms, there is already the core of this interactive model of learning when students make decisions about their own writing, when they write for real purposes and real readers, and when they learn from their peers.

In classrooms where the teacher proposes to learn with his or her students, roles of authority begin to break down even more. In a shared inquiry, students see the teacher learn, and they learn by teaching. Both students and teacher see themselves as makers of meaning and as providers and takers of skills and information. When this happens the writing classroom changes again. As Paulo Freire writes:

> Through dialogue, the teacher-of-the-students and the students-of-the-teacher cease to exist and a new term emerges: teacher-student with students-teachers. The teacher is no longer merely the one-who-teaches, but one who is himself taught in dialogue with the students, who in turn, while being taught, also teach. They become jointly responsible for a process in which all grow. (p. 67)

In a situation governed by real questions, students are involved not only in what they learn, but also how they learn. They have more invested in the class and therefore take more responsibility for their own learning.

I first conducted a shared inquiry in the fall of 1986. With the support of an NCTE Teacher/Researcher grant, I hired two students as partners in my research on what happens when high school students use an electronic network to create a real context for writing. Twenty-seven of my students at Sewickley Academy, a private suburban school outside of Pittsburgh, were engaged in an electronic writing exchange with students from Wilsall High School in a tiny ranching community in southwestern Montana, and from Little Wound High School on the Pine Ridge Sioux reservation in South Dakota. While the central questions of the course focused on similarities and differences among the three communities, my research partners and I were also interested in questions related to the role of computers in our exchange, the transformation of stereotypes, and writers' attention to context (i.e., the purpose, audience, persona, and type of discourse they were writing). The two student researchers were involved not only in the clerical end of research—photocopying, typing, transcribing, counting electronic messages— but they also shared in the collection and analysis of data (Schwartz, 1988). My two research partners prepared, conducted, taped, transcribed, and ana- lyzed group interviews, helped create surveys, and analyzed the written products of the course.

From working with these two students as research partners who partici- pated equally with me in a professional project, I learned three things about shared inquiry: (1) students discovered information I wouldn't have seen, (2) they acted responsibly as peer readers, and (3) when raising questions and analyzing data, we all learned about language together.

Essentially, what I found is that our roles shifted from teacher-student to colleague. It made me realize even more than I had before that students are capable of amazing things *if* we trust them with more authority. Researchers tell us that involving students in inquiry can make them better writers (Hillocks) and better leaners (Boomer). Garth Boomer even proposes

> that any learning sequence should begin with a negotiation of intentions to the point that both teacher and student intend in the same direction and mutually *own* the curriculum as *jointly planned*. Under this model, the unit of curriculum is itself a piece of action research into learning which can be reflected upon and evaluated by both teacher and student. . . . In such a "community of thinkers," intentions become shared, thinking power is increased, and, through reflection on the learning, teachers and students progressively learn more about how to learn. (pp. 11–12)

My inquiry project worked with two students outside of class. What would happen, I wondered, if I tried to involve a whole class in a shared inquiry? In the 1987–1988 school year I had a chance to investigate that question in an English course at Sewickley Academy called "The History of Pittsburgh," which was coordinated with a history class at Clairton High School, about an hour and a half away in Clairton, Pennsylvania. Six teachers in English, history, and computer science planned a course with common assignments that offered high school students a chance to do original research into their communities and to share that research, along with questions, notes, letters, and essays using the computer for electronic mail.

Clairton is a working-class town centered around what was once the biggest coke works in the world. In 1987 over half of the heads of households were unemployed. Since the town's bankruptcy, there has been no regular police or fire department, and in 1987 Clairton students had to attend a condemned elementary school in shifts while they waited for the state to finish rebuilding their former high school. The day my students and I visited Clairton, we drove through the Mon Valley, where Pittsburgh's industry had been centered for a hundred years. The enormous steel mills we passed in Homestead, Duquesne, Braddock, McKees Rocks, and, finally, Clairton were closed or nearly silent, "like ghost towns out west," one of my students said.

Sewickley, by contrast, is one of the towns where steel barons used to own summer homes. It's one of the most affluent towns in the Pittsburgh area. Students who live there are likely to go home to three-story, one-family houses—not segregated housing projects. Most students, some on scholarships, drive in to Sewickley from dozens of outlying areas, but all are eager for an education that will prepare them for college. The school they attend is beautiful and looked to the Clairton kids "like a college campus." The day the Clairton students visited Sewickley, they got off their bus and stood frozen, for what seemed like five minutes, till one student called another's name and they all met for the first time. By the end of the day, their teachers could barely coerce them to leave.

It would be easy to stereotype the kids at Sewickley as "stuck-up, rich wimps," as one of my students put it, or, as he continued, to stereotype Clairton kids as "poor, poorly dressed, [and living in] slum-like houses." Our course was an investigation into those images, where they come from, and how they change. In coming to terms with each other, the students had to confront their stereotypes about public and private education, as well as the economic, racial, religious, and ethnic differences between and also within the two schools. They had to leave their classroom to do that, they had to learn from each other, and they had to write about what they saw.

What made this course unusual was not just the collaboration between Sewickley and Clairton—two economically different communities that shared a common history in Pittsburgh—but also the focus of the course on inquiry. Writing was to be used for a real purpose—to investigate, reflect on, and communicate what we found. The computer would be the tool for writing and, with its local bulletin-board service, the tool for communicating as well. Ten students participated from Sewickley, twenty from Clairton. Six teachers worked on the project, with further support from other faculty and administration at the two schools, as well as grants from the Pennsylvania Museum Commission and the Bread Loaf School of English.

From the beginning of the course, I told the class we would focus on writing and inquiry as much as we would on local history. In the course description, I had written that "most of the activities you participate in will be as much about *how* to discover information as they are about *what* you discover. We are all learners when we conduct research by asking genuine questions, creating and testing hypotheses, observing, finding answers, and writing about what we find. Since writing is one of the best ways to learn, we will write often to explore ideas, to make connections, and to share results. This will lead us at times to examine language—how we use words to think and communicate, and how to be better writers."

In the History of Pittsburgh class, students and teacher shared the process of finding out. We welcomed questions as a basis for developing the course. Students began with questions about their own pasts:

What were the significant events of their lives?

Where did their parents and grandparents come from?

What did they want to learn about Sewickley, Pittsburgh, or the other towns they lived in?

Since it was the 150th anniversary of Sewickley Academy, what could we find out about that?

Questions continued as students prepared for the exchange:

What did they know about Clairton? What did they expect to find out?

How did they see the kids from Clairton?

How did they expect the kids from Clairton saw them?

How did my students see themselves?

What is similar or different between teenagers in both communities?

On what do we base our judgments?

When misperceptions arise, how do we change them?

How did it feel to be a minority?

How are we going to use telecommunications?

Students electronically mailed each other questions about town government, ethnic origins, career ambitions, jobs, school, percentage of minorities, religion, and what they did for fun in their spare time. Some questions could be answered from experience; others had to be discovered through outside research.

A LOT MORE THAN THE FACTS

As students pursued their own questions, they had to choose the best method for finding out. Would answers best be found in a book? A formal interview? An informal conversation? A class discussion? A survey? A lecture outside class? A phone call to town hall? A trip to the public library? By close observation? Students used all of these methods. They interviewed and wrote about parents, grandparents, administrators, teachers, older residents of their towns, the first woman architect in Pittsburgh, and a former managing director of the Civic Light Opera, among others. They brought to class an author, a filmmaker, an officer from the local historical society, and a long-time resident of Sewickley who had lived in the first post office west of the Allegheny Mountains. They conducted schoolwide surveys; assembled statistics from the public library, the town hall, and the school's development office; read books, dug up old photos, and attended outside lectures. They learned that different questions require different sources of information. In the process they also learned the difference between traditional research and what we called inquiry. In her self-assessment of her work at the end of the course, Heather wrote:

> I discovered more than any book or newspaper could tell me. I found out what it was like to actually live through those years. . . . Inquiry teaches a lot more than the facts. It teaches the feelings, the emotions, and most of all the truth about the people instead of the events. And isn't that really what history is about anyway?

Students further learned that new information leads to new questions. To become an independent learner, Andy wrote, "All it takes is a little know-how on how to find information. Once you find a book . . . you can then follow up the leads it drops, and become almost like a detective, searching for clues on whatever your particular interest is." When we read Thomas Bell's *Out of This Furnace* to find out about immigrant labor in the Pittsburgh steel mills, students supplemented the book with pamphlets about unions, books about the Orthodox Church and the Serbian alphabet, and a map of a local mill. We asked, where could we find out more about Braddock, the center of *Out of This Furnace?* Where could we find out more about Eastern European customs and food? What are *hruskas*, and how do they taste? One student, Lacey, invited the class to her home for her family's traditional Orthodox Christmas meal. Her father translated the names of the homemade breads, described the significance of the meal, and finished by telling of his own days working in the mills. Another student, Darren, interviewed his grandfather about working in Aliquippa, a mill town closer to Sewickley, and the interview was eventually published in a national magazine. Still another student, Laura, invited Dave Demarest (the writer who had had *Out of This Furnace* reprinted and who had written its afterword) to come to our school, show slides, and talk about Braddock and the history behind the book. Demarest was followed by Tony Buba, an internationally acclaimed documentary filmmaker, who specializes in films about Braddock, where he still lives. Buba came the same day the students from Clairton visited. He talked with pride (and anger) about changes in the Mon Valley, how community history had to be preserved, and how we can generalize about life in the Pittsburgh area by examining its particulars. Laura had arranged his visit too.

THE PROCESS OF KNOWING

The questions that persisted between Sewickley and Clairton showed the students struggling to know themselves and to communicate as truthfully as possible to someone else. Meaning is slippery, they discovered. Students grew to understand the power they had to influence how others saw them. One day in class, before they met in person, Lacey reported a three-hour phone conversation she had had with her Clairton correspondent the night before. She said they described who everyone was, what they looked like, and other information that hadn't been forthcoming in the letters. They were also more blunt than they had been in the letters. "Are you all rich? We're all poor," the Clairton student said. That was our first confirmation of how we feared Clairton would see us.

"I hope they don't think we're geeks," Kathy said. There was a lot of concern throughout the correspondence that Clairton wouldn't be able to see beyond the economic differences between the two schools. Both sides, though, tried hard to correct any false conceptions. In a letter from Clairton to Andy before they met, Fred wrote:

> What I meant when I said that everyone thinks that Clairton is a bad city is that because we're considered an economically distressed city people think

that a lot of bad things go on here. Like a lot of robbery and stuff like that. It's real surprising the stereotypes the surrounding areas have about us; like Pleasant Hills, T.J., and some other areas. I just wish I could show everyone like that, that it's not true. Our city isn't one big slum like some of them think either. I mean there are a few bad areas, but if you take for example the neighborhood I live in it would fit in almost any community, as a normal friendly place where the neighbors all get along and know that they can rely on one another if they need to.

Before the Clairton students visited Sewickley, a common expectation was:

> I think (but I don't hope) that the Clairton students are going to resent us big-time when they meet us. In letters we can hide the facts that we live in beautiful houses, wear expensive clothes, and attend an incredible, gorgeous, expensive school. I also think they might not want us to see their school now. But I'm not sure.

After the Clairton students visited, though, my students were delighted by how well it went:

> First of all, I had a great time! I think I expected a lot of differences, so many that they would get in the way of "the project." But they didn't, which was fabulous!
>
> In general, they (the kids) were really open (and open-minded) & it happily surprised me.

In building a more informed picture of her community, Lacey found:

> It was hard to explain that not everyone who goes to S.A. is affluent and that not all people who go to SA are from Sewickley. My guests were on the lighter side of shock when they found out that I chose SA over other schools. It was like . . . "How can your school be *that* good?"
>
> Another "topic" that surprised them was the number of kids here on scholarships. Why get a scholarship to a high school?

Because we were involved in an inquiry, we continued to examine our expectations, to raise questions, and—always—to write about what we found. Writing and talking heightened our sensitivity about stereotyping, but meeting in person made us confront even more how images are formed, how we make judgments and are judged, and how really difficult it is to change someone's mind. James Britton writes:

> As human beings, we meet every new situation armed with expectations derived from past experience or, more accurately, derived from our interpretations of past experience. We face the new, therefore, not only with knowledge drawn from the past but also with developed tendencies to interpret in certain ways. It is in submitting these to the test of fresh

experience—that is, in having our expectations and mode of interpreting either confirmed or modified—that the learning, the discovery, takes place. (p. 16)

Knowing, as Britton says, is a form of doing: "There is no simple sense in which we *apply* a poultice to a swelling. In any confrontation, what we know must be reformulated in the light of what we perceive and our knowledge is thus forever on the move" (p. 19). To learn, we found, meant we couldn't stand still. Sometimes we had to leave the classroom; other times we had to bring the outside in.

Certain questions became a framework for which we could test what we were learning against what we already knew:

What do I already know about this subject/ idea/ person/ place/ experience?

What do I expect to see? What questions do I have?

What did I observe?

What did my observations confirm? What surprises were there?

What questions were answered? What conclusions can I draw?

What new questions are raised?

In talk and in writing, students reflected continually on how their expectations were matched or not. They were always revising their preconceptions based on their observations, experiences, and reading. For the students and for me, the course was about coming to know—the process of raising questions, gathering information, and testing assumptions.

THE LIMITS OF COMMUNICATION

As students tested their expectations, they struggled to stay open-minded, to observe and listen carefully, and not to generalize too quickly based on one observation or one interview. We found that no matter how much information we had from primary or secondary sources, it was never enough. After she met her Clairton correspondent, one of my students said in class, "You think you knew them from letters, but now I feel like I don't know them at all." Every new point added to our understanding but also complicated the perspective. When we visited the Clairton students, we observed their school, their neighborhood, and even saw the outside of some of their homes. We were continuing to understand something about how they lived. As Laura said later, though, if we could have lived with the Clairton students in their houses, we would have come to understand even more. At the same time our knowledge grew, we recognized its limits. To be sensitive to that was to increase our understanding of how communication and language work. We are always trying to say what we mean (and to infer beyond what we see).

Katie became very aware of the relative completeness of any picture, when she was the first to describe the town of Sewickley for her outside readers:

> When I wrote about the intersection at Beaver and Broad Streets, I learned so much about Sewickley. I never had really examined where I lived before.
>
> Looking back, when I decided to write about the intersection, I thought that it would be a fairly easy job. I thought, "I live here, don't I?" Soon afterwards, I began my "easy" job. Immediately, I had to eat crow. I began to realize that I had never before ripped apart Sewickley to see what makes it tick. I quickly saw that the essay was going to be much more than description.
>
> As I sat at the corner in the park, I had the chance to observe people. I was already aware of the dichotomy between rich and poor. However, that corner came to symbolize the split. By that I mean that the poor rarely crossed Beaver Street to get to the specialty shops. They stayed for the most part in the front of Mellon Bank and on the benches of the park.
>
> As for being a teacher in this situation, it was such a strange feeling to know that I was going to be representing Sewickley to Clairton. It was both exciting and nerve-wracking. I felt great knowing that I would be the one to say that Sewickley is more than rich people, specialty shops, and big houses. However, I was very concerned with presenting the full picture. It was very tempting to emphasize the poorer people, because everyone thinks that everyone in Sewickley is rich. However, I had to present a balanced picture. I constantly worried that the picture would not have some type of equilibrium. In this case, I truly felt the responsibility of being a teacher.

Katie was beginning to understand where stereotypes come from, and she was struggling for that impossible balance she associated with teaching—or with a type of authority she recognized she, too, could share.

SHIFTING AUTHORITY IN THE CLASSROOM

As students participated in our collective inquiry, they learned that they, as well as the teacher, could contribute new information and affect the direction of the class. This new authority for them led us all to question the traditional roles of student and teacher. We became "jointly responsible for a process in which all grow" (Freire, p. 67).

In sharing inquiry our roles had to change. There were times when students saw me as a learner—not as someone with all the answers—and times when they saw themselves as teachers. The atmosphere of the classroom had to change too. "There was a special rapport among everyone in the class," one student wrote in her final evaluation of the course. Another wrote, "With all of the informality in the class structure itself, we had a chance to be both teachers and students." Even the notion of "teaching" had to be redefined not only as providing information and transmitting the answers, but also as raising questions, reflecting, creating and sharing ideas. Teaching—or learning—could happen with a whole class, between two partners, or even by oneself. One student wrote about what she taught herself after suffering through a painful misunderstanding with her Clairton partner: "In this experience, I was both a learner and a teacher. I taught myself that comments that I had felt were genuine and personal had been seen by another as impersonal and boring. This showed me how easy it is to misconstrue other's intentions."

Research suggests that building responsibility and sharing authority are crucial for secondary school students. In 1984, Theodore Sizer reported that "no more important finding has emerged from the inquiries of our study than that the American high school student, *as student*, is all too often docile, compliant, and without initiative" (p. 54). "Put the burden of learning on them," he says. "Such responsibility will liberate energy now lost because of the impersonality and the patronizing inherent in the lockstep routines of many schools" (p. 67). In their studies of writing and learning, Judith Langer and Arthur Applebee conclude that "despite the process- and context-oriented research of the past two decades, [the traditional teacher-centered classroom] continues to undergird contemporary approaches to schooling, including the approaches of the teachers we studied." They continue to report:

> Though persistent and widespread, this model of teaching militates against many of our goals for writing and learning. It emphasizes the teacher as transmitter of knowledge, rather than the students as active agents who must interpret and reinterpret what they are learning; it emphasizes testing and evaluation, rather than work in progress; and it emphasizes declarative rather than procedural knowledge (knowing *that* rather than knowing *how*). To summarize bluntly, given traditional notions of instruction, it may be impossible to implement successfully the approaches we have championed. (pp. 138–139)

We know from researchers such as Sondra Perl that when writing is taught effectively, students take on new roles of authority, and the structure of the classroom changes:

> Traditional assumptions about how writing happened, of who could learn from whom, or of who owned or had access to knowledge, had, for the most part, vanished. No longer were teachers the sole sources of knowledge in

their classrooms. Instead, they created settings in which students wrote for and learned from one another. And when they were no longer constrained by the need to write merely to please their teachers, some students, some of the time, discovered a freedom and depth of expression they had rarely known before. (p. 251)

Furthermore, Perl found that "teachers who inquired into the nature of their teaching taught writing in the same spirit of inquiry" (p. 253). Nancie Atwell, too, argues "for a redistribution of the power of ideas and a new kind of classroom seating plan. When each student initiates the writing process by taking responsibility for finding out what he or she has to say, everyone sits at a big desk" (p. 181). For effective writing and learning to happen, the classroom has to change. Students need to be trusted to be learners and to share authority with their teachers.

After the Pittsburgh history course was over, I met several times with two students to look at what was different about our course. What conditions made it possible for us to shift authority so that students and teacher learned together? One of those students, Laura Gratton, spoke with me later about the results of our project at the Miami University "Writing Teacher as Researcher" Conference in 1988. In sum, these are the conditions we found that created the shift in authority in our class:

1. *Posing real questions* (or, no more certainty)

   In order to learn with students and to show them that their answers matter, the teacher has to ask genuine questions. I had to accept the fact that I did not know every answer in order to encourage my students to teach me.

2. *Students and teachers sharing expertise* (or, helping someone like your teacher when he or she needs it)

   In class students shared their expertise about different religions, different ethnic backgrounds, working-class vs. upper-class neighborhoods, the history of US Steel's union, their own personal histories. When they wrote to Clairton, or when the Clairton students visited, Sewickley students had another audience with which they could share their expertise on school and community. Students also shared varying expertise with each other on the use of the computer for telecommunications and word processing.

   Students shared information they had to research. They conducted a survey at SA on public/private schools and student jobs; they attended lectures on local history and how to conduct oral histories; they interviewed outside experts; they compiled statistics on minorities, class size, and so on; they shared outside reading (such as Annie Dillard's *An American Childhood*).

At both schools there were students who had more expertise with electronic bulletin boards than their teachers. Fred, a student from Clairton, wrote, "Our teacher went to an orientation on computer usage yesterday and now she is all excited. She is sitting here right next to me typing a letter to Don (the sysop). It's really a good feeling when you're able to help someone like your teacher when they need it. God knows she is always here for us when we need her."

3. *Sharing decisions* (how we had a say in what we did)

In her final evaluation of the course, one student wrote, "most effective was all the freedom—how we had a say in what we did."

I had to plan, but also stay flexible enough for students to influence the direction of the course. Visiting Clairton, inviting speakers, and sharing a Serbian Christmas dinner were activities based on student suggestions. Students were able to choose their own topics, influence the pace of our reading, and—through midcourse surveys—comment on the success or failures of the course and make suggestions for change. In their final course assessments, they participated further in the evaluation process.

Students also took responsibility for managing aspects of the class. Each student had a different job that contributed to the group. These included managing the electronic bulletin board, keeping a class notebook, hosting guest speakers, and conducting outside research.

4. *Creating a sense of community* (a special rapport)

It was important to create an atmosphere, based on trust, that would allow students to experiment, to share their feelings and insights, and to try new things: "At first all of the informal writing and lack of grades frustrated me, and I'm sure I didn't make a secret of it. But, now, looking back, I realize how helpful it all was. My writing improved in that I'm a lot more honest than I used to be. I'm not afraid to add my opinions and feelings anymore. . . . By writing informally, without the pressure of being graded, we could be honest, experiment, without being afraid."

5. *Hands-on experience*

The course got students to go outside of the classroom and to learn by doing. Lisa wrote at the end of the course that "the process of inquiry is much more beneficial than regular research you do in history. The thing that makes it different is the hands-on experience. When you do research that's in a book or article the only thing you find out is what another person has learned. It isn't your own views. This is what separates inquiry from traditional research." She went on, "Taking action on a subject to find information with your own hands and eyes makes a person remember that forever."

When students exchanged writing with their Clairton partners, or when they shared results of their research with a wider audience, they wrote for real purposes and to real readers. They took pride in their work when it was quoted in a ceremony celebrating the school's anniversary or when it appeared in an anthology that was sent to local libraries and historical societies.

6. *Respect for the little guy*

Andy wrote, "I think the most important thing I learned, through all of my experiences with the History of Pittsburgh class, is that everyone, no matter how small, or seemingly insignificant they are has something important to offer his community. . . . I have discovered a new way to find information, to dig into the things the little guy has to say, because sometimes his story is more factual than any encyclopedia." From conducting original community research, examining their own histories, and reading about "the little guy" in the steel industry, they learned that they, too, can make history.

7. *Providing models of inquiry*

As the students wrote about and conducted research, they saw me model a process of raising questions, examining expectations, and writing before and after our class trips. Speakers who visited the class also spoke on their own research and, through films, slides, speaking and writing, demonstrated their own values about lifelong learning, respect for community, and methods of interpreting the universal in the particular.

8. *Focus on process of learning as well as the content* (the how and the what)

Laura wrote, "What you learn is only as interesting as how you learn it. If you copy information from an encyclopedia, your paper will probably be as boring as it was to write. And furthermore, what idiot couldn't look something up in the encyclopedia? You have to have fun when you research—you have to think of a way that will make it interesting to you personally. Then you can be enthused about it and your paper will show your enthusiasm."

Our ideas of learning had to be based on a model of shared inquiry and participation, not the old transmission model where expert information passes unidirectionally from teacher to student. Even the definition of the classroom changed to mean *where* we learn—outside as well as inside a school.

My students and I were involved in this inquiry together. Each of us taught; each of us learned. To allow that to happen, I had to give up the traditional authority I was used to bringing to the classroom. Since I was an English teacher in a collaborative, interdisciplinary course whose content material was history, it was easy for me to assume the role of learner. There was much I didn't know about Pittsburgh. I wanted to be able to learn with my students, and to build in the flexibility for them to follow their own leads. At the same time, I had to offer a structure and guidelines from which students could freely roam. That freedom is a funny thing in a school system. It angered colleagues who saw it as too lenient or breaking the rules. It made the teacher and students uncomfortable who are used to predictable routines and centralized authority. But when it works, it makes students responsible for their own learning. It redistributes the power of the class, not equally, but so that it's not exclusively in the hands of the teacher.

Four months after our original visit to Clairton, I drove back with Laura for the open house of the new Clairton High School. Despite the resignation of two superintendents, the three-months delay of the opening, and a lawsuit between the school and the city, the school opened to the excitement of the whole town. There were hundreds of visitors on tours of the new building when we were there. People seemed to share the sense that this beautiful school would be a fresh start for Clairton's children. Even the owner of the Blue Bird, a busy all-night restaurant, planned to go over to see the new school before he went home to bed. We had found him resting in the window of the Blue Bird, where he signaled us to come in. Listening to him tell about the history of the restaurant his father began in 1923, we were both—teacher and student—reminded how much fun it is to find out something unexpectedly and how the classroom doesn't have to stand still.

THE WRITING TEACHER
IN THE TECHNICAL
WRITING CLASSROOM

14

Storytelling in a Technical Writing Class: Classroom-Based Research and Community

ART YOUNG

The central problem of an education based upon experience is to select the kind of present experiences that live fruitfully and creatively in subsequent experiences.

John Dewey

In this chapter I report on classroom-based research conducted by students as part of the course "English 490/690: Advanced Business and Technical Writing," which I taught for the first time in spring semester 1988. In this course, students developed a sixty-page user manual for a telecommunications system, a manual for which funding had been secured for printing and distribution to the system's users. Here I will provide background about the development of this course, describe the students' classroom-based research projects, and consider what I have learned about the teaching of writing from the students' research. As this course developed over the term, it seemed to me to become more truly collaborative and inquiry-oriented than any class I had taught before. In seeking confirmation of my perception and a better understanding of what actually occurred in this class, I carefully examined the research the students conducted on their learning in the class. One important concept that emerged from this research and my analysis of it was the essential role that storytelling played in developing and sustaining our collaborative community. Stories helped us make sense of our experience and understand what we were about, and stories helped us build our supportive, collaborative community. In many ways, this chapter is the story of those stories.[1]

SETTING

The state of South Carolina has a telecommunications system called the Clemson University Forestry and Agricultural Network, mercifully abbreviated to CUFAN. This system is available for a subscription fee to all residents and businesses within the state. CUFAN contains an electronic mail system, a conferencing system, a database of forestry and agricultural information, and a database of student writing. Thus, farmers in our state with a personal computer and a modem can use this system to ask a question and get a response from an extension agent about a new fertilizer on the market, for example, or to call up on screen a database of the most recent information about soybean planting. And students and teachers in our state use the system to correspond with fellow students and teachers in schools considerable distances away. My colleague at Clemson, Dixie Goswami, who also serves as the director of the Bread Loaf School of English Writing, is spearheading an effort to make CUFAN serve as a local version of the international Breadnet System, the telecommunications network that links the teachers and students throughout the world associated with the Bread Loaf School of English. As I read student writing on Breadnet, I saw the potential of this enabling technology in the development of these writers' language abilities. Here is an example of correspondence between two high school students about a novel they are reading. Dawn writes from a rural school in the Appalachian Piedmont and Ken responds from a school in New York City.[2]

Dear Student,

I am student at Tamassee-Salem High School in South Carolina. My English Class is reading THE STRANGER by Albert Camus. My English teacher has told my class that your class has just finished reading this book.

I have just finished reading the second chapter. The ending of this chapter really psyched me out. He says, "Really, nothing in my life had changed." What does he mean? His mother just died. I know if my mother had died, my whole life would change.

Maybe he just doesn't want to admit his feelings. He acts as if his mother dying was just another day. When he slept with Marie, he didn't show any real emotions toward her except horniness. It may be just my belief that you have to care about someone to take part in love-making.

I am looking forward to reading more about this book. It seems like a very interesting book so far. How do you like it?

Dawn

Dear Dawn,

In your letter, you discussed Meursault's feeling of when his mother died, and his feelings and actions with Marie. It seems to me, that all through THE STRANGER, Camus represents Meursault's character as something of a loner. I was once a loner, and in my experience with other loners, I have found that a loner tends to draw into himself, not affording himself the luxury of showing emotions for fear of being hurt. Could this not be the reason for Meursault's actions?

There was something else I was wondering about. In our class, we got into a discussion about the old man, Salamano. We were discussing the treatment of his dog. There were many different reasons given as to why he treated his dog as he did. Some said that he hated the dog, but it was the only thing that would stay with him. Others thought he had an inferiority complex. I reserved judgement until I completed the book. When he lost the dog, he was upset at the loss one minute, cursing the dog for leaving the next, and then longing for his return again. This led me to believe that he might be slightly insane, what do you think?

Ken

Such writing convinced me that making such technology available to increasing numbers of students and teachers could produce important results. Dawn and Ken's writing and that of the other students I read exhibited many of the rhetorical and contextual features essential for growth in language abilities. They wrote to communicate with each other (and not to be tested/ evaluated), to initiate a dialogue that invites response, and to collaborate in creating a context in which to relate the story they were reading to their personal stories and thereby learn something about literature, about them-selves, and about each other. In Nancy Martin's words, these students used their everyday language ("psyched me out") and sense of wonder ("I was wondering") to develop new utterances, perspectives, and thoughts, "the dynamic by which we learn our mother tongue" (p. 10). In addition, this rhetorical context for writing about literature seems to have enabled students to respond to *The Stranger* as Louise Rosenblatt's ordinary readers, thus recognizing "the basic affinity of all readers of literary works of art" to establish an important relationship with literary texts (p. 140).

I learned about the potential of CUFAN and Breadnet from my colleagues at Clemson University—Dixie Goswami, Ike Coleman, and Jack Blodgett—and their innovative work in the schools. A central component of this work was using CUFAN to network K through 12 classrooms across South Carolina. From the Atlantic coastline to the upstate mountains, students and teachers were to be writing to one another, sharing their research, conferencing about their experiences with literature, and establishing a database of information on local history, customs, and folklore. Yet one problem consistently thwarted their efforts to engage teachers in the innovative technology. There was no manual that described how to set up and operate the system, and there was no information aimed at often computer-shy people on how to keep the system running after it had been set up. At one of our planning meetings, Dixie wondered aloud whether some enterprising class of technical writing students could be persuaded to produce such a manual. (How did she know what I was teaching the next term?) As the meeting ended, I promised to help find a technical writing teacher who might be willing to do such a thing—to develop a software manual for use by teachers and students in the schools, beginning with the schools in the rural and disadvantaged areas of South Carolina.

So, I spent some time over the next couple of days thinking about the cons and pros of such a course. I didn't know anything about this or any other telecommunications system. I had never designed and written a computer manual myself. I didn't know if the project was at all feasible—that is, whether it could be even reasonably attempted and even half-completed by under-graduates who might be as ignorant in these matters as I was. Risky business. On the other hand, I had seen the potential of this technology for English instruction in the writings of Dawn, Ken, and their classmates. Focusing a course on a project that would be important and worthwhile, and that would be immediately useful and helpful to others, was appealing. I had to admit that I had always wanted to teach such an experimental, project-oriented course, but I had never seemed to have the time or the foolhardiness to try it.

Also, I knew a technical writing course should be ideal for such a project. Frequently, such courses are among the most prescriptive and routine, involving predictable exercises in audience analysis, format practice, and report preparation. Yet technical writing courses have a mandate to explore options for instruction and research on writing in nonacademic settings. They should be courses that construct opportunities for writing outside the academy, courses that help students develop "street smarts" rather than "school smarts" in the complex world of communication in the workplace. So rather than being the least likely of places to discover innovation and practice in writing instruction, technical writing should be one of the most likely places. Indeed, the kind of experimentation essential to technical writing courses, if supported by classroom-based research, may well produce knowledge useful to the teaching of writing generally.

Teaching Journal

So I agreed that my technical writing course the next term would attempt to produce the needed computer manual, from inception to design, from field testing to final editing. As I review the planning notes contained in my teaching journal, the ones I wrote before the class actually began, I can see that I wanted to engage students in a project that would both serve others beyond our class and demand collaboration by the very nature of the task. Here are some of the strategies I hoped to implement:

- To make collaborative activity, in which students have to discriminate, negotiate, delegate, innovate, evaluate, cooperate, and be both supportive and critical, the very heart of the course—In other words, a course to develop and practice what Roger J. Peters calls "street smarts."[3]
- To establish a context in which students may come to know more about the subject to be studied and written about than the teacher does and in which the knowledge and expertise of the group surpasses that of any individual within it.
- To design, write, and deliver written products for and to audiences beyond the classroom—audiences that would provide feedback throughout the developmental process, audiences that, in the end, would evaluate the writing and its usefulness.
- To establish a context in which little is certain and in which creativity and risk-taking are encouraged, supported, and rewarded. To take on a task in which learning new information and new skills is a requirement to successfully completing it, a task that may or may not be completed in one term. Not even the teacher knows for sure.
- To establish a role for myself that "embraces the contraries" Peter Elbow describes so well in his book with a similar title. That is, to hold to the highest standards in developing a successful written product, yet to be a valuable and useful resource for the students in learning and risk-taking. And in James Britton's terms, I wanted to assume at various times the stance of both a participant and a spectator in this course (*Prospect and Retrospect*, pp. 48–54). I wanted to participate in creating a successful product, and I wanted to be a spectator observing the classroom experience that created it. Or to put it another way, I wanted to create opportunities to tell stories about the class and to encourage the students to tell stories as well.
- To develop a teacher-as-researcher strategy in order to learn from my students how they experienced the course. To integrate student research into the essential fabric of the course—research that would affect the ongoing instruction of the course and produce knowledge worthy of further reflection and action.[4]

The Class

Fifteen students—ten undergraduates and five MA students—assembled for that first class in early January. Most had no knowledge of computers beyond word processing, and none had experience with CUFAN. They listened patiently to my description of the interesting project in telecommunications we might do, a project that meant learning how to work with telecommunications as well as how to write about it, and about the unorthodox way the class would be run: we would work collaboratively, and we would set agendas, deadlines and grading procedures only after we got into the project, understood its scope and possibilities, and figured out the best way we could work together to learn something about technical writing in the process of getting our project done. As I found out later from the students' research, the course I described to them was not the course they expected—we were actually going to *do* technical writing, rather than study and practice doing it. However, soon there were only twelve students—seven undergraduates and five graduates— and all but four undergraduate students were English majors. They were a hearty twelve that, despite frequent doubts, continued with the course to the end.

Of course, there were some guidelines and structures from the beginning: a textbook of readings about research on writing in nonacademic settings, supplementary handouts, and books on library reserve about developing and writing user manuals. We each wrote a weekly memo to the class reporting on progress, problems, and forthcoming plans. And as the course progressed, we did an increasing amount of interactive writing (by EMail and on paper), the kind that requires a quick reply in order to build a cooperative community, to accomplish tasks, and to understand each other's strengths and potential contributions. Students were transformed into communication consultants, and I assumed a role of team coordinator and supervisor. We chose *Word-Works* as the name of our consulting firm.

In choosing our firm's name, we began developing group interaction and decision-making by consensus. We set about learning the telecommunications system, with special tutoring sessions in computer labs and numerous extra hours on our own. We met with our clients (consultants must have clients) and discovered that we had several—and also that they did not think alike or expect the same thing from the manual we had agreed to write for them. The "computer people," as I called them (the faculty and staff in the College of Agriculture who ran the system) wanted a manual for farmers and business people. They told us explicitly to de-emphasize readers who might be teachers and students, because they would be a minority of the users, and because it wasn't at all clear whether schools would really be able to incorporate telecommunications into instruction. On the other hand, the "English people"—Dixie, Jack, and Ike—told us that they had given a $15,000 grant to the computer people for the production of the manual—that the grant was even now paying for our class's computer time, and that they expected educational use to have a prominent role. Above all they wanted our manual to be user friendly. The computer people wanted it to be user friendly too; after all, who's against user-friendly manuals? But they wanted the manual to follow what the consultants felt was the decidedly unfriendly form of most computer manuals—such as the incessant numbering of each section, of almost every paragraph and sentence. (You've probably seen this convention: 1.0 turn on the machine, 1.1 insert the disk, 1.2 initialize the disk, 1.3 format the disk, and so on.)

The computer people insisted that we write for IBM PC compatible software, because that was the choice of their users; the English people insisted that we write for Apple computers, since Apples were most available in the schools.

The students wanted to know what to do about these mixed messages, and so did I. We used class time to struggle with these rhetorical and political problems, even as we further considered our audience: the computer clients, the English clients, and then the real users—farmers, bankers, extension agents, teachers, and students. Another thing I later learned from my students' research was that my own unfamiliarity and sometimes bewilderment with this project became a source of inspiration for them. For even though these conflicting mandates may have made the writing of the manual more difficult, the students felt they were significant in shaping our collaborative community. To quote Bill, one of the consultants: "We finally could only look to ourselves for resolutions to problems."

Consultants met frequently outside of class; there simply wasn't enough time for our collaborative activity in two 75-minute sessions a week. We divided into subgroups to take on different tasks related to the project. Each group learned a part of the system, such as electronic mail or CoSy (the conferencing component), drafted a section of the manual, arranged for field tests of that section, made revisions as indicated by the field tests, and then reported results quickly to the rest of the group. Some consultants visited project sites in the schools where teachers and students had the system installed to observe how they were using it, what their problems were, what would be most useful to them. We invited outsiders into the class to further our understanding of computers and manuals—Nancy Martin, a consultant from England, discussed her evaluation of the Bread Loaf computers in the schools project; Terry Thompson, a technical writer, talked about how IBM wrote and produced manuals.

There were numerous changes and adjustments as we went along. Individual deadlines became fluid, but it also became obvious that completion of the manual was possible before the end of the term if we organized our resources effectively, worked diligently (maybe a little overtime would be needed), collaborated successfully, delegated authority, and had a little luck.

CLASSROOM-BASED RESEARCH

In addition to their work on the manual, all consultants, individually or in collaboration, worked on research projects. Eight of the twelve chose projects related to the production of the manual. For example, two collaborated on a report about computer use in local schools—schools that were attempting to participate in the CUFAN project. They observed that new opportunities for writing and reading instruction in the schools made possible by computers and telecommunications were not being implemented—computers did not fit into the convenient structures of traditional classrooms, unless they were used for skill-and-drill or computer-literacy exercises. Four other consultants, however, undertook classroom-based research projects—that is, they conducted research on our classroom community to study the context for language and learning as we experienced it. These researchers became class historians, class ethnographers, and class rhetoricians. They began by tape-recording some of our meetings in and out of class.

Such research activity had an immediate impact on the course. Early on, for example, ethnography notes revealed that whenever the topic turned to hardware and software, the computer knowledgeable men in the class dominated discussion in such a way that the members who were not computer knowledgeable, mostly female, felt excluded. The computer jocks, as they were fondly labeled, talked to one another in the jargon of insiders.

Here is an example from Paramita's notebook. She is from India and had lived in the United States for less than a year.

> Feb. 4. The Dec Lab machines do not have internal lens drives programs, applications are loaded every morning with a RAM DISK. Every time the machines are shut off, the applications are lost. (Memory space is used to load the Apple files.) The users never have to power the systems off. They are asked to come and use the applications directly.
>
> There is probably some tension in the class, a division of interests between the "writing experts," and the "computer buffs." The class conversation

always moves too much in one direction—either totally "letters" or totally "technical achievements." Donna has also noticed this tension, and Jim obviously feels uncomfortable.

The first paragraph is written as a participant in the class. Paramita was not trained in computer use, and she diligently tries to take down the important information provided by a computer-knowledgeable classmate. In the second paragraph she switches her point of view to become an observer/recorder of the social dynamics of the class. She might best be described as a participant-observer, as she both observes and feels the tension in the class. She records informally a piece of gossip, creates the beginnings of a story, becomes a spectator on her own experience. James Britton and his colleagues, building on the work of the British psychologist D. W. Harding, note that the spectator role "is not simply concerned to perceive and understand," clearly Paramita's concern in her first paragraph, but rather in engaging feelings and applying a sense of values to what is perceived, as Paramita attempts in paragraph two (*Development of Writing Abilities 11–18*, p. 80).

As the supervisor who knew as little about the computer system as the least knowledgeable students, I was impressed by the use of jargon so freely spouted and thankful that someone in the class could talk like that, assuming that such talk would manifest itself in the technical expertise needed to complete the project. But the female consultants were annoyed rather than impressed. This issue needed to be confronted now and not later. I began to feel that my previous experience as the department head for fifty faculty (who also frequently didn't see eye to eye) might be useful.

What I found interesting was that this tension between the computer "haves and have nots" was a point of reference in three of the classroom-based research projects. All three described the tension and interpreted its significance, and all agreed that it had dissipated by the last few weeks of the course. However, at midpoint the students were troubled by the existence of this tension and clearly wanted to work beyond it, while I more or less assumed such tension was inevitable among groups of diverse people. In any event, I got a fuller and richer explanation for this tension and its gradual amelioration from the research of the consultants.

Paramita's Research

Paramita did a discourse analysis of the oral and written language of our classroom community (our consulting firm if you will) over the course of the term. From an analysis of our memos, EMail messages, and discussions in and out of class, she documented patterns of oral and written language use and was able to draw some conclusions about the development and use of specialized language within our discourse community. Here are some excerpts from her research report.

> When two computer-oriented consultants, John and Martin, indulge in a highly technical discussion about the problems of using a Hayes incompatible modem, then another consultant Pearl may find it extremely annoying that the whole conversation seems to fly over her head, even though she may consider herself technically knowledgeable, or at least technically competent in class. . . .
>
> The most logical conclusion I should draw is that the discourse patterns in our class must have reflected a dominance of English majors—maximum use of writing or literary skills. But the baffling truth is the actual interactions both in class (discussions, brainstorming, meetings) and outside of class (EMail messages, memos) show a widespread technical orientation of our members. . . .
>
> My aim in bringing in this issue at this point is showing the inception, growth and maturity of a parallel discourse community. The point worth noting is that this time the technical gobbledegook is not limited to a few professional individuals in the class, it has contaminated the masses. I have been noticing that memos falling under the time span of the last one and half months have an amazing degree of thematic unity. The major theme is almost always a topic of the computer manual: EMail, CoSy, ProComm, CUFAN, templates, etc. The discussions do not stop with specific task-oriented problems but proceed at length with speculations, conjectures and assumptions regarding the political issues at stake. The "manual" fever seems to be very much there. Surprisingly enough, this project has not widened the gap between the writing experts and the technical experts, in fact, the gap has been bridged. The "manual" community members have developed a keen sense of unity, interdependence, and trust.

Studying Paramita's research, listening to the stories she and the other researchers told, provided me with a broader interpretation of my own experience in this course. To summarize this research in my own words: tension developed early in the class between those students who could use computer jargon and those who could not. One very human response was to try to remove the tension, and the most commonsense way appeared to be to restrain the computer buffs from speaking over the heads of the rest of us. And yet as the course developed, the tension did disappear—but not because less jargon was spoken, because these researchers had documented that, in fact, more jargon was spoken. As consultants became familiar with the technical aspects of the telecommunications system, they found it natural to speak in the most available language, and that was technical language.

The class historian, Christi, pointed out that while we all came to speak confidently in technical language about our area of expertise, not all members of the class were conversant with other areas, and thus the problem of incomprehensible technical language remained. But the technical language did not cause tension at the end of the course as it had at the beginning. Her research revealed two reasons for the change—we knew each other better and felt free to interrupt to get alternative explanations when we thought they were necessary; and we now were on equal footing (each of us knew some technical jargon unknown to others, a clear contrast to the beginning of the class). The irony of our consulting firm's developing a technically and linguistically sophisticated discourse community while contracting to write a computer manual in clear, jargon-free prose for uninitiated students, teachers, and farmers was not lost on the consultants. They realized they had experienced in a "street smarts" sense the problem of technical writers who translate and interpret the language of one discourse community into the language of others (i.e., the language of computer engineers into the language of nontechnical consumers of computer products).

Just how parochial our language use had become became evident when my twelve-year-old daughter Sarah took the day off from seventh grade to visit our class on the last day of the course—the day we gave our final oral report to our clients, to interested students and faculty, and to representative users. On this day the consultants arrived anxious about their presentation but relieved that the project was finally coming to an end. But before the presentation began, we learned from one of the computer clients that the CoSy conferencing system had been scrapped. The university had purchased a more efficient, more user-friendly system. The word spread among the consultants quickly and incredulously: "CoSy has been killed!" Those consultants who had worked so hard to make this very-much-less-than-friendly system friendly to users poignantly realized that their writing was headed for the trash can—a hard way to learn "street smarts"!

We were all relieved, however, that we had designed the manual in anticipation of such murderous acts. The CoSy section could be lifted out and laid to rest without disrupting the sectioning, pagination, or indexing of the rest of the manual. But my daughter Sarah had picked up on our affection for and emotional investment in something with the cuddly name CoSy. On our drive home that day, she queried me about who killed CoSy, why did he have to die, exactly what was my role in the death, why wasn't I working to bring him back to life. To this day, she partially blames me for the death of CoSy, a death she knows upset my students very much. She was there. She heard their talk, listened to their stories, and witnessed their actions.

Bill's Research

Another researcher in the class, Bill, wrote case studies of two of the other consultants. After surveying the attitudes of the class as a whole (using the research data of others), Bill wrote case studies of Donna and Mike. Donna was an MA student in English who apprehensively entered the class because she had little prior experience with computers or technical writing. Mike was an undergraduate majoring in math and computer science who was the most knowledgeable computer person in the class, but he too was apprehensive about being a technical major in an English class full of English majors. Bill conducted taped interviews with these two students and then focused his case studies on how they experienced collaboration. Here is part of Bill's case study of Mike:

> The consensus seems to be that the kind of writing that was done in the class would not have been possible if there hadn't been the freedom from grades so that each writer could focus on the project and not on personal recognition. . . . [Mike] said that he likes the "less structured approach" because it "takes the pressure off because we already have enough pressure to meet deadlines, to get this project done. And I think the students are committed to this project. They want to see a product, they want to see it look nice."

> Both Donna and Mike commented on the fact that they appreciated having the "pressure off." This seemed ironic to me, since the deadlines and pressure to finish the product were very real. The pressure that was removed was the pressure to impress the teachers so that they could prove they had earned an "A" for whatever thing they were doing. As long as there were grades there would be ownership, and resentment towards editing and change. Everyone would defend his or her opinion to the death if there was a sense that a grade was riding on it. Without this pressure, however, the participants were able to focus on what was best for the manual and not on what was best for the individual. This allowed everyone to spend time on what had to be done and not on polishing their list of contributions.

> [Mike] felt that the project had one great advantage; that it simulated "real world" experience.

> "It's a big project; a lot of people are working on it. I've never worked on a project with this many people before. Covering so much material, and a . . . you referred to a technical background; I was looking through this document; I know how to do like the EMail, and the Procomm. I don't know a thing about CoSy, I don't know a thing about Smarterm, so I've been involved in a project where a lot's going on that I don't know about. And that I think will be a lot like the real world. Because you can't go into industry knowing all products and things like that."

> So the idea has come full circle. To make a collaborative writing project effective there has to be a sense of community among members of the group,

and a sense of security and creativity that is fostered by that community. Each participant must, ironically, personalize the project in order to produce a final product that bears no one individual's stamp. Each individual must be allowed the freedom to express himself or herself to address the problem that is before the group. This seems to allow each participant to feel that the project is in some way theirs. As a group, however, the individual abilities and achievements of the members are absorbed into the larger consciousness of the community. There, somehow, all of the disparate pieces are melded and blended to fit together. The final project is then both a reflection of each individual participant, but also the product of a group that bears no thumbprint of any individual contributor. And it is this seeming dichotomy of direction that makes the collaborative writing experience both positive and unique.

As I listen to Mike tell his story to Bill, and to Bill synthesizing his research for me, I learn that my strategies about developing "street smarts" and about tackling a project in which the knowledge and expertise of the group surpasses that of any individual within the group were apparently successful. But I also learn some new things from Bill's research, about how collaboration, as he and his fellow consultants experienced it, meant the ability to develop a personal and individual contribution and then be able to lose it within the community effort. Or, to say it another way, group members needed to have a strong voice in order to make a significant contribution and yet be willing to see that strong voice absorbed and irrevocably transformed by collaboration. As interesting as this insight in Bill's research report is, I was further surprised by his response to this section in an early draft of this chapter. In the margin, he wrote: "What motivated us to give up so much free time? It was *our* manual. I still feel that way. In fact, I almost resent other classes working on it and not recognizing what we did. The community that evolved was magical, and to me, the manual has an almost spiritual significance. (I'm really at a loss for words to describe my attachment to a technical manual.)" Bill doesn't appreciate the other technical writing classes that continue to work on the manual, writing user-friendly directions for new applications and revising existing ones. While he and his classmates agreed to have their individual voices transformed through collaboration, Bill doesn't like his group's voice and *their* manual, which he views as emblematic of their collaborative experience, reconstituted and changed by writers who did not share their experience. Bill, a graduate student in literature, says that he cannot explain his attachment to a technical manual, but he says much about what he left unsaid. It has to do with purposeful activity, successful collaboration, and a magical sense of community.

Bill's further interpretation—that this collaborative experience would not have been possible if I had used traditional grading procedures—was a matter that I had not thoughtfully considered prior to the course. Discussion of grading practices appears nowhere in my teaching journal until after the class began. I long ago gave up grading each individual piece of student writing, but I usually provide commentary and a grade for work completed two or three times during the term. But as we got into this course, and as the inevitable student anxiety about grades emerged, I determined (I'm not quite sure why or how) that assigning individual grades would not be appropriate at any point in the course, except at its conclusion. I can now tell from several of the research projects that the problem of feedback and of grades was a major concern for most of the students, but that the anxiety, perhaps contrary to expectations, was tempered as the course progressed. As the class historian noted, not having grades was interpreted by several students as having to produce more rather than less as the term progressed. Individual and collective goals merged into one: to complete the manual on time and to have it accepted as an effective document by our clients and distributed to the users on the farms and in the schools of South Carolina. From reading Bill's report, I can see how his research led him to believe that this one "seat of the pants" decision I made about grades was most important in enabling students, admittedly unfamiliar with collaboration, to have a positive and productive experience.

Issues of competition, power, and interpersonal tension did not completely disappear from our collaborative community, of course. We did, however, develop interesting methods for acknowledging tension and resolving conflicts. For example, about halfway through the term, one consultant became upset when another consultant completely rewrote a section of the manual he had written without first checking with him. He complained not to me, the teacher, but to other consultants, who quickly intervened to mediate the miscommunication, the poor etiquette, the hurt feelings, and the potential danger to further productive collaboration. I found out about the "blow up" only after the incident was considered history. I was part of a classroom community in which I did not have to be the absolute authority, exercising control and ruling on contentious issues. The consultants themselves found ways to ameliorate tensions, reinforce collegiality, create a successful product, and evolve a community that, at least for Bill, "was magical." We seemed to have experienced what John Dewey meant when he wrote of educational democracy: "It is not the will or desire of any one person which establishes order but the moving spirit of the whole group. The control is social, but individuals are parts of a community, not outside of it" (p. 54).

REFLECTIONS

Two consultants, Christi and Donna, the class historian and the class ethnographer, in addition to their research reports, collaborated on a composite from tape recordings of a typical class day—a mock transcript from which I have learned a great deal, and which the consultants themselves seemed to appreciate when it was read aloud to the class. Here is an excerpt:

Michael begins, "First of all, does anyone have any general comments about this article? I thought it brought up some interesting points about how management can affect how the computer manual gets used. . . ." Once Michael initiates the conversation, the discussion takes off.

"It sounded about right in my experience—I'm not sure about management style, but I know that I've used quite a few user's manuals, and on most of them you just want to be able to go to the specific information you need and use that—"

"Really!" someone interrupts. "I want to be able to sit down and turn the computer on and go! So what I use is the part on getting started, and then I just look at what I need to—if I can find it—after that."

"Maybe we should do something like that for our manual. . . . You know, organize information in the order you'll use it or something," one consultant volunteers.

This prompts a reply from one usually silent member. "Or maybe provide an index for each section instead of at the end so users can look in each area—that way they won't have to wade through so much other stuff."

"Each group will need to develop indexes for their sections—and hopefully make them as 'user-friendly' as possible," interjects Art.

"What about making each index 'goal-oriented?' I've used some manuals like this and they seemed to help me out a lot," suggests one consultant with plenty of computer experience.

Another consultant with less technical exposure wants to know exactly what the first consultant is talking about. "What do you mean by 'goal-oriented.'?"

"It's organized by the actions and tasks you need to perform—if you want to do something, you look up that idea."

"Oh . . . Then that might work well, because when you're not sure of the technical name, it's impossible to look it up!" she laughs.

"Not only that—" contributes another member, "but you don't always have time to figure out where to look. When I worked at Sears, we got computerized cash registers and none of us really knew what we were doing, even after we went through this training seminar. And when five customers are standing there in line, you don't have time to call the manager for help. So they gave us flipcards—little three-by-five index cards—on a rolodex-kind-of-holder that had tabs with an action printed on them. So if you had to enter in 'cash return' and you didn't know how, all you had to do was look for 'cash return' on the tab and flip to it and then follow the real simple directions on that. That way, we'd been exposed to it once in training and still could use it for real almost immediately. And none of us were too nervous about it 'cause we knew we could look it up by ourselves in less than a minute.

"We needed something like that in this hospital where I worked last summer," another consultant tells us. "We got this brand new computer system in and they wanted us to use it immediately. I mean these doctors would come in and stand over your shoulder and it was hard to tell them, 'wait just a minute—I'm just learning this!' They didn't like that too much," she laughs. "We didn't have anything like you used at Sears, so we'd make the doctors mad and say, 'hang on!' and we'd run ask our supervisor, who'd come help us do what we needed. But there was only one manual and he kept that in his office so no one but him could use it—just like this article talked about. We need something to help us look stuff up quickly."

"I've found that templates really help a lot," someone suggests. "Just quick at-a-glance information like what keys stand for what function that's all printed on laminated cardboard that I prop up on my PC—then if I need it I just look down and there it is. I was thinking something like that might be a good thing to include in our CUFAN manual."

This hypothetical transcript, constructed from tapes and observations and transformed by the students' imaginative power, describes a day about two-thirds through the course. While there are many context-specific references (for example, the inside jokes associated with our numerous discussions of "templates," or the gender dynamics of who speaks how), I believe others can join with me in constructing generalizable meaning from their playful story. We notice that the conversation moves comfortably and deftly among the assigned reading selection, the students' personal experiences with computers, considerations of the writing project (the manual), and the telling of stories designed to build community among members and to make points about the social context in which manuals are sometimes used. The tension I noted earlier between those consultants who were technically knowledgeable and those who were not is displayed here ("Another consultant with less technical exposure wants to know exactly what the first consultant is taking about"), but this tension is handled by a pointed question followed by a friendly yet knowledgeable laugh. This transcript shows focused discussion as a problem-solving activity—not discussing the reading for its own sake, not telling stories for their own sake, but rather to generate perspectives and solutions for the principal problems at hand: the production of an effective and usable computer manual, the relating of new knowledge to past personal experience, and the development of a collaborative community. And perhaps most of all, this slice of classroom conversation documents the important role "talk" played in the group's learning, problem solving, and successful collaboration. Through this narrative, Christi and Donna have created a vehicle in which they can stand back as spectators and imaginatively depict their participation in a transactional, vocational, practical technical writing experience.

In writing this narrative, Christi and Donna chose to tell a story about the stories we told: about computer use, about manual use, about working at Sears, about working in a hospital, about templates. In selecting these stories for their story, they were capturing what many of us valued most about our classroom conversations and our experience in collaboration. We valued each other's stories, we valued what each person brought to this collaborative experience, we valued those times when usually silent members spoke, we valued the way we had come to handle interpersonal tensions and conflicts, we valued the way we had learned to talk with each other, and we valued the knowledge each of us had gained and that the entire group had gained in order to write a document of which we could be proud, one that we envisioned would change the way students and teachers communicated with others within South Carolina's classrooms and beyond. In responding to an early draft of this chapter, one in which storytelling was alluded to but had not yet emerged as a major focus in the retelling of this classroom experience, Christi wrote:

> I'm afraid I don't have too much to say—I think you should focus on storytelling and collaboration—in the light of how we collaborated to form a group that produced a good product, and how, to collaborate and form that group, we used stories. Stories helped us when we couldn't speak the jargon, helped explain why we thought/felt/suggested certain things, helped us understand *some* of the politics of CUFAN (the computer people and the English people told us *their* individual stories); stories helped prompt other stories to brainstorm and jog new ideas, helped us relate to the readings, helped us do research on the class (people told stories about the class on the tapes). So all this storytelling came together to the point that the class had its own "history"—with individual stories being stored in our collective memory. Anyway, so the class as a whole had (has) a common experience about which we can tell stories—and you are now doing so—but all of the individual stories told in class or at night meetings and at Nick's Tavern help make up the final product and collaboration—and the stories therefore colored the manual—sometimes overtly (the ordering of sections, how to be user-friendly) and sometimes subtly (personal relationships that very likely influenced give-and-take in discussions and decisions about the final product). So I guess what I'm saying is that we collaborated daily in class, and we told stories to collaborate. (I guess I had more to say than I thought I did!!)

For most of us who were involved in this course, the story has not ended. We still talk about our experience, and we still think about it as we go about our lives in teaching, technical writing, tending the sick, raising children, developing "school smarts" and "street smarts," listening to and telling stories. Paulo Freire, in *Pedagogy of the Oppressed*, discusses the "fundamentally *narrative* character" of the student-teacher relationship and concludes that "education is suffering from narration sickness." This sickness exists because the teacher constantly narrates to the patient listening students, who "tend in the process of being narrated to to become lifeless and petrified," as they "memorize mechanically the narrated content." The narrative character of instruction leads to Freire's banking concept of education, in which the teacher knows everything and the students know nothing—in which the students are the depositories and the teacher is the depositor" (pp. 57–59). Freire's indictment of "banking" classroom methodology is warranted, but his suggestion that narrative is the inherent cause of the malaise is not. Freire's banker-teachers orate rather than narrate, make pronouncements rather than tell stories. And most importantly, these banker-teachers do not allow students, whom they view as empty containers to be filled up, to speak at all, except to repeat what the teacher has already spoken. The issue might be phrased differently: "Who gets to tell the stories?" When students and teachers both contribute stories as part of the educational process of asking questions and developing knowledge, then a collaborative and democratic method of education is possible, one similar to Freire's "problem-posing" method (pp. 68–74).

Christi and Donna's narrative was a gift. They were not required or expected to produce such a narrative. I believe they were motivated to write and share it with the rest of us, whom they perceived as trusted friends with shared mutual experience, in order to reflect in the spectator role on their experience in this class. They wanted to verbalize this experience, make sense of it, give value to it. They recognized with James Britton that "one of the important ways in which we frame an evaluation and communicate it is by giving a particular shape to the events in narrating them" (*Prospect and Retrospect*, p. 52). Narrative is an important way of knowing, of coming to know, and all learners—students and teachers alike—should have opportunities to tell stories in order to make new knowledge meaningful and to put difficult problems in perspective. Narrative thus considered becomes a tool for attaining Paulo Freire's goal in which "learners penetrate or enter into the discourse of the teacher, appropriating for themselves the deepest significance of the subject being taught. The indisputable responsibility of the teacher to teach is thus shared by the learners through their own act of intimately knowing what is taught. . . . To teach, then, is the form that knowing takes as the teacher searches for a particular way of teaching that will challenge and call forth in students their own act of knowing" ("Letter to North American Teachers," p. 213).

In conclusion, based on my experience in this course, the student's research, and my collaborative experience with these researchers in the writing of this chapter, I offer some tentative generalities about our experience in this course:

- We did not learn the skills of technical writing or of collaboration independent of context. We saw clearly the social and political nature of our writing and the process that created it. We wanted to write an effective manual because we wanted to create further opportunities for learning and communicating in the schools and on the farms of South Carolina. We saw ourselves as agents in the making of a better world. We came to know the meaning of John Dewey's statement: "There is no such thing as educational value in the abstract" (p. 46).

- We, teachers and students, became empowered as writers by developing the knowledge necessary to engender our discourse community. We made ourselves experts and thus developed the authority to speak to each other in one discourse and to nonexperts in another.

- We learned that interactive teaching, in which students learn from the teacher and the teacher learns from the students, is essential to the establishment of a collaborative community of learners in the classroom.

- We learned about community: what it is, how to get it, and what happens when individuals become a community. Within our classroom community, we know that individual roles changed, that people learned to talk differently to each other, to perceive each other differently, and that without these changes genuine collaboration would have been impossible.

- We performed research that mattered. We created opportunities for each other to think critically about our own education. When we examined how we talked to each other, wrote to each other, talked to students and teachers in the schools, wrote to others who needed the technical knowledge and the rhetorical expertise that we possessed, we deepened our understanding of how we and other people learn.

- We used and enhanced both our "street smarts" and our "school smarts." We learned that classroom-based research projects are powerful pedagogy, for in the process of learning what went on in our course we were shaping what went on. We participated in an experiment and observed how we performed, and we performed much better than expected because we were involved in an experiment. All classes perhaps should be experiments in learning.

- We talked expressively to each other within and without the classroom. We related new knowledge and unfamiliar problems to previous experiences, we developed trust in each other, we defined problems, assessed resources, and rehearsed solutions. We realized we were storytellers and that the stories we created were indispensable to what we were about.

NOTES

1. I wish to express my gratitude to several students for permission to tell their contributions to our story: Mike Brown, Paramita Ghosh, Bill McGee, Donna McKamy, Christi Morrison. My thanks to several colleagues who read and commented on this chapter in draft: Denise Boerckle, Dixie Goswami, Susan Hilligoss, Liz Lamont, Bill McGee, Christi Morrison, Wendy Price, and Leslie Robinson. I also want to thank Michael Strickland, currently a doctoral student at the University of Georgia, who assisted me in organizing and supervising the day-to-day activities of the course.

2. My thanks to Ike Coleman, coordinator of the Bread Loaf/South Carolina Project, for permission to use the writing from Breadnet.

3. I am indebted to Roger J. Peters and his work on practical intelligence for his distinction and discussion of "street smarts" vs. "school smarts." For further information on collaborative learning and the teaching of writing, see: Kenneth A. Bruffee, "Collaborative Learning and the 'Conversation of Mankind,'" *College English* 46 (November 1984): 635–52, and his "Social Construction, Language, and the Authority of Knowledge: A Bibliographical Essay," *College English* 48 (December 1986): 773–90; Jeff Golub, ed., *Focus on Collaborative Learning* (Urbana, IL: NCTE, 1988); and Harvey S. Wiener, "Collaborative Learning in the Classroom: A Guide to Evaluation," *College English* 48 (January 1986): 52–61.

4. For further information about the teacher as researcher, see: Glenda L. Bissex and Richard H. Bullock, eds., *Seeing for Ourselves: Case-Study Research by Teachers of Writing* (Portsmouth, NH: Heinemann, 1987); Dixie Goswami and Peter R. Stillman, eds., *Reclaiming the Classroom: Teacher Research as an Agency for Change* (Portsmouth, NH: Boynton/Cook, 1987); and Marian M. Mohr and Marion S. MacLean, *Working Together: A Guide for Teacher-Researchers* (Urbana, IL: NCTE, 1987.)

15

Critical Inquiry in a Technical Writing Course

JACK SELZER

Once upon a time, the idea of the teacher (or student) as researcher might have been greeted with skepticism by those who teach technical writing. After all, ever since the first technical writing courses emerged in the decade before World War I—especially as the result of the industrializing of America, the establishment of professional colleges of engineering, and the "scientific management" of the new assembly-line industries—technical writing has been seen as fundamentally instrumental. Samuel Chandler Earle, Sada Harbarger, T. A. Richard, and other pioneer textbook writers regarded language in general as a tool and technical language in particular as a tool of technology—a means of helping the gears of a technological culture to run smoothly.[1] The followers of those early teachers have been encouraged to see their job as instrumental too: their task has been to help people become useful employees—effective tools themselves within modern corporations and complex bureaucracies. Even now most technical writing teachers are quite sympathetic with David Dobrin's elegant definition of technical writing as "writing that accommodates technology to the user," and most practitioners, users, and teachers—armed with readability formulas and user-testing procedures—judge technical prose in terms of its utility and efficiency. As the authors of one of the most influential textbooks ever written on technical writing put it, technical writing "is an act of communication by a professional in an organizational system to transfer information necessary for the system to continue to function" (Mathes and Stevenson, p. 1). From that perspective the technical writing teacher's job can become just as instrumental: the teacher-as-technician transfers as efficiently as possible to relatively less efficient students the rhetorical strategies and tactics most likely to be productive in complex technological endeavors and organizations.

Now, however, a number of developments are encouraging different attitudes toward technical writing instruction, attitudes that can accommodate the idea of the teacher as researcher. One is a change in approaches to writing instruction in general. As teachers have begun to attend to the dynamics of the writing process and to the implications of the notion of interpretive communities, they have inevitably become less persistent dealers in efficient textual moves (or narrow readability or usability measures) and more commonly advisors who help students to study and then manage the constraints and demands and implications of different composing circumstances. Another is that technical writing teachers less often see technical writing as just a tool. Certainly technical writing is still regarded as a tool; anyone who has read the latest textbooks in the field knows that. But it is not *just* a tool, any more than the assembly line is *just* a tool. If language is epistemic and knowledge-making is social and collaborative, if knowledge is constructed and negotiated through language in a community, if rhetoric even in science and technology involves not only the instrumental transmission of knowledge but also its generation, then writing (including technical and scientific writing) becomes a reality itself as well as a tool for mediating reality. Like the assembly line, technical writing is an artifact as well as a tool. It is not simply a tool for the mere transmission of knowledge but a tool for the discovery of knowledge as well, a technology for inquiry about the world and other tools.[2]

Accordingly—and this is the third development I want to mention— technical writing (or the rhetoric of science and technology) has become an object of study in its own right, a phenomenon of interest in itself. One of the more significant developments within rhetorical studies in the past decade has been the scrutiny of scientific and technical discourse. For instance, the contributions in Lee Odell and Dixie Goswami's collection of essays focus not just in general on "writing in nonacademic settings" but in particular on the rhetoric employed in technical and institutional settings. New journals (e.g., *The Journal of Business and Technical Communication* and *Management Communication Quarterly*) have been founded with an explicit emphasis on technical, scientific, and business prose; and journals with an established commitment to publishing work on rhetoric—journals in English (e.g., *CCC* and *College English*), in speech communication (e.g., *Quarterly Journal of Speech*), and with an interdisciplinary slant (e.g., *Written Communication*)—now regularly publish studies of scientific or technical discourse. The University of Wisconsin Press is producing a series of volumes about "the rhetoric of the human sciences" (sample titles: *The Rhetoric of Economics* and *Heracles' Bow: Essays on the Rhetoric and Poetics of the Law*), and SUNY Press has just announced plans for a similar series—Studies in Scientific and Technical Communication—under the editorship of James Zappen. Even "insiders" are becoming interested in the dynamics of scientific and technical discourse: I'm thinking of works such as *The Mismeasure of Man* and *Time's Arrow, Time's*

Cycle by Stephen J. Gould, the anthropologist Clifford Geertz's *Works and Lives* (essentially a close rhetorical analysis of ethnographic accounts), and Bruno Latour and Steve Woolgar's *Laboratory Life* (an account of how setting influences the discourse produced in a scientific community). Most of this work concentrates not on the "how to do it" side of writing but on understanding "how it works."

In the light of this scholarship, the technical writing classroom continues to be a place where students acquire and master certain language tools, but it also offers an occasion for studying those tools as artifacts, for studying language and its uses in technical, scientific, and institutional settings. "Know how" is still central to the technical writing course, but so is "know that." After all, technical students can know how to use language most effectively only if they understand something of the various ways that language does function in different communities, and only if they are flexible enough and rhetorically savvy enough to change when new circumstances call for change. And they can understand their own roles in technical organizations—for example, does a particular organization treat its employees, its engineers, as so many tools themselves? is the organization conscious of that?—only when they understand how writing functions in particular technical settings. Technical writing is still a "how-to" course in how to empower students with rhetorical strategies and tactics that "work" in technical cultures; but it is also a subject matter, an object for inquiry—a body of knowledge and practices, habits and conventions, that is worth studying.

From the perspective of these three developments, of course, the technical writing teacher's role also changes. If the course is not merely a matter of imparting skills and competencies and efficiencies, the teacher is less likely to be a technician, a "delivery system"—and more likely to be a fellow student engaged in the body of knowledge called technical writing and committed to initiating other students into the same body of knowledge. No longer is the course a process of transferring knowledge from the teacher who has it to the student who doesn't. Instead (or in addition, since there is no reason why authoritative guides cannot be retained), the course becomes a directed kind of inquiry during which students and the teacher-student collaborate to further knowledge in the field. A technical writing teacher can still recommend specific tactics to student writers, can still help students stretch their writing skills and their knowledge of what makes technical writing work, can still assign and evaluate papers—indeed, I would say that a technical writing teacher *should* continue those activities: there is no reason that the authoritative voice of the teacher must be at odds with a course that is an inquiry. But there is no reason to reduce the course to *only* the transferring of information or "skills." A course in technical writing can become as well the occasion for a sophisticated investigation into the nature of language and its uses in technical and scientific communities.

How might that investigation be carried out? This chapter outlines some specific suggestions—only *some* of them, and only *suggestions*—for turning technical writing into an arena of shared inquiry. I want to concentrate only on writing assignments because my central point is that technical writing teachers can be researchers without compromising (and in fact while enhancing) the traditional instrumental goals of the course. At the root of these assignments are the teacher's commitment to become as much the receiver as the giver of information; the teacher's willingness to abrogate the role of expert, at least on occasion; and the activity of rhetorical analysis. The assignments that I discuss here are designed for the standard, beginning technical writing course offered to juniors and seniors majoring in scientific and applied-scientific disciplines. To give readers a sense of how these assignments—these snapshots of moments in a semester—might fit into the broader goals of such a course, I have provided a typical course overview (see Appendix A); the overview lists the writing principles taken up in the course and the possible assignments (most teachers at Penn State choose between six and eight) that might give students the opportunity to practice those principles. But while the assignments I will discuss are designed for one kind of technical writing course, the thinking behind them might easily be applied to the construction of assignments in other technical writing courses, either those more specialized (e.g., courses in a particular genre, such as Proposal Writing) or those more advanced (where in fact more "inquiry" might be expected as a matter of course). There are certainly many other ways to turn a course into an inquiry besides using the writing assignments; indeed, the act of inquiry should probably figure in some way into every class meeting. But I do contend that the two kinds of assignments that I will describe—those that ask students to serve as "research assistants" and those that are exercises in rhetorical analysis—provide particularly interesting and fruitful occasions for inquiry.

THE STUDENT AS RESEARCH ASSISTANT

Included in the appendices are several examples—two versions of one assignment, three of another—of what I mean by asking students to become research assistants. Essentially these assignments require students to begin to do informally what they will do in a more formal way later in the course: write a report that solves a specific problem for someone. Only this time, early in the course, they report information that will be useful to the teacher and to their classmates and that is relevant to the subject matter of the early stages of my course.[3] Essentially students are asked to do an informal study of writers at work in order to advance my own understanding of technical writing (technical writing as process and as product) as well as their own. All of the exercises described in this section appropriate a cornerstone of classroom research: the case study, the hard look at a small sample.

Project 1 has two general forms (see Appendices B and C). I used the first version for several years as a way to deepen my knowledge of the kinds of writing done in various fields. At a time when I had only the most general hunches about what kinds of documents were being produced in various fields, I asked each of my students to do a modest inquiry into the genres and writing situations they would encounter after graduation. After interviewing and/or observing a professional working in their particular fields and sub-fields, students reported to me in writing specifics about the amounts and kinds of writing done in those disciplines.[4] The students' reports were often enlightening and sometimes fascinating to me, for the students were able to provide information about a dizzying range of documents from a dizzying range of subfields. Moreover—and more important—the students themselves learned in a concrete if indirect way some of the things I try to emphasize early in my technical writing courses: (1) the importance of writing to one's professional—and technical—success; (2) the variety of writing tasks required on the job; (3) the need for flexibility and resourcefulness as a way of handling that variety; and (4) the value of audience and purpose as concepts for directing that flexibility and resourcefulness. The introductory lessons provided by this assignment, in short, cut two ways—they give an instructor far greater understanding of the field circumscribed by the term "technical writing"; and they indoctrinate students into some of the basic principles of that kind of writing, principles that the remainder of the course can deepen, qualify, and elaborate.

After using this assignment in one form or another for several years, I noticed that the students' reports were becoming less informative to me. Apparently the reports had succeeded in domesticating for me the mysteries of many technical fields, because each semester the students' results struck me as less and less surprising. At the same time, my own professional interests were shifting somewhat away from written products and toward the processes involved in composing those products in a technical or scientific setting. Consequently I decided to modify my first assignment to the form reproduced in Appendix C. The first part of the assignment specifies the kinds of information I am interested in gaining about the composing processes of technical writers: How do they plan, invent, arrange, revise? What are the dynamics of collaborative writing at work? Which aspects of the rhetorical situation affect which aspects of composing, and how? How do composing practices change over time? The second half of the assignment asks students to try to find some information relevant to those questions and to report those findings to me. Again, I have found the student reports to be both useful and interesting; again, I have watched students learn just the things I try to emphasize early in the course. And since the students submit their reports to a real reader—me—who has requested the information and who can judge the success of the reports, the assignment satisfies the instrumental goals of the course as well.

This chapter does not permit me the space to quote student examples at length, but here is a fairly typical excerpt from a report by a geography major named Nancy Anderson that describes the actual composition (after some planning and invention) of a document by an "environmental photogrammetry interpreter" employed by Bionetics, a private contractor for the Environmental Protection Agency:

> When Mr. Mata actually sits down to write the text, he begins with an introduction. This restates the assignment and gives an overview of how he is planning to attack the problems of the site. Next, Mr. Mata writes the main body of the text, a purely descriptive annotation of the aerial photographs. He writes this while referring to his original annotations and to the photographs, which he has spread out on a light table beside his desk. This writing he calls "guts writing," not worrying about grammar or spelling. His main concern is getting his thoughts down on paper. He writes in sections, leaving big gaps between sections for additions. He writes, rewrites, scribbles out as well as "cuts and pastes" sections of his writing. Mr. Mata used to throw away parts of the text with which he was not happy when he first started working a year and half ago, but now he is not concerned with how well he phrases the text the first time through, but is concerned that all of the pertinent information is included. After his initial draft of the text, Mr. Mata stressed that he "goes back and makes it pretty . . . making sure it's written efficiently and in a clear manner." Mr. Mata finds that when he writes the "creative process" is still going on. In fact, he finds that his best insights "pop into his head" while he is in the writing stage. In other words, while he is writing he makes new discoveries and sees new relationships within and among the information contained on the aerial photographs that he did not see as important before he started writing.

Later the report describes the processes of checking, approval, and revision that documents endure at Bionetics, as well as some of the political and legal factors that constrain writers there. It all amounts to one informal but relatively thick description of one document by one writer in one location, one report among many that together have taught me much of what I now think I know about how technical writers operate. What the students report may not be scientifically valid (whatever that means), and I have not yet felt that it is legitimate for my students to report their findings in a journal article. Although I give students a short primer on ethnography in the course of the assignment (just as I speak to them informally about interviewing techniques in connection with the other assignment that I have mentioned), I have no illusions about the reliability and generalizability of the students' accounts. However, I can attest to the fact that when students are asked to pursue answers to substantial questions and to report their results to a teacher who is honestly interested in what can be learned from those reports, and when the substantial questions relate explicitly to the subject matter of the course, both students and teachers benefit.

One final note on these first two assignments. My university offers a very large number of sections of technical writing each semester. The demand for the course, coupled with the desire of many advanced graduate students to teach it, has meant that our staff is relatively inexperienced. But assignments like these, and the perspective of the teacher as researcher, have the effect of making inexperience something of an asset rather than a liability. Instead of taking on (with no little discomfort and a fair amount of dissembling) the role of Authoritative Guide to Technical Prose, new teachers can assume the more comfortable role of a fellow explorer into the nature of technical writing. When new teachers are encouraged to see their courses as inquiries, and when their students are directed to assist teachers' explorations, then those teachers gain knowledge and confidence alongside their students.

Before I leave this section on "the student as research assistant," I want to mention briefly some other offspring of these assignments—three follow-up exercises collectively entitled Project 2 in the appendices. Depending on what I want to accomplish in a given semester and on what other assignments I make in a given term, I usually require my students to do one of the three. The first version (see Appendix D) is useful when I want students to learn something about how to work under time constraints (in this case, the limits of one class period) and about how to "boilerplate"—how to adapt and to use information contained in one kind of document (for one kind of reader) to meet the requirements of another rhetorical situation; both skills, I have learned, are important ones for effective technical writers to have. In the first weeks of the course I am usually intent on impressing on students the importance of audience and purpose to the substance and form of a successful document, and the need for flexibility and resourcefulness in their composing habits: this short in-class assignment gives me a chance to dramatize both points. It also satisfies another goal that I try to achieve whenever possible— the assignment has a real goal for real readers who can make real use of the written product. In the course of completing the assignment—a report for a friend concerning the kind of writing the friend can expect to find in a given field—the technical writer again assumes the role of a research assistant. Only this time the beneficiary of the research is not the teacher but the friend (who receives the writer's revised version of the assignment, after my suggestions have been considered and incorporated).

The same rhetorical situation prevails in the other two versions of Project 2, with the attendant benefits to the same intended reader. In both of these versions the student once again is asked to adapt information in one document to another rhetorical situation. Only here different composing activities are required. Instead of writing a document in class, within a 50- or 75-minute period, the student writer gets plenty of time to accomplish the task but different circumstances to adjust to. The first set of circumstances (see Appendix E) amounts to a simple way of helping students learn how to collaborate with others in making knowledge. After Project 1 is completed and collected, I provide each student with three or four reports by students in the same or similar disciplines. (Sometimes that requires me to reach into my files of student papers from previous semesters or to rely on colleagues who now assign the same first project as I do.) Then each student constructs a new report for a new reader, a report that incorporates the additional information into the "original" report. Students must decide which information to keep, delete, substitute, qualify, and emphasize; after all, part of the point once again is to teach students that content, arrangement, and style must be adjusted in response to every new rhetorical situation. But part of the point is also to mimic the conditions of technical employment, where documents are less often private and self-contained productions and more often public and socially constructed links in communicative chains that together create knowledge in a given setting. And of course through it all the student's knowledge of technical writing benefits: from reading other accounts about writers in similar disciplines, by experiencing and weighing other information about the writing he or she will do after graduation, each student becomes more authoritative about the composing practices of given communities.

From here it is a short step to the third version of this follow-up assignment (Appendix F). In this case students collaborate with colleagues not only in making knowledge, as in the previous version, but also in the act of composing a document for a reader whose needs direct the knowledge-making activity and who benefits directly from it. For this time the report is actually produced collaboratively: in the words of the assignment sheet, "all four members of [the] group must cooperate to produce one report. You will have to negotiate [with other members of the group] what goes into the report, how it will be organized, and how long the report will be; you will have to work together in drafting and revising (and typing) the report; and you will have to work out efficient and equitable work assignments." This is a challenging assignment, especially since I make it early in the course, before there has been much occasion for discussing collaboration or practicing it even informally (e.g., in peer review sessions). I do provide some advice about collaboration, enough to allow students to complete the work; but I also must admit that a major purpose of the assignment is to generate difficulties in collaboration that the rest of the course can address and ameliorate. The course addresses collaboration in many forms[5] and through many venues—through everything from informal editing pairs to full-fledged group projects—and suggests, only through reflection on all of them, successful modes of collaboration. Perhaps this is a fitting place to close this section because collaboration is another essential activity for teachers who are researchers and because collaboration is especially relevant to a section with the theme, "the student as research assistant."

THE STUDENT AS RHETORICAL ANALYST

A second set of assignments, one or more of which might easily be incorporated into any technical writing course, involves students in the act of rhetorical analysis. By examining carefully the rhetorical choices made by themselves and by other technical writers, students inevitably become more self-conscious rhetors who are better able to construct effective documents. This is a central aim of the assignment. But another result is that the students generate new knowledge about the dynamics of technical prose and about the conventions of specific discourse communities, new knowledge valuable to themselves and their teachers alike. Teachers who assign analyses of works in courses that consider belletristic literature know very well that students can create new knowledge about literary texts; technical writing teachers can do the same. When students for the benefit of their teachers analyze scientific and technical prose (what I call scientific and technical literature), those students in the process grow as writers and through their written products help their teachers become more knowledgeable about technical writing.

Rhetorical analysis is possible just about anytime, of course. I have provided one example (Appendix G) that illustrates just how easily rhetorical analysis can be incorporated into the most common and routine assignments, in this case the résumé assignment. In fact, there is probably no more common assignment in technical writing pedagogy than the one that asks students to develop a résumé and application letter for a specific employer. But even such a standard assignment can offer an occasion for students to reflect on their choices. My colleague Davida Charney (who first suggested this twist to me) and I have been able to get students to stand back from their work by requiring them to explain in a cover memo how their résumés and application letters are appropriate to given circumstances (i.e., to a given application situation for a given employer). Such a cover memo is useful in several respects, I have found. It forces students to become more self-conscious about the shape and substance of every detail of their work. (This is especially important in highly conventional forms like the résumé, when the temptation is for a student to be more an imitator than a rhetor.) But it also offers an opportunity for teachers to learn as well. When students comment in detail about the kinds of employers and positions their applications are designed for, teachers learn more about the world of technical work. They also, incidentally, gain insights into student motives and choices that make their comments on the applications more pointed and useful.[6]

A rhetorical analysis can also be useful if it is taken up as an interim part of a larger writing enterprise, if it is used to give writers perspective on documents in the process of development. That is the point of the analysis that I require in my course in connection with the students' production of a set of instructions or of a formal report or both. Like many technical writing teachers, I require an "instructions" assignment (it essentially asks students to teach an untutored potential user how to employ some tool) because it offers an occasion for students to practice certain things that I cover in my course— achieving multiple purposes, for example; partitioning; revealing arrangement; adapting to an audience; devising illustrations; and so forth. In order to make students more conscious of the rhetoric of instructions and thereby to help them improve their own instructions, I also assign a preliminary task, something along the lines of the "Project 5" reproduced in Appendices H through J.

The first version of this assignment, though it is the least "functional" in contributing insights into how to write a particular set of instructions, nevertheless invariably produces interesting and instructive results (see Appendix H). In keeping with the current interest in social perspectives on writing,[7] the assignment is designed to make students more conscious of how "setting" or "culture" influences writers and their writing. As the second paragraph of the assignment sheet explains, students are asked to compare two documents (a conventional car owner's manual and the counterculture classic *How to Keep Your Volkswagen*) and to explain differences in the documents in terms of the cultures that the documents emerge from.[8] How are writers and their texts shaped by the beliefs and expectations of other members of their community? How does a corporation's ethos affect the production of documents in that corporation? How do individuals "cope" with texts—as writers and as readers—within given institutions? How do texts "socialize" (or is the word "coerce"?) readers into adopting certain attitudes and roles? This assignment is meant to invite students to begin to consider such questions. It is calculated less to make students conscious of the particular rhetorical choices that pay off in a particular set of instructions and more to make students generally aware that setting indeed constrains all rhetorical decision making—and that writers (and readers) should attend to the implications of setting whenever they write (or read) in an organizational setting. This assignment is challenging because students have not often practiced this kind of analysis and because many institutional values are understated or implicit in documents. Nonetheless, I can say that students are often remarkably insightful about the political and social values contained in technical documents. Armed with the perspective that they gain through comparison, students are quite shrewd in uncovering the subtext of an auto manual or other kinds of instructions. And armed with the students' analyses, teachers themselves grow more prescient about the cultural values stated or implied or reflected in technical documents.

A second version of this assignment (Appendix I) is more immediately and obviously practical for students engaged in the process of writing instructions. Here again students are asked to compare two documents—"the instructions that come with two very similar products"—because comparison gives inexperienced analysts the perspective necessary for them to uncover rhetorical choices that might otherwise seem inevitable; as Lee Odell explains elsewhere in this volume, comparison creates "dissonance." And here once more students are asked to consider the implications for writing of "cultural" considerations—for instance, "How can you tell from the instructions that it's an IBM personal computer, not someone else's?" This time, however, students are also required to "assess the relative success of the two documents." As a direct consequence, students uncover rhetorical maneuvers that they find quite practical when they come to write a set of instructions themselves. They observe the pitfalls of certain choices; they learn how skilled writers attempt to accommodate readers with different and sometimes conflicting needs; through careful analysis they generate good ideas for their own instructions—and discard bad ones. And as a result of reading the analyses, teachers themselves grow wiser about ways to handle the exigencies contained in the genre called "instructions." In short, as a result of the assignment teacher and student can collaborate to generate new knowledge about technical writing.

The third version of this assignment is even more pointed toward the particular instructions that students will be writing. If the first version is a bit abstract and general in its applicability to the student's own instructions-in-progress, then this version is eminently concrete and practical. Let me first quickly set the context: sometimes I make my instructions assignment in connection with a specific need (a set of clearly inadequate instructions currently exists somewhere, usually in connection with the student's discipline; the student then takes on the job of rewriting those instructions). If my instructions assignment takes that form, then the analysis assignment can play right into it, as Appendix J notes: students "do a careful rhetorical analysis of the 'flawed' set of instructions that [their] project will replace" so that I can understand better why the student chose to revise those particular instructions, so that I can judge better the success of the revision—and so that the student is better prepared to do a successful revision. The attraction of this particular assignment is that it serves so well the instrumental nature of the instructions assignment. The liability is the other side of that same coin: because it so narrowly serves instrumental goals, the assignment obviates in large measure the opportunity for students to create new knowledge.

Nevertheless, a rhetorical analysis with an instrumental aim still serves the goals of a course in technical writing, and I am therefore quite comfortable with it—especially since my formal report assignment gives me another opportunity to direct students in the development of new knowledge. As it does in a great many technical writing courses, my formal report assignment generates toward the end of the semester a substantial piece of writing that I can use to determine how well students have mastered everything that is covered by the course. Students may meet the requirements of this task in several possible ways: (1) they can prepare a literature review in order to bring someone up to date on a given topic; (2) they can prepare a feasibility report for some organization; or (3) they can write a recommendation report that helps readers decide on a course of action. No matter which genre a student chooses, however, I first force him or her to reflect on the rhetoric of a particular species of the genre by requiring a rhetorical analysis of it.

The rhetorical analysis of the report essentially repeats the goals of the rhetorical analysis of instructions: students are supposed to become wiser rhetors, wiser report writers, as a result of their analysis of a text analogous to the one they are producing; and there is an occasion for students to generate new knowledge about reports that will benefit student and teacher alike. The first version of this assignment (Appendix K) resembles the third version of the rhetorical-analysis-of-instructions task that I just described. Each student finds a report that is a reasonable facsimile of the one he or she will be writing for my course, a report written for similar readers on a comparable problem of roughly the same scope; then the student assesses the strengths and weaknesses of that document. The benefit to the student is obvious; like the third analysis-of-instructions assignment, this one enables students to learn the conventions of a genre and ways of meeting readers' needs successfully within those conventions. Like the third analysis-of-instructions assignment, it is geared to the instrumental goals of the course, although the best student analyses do make their readers more knowledgeable about the dynamics of technical prose.

Less instrumental but more instructive, in my opinion, is the other version of this assignment (Appendix L). The assignment asks students to address the specific problem of a specific reader—one who wants to "know more about the way disciplines and institutions affect writing"—by means of another comparative analysis of two documents: one a report not in the student's discipline, and the other a report comparable to the one the student is in the process of writing. When the student reports on the results of that comparison, he or she usually has become more knowledgeable about reports; in that sense, this version of the assignment serves (if to a lesser extent) the same instrumental goals as the other version. In addition, however, the student also usually has grown more sensitive to the way institutions and disciplines shape discourse; in that sense, this version serves the same instructional goals as the first analysis-of-instructions assignment—namely, to deepen students' (and teachers') appreciation of the cultural and political dimensions of composing. The key to this assignment is giving students a genuine twofold opportunity— to generate new knowledge and to report that new knowledge to a reader (the teacher) who is anxious to learn. I very much like assignments like this one because of their versatility. They further the traditional instrumental goals of the course; they produce sample prose from students so that I can monitor and encourage each student's writing progress; and they amount to "real writing"—writing designed to influence the thinking and/or actions of the reader (in this case me). By making assignments like this, by cooperating with students in this way, I have grown substantially in my own knowledge of technical prose while at the same time helping my students master the techniques called for in technical writing.

Let me conclude with some qualifiers. Of course I recognize that I have barely begun to detail the ways that a technical writing course can become an inquiry, the ways that the course can make writing teachers and their students into original researchers. My emphasis has been on writing assignments, but I have mentioned only a few of the possibilities for using assignments to generate genuine inquiry. (Assigning journals and requiring detailed revisions strike me as two other possibilities, and I have even toyed with the idea of requiring students to write a parody as a way of alerting them to the highly conventional yet explicitly rhetorical nature of writing in scientific and techni- cal disciplines.) And I certainly do not want to leave the impression that making a course into an inquiry involves only the assignments, or that a writing course amounts only to a series of assignments.

For there are many other ways to encourage inquiry in the technical writing classroom. The readings in the course, to take an obvious example, can be used to encourage a critical attitude toward technical documents. I have used Gould's *The Mismeasure of Man* in an advanced technical writing course to sensitize students to the cultural, political, and rhetorical biases that inevitably influence the making of knowledge and the conduct of business in any field; Geertz's *The Anthropologist as Author* or Latour and Woolgar's *Laboratory Life* could be used to the same end with equally advanced students. Or activities like the ones described by Art Young elsewhere in this book can be used to transform a merely instrumental course into one that involves inquiry as well. Teachers can also turn their class discussions of sample scientific and technical documents into occasions for inquiry: instead of forever looking at documents for what is "effective" or "ineffective" about them (though there is certainly a place for that), simply ask broader, less directive, less prescriptive questions designed to get at descriptions of how specific documents work. Simply encourage, on a daily basis, a habit of mind alert to what students can teach and an attitude toward students that shows that they are expected to teach as much as to learn. And then teach you they will.

Appendix A
The Undergraduate Technical Writing Course at Penn State

English 202C
Schematic Overview

Writing Principles	Possible Assignments
(fixed from section to section)	(variable with each instructor)
Planning: the rhetorical situation	Interview of a professional
The writing process at work: special resources and constraints; collaboration	Collaborative report
Purpose: purpose statements for solicited and unsolicited documents; simple and multiple (and conflicting) aims	Comparison (in-class?) of writing at school and at work
Invention: interviewing techniques; exploring a subject (review the "modes": description, definition, comparison, etc.); considering audience: homogeneous, heterogeneous, and multiple	Proposal
Invention (continued): genre constraints; audience analysis continued (knowledge, attitudes, needs/expectations)	Résumé and application letter
Arrangement: overall patterns and general principles; segments and paragraph blocks	Description of mechanism or instructions
Revealing arrangement: headings, forecasting, layout, transitions, numerical and alphabetical systems	
Review of paragraph principles: topic sentences, main-idea emphasis, transitions	Rhetorical analysis of instructions
Invention (continued): principles of argument and persuasion; library research tools; documentation; reusing previous work	Letter of inquiry
Visuals: page format (white space, significant placement of text and visual elements)	Exercise on visuals
Graphics: tables, graphs, charts, illustrations, labeling	
Writing abstracts and summaries	Abstract or summary (in-class?)
Revision principles	Portfolio

Writing Principles (fixed from section to section)	**Possible Assignments** (variable with each instructor)
Sentencing principles: passive and active voice, nominalizations, noun strings, common schemes and tropes, old/new information, transitions	Progress report
Voice and tone	User-test report
Evaluation tactics	Peer review
Conventions of correspondence, memos, résumés, proposals, instructions, and various kinds of reports	Article for readers outside discipline
Kinds of reports: literature reviews, recommendation reports, feasibility studies. Two-part structure to meet the needs of complex audiences: forewords, summaries, tables of contents; appendices; introductions and conclusions; report bodies.	Formal report or manual Rhetorical analysis of report

Appendix B
Assignment Sheet for Project 1:
Writing in Your Profession

For your first project, interview a member of a profession you wish to join and report to me on the writing you are likely to do on the job. The purpose of the assignment is to reinforce what you have learned so far about the writing process, to introduce you to the kind of writing you will do outside of college, and to give you practice in assessing the rhetorical context of a piece of writing.

RHETORICAL CONTEXT

As a teacher of technical writing, I am interested in learning about how people write on the job. In particular, I want to know how important writing will be to you in your professional life, what kinds of writing you might be asked to do, and how people in your profession go about their writing tasks. However, I don't know very much about the specifics of any particular position in your profession. Therefore, your job is to present "insider" information to an interested "outsider." You must carefully select background information, details, and vocabulary that I will understand and find appropriate. You must also organize your report clearly so that I will find it easy to follow.

REQUIREMENTS FOR THE INTERVIEW

1. The person you choose to interview must be a professional already on the job or recently retired. The person may be a relative or friend, a former employer, or someone you have never met before. Ideally, this person holds a job similar to one you would like to hold someday, preferably one you might reasonably hope to have within the next ten years.

2. *THE PERSON MAY NOT LIVE WITHIN A 50-MILE RADIUS OF STATE COLLEGE* unless you can prove that you have lived in State College your whole life. Obviously you may conduct the interview either in person or on the telephone. During class, we will discuss strategies of interviewing that should help you complete this part of the project.

REQUIREMENTS FOR THE REPORT

When evaluating your project, I will use the general criteria described in the course syllabus and the following specific requirements for this project:

1. You must identify the interviewee clearly, including his or her role in the organization. What are his or her major responsibilities?
2. You must present findings on at least the following topics:
   a. The *amount* and *kinds* of writing the interviewee does on the job
   b. The range of rhetorical situations the interviewee addresses (i.e., audiences and purposes)
   c. An overall evaluation of the role of writing in his or her job; if possible, extend your evaluation to the profession as a whole
3. You must use specific examples and instances to document your analysis.
4. You must write your report in the form of a memo addressed to me, your instructor. The memo must be no more than 1,500 words long.

While you should explore each topic listed above in your interview, you may find that one area turns out to be particularly fruitful. You may choose to concentrate on that topic in your report, as long as you briefly address the others. For example, you may report on the writing process the interviewee employed in producing one particularly important document, perhaps in collaboration with others. Or you may report on how the interviewee's writing habits have changed over time. Just remember to address my need for information in some substantial way.

Appendix C
Assignment Sheet for Project 1:
The Writing Process in Your Profession

There are two main purposes for your first assignment: to reinforce what you have learned so far this semester about the writing process; and to give you practice in assessing the rhetorical context of a piece of writing. (A secondary purpose is to introduce you to the kind of writing you might be doing after you graduate.)

YOUR PROBLEM

As you know, your instructor is particularly interested in how people write on the job. I want to know how people conceive of rhetorical situations before they write; where they get the information that goes into their writing; how they go about organizing their material; how they transcribe what they write; and when and how—and how much—they revise. How do engineers and scientists and managers cooperate with their coworkers when they write? Moreover, how does their writing process change when *what* they write changes, or when time is short, or when the document is routine or especially important or unimportant? How have their habits changed over the years? What little "tricks" or idiosyncracies do they have? And so on.

Your job is to help your instructor out. First, locate someone who has a job like you might have in the next five years; that person might be a relative, friend, or professional acquaintance. *That person may not reside within a 50-mile radius of State College*, unless you can prove that you have lived in State College your whole life.

Finally, in a short report (it may not exceed 1,500 words) give me the information I am interested in. Obviously you will not be able to give me all the information I seek, so concentrate on one or two particular questions or documents. Please be as detailed and complete as possible. And be sure to set the stage for the description: explain who you observed, what the document was, what its aim and audience were, and what (if anything) "constrained" the writing (e.g., time, resources, etc.). You may interview me during class to find out what I particularly hope to learn from you in your report.

Appendix D
Assignment Sheet for Project 2:
Informal Correspondence (in class)

The purpose of this assignment is to begin teaching you three things: how to operate under time constraints, how to adapt information in one communication to another assignment, and how an audience affects a writing task. In addition, I want you to practice what I've been preaching so far in the course about purpose and audience.

YOUR PROBLEM

Imagine (or remember) that you have a friend who has just decided to major in your discipline (and who hasn't yet taken English 202C). Your friend doesn't know very well what people who work in your field do each day on the job; especially is your friend rather naive about the way people write at work and the importance of writing on the job.

Your job is to write a letter to your friend that gives him or her an idea of what to expect after graduation. Answer this question for your friend: how does *what* or *how* you write at school compare to *what* or *how* professionals in your field write at work? In answering, feel free to call upon the same information you used in Project 1 and upon any other information you learned in the interview. And in composing your letter, remember to let your purpose and audience and time constraints shape all the decisions you make about format, length, arrangement, content, and style.

Appendix E
Assignment Sheet for Project 2:
Informal Correspondence

The purpose of this assignment is to begin teaching you two things—how to adapt information in one communication to another assignment, and how to adapt information to an audience.

YOUR PROBLEM

Imagine (or remember) that you have a friend who has just decided to major in your discipline (and who hasn't yet taken English 202C). Your friend doesn't know very well what people who work in your field do each day on the job; especially is your friend rather naive about the way people write at work and the importance of writing on the job.

Your job is to write a letter to your friend that gives him or her an idea of what to expect after graduation. Answer this question for your friend: how does *what* or *how* you write at school compare to *what* or *how* professionals in your field write at work? In answering, feel free to call upon the same information you used in Project 1 and upon any information you learned in the interview. In addition, make use of the information recently collected on this topic by the classmates whose reports I will provide for you. And in composing your letter, remember to let your purpose and audience shape all the decisions you make about format, length, arrangement, content, and style.

Appendix F
Assignment Sheet for Project 2:
Collaborative Report

The purpose of this assignment is to begin teaching you three things: how to adapt information in one communication to another assignment, how to adapt information to an audience, and how to collaborate with other writers.

YOUR PROBLEM

Your task is *precisely* the same one as your first project: to inform me about the writing you will be doing on the job. Address and solve the same problem you addressed earlier.

There are two significant differences, however. First, you will benefit not only from the research you did on your first project but also from the research done by three of your classmates whose reports I will provide for you. In other words, you must look at all the information gathered by all four researchers, and decide which information should be presented in this new report.

Second, you must produce your report collaboratively; that is, all four members of your group must cooperate to produce one report. You will have to negotiate among yourselves what goes into the report, how it will be organized, and how long the report will be; you will have to work together in drafting and revising (and typing) the report; and you will have to work out efficient and equitable work assignments. (As you can see from the syllabus, I will have something to say in today's class and in our next one about how to collaborate effectively.)

Appendix G
Assignment Sheet for Project 3:
Job Application Package

Most people obtain jobs through a multistage process. To obtain a job, you must first research the types of jobs you are qualified for and the types of employer you would like to work for. Then you must convince specific employers to consider you for a job. These days, most employers have too many applicants per job to interview each one personally. These employers sort through job application packages (résumés and cover letters) to decide which applicants to consider further. So your first communication with your future employer is likely to be in writing and must persuade him or her to continue the conversation.

For this assignment, you will write two job applications that are addressed to different possible employers and that apply for two different types of jobs. (Juniors may apply for summer work, for internships, or for scholarships or other awards.) Each application will include two parts: (1) a cover letter addressed to the employer that introduces yourself and highlights particularly relevant aspects of your experience, and (2) a résumé. In addition, you will turn in a cover memo addressed to me that overviews the two jobs, reviews what you know about these particular employers, and describes how you have adapted your applications to meet these two different rhetorical situations.

MEMO

Write a brief memo (no more than three pages, double-spaced), addressed to me. For each of the two jobs, the memo must contain a separate job description and audience analysis. The memo must also include a rhetorical analysis, highlighting how you adapted your résumé and cover letter to meet the different requirements for these two jobs.

RÉSUMÉS

Selection of Material: The heading of your résumés should state your name, address, telephone number, and professional objective. The body of your résumés should provide your reader with evidence that you would make a capable, responsible, and pleasant employee.

Arrangement of Material: The facts in the body of your résumés should be ordered from most to least important—from your reader's point of view.

Presentation of Material: Your résumés should neatly present your facts in an appropriate format for résumés, and your prose should present your facts in a brief but easily understandable manner. Your format can be "traditional" or "innovative," depending on what would best serve your and your reader's interests.

LETTER OF APPLICATION

Selection of material: The opening of your letter should establish a personal relationship between you and your reader in which your reader knows who you are, what you want, and why you are writing. The body of your letter should explain the special relevance of the facts presented in your résumé to the particular job you want your reader to help you get. Your closing should prompt your reader to make some response to your correspondence.

Arrangement of Material: The material in the body of your letter should be ordered in some clearly obvious way (e.g., around your training and experience, or around what the job requires). Paragraphs should move from the general to the particular.

Presentation of Material: Your letter should neatly present your facts in a conventional format for business correspondence, and it should present the facts in a brief but readily understandable manner. Also, your letter should support all of your generalizations with specific evidence. Cover letters are difficult to write because they aim at somewhat conflicting goals. On the one hand, you want to make a good first impression. So you want to sound polite and fairly formal. On the other hand, you want to stand out from the crowd—otherwise, why should the employer hire you rather than any of the other applicants? The best policy is probably to talk to your reader as directly and naturally as possible. Avoid hype.

Appendix H
Assignment Sheet for Project 5:
Rhetorical Analysis

To prepare you better for Project 6 (Instructions), I want you to do a rhetorical analysis of a set of instructions. The assignment is designed to make you (and me) more sensitive to the range of rhetorical and "cultural" considerations involved in a given set of instructions. To put it another way, the assignment is designed to make you more aware of the various rhetorical and "political" dimensions of a set of instructions, so that you will be able to be more sensitive to those dimensions when you write your own instructions. (The assignment is also designed to give you a chance to educate me, as well.)

YOUR JOB

Compare John Muir and Tosh Gregg's *How to Keep Your Volkswagen* (on reserve in Pattee Library) with a *specific* "conventional" owner's manual that comes with a car (yours or a friend's). The differences in the two documents will be many—some of them readily apparent, some of them subtle. I want you to try to answer this question: to what extent are those differences the result of their authors' social situation? In other words, consider the fact that the Volkswagen manual was written (and published) by "independent" writers while the other owner's manual was produced by document designers who work for an auto manufacturer: how does that fact manifest itself in the two finished products?

Answer that question in a memo to me. Your job is to educate me in the "cultural" and "institutional" constraints that affect writers' choices, with specific reference to the case in question. Your memo should be no more than 1,500 words. Be sure you practice what I've been preaching in class recently: organize carefully, with your reader in mind; reveal your organization; and practice the principles of argument we've been considering.

Appendix I
Assignment Sheet for Project 5:
Rhetorical Analysis

To prepare you better for Project 6 (Instructions), I want you to do a rhetorical analysis of a set of instructions. The assignment is designed to make you (and me) more sensitive to the range of rhetorical and "cultural" considerations involved in a given set of instructions. To put it another way, the assignment is designed to make you more aware of the various rhetorical and "political" dimensions of a set of instructions, so that you will be able to be more sensitive to those dimensions when you write your own instructions. (The assignment is also designed to give you a chance to educate me, as well.)

YOUR JOB

Compare the instructions that come with two very similar products made by two different companies (e.g., two personal computers with the same capabilities, or two microwave ovens, or two similar lawn mowers, or two college catalogs, or two similar pieces of lab equipment, etc.). Do two things— assess the relative "success" of the two documents (which is better at empowering its readers? what are the relative merits of each?); and consider how each document reflects the relative merits of each?); and consider how each document reflects the "cultural" values of the organization that produced it (for instance, how can you tell from the instructions that it's an IBM PC, not someone else's?). Then, in a memo of no more than 1,500 words, explain to me what you've found. Be sure to use the memo to practice what you've learned about organization, revealing organization, and argument. Please append to your memo the sets of instructions that you discuss; I'll return them when I return your memo.

Essentially it all comes down to this: what are the differences in the two sets of instructions, and how can you explain the differences? Some differences are likely to be in the quality of the instructions or in the authors' approach to them; other differences are likely to reflect on the organizations that produced the instructions. Your job is to write a memo that makes me understand in a sophisticated way the instructions you discuss.

Appendix J
Assignment Sheet for Project 5:
Rhetorical Analysis

To prepare you better for Project 6 (Instructions), I want you to do a rhetorical analysis of a set of instructions. The assignment is designed to make you (and me) more sensitive to the range of rhetorical and "cultural" considerations involved in a given set of instructions. To put it another way, the assignment is designed to make you more aware of the various rhetorical and "political" dimensions of a set of instructions, so that you will be able to be more sensitive to those dimensions when you write your own instructions. (The assignment is also designed to give you a chance to educate me, as well.)

YOUR JOB

Do a careful rhetorical analysis of the "flawed" set of instructions that your Project 6 will replace. Your job is to assess the relative strengths and weaknesses of the document in question. Be sure to make a convincing case for your assessment: if you think the document has weaknesses, support your contentions by discussing the text in detail and/or by documenting the problems (confusion, mistakes, wasted time and effort, etc.) created by the document; if you think the document has strengths, defend that assessment as well with hard evidence.

Then explain what you find to me in a memo of no more than 1,500 words. Your job is to enable me to understand better why you chose the task for Project 6 that you did choose and to give me the background necessary for me to judge your success in Project 6. In your final paragraph or two, I want you to speculate about the possible *causes* of the shortcomings in the document in question: Was it the author's failure to consider all his or her readers? Was it a failure to understand the task in all its complexity? Did the writer misjudge the capabilities of his or her readers? Are there "cultural" or "institutional" explanations for the weaknesses? Or what? Otherwise, write the memo as you see fit—remembering, of course, to use this occasion to practice what we're now emphasizing in class: organization, revealing of organization, and argument. And remember to append to your report the document in question so that I can see what you're talking about.

Appendix K
Assignment Sheet for Project 7:
Rhetorical Analysis

This project is designed to help you write a better report for Project 8 (because you understand better the rhetorical choices involved in a report)—and to help me better understand technical reports as well.

THE PROBLEM

Your teacher (that's me) understands some things about scientific and technical writing, but certainly not everything. In particular, I am interested in knowing more about the way audiences affect writing that is directed to them. Will you help me by explaining how a particular report was adapted to a specific audience in your field?

YOUR JOB

Find a report comparable to the one you will write for this course—as comparable as possible. That report should address a problem similar to the one you are addressing, and it should have a similar scope; if you are writing your own report from the perspective of a particular company or institution or discipline, simply choose a report produced by that company or institution or discipline. (I'll discuss easy ways of finding such reports in our next class.)

Your job is to comment on that report. Answer this question: how is the report in question suited (or unsuited) to the needs of its reader(s)? To put the question another way, how (and how well) has the author of the report adapted the presentation to the needs of his or her reader(s)? (To stimulate your thinking, consider this question: how would the report be different if it had been directed to a different audience or audiences?) If possible, you might wish to interview the author of the report to get a feel for the goals of the report and for how (and how well) the document is directed to its readers; but most of your ideas should emerge from a careful analysis of the document, an analysis like the ones we carry out in class.

Once you've answered the question satisfactorily, tell me the answer in a short report of *no more than 1,500 words*. Remember, as you write, what you are learning in class about reports; and remember to use the occasion as well to practice the sentencing techniques we've been working on for the past few weeks. Please append the report you are discussing to your memo so that I can see what you're talking about; I'll return the report with your graded analysis.

Appendix L
Assignment Sheet for Project 7:
Rhetorical Analysis

This project is designed to help you write a better report for Project 8 (because you understand better the rhetorical choices involved in a report)—and to help me better understand technical reports as well.

THE PROBLEM

Your teacher (that's me) understands some things about scientific and technical writing, but certainly not everything. In particular, I am interested in knowing more about the way *disciplines* and *institutions* affect the writing that emerges from them. Will you help me by explaining how a particular report is the product of a particular community?

YOUR JOB

Find two reports: one from any source *not* in your discipline, and the other a report comparable to the one you will write for this course—as comparable as possible. The second report should address a problem similar to the one you are addressing, and it should have a similar scope; if you are writing your own report from the perspective of a particular company or institution or discipline, simply choose a report produced by that company or institution or discipline. (I'll discuss easy ways of finding such reports in our next class.)

Your job is to comment on the second report, the one like the report you'll be writing. Answer this question: how is the report in question a product of its particular *institution* and *discipline*? (To stimulate your thinking, consider this question: how would the report be different if it had been produced by a writer in a different discipline or institution? The other report you've collected can suggest alternatives to you, and you can also interview the writers involved, if they are available. Otherwise, stick to a careful analysis of the report itself.)

Once you've answered the question satisfactorily, tell me the answer in a short report of *no more than 1,500 words*. Remember, as you write, what you are learning in class about reports; and remember to use the occasion as well to practice the sentencing techniques we've been working on for the past few weeks.

NOTES

1. Outlines of a history of technical writing instruction in America have been delineated by Robert C. Connors and Rhonda C. Grego. Louise Dunlap has begun the job of explaining how that history is tied to the "scientific management" approach to large manufacturing concerns. On the relationship between technology and technological language, see Carolyn Miller.

2. For a fine introductory overview of epistemic rhetoric, see Michael Leff; for an overview of how meaning is negotiated in communities, see Kenneth Bruffee; for an introduction to the social and rhetorical nature of rhetoric in science and technology, see Charles Bazerman.

3. The initial idea for this assignment, as far as I can remember, was contained in suggestions found in the Document Design Center's *Writing in the Professions*, edited by Dixie Goswami et al. See especially the suggestions for conducting case studies on pp. 26–29; my first assignments are elaborations, particularizations, and extensions of those suggestions.

4. Some local constraints in these assignments probably need to be explained. First, my students are prohibited from interviewing people in the State College area in order to protect the time of professionals in our small town. Since many teachers in our program now use this assignment, local engineering firms (for instance) would be inundated with calls and written requests for interviews. Consequently, students are encouraged to gather information outside the university community. Because our fall semester begins late in August, the Labor Day holiday weekend gives most students an occasion to gather information outside State College. I have also resorted to other ruses (e.g., group interviews) to make it practical for students to complete the assignment satisfactorily; teachers who have the good sense to teach at a smaller institution or in a larger city would have an easier time making this assignment without alienating their colleagues in the technical professions.

5. A useful taxonomy for collaboration is contained in Stephen Witte's unpublished manuscript, "Some Contexts for Understanding Written Literacy."

6. The same kind of student reflection on completed documents can be accomplished more informally, I recognize. For example, before they ask students to turn in any writing assignment, many teachers require students to do an informal handwritten self-analysis of their success in that particular task. I certainly do not intend to discourage that kind of practice; my only point is that making that activity more formal can make it even more useful.

7. For an introduction to this perspective, see Lester Faigley.

8. This assignment was conceived in part as a result of conversations with my colleague Jeff Purvis. For other suggestions on rhetorical analysis assignments suited to writing in particular disciplines, see Kate Ronald.

THE WRITING TEACHER
IN THE LITERATURE
CLASSROOM

16

The Construction of Meaning: Practicing What We Preach

LEE ODELL

Some time ago, a colleague described to me a conversation he had just had with a student in his undergraduate writing course. The student had asked exactly what he (the student) would need to do in order to get A's on all the essays that would be assigned during the rest of the semester. My colleague tried to explain to the student that his question was not readily answerable. Thereupon, my colleague told me, "The kid looked at me as though I was either a fool or a knave. A fool, because I couldn't answer an obviously important question about my discipline. Or a knave, because I knew the answer and just wouldn't tell him."

The predicament is, surely, familiar enough. Students come to us expecting not just an answer but *the* answer to questions that are complex in ways that they don't even imagine. We are not helpless in these cases. We can say things that can help students deal intelligently with complexity. But, unless we are dealing with a very well-defined question, we assume that the answer does not lie within one individual; rather it comes to exist only as the result of, to borrow Louise Rosenblatt's term, a transaction between a particular learner, a subject matter, and other learners (a group that may or may not include us). When we do not succumb to the flattery of having our opinions asked, we tell students they will have to construct their own answers, their own meaning.

One reason we do this is that we are coming to see all the language arts—reading, writing, talking, listening—as meaning-creating activities. For some time now, we have recognized that writing and talking are more than ways of expressing what people already have on their minds; they are ways of generating ideas and discovering what one thinks or feels or values. More recently we have begun to see that reading and listening are not simply

This chapter is based on work done for a three-year study sponsored by the Sid W. Richardson Foundation.

processes of receiving a message that is already present in a written or spoken text; rather they are processes of constructing a message, one that is based partly on the text at hand and partly on the reader/listener's prior experiences, knowledge of other texts, purposes for reading, and so on.

At about the same time we have begun to come to this view of the language arts, we have also been developing classroom procedures that seem uniquely suited to our goal of helping students engage in the construction of meaning. We have begun to ask students to keep journals or learning logs as a way of reflecting upon experience and stimulating thought; we are learning how to show students that the processes of drafting and revising can lead a writer to think about things in ways that might not otherwise be possible; and we are asking students to work in small groups, either to begin or to refine their thinking about a particular subject.

None of these teaching procedures works perfectly all the time. But enough of them work enough of the time for us to think we may have something valuable here. On a good day, at least, something seems to be happening. But what is it? What's going on in those discussion groups, learning logs, and essays? How can we describe the meaning-making that is present in (or significantly absent from) students' work? What are students doing that's useful, that will stand them in good stead once they leave our classes? What are they doing that's not so useful?

When it comes to answering these questions, we find ourselves in pretty much the same boat we like our students to be in. There is no single, fore-ordained, correct answer. There can't be. Consequently, we have to draw on all our resources—prior experiences, theory, values, personal observation—to make our own sense of a complex experience (in this case, the writing, talking, and thinking of our students) without being able to rely on someone else for the correct answer, the one infallible interpretation of what is happening. We must come to our own conclusions, we must make our own meaning. We must practice what we preach.

For many, this is a terribly disconcerting thought, if only because it's almost certain that our prior education has not prepared us to do this sort of work. From our own experience as students, we have probably learned that teaching is in large measure a process of imparting information. If we have been fortunate, perhaps there were times when we were genuinely engaged in a process of inquiry and were shown how to construct our own meaning on a topic that mattered to us. I would like to believe that this sort of experience is the rule rather than the exception, but it doesn't seem to be—at least not in my experience as a student or as someone who attends classes and reads student papers in a number of different disciplines at grade levels ranging from second grade through graduate school. Typically, the values conveyed through those classes can be represented by one professor's comment on a student essay: "I can almost hear myself talking in this essay. It's nice to know someone was listening. A + ." The self-incrimination is rarely so blatant. But frequently the assumption seems to be that the teacher's primary job is to impart information and the student's job is to receive that information, distorting it as little as possible in the process.

Even when our teachers have set out to teach us how to, as the phrase goes, "think for ourselves," there is a good chance they have subverted their own efforts. As Robert Sternberg and Marie Martin have shown, when teachers and textbooks purport to teach "critical thinking," it is likely that work in this area will be relegated to moments when there is extra class time to be filled; or it will not be integrated into the study of the subject matter at hand; or the teacher will conduct the class session in ways that preempt students' thinking for themselves. An example of this last point: a calculus teacher begins class by putting a complicated problem on the overhead projector and asking students not to give the answer to the problem but rather to decide upon the most logical point at which to attack the problem. This would seem to be an excellent way to engage students in a process of inquiry and help them develop problem-solving strategies that would let them become independent learners. Unfortunately, this is not what happens. Having posed the question, the teacher proceeds to answer it, not only doing the work for the students but excluding them from the process of inquiry and increasing rather than reducing their dependence on the teacher.

Unfortunately, I suspect that all these difficulties are compounded by our professional training as teachers. Typically this training has focused our attention on what teachers do when they plan a class, put together a lecture, or design a classroom activity. But we have not been asked to focus on what students do. We have not been taught how to describe and learn from our students' attempts to construct their own meaning. Consequently, we find ourselves in a paradoxical situation: current theory and practice emphasize the processes of learning, but we find ourselves ill-prepared to understand students' work with those processes. We have difficulty in saying where students are doing well, where they are having trouble, and what they need to do in order to improve.

Given our experience as students and our training as teachers, this difficulty is substantial. But it is not insurmountable. We can, in fact, learn how to learn from our students. But to do so, we will need to make a couple of basic assumptions. The first is that the processes of meaning-making are not completely random or mysterious. Granted, these processes are complex, they occur with great speed, and their outcome is often unpredictable. Nonetheless, there are usually methods in this madness. More specifically: when we look at students working in small groups, we can begin to see patterns of interaction, types of interpersonal behavior that can enhance or hinder students' collaborative efforts to construct meaning. Similarly, whether we are listening to a discussion or reading a piece of student writing, we can draw some conclusions about the mind at work; we can find evidence of thinking processes that are, at least in part, conscious, knowable, and learnable.

The second assumption is that our efforts to understand students' meaning-making must be grounded in theory and research. This is not to suggest that we should accept any one view of the processes of thinking and interacting. Most likely, we will synthesize a number of such views and then modify that synthesis as we learn more about a particular group of students. But these views do exist. At the very least, they can help us see more clearly what we do not believe to be true about the processes of thinking and interacting. At best, they can provide a carefully reasoned perspective from which we can examine and perhaps revise our own notions about thinking.

In the remainder of this chapter I will show that these assumptions can guide our efforts to learn from students. After presenting a synthesis of some current work on thinking and interacting, I will use it in analyzing some students' work and making recommendations for teaching. Although I will look very specifically at one group of students who are talking and writing about the novel *Wuthering Heights*, my primary concern is not to analyze and improve the meaning-making processes of these students, but to illustrate a meaning-making process that teachers must go through, a process of learning from students and using what we learn to help students grow.

SYNTHESIZING THEORY AND RESEARCH

Thinking

In light of current theory and research, this topic may seem a bit intimidating. We have to acknowledge that some aspects of the thinking process may never be knowable. And those aspects that are knowable have been described in a great variety of ways. Thus one review of work on thinking has produced a list of over fifty terms pertaining to such familiar topics as problem solving, decision making, inductive thinking, and so on (Gubbins, cited in Sternberg, p. 52). We can reduce this list substantially if we set up one basic criterion: any terminology we use must let us describe students' work in ways that are useful to both teachers and students. That is, our descriptions must let teachers identify students' strengths and weaknesses and determine the kinds of experiences students will need if they are to improve. Further, these descriptions must have heuristic value for students; they must help students see what conscious actions they might take in order to direct the process of inquiry. With this criterion in mind, I want to concentrate on two types of intellectual activities. By no means do these two types of activities include all the conscious activity that goes on when we think. But they do allow us to account for much of what is going on in the student talk and writing analyzed later in this chapter. From my discussion, it will be obvious that I have drawn heavily from a number of sources, most notably from the work of Leon Festinger, Jean Piaget, Robert Sternberg, and Peter Elbow.

The first basic activity is *acknowledging dissonance*. We feel dissonance when there is some disparity between what we expect and what we encounter, when there is some gap in our understanding of the world, when we realize that a particular fact or value or belief is incompatible with some other. Most often dissonance is expressed as a question, a disagreement, a criticism, a feeling of uncertainty. Or we may not acknowledge the dissonance directly; instead we might imply that something is wrong by making a negative value judgment or proposing changes in our own or someone else's behavior. For some scholars (e.g., Jean Piaget and Leon Festinger) an awareness of dissonance is the motivation for all human activity, whether cognitive, affective, or physical.

The second basic activity, *considering alternatives*, subsumes at least three slightly different activities. The first is represented by terms such as "formulating alternative solutions," "generating multiple ideas," and "generating different ideas" (Gubbins, cited in Sternberg). For many of us, the most familiar form of this activity may be brainstorming: we try to think of as many possibilities—and as many different kinds of possibilities—as we can. Thinking of possibilities necessarily entails a second sort of activity, that of assessing the possibilities we come up with; we try to think of facts or ideas that will either refute or support a claim, that will justify or repudiate a way of expressing or organizing our ideas. And finally, considering alternatives entails what philosopher Richard Paul has called "dialogical thinking," considering perspectives that differ from our own (cited in Sternberg). Inevitably, we approach any subject from our own perspective. But we can at least enlarge that perspective. When we are inclined to play what Peter Elbow calls the "doubting game," we can try to play the "believing game"; we can try to empathize with our readers, anticipating points where readers may disagree or become confused; we can try to consider an event from the perspective of various people who participate in that event.

Interacting

When we look for ways to describe students' interaction, we do not find quite as many options as there are for labeling thinking. But there is some useful work to draw on. Robert Bales, for example, has developed very carefully tested procedures for what he refers to as "interaction analysis." Sarah Freedman has explored ways linguists' notions of "turn-taking" might help us account for what goes on in student-teacher writing conferences. And Anne Gere has shown how statements in a small group discussion might be categorized as to their topic and function.

In deciding how we will proceed with our analysis, we have to bear in mind what we want to avoid and what we hope to accomplish through small group discussions. Surely we don't want these discussions to become highly adversarial situations where participants, engaging exclusively in Elbow's "doubting game," focus solely on the inadequacies of what others say or write. Instead, these discussions have to be occasions where people seriously consider perspectives that may differ from their own. Ultimately, participants in the discussion may decide to modify or reject these perspectives. But they must at least know what those perspectives are—their strengths as well as their weaknesses.

In order to do this, they must, among other things, listen to each other. They must attend thoughtfully to what others say or write. On a relatively simple level, this means that we want students to:

- Avoid interruptions
- Paraphrase/reiterate what someone says, especially to make sure that they've understood correctly
- Answer each other's questions, respond to requests, follow suggestions

We also need to determine whether students are interacting in more sophisticated ways that allow the dialogical thinking I mentioned earlier. We want students to be able to:

- Develop someone else's statement by
  asking for clarification or elaboration
  elaborating on or corroborating what someone else has said
  drawing a conclusion based on what someone else has said
- Limit or clarify the point(s) on which they disagree with another group member
- Agree/find common ground, especially when inclined to disagree
- Consider modifying their own position

ANALYZING STUDENTS' WORK

Even if we have some clear definitions of *thinking* and *interacting*, any attempt to analyze students' work immediately runs into a couple of problems. For one thing, we have to account not only for what our students are doing but also for what we are doing. If we want to understand our students' thinking, we must also be aware of our own thinking. Furthermore, it sometimes seems that we must understand everything all at once. To assess what is going on in, for example, a small group discussion, we must also understand what's going on in students' journal writing, in the drafts of their essays, in their revisions, and in whole-class discussions. No matter where we decide to begin our analysis, it's likely that we'll wish we had previously analyzed something else. But we must begin somewhere.

Whole-Class Discussion

At the risk of seeming arbitrary, I want to begin my analysis with an excerpt from a class discussion that took place after students had finished reading *Wuthering Heights* but before they wrote their essays on the novel. In the excerpt below, students consider the causes of Heathcliff's actions at the end of the novel.

MANASA: Whose fault was it? Was it Heathcliff's fault that he turned out the way he did, or was it . . .

MARC: It was the environment.

MANASA: The environment.

DOUG: No, his personality.

MARC: His personality which developed due to his being at Wuthering Heights.

DOUG: Are you saying people have no previous characteristics?

MARC: Yes, they do. When you're a little kid and someone takes you to another place, you're most likely going to develop a personality there.

ADAM: A child develops his personality before the age of six.

MARC: I . . . the whole thing was based on jealousy.

DENNIS: I think he was . . . I think he was jealous. The whole thing . . . if he wasn't jealous, he wouldn't love nor would he hate.

TAMMY: It was brought on by his environment that he was jealous. [Rumble of class]

DENNIS: Why? Could he not love anyone else? He fell in love with Isabella later.

CLASS: No! No! [Confusion]

DENNIS: OK, he didn't fall in love with her, but he married her later.

TAMMY: That was . . .

DENNIS: Wait a minute. I'm saying . . . I'm saying . . . no, I'm saying that he's jealous because . . . because he finds that everybody is liking the person that he likes.

TAMMY: So it's his environment that is influencing his life. If there wasn't someone making him jealous, he wouldn't *be* jealous.

CLASS: Ooooh!

As students think about the cause-effect relationships that might explain Heathcliff's behavior, they become aware of a good bit of dissonance. They hear three conflicting views: Tammy and Marc claim that Heathcliff's behavior is caused by his environment, specifically by his experiences at Wuthering Heights; Doug sees Heathcliff's "personality" as the cause; and Marc and Dennis attribute his actions to "jealousy." Furthermore, there is a certain amount of listening. Directly or indirectly, all the students respond to Manasa's question, "Whose fault was it?" Doug and Dennis ask what might be construed as questions of clarification ("Are you saying people have no previous characteristics?" and "Why? Could he not love anyone else?"). At one point Dennis slightly modifies his position ("OK," he concedes, "he didn't fall in love with her . . ."). And Marc and Tammy base a couple of their statements on a preceding comment. In response to Doug's claim about personality causing Heathcliff's actions, Marc says, "His personality which developed due to his being at Wuthering Heights." When Dennis remarks that Heathcliff is "jealous because . . . because he finds that everybody is liking the person that he likes," Tammy uses Dennis's statement as a basis for her conclusion: "So it's his environment that is influencing his life. If there wasn't someone making him jealous, he wouldn't *be* jealous."

The last comment epitomizes not only the strengths of this discussion but also some of its weaknesses. Tammy doesn't really seem to be listening to Dennis's statement. She doesn't try to think of ways in which it might be a legitimate claim; rather, she simply uses it as a starting point for expressing her own contradictory view. Something like this also happens in Marc's comment about "personality," mentioned earlier. Furthermore, the "questions of clarification," mentioned above, could also be seen as politely veiled rejections of other students' claims. Nonetheless, the discussion is lively and students seem engaged in thinking about the novel.

Response Journal

During the time students were reading *Wuthering Heights*, they were to write three journal entries in response to the novel. Here is Adam's third journal entry:

> As I read toward the end of *Wuthering Heights* I had hopes of a tragic ending, but as I suspected the survivors lived happily ever after.
>
> I felt it was almost too coincidental that Nelly became ill, confined to her bed, in chapter twenty-three. By doing this Emily Bronte made it possible for Cathy to visit Wuthering Heights undetected.
>
> My pity for Hareton grew as Linton and Cathy became closer. I didn't feel it followed Cathy's character when she would ridicule Hareton about his illiteracy.
>
> Heathcliff's act of kidnapping would have been too melodramatic had Emily not built up such a villainous and undeterred character. I was impressed by Heathcliff's ability to bribe Edgar's lawyer to avoid going to the grange until after his death. I do not sympathize with Heathcliff's haunted feelings, after all, he did ask for it.
>
> The last chapter just sums up Emily Bronte's statement, "love conquers all."

In this piece, Adam notices several dissonances: between the way he wanted the novel to end (tragically) and the way it did end (happily); between Adam's understanding of Cathy's character and Cathy's action in ridiculing Hareton; between the way one might feel about Heathcliff's "haunted feelings" and the way he did feel ("I do not sympathize with Heathcliff's haunted feelings"). Adam does not specifically mention alternative perspectives or interpretations. But he does raise topics (the appropriateness of the ending; the way one feels about Heathcliff) about which there might be differing points of view.

Initial Draft

After taking part in the class discussion and completing his journal entries, Adam comes to his peer response group with the following draft.

Character Development

Environment plays the major role in the development of people. Therefore, it goes unsaid that environment also forms characters in a story. We have all heard the anecdote "We are products of our environment." I think *Wuthering Heights* is an explicit example of this. The personalities of Catherine, Linton, Isabella, and Edgar are direct products of their environment.

As a reader of *Wuthering Heights* we are not informed of Mr. and Mrs. Earnshaw's background, but they seem to have initiated the problems in our story. By favoring Heathcliff over his own son, Mr. Earnshaw put incredible pressure on Hindley as a child. Hindley's only caring parent was his mother. She loved him dearly but didn't have the character to stand up for him. When she died Hindley's world warped even more. Hindley was uncontrollably pitted against Heathcliff as a child by having to compete with him for his father's love.

Catherine Earnshaw's free spirit can be attributed to her mother's death. Her father may advise her but I doubt the family support was there. The introduction of Heathcliff into her life was bizarre. Imagine the stories he told her of life on the streets. He was new and exciting, elements Catherine admired.

Isabella Linton was a very spoiled young lady. Her family's social attitude made it so she would only meet youngster's such as herself, rich. This only added to her brattish attitude.

Edgar Linton grew up in the same house yet developed a self of constancy and tenderness. Such is how rich gentlemen of the day were. He contains all the qualities one associates with the hero of a Victorian novel. He grew up filling this mold because that was what was expected of him in his social ranking. His self development as a gentleman's gentleman backfired when he fell in love with Catherine. He wasn't much to hold her as a husband.

Linton's childhood was a sad one. Being creatively bent his main interest was ignored by his father. This hindered him throughout his life. He was never confident or an achiever.

The social position held by these families along with their rural standing developed these characters into the driving forces of Emily Bronte's *Wuthering Heights*. If Catherine had been exposed to more eligible bachelors I don't see how she could have married Edgar. Isabella married Heathcliff more out of romantic delusion and flat out rebellion than love. The events were directly caused by the characters social standing and the relative distance between their homes.

Although a draft of an essay can't tell us about all the thinking that went on while the essay was being written, it can show some evidence of the thinking processes I've mentioned. This essay indicates that Adam was aware of several dissonances. At one point (paragraph three), he indicates a disparity between Catherine's background and the novelty and excitement of Heathcliff's "life on the streets." At another point (paragraph seven), Adam makes a claim that indicates two conflicting perspectives on a character's actions; when Isabella marries Heathcliff, she does so "more out of romantic delusion and flat out rebellion than love."

Other dissonances in the essay do not reflect conflicts between two points of view or interpretations; rather they reflect discrepancies between what the student finds in the novel and what he expects, needs, or values. For example,

Adam indicates that several of the characters grow up in family circumstances that he finds regrettable: both Hindley and Catherine lack the family support they might have had; Linton's father ignores Linton's creative potential; Isabella's family displays a harmful "social attitude." Furthermore, Adam suggests that most of the characters fall short in one way or another: Mr. Earnshaw put too much pressure on Hindley; Isabella is "a very spoiled young lady" who displays a "brattish attitude"; although Linton is a typical hero of a Victorian novel, "he isn't much to hold [Catherine] as a husband"; moreover, "he was never . . . an achiever." And finally, Adam indicates a disparity between the information the novel might have included and that which it actually contains; he points out that there is no information about the "background" of Mr. and Mrs. Earnshaw.

As I shall suggest in a moment, the work reflected in this draft is not perfect. But it is extremely valuable. For one thing, Adam does not distance himself from the novel, as high school students sometimes do. Instead, the dissonances I've mentioned suggest some personal engagement with the story; he's related aspects of the novel to his own needs, values, expectations. Moreover, he has avoided a "safe" topic, one that allows a single, unambiguous—and, ultimately, boring—perspective. As we saw in the class discussion, the topic invites different perspectives, differing opinions from perfectly reasonable people. Finally, even what I see as problems in this essay strikes me as potentially useful. As Adam learns to recognize and solve these problems, he will be learning things he can use in other essays, especially argumentative or persuasive papers.

To be more specific about what I see as problems: in most of the paragraphs, I can follow Adam's claims about how some aspect of environment has influenced a particular character's development. But paragraph three is not so clear to me. Exactly how did the death of Catherine's mother create Catherine's "free spirit"? What is the sequence of events set in motion by the death of Catherine's mother? What are the assumptions that lead one to assume that this sequence had anything to do with Catherine's free spirit? My point here is not to deny that this relationship exists; it is that Adam has not made explicit a series of facts and assumptions that link Fact A with Conclusion B. This problem is not, of course, unique to this essay. If we can get this student to understand what he needs to do here, we can help him understand something he will need to do fairly frequently in this sort of essay.

Another problem appears in paragraph five, where the essay contains some anomalous information about Edgar, information that seems inconsistent with the basic point that environment shapes character. Since Edgar and Isabella grew up in the same household, how is it that they developed into such different people, he a gentleman and she a brat? And if the social expectations of the era molded him into a "gentlemen's gentleman," why is it that all this development "backfired when he fell in love with Catherine"? Often students respond to this sort of question by offering to remove the offending statements. But that, of course, misses the point. Unless one is dealing with the most simple-minded truisms, there are often facts that, at first glance, appear not to fit in with the claims one wants to make. In order to develop a really thoughtful interpretation, one must deal with these facts, either explaining how they are consistent with one's ideas or modifying those ideas.

One final problem concerns the way the essay sets up and fulfills expectations. At the end of the first paragraph, the student writes, "The personalities of Catherine, Linton, Isabella, and Edgar are direct products of their environment." This series of names—as is often the case with a series of nouns, especially in such a prominent position—creates some expectations not only about the characters to be discussed in the essay but also about the sequence in which they will be discussed. But paragraph two violates those expectations by talking about Hindley, a character not mentioned at the outset. This apparent digression is quite appropriate for an early draft, where a writer's initial organizational plan may change drastically as the writer produces the draft. But since the problem also appears in Adam's final draft, it may be that Adam needs to think about the way he sets up and fulfills a reader's expectations.

Peer Response Group

Having looked at the thinking reflected in a draft of Adam's essay, we are now in a position to consider some of the thinking and listening that went on when a group of four students discussed Adam's draft. About ten minutes into the discussion, the following talk occurred:

MIKE: Okay, you say you know that it's an explicit example of . . .

ADAM: Excuse me?

MIKE: What did you put about Heathcliff in here?

ADAM: Just that . . .

MIKE: How's he a product of his environment?

WENDY: Yeah, you could add that in because he's a central character.

MIKE: I mean like his . . . his beginnings as a child and talk about that.

ADAM: Yeah, let's see . . . how old was he when he was introduced in the story?

JAMES: Wasn't he like about eleven or something?

WENDY: Yeah, it never really said, but we decided that he was about that.

JAMES: I mean from the movie you'd think he was about ten or eleven.

ADAM: He was old enough to . . . he had developed enough to where he . . . his character and his attitude and his personality had already been developed.

JAMES: See, his . . .

WENDY: Yeah, he got all that from when he was on the streets.

JAMES: His personality was developed, I think, from the Earnshaw household.

ADAM: How's that?

JAMES: Well, see, if you think about it, if Hindley hadn't got on the wrong start with him, . . .

ADAM: Uh-huh.

JAMES: . . . then the story would have been a whole different change you know. Hindley wouldn't have been so vengeful and cruel, you know, during childhood days, and then, you know, in the early part of their adulthood.

ADAM: You think he had the right to be kinda vengeful.

JAMES: Not really.

WENDY: So that's the social environment that shaped him.

JAMES: Yeah. No, but see, just because his Dad paid more attention to Heathcliff, that's Hindley's fault for not, you know, giving his Dad the love and affection that Heathcliff gave him.

ADAM: Well, basically he was rebelling against his Dad, because his Dad didn't respect him as a person. He was more . . .

JAMES: Yeah, he took it out on Heathcliff.

ADAM: Okay. Yeah.

JAMES: And I think if he hadn't done that to Heathcliff, then the story would have been all different towards the end.

WENDY: So you could put that in your story—to discuss the social environment and the development of the story.

ADAM: All right.

In some respects, this is an exemplary small group discussion. For one thing, the students listen to each other. They answer each other's questions; when they interrupt, it's usually to agree with the previous speaker; and they ask for elaboration or clarification (for example, when James asserts that "[Heathcliff's] personality was developed, I think, from the Earnshaw household," Adam's response is "How's that?"). Furthermore, the students are thinking about the novel and Adam's draft. They raise several kinds of dissonances:

between what Adam did do and what he might do (Mike and Wendy suggest that Adam add information about Heathcliff's early childhood); between the way Hindley actually treated his father and the way he might have treated him (James implies that Hindley should have given his father "the love and affection that Heathcliff gave him"); and about the facts of the story (Adam raises the question of how old Heathcliff was when he was introduced into the novel).

This discussion begins to bother me only when I relate it to what happened in the whole-class discussion and in Adam's draft. In the class discussion, some of the dissonance arose because students had strongly conflicting points of view concerning the influence of the environment on character development. In the peer response group, conflicting interpretations of the novel almost never arise; one possible exception is in James and Adam's brief exchange about whether a character did or did not have "the right to be kinda vengeful." Even more important, the dissonances that do arise are not prompted by students' efforts to follow or assess Adam's line of argument. No one, for example, asks Adam to clarify the relationship between the death of Catherine's mother and Catherine's free spirit; no one points out that the paragraph about Edgar doesn't seem to fit with Adam's thesis that environment shapes character.

One way to summarize my point is to say that the students weren't bothered by the same things that bothered me. This may be inescapable, since our understanding of how students are responding to an essay will be at least somewhat influenced by our own response to that essay. Nor is this altogether bad; students have a right to expect their teachers to have some skill in analyzing arguments and some knowledge of features that can make a particular sort of discourse effective or ineffective. But a more serious problem, for me, is that the students' comments do not seem designed to help Adam achieve the purposes he has set out to achieve. When they identify a dissonance, they don't focus on some feature of the text that helps or hinders Adam's effort to make his point. Thus it's not entirely surprising that Adam's final draft is virtually the same as his earlier one. For all their hard work, the peer response group made almost no impact on Adam's writing.

MAKING RECOMMENDATIONS

Throughout the process of analyzing the work of Adam and his classmates, I have become increasingly aware of a couple of patterns that appear not only in Adam's work but in that of his classmates as well. The first of these is based on students' journal and essay writing and, since I have access to every student's writing, can be documented thoroughly. The second concerns students' talking and must be more tentative, since not all students took part in the class discussion and not all peer response groups for this assignment were recorded. Nonetheless, I think there is enough information here to allow several recommendations, based on the patterns in these students' work.

One pattern is that Adam and his classmates tend to avoid considering divergent perspectives or conflicting points of view. It is true that differing viewpoints appear in the class discussion, when students argue as to whether Heathcliff's behavior was caused by the environment, his personality, or his jealousy. But this conflict does not appear at all in Adam's essay; from reading it, you would never know that he had taken part in a class discussion where people had challenged the claim that environment influences character development. As noted earlier, one possible conflict of opinion appears briefly in the peer response group, when Adam asks James if he feels Heathcliff had a right to be vengeful. But the conflict doesn't go beyond Adam's question and James's response. Similarly, Adam's journal entries imply topics that might allow divergent opinions, but those topics are not developed in the journal entries and they don't appear in the draft of his essay.

The same sort of pattern appears in the drafts and journal entries of almost all of Adam's classmates. With the exception of six students (whose journal entries consisted mainly of plot summaries), students mentioned topics that seemed to invite divergent points of view. But in almost all of the essays, students avoided this sort of conflict. Either they wrote on topics that seemed to me, at least, unlikely to generate much controversy (e.g., the "gothic" qualities of *Wuthering Heights*) or they chose controversial topics (e.g., the influence of environment upon character) without referring to viewpoints that differed from their own. In the six essays that did refer to different points of view, those perspectives were usually mentioned and then rejected without much explanation as to why they were rejected.

Perhaps not surprisingly, this pattern in students' writing is closely related to one that appears in their talk. As in their writing, students tend to avoid considering different perspectives. Although their comments in the peer response group show that they have rather impressive listening skills, students' comments in the whole-class discussion suggest that they might not use them very extensively when they hear conclusions that differ from their own. Furthermore, at least when they talk about classmates' writing, students in the peer response group discussed above tend to avoid proposing conflicting facts or interpretations. For example, no one, as noted earlier, points out that the paragraph about Edgar Linton seems inconsistent with Adam's thesis. Finally, and perhaps paradoxically, members of the peer response group don't seem to entertain Adam's perspective on his own essay. When they comment specifically on the essay, students seem concerned with saying what they think Adam needs to do and not with determining whether Adam is successfully making the point he set out to make. For example, Wendy urges Adam to include a discussion of Heathcliff "because he's a central character." This may be very good advice. But it doesn't help Adam see whether he's made the point he set out to make about Catherine, Linton, Isabella, and Edgar.

These patterns seem significant because they did not have to hold true. These students were capable of listening to each other and thinking collaboratively. In their class discussion, these students showed that they were, in fact, capable of advancing alternative points of view. And the teacher had done a superb job of helping students develop a high level of personal engagement with the novel, one that would give them a basis for meaningful argument about divergent perspectives.

All of this—the patterns that emerge from the analysis and the significance of those patterns—leads me to believe that these students might benefit from working toward several goals, all, of course, related to the ability to consider alternative perspectives. For one thing, it would probably be useful for students to learn to look at specific experiences from several different points of view. How, for example, might different characters in a scene react to or interpret what goes on in that scene? What are the different ways a reader might respond to a particular character? How could the character's actions be seen as plausible? How implausible? Why might one be sympathetic with this character? Why unsympathetic? This sort of analysis might go on in whole-class discussions, in small group interactions, and in response journals, as well as in formal essays.

In addition to this work, it might make sense to show students how peer response groups might—helpfully, tactfully—play both the "doubting game" and the "believing game." What claims can group members confirm by citing additional evidence? Where can group members find conflicting information or alternative interpretations? And finally, it would be useful to show students how to look back through their response journals to identify topics that might allow a writer to consider different perspectives.

Everything I have said thus far is in some ways quite personal. I have presented my attempt to construct my own meaning of these students' work, an attempt based on my analysis and on values that I personally believe in. Consequently, a logical question is: How much confidence can one place in this constructed meaning? My answer has to be: A great deal—and very little. My analysis is based on evidence that comes not from a single source but from a range of sources: class discussion, small group discussion, journal writing, and essay writing. Thus I feel reasonably confident that I am not responding to some isolated phenomenon that may never again appear in the work of these students. Further, my recommendations are consistent with a need identified in a report from the National Assessment of Educational Progress (NAEP). The most recent report claims that students' efforts to write persuasive discourse were "dismaying." Fewer than 25 percent of the students tested wrote persuasive essays that could be called adequate. Not *excellent*. *Adequate*. Since students badly need to improve on this type of writing, and since awareness of divergent points of view seems to be a prerequisite for this improvement, I feel reasonably confident about the potential value of my recommendations.

In summary, the problems I've identified seem real and the solution seems worth pursuing. So why the tentativeness I expressed earlier? One answer is that someone else might look at these students' work and come to different conclusions. That's always possible, even likely, especially if one approaches these students' work with assumptions that differ from mine. But my caution does not stem from a fear of disagreement. It stems, rather, from a fear of our profession's tendency to overgeneralize. Sometimes we assume that a principle or a teaching procedure that is appropriate for one set of circumstances automatically applies to other circumstances.

Quite possibly there are other groups of students for whom my recommendations would make sense. But almost certainly there are groups of students for whom these recommendations would be inappropriate, even destructive. My intent is not to generalize about the work of our students; my intent is to generalize about our responsibility as professionals. We are obliged, I think, to pay careful attention to what our students do when they go about constructing meaning.

As we do so, we will find that we ourselves are engaged in the process of constructing meaning. Consequently, we will change our relation to our students and to our subject matter. Instead of acting as purveyors of information, we can share in the satisfaction we recommend to our students, the satisfaction of coming to our own conclusions, constructing our own meaning. In doing this, we change our teaching; what we do on a given day is not governed solely by a preordained curriculum but by our sense of what Arthur Applebee has referred to as "the emerging life of the classroom." And, finally, we may help change the way other teachers are educated. If we can establish the premise that the construction of meaning is a central part of every teacher's responsibility, perhaps colleges and universities will offer courses that show students how to engage in this process and how to understand other people's efforts to engage in this process. This last may be asking for too much; higher education changes at a rate that gives new meaning to the phrase "deliberate speed." But the rest is within our grasp. Right now. All we have to do is practice what we preach.

17

Observing Students' Reflective Thinking: A Teacher-Research Project

Barry M. Kroll

The teacher must have his [or her] mind free to observe the mental responses and movements of the student. . . . The problem of the pupils is found in subject matter; the problem of teachers is what the minds of pupils are doing with this subject matter.

John Dewey, How We Think *(1933)*

The teacher-research movement has helped many composition teachers reconsider the distinction between "teachers" and "researchers," both by demonstrating that insightful research can occur when teachers observe their own students, and by showing that the practices of good teaching can embody many elements of research, understood in its broadest sense as a process of inquiry and observation. In my own recent classroom projects, I have found it increasingly difficult to separate my role as "teacher" from my role as "researcher." For if, as Dewey claims, I must pay close attention to what my students are thinking and feeling, then instruction and investigation are going to be inseparable activities, and my role in the classroom is almost inevitably going to be one of "teacher-researcher."

Recently, my teaching and research efforts have been focused on college students' reflections about issues of knowledge and moral action, as these reflections are displayed in the context of a composition and literature course that I have been teaching for the last few years, a course that takes the Vietnam War as its topic. Through a series of reading and writing projects, students examine the ways that the war has been represented in memoirs, histories, journalism, and fiction. But a number of the reading and writing assignments raise two key questions: How do we know what to believe when there are conflicting versions of the truth, all of them based on facts? And how do we know what is right or how to act when there are several courses of action, none of them clearly right, all of them partially wrong?

What has interested me a great deal is how my students grapple with those questions, and how their orientations to knowledge and moral action evolve as a result of their participation in the course. Therefore, I have tried, at the outset of the course, to get a sense of how my students tend to think about issues of war, truth, and moral action. Then, throughout the course, I have looked for ways to monitor students' reactions to particular books and writing assignments that pose ethical or epistemological dilemmas, and thus promise to challenge their beliefs and ways of knowing. Finally, at the end of the semester, I have tried to find out how students see their original responses, as they look back at them with the course under their belts.

Let me share some of what I have found out during this project, focusing on what I have learned from two students, both of whom grappled with complex and vexing issues in the course of reading and writing about the war. In the first case, I'll focus on a student (Kristin) who is trying to decide what to believe when faced with conflicting accounts of an event, while in the second I'll focus on one of her classmates (Sarah) who is struggling to determine what action, among several disturbing alternatives, is right.

During the first class meeting, I gave the students a set of written "situations" that posed hypothetical but plausible dilemmas of knowledge and moral action in the context of war. I asked students to read over the situations and to think about them before they came to an individual conference, scheduled for later that week (or the next), a conference in which I planned to talk with them about their reactions to the situations.

One of the situations contained two quite different accounts of the same battle—the battle of Ap Bac, a skirmish that took place early in the war, when Americans were present only as advisors to the South Vietnamese Army. I designed these two accounts so that they were nearly the same length, with an equal number of references to sources, and so that both cited observers or analysts to support a particular view of the battle. And yet the accounts themselves differed markedly, both in their presentation of the "facts" of what took place during the battle and in their interpretation of the outcome. By talking with students about their reactions to these accounts, I hoped to get an idea of how they responded to situations in which there were several versions of the truth—a situation they would encounter again in the course. With the students' permission, I made a tape recording of each conference, so that I could review the students' responses later. (I also had other plans for the tapes.)

During her conference, Kristin (a junior majoring in English) seemed relatively unperturbed about the existence of two different accounts of the battle. She appeared to accept the fact that people usually see things from different perspectives and thus tell different stories about what they have observed. Our conversation went as follows:

> *Did you have any reactions to those two accounts of the battle?*
> There's two sides to every story. I don't know . . . it happens in everything it seems, that, you know, depending on which side you're looking at it from you're going to get a different story, you know. And this one, I couldn't BELIEVE the difference in this story. I mean, it's, it's so hard to . . . see, people have different perspectives, you know, and they're going to . . . back from their past experiences . . . they're going to tell things differently, they're going to look at different things, and they're going to make it, you know, look better from that perspective, and they're not going to try to tell it, you know, if it makes them look bad. . . .
>
> *Given that situation that you talk about—that people have different perspectives, and see things different ways, and tell different stories about the same events—if that's the case, how is it ever possible to know anything, to know what really happened?*
> I don't, I don't, really don't think you can know what really happened. *Really?* Yeah. . . . You can take things in that people tell you, and then make your own judgments. I mean, you never really know for sure what . . . if they're telling you everything, if they're holding back some things, or they're adding some things. I don't think you can really ever know. You can just take it in and, you know, think about it and make your own judgments.
>
> *Do you think you can get close to the truth?*
> Hmm. Somewhat close . . . yeah, I think you can. Well, you can get an idea of what happened. You know—I have kind of an idea of what happened. But you're just . . . you yourself, I think you have to make the final judgment as to what you think is true.

Kristin seems to recognize that it is difficult to know with any certainty what happened in a particular situation, not only because people see events differently and so tell different stories, but also because they may deliberately distort their accounts to make themselves look good. In addition, Kristin seems to believe that through a process of deliberation—taking in all the accounts and thinking about them—a person can arrive at a personally valid assessment of what happened, a "judgment as to what you think is true."

But if Kristin really subscribes to this view of deliberation and contingent judgment, she should be prepared to handle a subsequent unit in the course, a unit in which she and her classmates will read conflicting accounts of another incident, the "Hué Massacre" of 1968. During this unit, students read a series of articles that supported two different accounts of events in the city of Hué. According to one version, communist forces entered the city with blacklists and carried out ruthless executions of thousands of Vietnamese civilians. But in another version, the story of the massacre is portrayed as a myth, an elaborate attempt to conceal the destructiveness of the massive U.S. firepower used in recapturing the city, as well as an effort to score a propaganda victory against the communists (just at the time the My Lai massacre was coming to light). The assignment was to write a paper that proposed what "really happened" in Hué during the 1968 Tet Offensive.

Throughout the course, students kept a detailed journal of their thoughts and reactions. I collected the journals five times and wrote comments and replies to the students' entries. The journals were my primary mechanism for monitoring students' responses and evolving orientations. How did Kristin respond to the Hué assignment? Her journal entries during the unit are both revealing and surprising:

> The section of historical accounts . . . has me pretty confused. It's kind of scary thinking back upon all the information that I just took in without any questions. So many things in history can be distorted just through simple biases. I really wonder if anyone can really know the truth about things that have happened in the past. All the accounts I have read so far might just be only mere exaggerations, exaggerations that I took in and felt and wrote about. Sometimes living in the present is difficult, and now I must analyze and determine what actually happened several years ago. I'm sure with the guidance of Professor Kroll everything will become clear, but until then, I don't know, I am still apprehensive.

I was puzzled by several features of Kristin's response. To begin with, there seems to be a discrepancy between her self-confident response to the two accounts of Ap Bac and the anxiety reflected in this journal entry on the Hué material. Why is she so disturbed by alternative histories of the massacre when she seemed to accept so readily the existence of divergent accounts of a battle? Furthermore, why can Kristin talk so convincingly, during her conference, about taking everything in and making a personal judgment, while in her response to the Hué materials she seems unable—or unwilling—to make judgments about which accounts are more plausible? Why, given the epistemological orientation she appears to display in her response to the Ap Bac problem, does she founder on the realization that there can be multiple and discrepant histories—rather than a single and authoritative truth? In her next journal entry, three days later, Kristin carries her reflections further:

> How do I feel about all of this? So damn confused. So far I have done the reading assignment . . . and I still really do not know what to believe or who to trust. The possibilities either way are scary. . . . I just don't know. Perhaps as I read more accounts of the massacre things will begin to fall into place.

Perhaps I suppose really all anyone can do in interpreting history is to make an educated guess. Sometimes I just want to ignore history, just not care. . . . For me it is especially frustrating to be unable to get a cut and dry, "yes" or "no" response. The very use of historically vital information as propaganda scares me. How much do I really—I mean really—know about the things that are going on around me? How much is propaganda? Who is telling the truth?

Again, despite claims during her conference that one "can never really know for sure" what happened and that each person has to "make the final judgment as to what you think is true," at this point Kristin is clearly wrestling with the implications of what seems to be a new and particularly vexing sense of uncertainty. Beneath her assertion that one can never know the truth seems to lie a deeper desire for a "cut and dry, yes or no" set of answers.

At the end of the course, about two months later, I gave students back the tape recording I had made during their conferences, and I asked them to use the tape and their journals to write a paper in which they summarized how their ideas about such issues as aggression, war, knowledge, truth, and morality had either solidified or changed throughout the course. Kristin's essay reveals the centrality of her struggle during the Hué unit:

My first battle was Hué. I was bombarded with page after page of conflicting historical information. I was confused and frustrated. There were so many different accounts of Hué. How can all of them be right? How can all of them be wrong? I was disillusioned. Don't believe everything you read! Dr. Kroll realized my confusion and threw some vital advice my way. "Take it all in," he said, "and then draw your own conclusion." And so I did. For seven nights and eight days I pored over the Hué literature (the nights were especially bad). Each day I became more skeptical, less gullible. I felt myself become stronger, more critical. In the end I mastered the material, I drew my own conclusions, and ended my Hué experience with a 12-page masterpiece (if I do say so myself).

I want to point to one particularly intriguing feature of this reflection: the "vital" advice attributed to Dr. Kroll is strikingly similar to statements Kristin herself made in her conference, during the first week of the course. At one point in that conference, for example, Kristin said, "*take it in and . . . think about it and make your own judgments*." In her final reflections she quotes me as saying to "*take it all in . . . and then draw your own conclusion*." How can she regard my advice as an answer to her quandary when she had said very nearly the same thing herself at the outset of the course? I want to leave that question unanswered while I turn to the case of another student in the course—Sarah (a senior who was majoring in psychology).

Whereas Kristin's struggle was with issues of knowledge and truth, Sarah's main concern was with issues of right and wrong. During their conferences, students talked about their responses to a hypothetical dilemma in which a soldier has to make a decision about whether to shoot a Vietnamese woman who is in a position to harm the soldier's fellow squad members. This woman looks as if she might be planting a mine or booby trap, but she could also be an innocent bystander, caught in a situation that makes her look suspicious. I asked students whether the soldier should shoot or hold his fire—and why. From their responses, I hoped to discover students' orientations to the same kinds of ethical issues they would confront later in the course, in the books they would read. In our conference Sarah's response to the dilemma is quite intriguing:

> That one was really hard and I had to look at it . . . it's hard on paper especially because it's so hard to say what you would do. And I guess, though, I think, if it was me, I probably would have shot her because . . . of my friends. And I would have just had to think, well, sometimes you have to—you know it's really hard to make those decisions—but you have to weigh a life against another life. And I would have felt terrible if it had been the wrong decision, but that's probably what I would have done. . . .
>
> *Why does the fact that these people are your friends make a difference?*
>
> Because I'm selfish. Because you know this could be somebody else's mother, but at the same time I guess you've got to go with what's important to you and it would make a difference to me.
>
> *What if this soldier decides to shoot the woman and it turns out she was just an innocent peasant, caught in a bad set of circumstances, and she's dead. Do you think he's done anything morally wrong?*
>
> Well, I know if it was me I'd feel really bad, so I guess when you feel bad it's sort of like you're breaking some sort of morals. But at the same time I think I would justify it by saying I'm in a war and I have to . . . so I guess—no, if the morals of war are OK. And if they're not OK then you're . . . but, if that's what you're going on, if that's your basis for morals . . .
>
> *What do you think the morals of war are?*
>
> Well, you have to be willing to make judgments like this and maybe be wrong. And that's saying that I guess that you don't always have time to think things over, so you have to, I mean, the morals of war are, if you protect your side and do what, you know, and try to keep it as good as you can for your side. And try not to worry too much about the other side. . . .
>
> *If this guy did it, would you be willing to call him a murderer?*
>
> No, because I really believe that any situation, that there's no act that is inherently right or wrong, it's the reasons. I mean, you know, I think that if you look at the situation and you really do what you think is best, then really you've done all you can do. And I'm sure he would regret it, and it probably would make him do a lot of thinking about things, and maybe next time he

wouldn't shoot but then maybe next time it would be a booby trap, you know. And I really think that probably he would have felt a lot worse if he had let all his friends die. And it probably would have been . . . Well, I don't really think it would have been more right or really more wrong, but it just would have been what he would have had to deal with. And I know I couldn't deal with the idea that I just choked and I couldn't decide and therefore I let a whole bunch of people die rather than one.

At the outset of the course, it seems that Sarah believes that people can't know in absolute or abstract terms what the right course of action will be for a particular situation; instead, people must work out their own solutions for specific circumstances, using human judgment and practical reasoning as a guide. How does this moral orientation fare as Sarah continues to reflect on ethical issues?

The first thing that happens is that Sarah becomes uneasy about her position. After all, if she really believes that "no act . . . is inherently right or wrong" and that it is moral to "protect your side . . . and try not to worry too much about the other side," she has little basis for condemning any act, however heinous. A few days after her interview, Sarah makes the following entry in her journal:

> After my interview I really started to think about the morals of war. And after some reading I wonder if there are any. Certainly there should be some limits to what's fair and what's not. Murder is a given—that's war; booby-trapping children is wrong. Is killing a man OK but killing a woman wrong? I guess it depends on whether she's holding a gun or not. What about raping and taking of goods? What about torture and mutilation of bodies? The lines are very fine but if I wrote the rules for war it would be a much cleaner fight. Children would always be off limits. Rape would be off limits. . . . It's naive to think it could be like that. That you could only kill someone who was going to kill you, but that's the way it should be if it should be at all.

I believe Sarah is struggling here to revise her ethic so that it can embrace some moral rules ("children would always be off limits") but still remain sensitive to contextual factors—so that individual judgment, rather than some absolute principle, is central to moral deliberation.

Later in the course, Sarah reads two books in which there are controversial killings of Vietnamese. In Philip Caputo's memoir *A Rumor of War* Lieutenant Caputo sends his men into a village to capture some Vietcong suspects, giving his soldiers the impression that the suspects could be brought back "dead or alive." The men shoot one suspect, capture the wrong Vietnamese boy, and end up killing him on the way back to the base camp. Caputo and his men are charged with murder. In James Webb's novel *Fields of Fire* a squad leader called Snake takes his men in search of the VC who have ambushed and carried off two of their comrades. They find two suspects—an old man and a young woman—in a village, where they also discover the buried remains of their two friends. Although the Vietnamese claim they are innocent, they appear to be guilty, and so the squad kills them—over the protests of only one of the Americans, a Harvard-educated misfit named Goodrich (also called "Senator"). Goodrich, who has survived the war by looking out for himself, later reports the incident to the authorities.

Near the end of the course (but before she gets back the tape of her conference), Sarah looks back on the dilemma the soldier faced when confronted with the suspicious woman, and she compares it to the moral dilemmas she has read about during the course. She writes in her journal:

> Since this will be the last time we turn in our journals, I thought I'd try to look back a little and see how I've changed. What I'd really like to focus on is the morals of war. I remember reading those first handouts . . . the situation I remember best was the rifleman who had to choose whether to kill the woman in the road. At the time I knew very little about Vietnam, and it was hard for me. Now, no more blood-thirsty than I've ever been, I would shoot the woman. I wouldn't be like Goodrich in the war. I would think of my buddies and protect them. It's a risk the woman may be an innocent villager, but the way it was in Vietnam it's a risk you'd have to take.
>
> I don't think I would have involved myself in either of the killings in *Fields of Fire* or Caputo's book. These men took justice into their own hands, which even in wartime isn't fair. The line between killing a woman who might very likely be innocent and killing two people who are very likely VC and killed your friends is fine. But . . . killing the VC after the fact without real proof is an act of vengeance. . . . I guess what I'm saying is the wrong act for the right reason is better than the right act for the wrong reason.

When she reexamines the dilemma, Sarah again decides that the soldier must shoot the woman. Surprisingly, she presents this decision as if it were a new or different one: "*Now* . . . I would shoot the woman." And her main reason is that she is obligated to "think of my buddies and protect them"—virtually the same reason she gave during her conference three months before, when she said: "I probably would have shot her because of my friends." But to conclude that Sarah's ethical reasoning has remained stagnant throughout the course would be quite erroneous. For it is clear that Sarah's ethical views—while they may not have changed radically—have evolved as a result of her reflection and her interaction with material in the course.

At the beginning of the course, Sarah claimed that "no act is inherently right or wrong, it's the reasons." But her reading has helped her modify that position in two ways. First, she has encountered some actions that she cannot condone, no matter what the reasons or circumstances. And even more importantly, she has elaborated and refined her ideas about what kinds of reasons should be considered when one is trying to decide whether killing is morally justified. For example, actions that seem similar (such as killing Vietnamese suspects) must, in her view, be differentiated: Sarah struggles to distinguish between the case of killing a woman, even if she turns out to be innocent, when that act has a good chance of protecting the lives of comrades ("the wrong act for the right reason") and cases in which even Vietnamese who are very likely guilty of killing one's comrades are murdered as an act of revenge ("the right act for the wrong reason"). Yes, at the end of the course Sarah arrives at the same conclusion about the soldier's dilemma that she did at the beginning; but it *feels* like a new conclusion, because she arrives at it through a more complex process of reasoning, one informed by reflecting on situations depicted in the reading she has done for the course.

Similarly, Kristin's orientation to conflicting accounts appears to be about the same at the beginning and end of the course: on both occasions she says that knowing what is true depends on recognizing differences in perspective and using human judgment to sort them out. But her initial statements seem to express an orientation that she has difficulty putting into practice: when she is faced with an occasion that calls for critical analysis, Kristin becomes paralyzed by uncertainty, apprehensive about judging divergent accounts. In that situation, advice that echoes her own statements about deliberative judgment is perceived as new—or at least heard in a different way. Because she is expected to write a paper based on conflicting accounts, Kristin must try to practice the comparative-critical thinking she has explained so well at the beginning of the course: "you can just take it in and . . . think about it and make your own judgments." When she looks back at the painful experience of assessing divergent views and writing her paper, Kristin can express legitimate pleasure in becoming "more skeptical, less gullible," as well as pride in producing a paper in which she has drawn her "own conclusion."

When I ask myself whether reading and writing about the Vietnam War had any influence on my students' reflections about knowledge and moral action, I have a renewed appreciation for the complexity of that question. From observing students like Kristin and Sarah, I am reminded that the influence of a course may be subtle, that it will not always provoke a dramatic shift of orientation, a transition from one kind of epistemological or ethical stance to a different one. Instead, students like Kristin and Sarah often need time and opportunity to work out the implications of whatever views they say they hold when they come into a course. I also realize that if I want to find out whether students have refined their views, I have to look beyond their initial and final responses to dilemmas, because these responses do not always register the extent to which students have wrestled with issues and modified the ideas that lie beneath their responses.

But these realizations renew my commitment to teacher-research, since the activities of good teaching—such as talking with students about their ideas, asking them to keep a course journal, and encouraging reflective writing—are precisely the methods through which I will obtain more adequate answers to my questions about the evolution of college students' intellectual and ethical orientations. As I watch my students read, write, and reflect about difficult issues and disturbing choices, I'm often uncertain whether I'm acting as a teacher or a researcher. When I try to find out what's going on in my students' heads and hearts, am I conducting "research"? Or am I "teaching"? I am really at a loss to know where to draw the line.

18

The Writing Student as Researcher: Learning from Our Students

James A. Reither

I want to begin by advancing what I hope is a relatively innocuous claim—that *the business of discourse communities is inquiry*. That is, what members of discourse communities are about is not so much the accumulation of knowledge as it is change and the advancement of knowing—their own and that of the community. This is not, to be sure, a new claim (Reither); but it is nevertheless an interesting one in that it is not part of the assumption ground of writing teachers (Davis). It is not part of our ideology, not implicit in how we think and what we do. So, although the idea that the business of discourse communities is inquiry may not be new, it is nevertheless novel enough to urge us to look again, harder, at our thinking and at our practice.

Let me state the proposition another way: the ability to carry out inquiry is a more significant sign of an educated person than is any accumulated body of knowledge. It is not so much what we know that is important; it is what we can find out when circumstances call upon us to learn what we do not already know. It is that we see personal inquiry and coming to know as possible and important acts. Continued change, flexibility, and growth depend, certainly, upon having amassed knowledge; but they depend even more upon an ability to carry on the kinds of inquiry that result in knowing. What empowers "the educated" is not so much what they know; it is, more importantly, how thoroughly they are capable of finding out.

So, for instance, a medical doctor's abilities cannot be cemented in knowledge and practice accumulated in medical school and internship. Her abilities to prevent and treat illness depend upon continued inquiry into developing theory, technology, and practice. More to the point of this book's theme, our abilities as composition scholars and teachers cannot be fixed in past theory and practice—especially as we are confronted by evidence that the ways we think about and teach writing fail to produce the kinds of results we and our students would hope for. To become better theorists and teachers of writing, we must constantly renew our knowing through inquiry.

The key to continuing personal and disciplinary development, then, is learning how to find out more—to modify old knowing, to make new knowledge.

If that is true, it follows that perhaps the most important lesson we can teach our students is how and why to conduct inquiry on their own. We want them to accumulate knowledge; but, just as important, we want them also to learn why and how to undertake and organize their own inquiry, so they can continue to modify and develop their knowing as they find themselves in situations where what they presently know is inadequate to their needs.

Which brings me to the issues I want to address here: how we can help students become researchers, and what they and we learn when we do so. There are many kinds of research, many ways to be researchers. Because our focus is on the teaching of writing, because writing and learning to write are so intimately connected with reading and learning to read, and because it's the form of research I know best, I will talk about just one kind of inquiry, what Stephen North calls "standard humanist scholarship— . . . developing rational arguments founded on textual evidence" (p. 5). Like most kinds of research, such inquiry is grounded in serious, critical reading in a field's literature. For students, this most often means library research.[1] For us, it means working in the library, subscribing to journals, buying books, participating in workshops and conferences.

So, to get down to cases, how do we transform students into researchers? Let me answer this question indirectly, through a lengthy series of *supposes*—based not on a hypothetical situation, however, but rather on a course I taught in the academic year 1988–1989.

Suppose, first, that you set up a senior Shakespeare course to answer this kind of question: "How and where did Shakespeare learn to do what he did?"

But suppose also that instead of your assuming the responsibility for teaching the texts and gathering and structuring the information necessary to answer that question, you organize the course so your students find, organize, and teach that information to each other.

Suppose that the way the students do this is, first, by reading in the scholarly, secondary literature, as a way of learning not just "content" but also what kinds of questions can be asked and how they can be answered; second, by chunking the subject into smaller questions—as, for instance, "What kinds of texts did Shakespeare read in school that later showed up as traces in his plays?"; third, by dividing into teams which take responsibility for reading more deeply in the secondary literature and for reading some of the texts that Shakespeare himself would have read or seen; and fourth, by having the teams report their findings to one another in regular group reports, both individually and collaboratively written. (Suppose, too, that as circumstances and questions change, membership on teams changes.)

Suppose these reports are eventually revised and bound into a kind of publication of the students' findings on the question of how and where Shakespeare learned to write the kinds of plays he wrote.

Suppose that, because the purpose of the research reports is solely to advance the overall class research project, and because the important readers of these reports are the students themselves, these reports are not graded; and, further, that much of the burden for evaluation rests with those who know best the extent to which a student has contributed to the learning of others— her fellow students.

And, finally, suppose *your* responsibilities in all this are to suggest research procedures and directions, and to orchestrate and—acting as an expert coresearcher—model the process.

In other words, suppose you designed a course that stood the traditional, commonsensical roles of teachers and students on their heads. In "normal" teaching practice teachers function as knowers who organize and present course content to students. What might our students and we learn if these roles are radically redefined—if, that is, students are cast as researchers, organizers, and reporters who gather and put shape to information that they then report to one another, for each other's use, and teachers assume the functions of research or project directors?

What can students learn when a course is organized this way and when they are cast in such roles? I suggest they can learn several different kinds of things: they learn content, of course; but they also learn the mechanics and processes of library research; they learn how to learn, through their own question-driven inquiry, enough to become engaged, independent, analytical, and critical readers and thinkers; and they learn important lessons about writing and how to write.

The lessons students can learn about content seem obvious. They gather enough general background information to allow them to see ways to carve their subject into manageable chunks, and then, individually or in pairs or trios, they go on to find more detailed answers to their now more detailed questions.[2] They thus form a local community of inquirers and writers whose learning arises primarily and collaboratively out of a relationship between them and the larger disciplinary community represented in the field's published scholarship. They work up reports answering research questions they have come to pose as a result of their reading. Thus, for instance, by reading the scholarly literature, some of the plays Shakespeare must have seen and read, and some of Shakespeare's own plays, they become aware of ways the playwright went to school on the texts of others. Insofar as they can in the time they have, the students create for themselves the historical, political, social, literary, and dramatic context in which Shakespeare wrote. This kind of learning makes them more knowledgeable, more insightful readers of the scholarly work of others, of Renaissance literature in general, and of Shakespeare in particular. As their learning accumulates, they construct, for themselves—however arbitrarily and incompletely—the field's knowing. (The arbitrariness and incompleteness of their understanding echo our own: since we cannot know the entire field, we too carve it up into manageable chunks that we then "make whole" as best we can.)

Much of what they learn has to do with language. In the Shakespeare course I've been using as an example, they learn to talk knowledgeably about, for instance, miracle, morality, and Corpus Christi cycle plays; about Seneca, Plautus, Ovid, Kyd, Lyly, Greene, Marlowe, Jonson; about quartos and folios, English history plays and the Romance; about Samuel Schoenbaum, Irving Ribner, E. K. Chambers, A. C. Bradley. They learn how to pronounce Ovid, Antipholus, Jacques, Gloucester, Iago. They come across these terms and names (the genres, playwrights, poets, scholars, critics) in their reading. They learn their pronunciations, meanings, and uses because they must if they are to share their learning with others. To do that, they need to learn, talk, and write as members of the discourse community. In other words, the students' reading, talking, and writing as members of a research team enable them to develop a kind of situated disciplinary literacy.[3]

Students also learn lessons about the mechanics and processes of library research. Among other things, they learn how to find books and articles; how to find bibliographies; how to find literary texts in anthologies. They learn how to follow the trails authors blaze in footnotes, endnotes, and lists of references. That is, they learn how scholarly citations lead readers into and through the literature of a field; they learn how "exploration leads to still further exploration, discovery to still further discovery" (Odell, p.129). They come to understand, in addition, the kinds of questions that drive research; they understand where those questions come from, how they are generated. They do enough background reading in the secondary literature to learn what kinds of things Shakespeare had to have seen, read, and known about to write a given play; they read in the primary sources and analogues and they read Shakespeare's own play; and then they write reports whose function is to recreate for their colleagues key elements of the context in which the master's own play was written and viewed. In this way the students learn how scholarly inquiry is always situated in personal and community standards, conventions, expectations, and needs. In short, they learn not just how to work a library, how to take notes, and how to keep "bib" cards, but also something about where research might originate and fit into the schemes of things, what kinds of people do research, who they do it for, how and why they learn to do it, and how and why it gets written.

These seemingly elementary lessons about working a library and immersing oneself in a field's literature can be profoundly liberating for students. Jerome Bruner says that

> curiosity is almost a prototype of the intrinsic motive. Our attention is attracted to something that is unclear, unfinished, or uncertain. We sustain our attention until the matter in hand becomes clear, finished, or certain. The achievement of clarity or merely the search for it is what satisfies. (p. 114)

But what if we do not know how to satisfy our curiosity? What if we do not know how to achieve clarity, or even how to search for it? How satisfying is that? The answer seems to be that an inability to find things out kills curiosity: we tend to stop wondering if we do not know how to find out. (A few pages later in the same book Bruner himself says, "We get interested in what we get good at. In general, it is difficult to sustain interest [i.e., curiosity] unless one achieves some degree of competence" [p.118].) And, just as important, when we don't know how to find things out, we are utterly at the mercy of those who do. Learning how to work a library can reawaken curiosity because it can free students from the tyranny of ignorance and thus from the tyranny of those who would tell them how and what they ought to know.[4]

A third thing students learn as they become researchers is how to be more critical, analytical readers and thinkers. Being a critical reader is prerequisite to developing one's own knowledge claims and arguments out of textual evidence. A number of conditions encourage students to read and think more critically and analytically. One of these has to do with the kinds of learning I have already alluded to:

> We do not fully understand any particular text until we have some concept of the discipline into which it fits, and in which it has sense and significance. Conversely, we do not understand the discipline adequately until we are familiar with the historical works which make it up. (Luke, De Castell, and Luke, p. 115)

Wide reading in a field's literature familiarizes researchers with the meaning-making ways of the discipline. That familiarity—developed through reading, making sense, talking, writing—is what turns disciplinary outsiders into

insiders who know enough to recognize "what counts as a relevant premise
. . . [and] what counts as an argument" (Luke, De Castell, and Luke, p. 115)
in a discipline's discourse. Knowing enough to spot inadequate premises and
ineffectual arguments gives inquirers the kind of independence that allows
them to read and think against the grain—something possible only for
members of the community. In other words, the only way to read disciplinary
texts analytically, skeptically, and critically is "from the inside out," as an
independent member of the community.

Another condition encouraging critical thinking and reading has to do with
the contexts and sources of researchers' knowledge claims. It doesn't take a
vast amount of reading in a field's literature before one begins to come across
the differences, disagreements, and contradictions (Coe) among scholars and
critics. Thus, reading in a field's literature demonstrates to students the ways
these gaps vitalize a field, keeping its frontiers open and susceptible to inquiry.
And finding these gaps gives all researchers—old hands and novices alike—the
angles, purposes, focuses, and structures they need for their writing (Coe, pp.
275–76).

Finally, students functioning as researchers learn important lessons about
writing and how to write. The texts they read in a field's literature model the
language, functions, conventions, forms, values, and persuasion strategies of
the field's writing. Thus they learn what the field's texts look and sound like;
what kinds of questions the authors of those texts have asked, and what kinds
of answers they have found; what kinds of inquiry are recognized, afforded,
not blocked; what kinds of knowledge claims can be advanced in the field, and
what kinds of arguments and evidence can be used to support those claims. In
short, through an imitative process they are for the most part unaware of,
students learn what their own writing should look and feel like, what kinds of
claims they can advance, and what kind of arguments are likely to persuade.
Their regular oral and written reports to one another give them opportunities
to use and practice what these models teach them.

Perhaps the most important lesson the literature offers about writing has to
do with its conversational, dialogical nature. Students often see this soonest
and most clearly in the ways scholarly texts explicitly contextualize their
claims in the work of others—in the ways their authors ground their own texts
in previous texts in the field. Those textual environments are made most
explicit in an introduction, where an "author briefly states the present
position of research on his subject and the views currently held on it"
(McKerrow, p. 117). But scholarly writing is situated in other scholarly
writing in subtler ways as well. Students who read very far into a field's
literature and who report their findings to others learn more profound lessons
about the intertextuality of their project and about social-collaborative dimen-

sions of writing and knowing. They learn, for example, that even when they are being their most creative and contrarian, they do not write alone. They discover that what they have to say is always conditioned by an awareness of the knowing of those to whom they are trying to say it. They learn that they are always bound by conventions of community language, forms, and means of persuasion. And they gradually realize how to take advantage of the fact that everyone who looks even reasonably thoroughly at the primary and secondary literature of a field sees things differently from everyone else who reads in that literature. Seeing differently is the source of dissonance, uncertainty, incongruity, contradiction. Seeing differently gives inquirers issues to wonder about, question, rethink, disagree over. Seeing differently is the entryway into the ongoing conversation of a field.

Now, then, what might *we* learn if we cast ourselves as research or project directors who oversee the collaborative research projects undertaken by our students? First of all, obviously, we learn new ways of thinking about our roles as teachers and our students' roles as students. The most important of these, especially for the students, is that we can learn that it isn't always our job to make things easier for our students. As Luke, De Castell, and Luke tell us, in conventional classrooms that depend upon textbooks,

> teachers are the modern day arbiters of textual knowledge. They are the elders, the "clerics" who initiate children . . . into the literate processes requisite to the acquisition and application of . . . knowledge. Moreover, it is from teachers that students acquire not only a corpus of knowledge and skills, but also an attitude towards learning—in literary terms, a "sensibility" towards the text. In this respect, the teacher is like the literary critic, an arbiter of questions of style, aesthetic taste, propositional validity, and rhetorical force, who provides student readers with a running metatextual commentary with which to process the text.
>
> Thus, the school text is always the object of teacher mediation. One instructs with and through the text; a student confronts textual knowledge via teacher mediation. In the classroom situation, the text is the locus of information exchange. Inasmuch as the text for a particular subject, theme, or topic constrains the content of classroom information exchange, so does the teacher mediate the exchange between student and text. And within this communicational system of the classroom—a system supporting a particular structure of information exchange—the student assumes an acquiescent, *nonauthoritative status* in relation to both text and teacher. (p. 118)

If we can see ourselves less as "teachers" and more as "organizers," "coaches," "directors," or "managers," we free our students to find their own meanings in the texts they read. Because neither we nor our students are accustomed to these roles, however, we both find them difficult to assume.

Our students don't know how to work libraries, don't know which kinds of texts will help them quickly to construct a context for other texts, don't know that if they read just a few of the jargon-filled texts of most any field they will shortly become familiar enough with that jargon that their reading tasks will become easier. We see them struggling with the seemingly impossible task of making sense out of apparent chaos, and we want to help them out by telling them what to see and how to make order. Because we are "teachers," our impulse is to step between the students and the texts they are struggling with. We want to make this sense-making process easier for them; we want to explain things.

The trick, however, is in getting out of the way, by setting up situations that encourage students to develop their own reading and sense-making abilities, to let them develop independence from teachers. This step-by-step process works because the researching-and-reporting sequence is organized so that, as they learn how to carry it out, the students need to rely less and less on the teacher's guidance.

Second, we also stand to learn content. If the research project is a real one, and if we can resist our habitual impulse to intrude as "arbiters of textual knowledge," our students (because they are different from us) will come to see in ways we cannot. So, we have to encourage them to dig deeply and then pay attention to what they find and what they have to say about what they find. They will come up with new information, new ideas, and new insights. And we will learn from them: they will teach us, so that our knowledge of the field will be deepened in areas we have not extensively explored on our own. (Thus, for example, my students looked at sources for Shakespeare's plays that I had never seen—some, in fact, that I had not known of.)

Third and finally, we stand to learn powerful lessons about the processes of inquiry and learning. Because we are working with students just learning how to be researchers, we are forced to watch carefully what they do and how they do it. And we have to learn from what we see. Ann Berthoff says that "The centrally important question in all teaching is, 'What comes next?'" (p. 32). In a course where students are researchers and teachers are project directors, teachers must also continually ask: "Now that the students know this, what do they have to learn next?" "Where and how can they learn it?" "What would I do next if I were doing this research?" Because we ask such questions as these, we gain a clearer—and more clearly articulated—understanding of the processes of inquiring and learning. We come to understand better just what does come next, and why. We come to understand that situation precedes topic selection and focus. We come to understand the deep signifi- cance of reviews of research and scholarly citation (that is, we come to understand that such things are neither mere name-dropping nor simply ways to avoid charges of plagiarism). And we come to understand better the extent to which research, writing, and knowing are things we do with other people (Reither and Vipond). In short, we come to understand better just what "teaching" means.

NOTES

1. As will be abundantly clear in what follows, I am not here referring to the kind of inquiry that produces so-called "research papers" in composition courses—about which I share Richard Larson's "deep skepticism" (p. 812); and neither am I talking about the production of "term papers" for conventional content courses.

2. So, for example, my students asked such questions as these: What did Shakespeare learn from seeing or reading the anonymous *Famous Victories of King Henry the Fifth*? Or, how did Samuel Daniel's view of English history shape Shakespeare's view when he wrote his *Henry IV* plays? Or, in what ways did Ben Jonson's idea of "humours comedy" help Shakespeare write *The Merry Wives of Windsor*? And then, later, after they had accumulated sufficient knowledge, they asked questions about pattern: can we, by comparing Shakespeare's plays to those of his predecessors and contemporaries, find evidence that Shakespeare might have learned how to create effect through structure by alternating scenes among story lines (as he does, for example, in *2 Henry IV*)?

3. I hope readers will see in this phrase—"situated disciplinary reading"—an implicitly critical allusion to E. D. Hirsch's notion of cultural literacy as bits of information that may or may not constitute real or useful knowledge.

4. My colleague Douglas Vipond organizes his psychology courses along lines similar to those described here. One of the questions on his course evaluation questionnaire last spring was, "On the basis of this course, do you have any interest in pursuing the study of psychology further?" Although we're not exactly sure what to make of it, one of his students' answers was this: "No," she said, "because if I have to know something or if I am anxious to find out about something in psychology I will just follow the same route as I have all year—that being the resources at all the libraries and journals and psychology books."

19

Interaction and Assessment: Some Applications of Reader-Response Criticism to the Evaluation of Student Writing in a Poetry Writing Class

Patrick Bizzaro

Probably no area of writing instruction has received less attention than the problem of evaluation in creative poetry writing classes. After all, there is a much greater problem than procedure when a teacher evaluates a student's poem. On the one hand, there does not exist in our learned journals a body of research on evaluating a poem that would lend credence to any of the current, well-advertised systems of evaluation, including those methods of evaluating student writing mirroring New Critical approaches to literary texts. What's even more troubling (even for literary critics), there is no consensus about what constitutes poetry, let alone how to judge one poem as better than another. Teachers have great difficulty isolating what they hope to evaluate in student poems.

Close analysis of student writing over a period of time, such as a sixteen-week semester, is well suited to what we have come to call classroom-based research. In light of the well-known difficulties teachers experience in evaluating student poetry writing, I have undertaken a study to see what changes occur in students' perceptions of what poetry is and in the texts they produce and call poems. In other words, I seek at least a tentative answer to the following questions: Can reader-response critical tools be profitably employed in the evaluation of student poetry writing? And, as a corollary to the first question, a second: Where and how does meaning occur?

In this chapter, I set out to do four things: (1) to give some background to my interest in this subject—as a poet teaching poetry writing, (2) to make a case for using reader-response criticism in evaluating writing—as a student of literary history, (3) to report on the classroom-based research I am currently performing, and (4) to look at the changes in the writing of two beginning poets, Lisa and Chris, in an attempt to suggest some further implications for using reader-response critical tools in evaluating and shaping student writing.

1

Following the excellent advice of Dixie Goswami, who advocates that prior to performing classroom-based research, prospective teacher-researchers should analyze their own processes of writing, I examined closely my own writing and revising strategies. In an article in *Language Arts*, I reported on what I had discovered: I teach my students to write and revise by teaching them strategies I use when I write and revise. This finding has become the basis for my subsequent study.

In a paper presented to the Southeastern Conference on English in the Two-Year College, I discussed how a writer might publish poems in one of the journals on which I serve as poetry editor. In this talk, I attempted to answer the following question: Do my judgments about accepting or rejecting poems arise from personal biases reflected in my own poetry? A cursory glance at the kinds of poems I had accepted for publication revealed that I had selected poems I wish I had written, poems with strong image patterns rather than poems involved primarily with statement.

The significance of these two studies in light of my current research is that they underscore my growing awareness of the reader's role in determining a text's meaning and worth. Beginning as I believe all classroom-based research should, with self-analysis, I was led to a realization I might not have made without paying such close attention to myself in various roles, as writer, critic, and teacher: it is virtually impossible to evaluate objectively, as though all meaning resides in the text itself. In short, I could no longer ignore the role I play in making meaning when I evaluate a text.

Why study poetry writing, though, to determine the influence of personal biases on the evaluation of student writing? For one thing, when I examine a poem, I ordinarily approach it as most evaluators would like to approach student essays, by focusing first and foremost on the content and then by moving to matters of form or technique. I have found that I can approach an examination of my system for evaluating poetry without the kinds of biases I bring with me when I study my system for evaluating nonliterary texts. For a second reason, literary-critical theory introduces a question so basic to meaning that we often assume it is too complex to be asked of the way we criticize student compositions: Where does meaning reside?

One important conclusion I reached in my first two studies of the impact of my biases on my teaching and evaluating strategies is that any method employed in evaluating writing—that is, literary or nonliterary writing—reflects a teacher's understanding of where meaning occurs: in the author, the text, or the reader. I believe that reconsideration of meaning will, in turn, change evaluation methods. In other words, if we believe meaning resides in the reader's reinvention of the text, then we must reevaluate the methods we employ in evaluation.

2

To incorporate reader-response critical tools in our strategies for evaluating student writing, we must begin to view writing not so much as a process of working and reworking a text, but as an unfolding of meaning that somehow parallels the reader's process of understanding. Clearly, replying to a student "I know what you mean, but you haven't said it in this text" is an unsatisfying and false evaluation. Instead of focusing on the writer and on the text in isolation, any theories employing reader-response criticism will shift emphasis to the writer establishing a relationship with a reader and to the text as an entity vulnerable to repeated construction and reconstruction.

What exactly does this imply? It suggests that the way an evaluator finds meaning in a text is reflected in the method employed in evaluation. Most of us who have taught in the 1980s were taught, as students, that meaning resides in the text (though, of course, many of us now question our roots). As a result, when we read a student text—literary or nonliterary—we find meaning in the agreement of subject and verb and pronoun and antecedent, in the well-placed comma and period, in the correctly placed word. If this weren't at least the wrong-headed implications of our dominant methods for evaluating writing, then why would we spend so much time on such matters?

This view of meaning (which when applied to literary texts is called New Criticism) is reflected in many of our theories for evaluating student writing. But what if we believe meaning exists not in the text but in the reader's reinvention of the text? Let's explore this notion, first, by looking to literary history, for it is there that we typically find models for our own thinking.

I like to ask my students, repeatedly during the semester, the following question: "What kinds of things would you take into consideration in evaluating a poem?" The idea for this question came from my close reading of Wordsworth's *Preface to the Second Edition of the Lyrical Ballads*, since it strikes me as a question most serious poets eventually must ask themselves and, in fact, the question Wordsworth answers. In describing an experiment he and Coleridge set out to perform, Wordsworth wrote the following:

> The principal object, then, proposed in these Poems was to choose incidents and situations from common life, and to relate or describe them throughout, as far as was possible, in a selection of language really used by men, and, at the same time, to throw over them a certain colouring of imagination, whereby ordinary things should be presented to the mind in an unusual aspect. (Stillinger, p. 446)

Let's accept this passage, then, as Wordsworth's statement of his understanding of what constitutes poetry (at least in 1800). Now we are forced to consider a crucial question: Does the meaning of Wordsworth's poems exist in his plan as described in the *Preface*, in the poems themselves, or in the reader's perception of the writer's aspiration and accomplishment?

This is an important question because the methods we employ in evaluating literary texts often reflect the methods we use in determining meaning. Look at Coleridge's response to Wordsworth's efforts as an example of this point:

> To this I reply; that a rustic's language, purified from all provincialism and grossness, and so far reconstructed as to be made consistent with the rules of grammar . . . will not differ from the language of any other man of common-sense, however learned or refined he may be, except as far as the notions, which the rustic has to convey, are fewer and more indiscriminate. (Perkins, p. 463)

So Wordsworth gets a C + and decides not to take Advanced Poetry Writing.

No doubt Coleridge's estimation of Wordsworth's success or failure is based on Coleridge's reinvention of a text Wordsworth described and wrote, earnestly reiterating the language of the rustic. In any event, the texts Wordsworth produced mirrored *his* understanding of what a poem should be. Unfortunately, Coleridge could only understand—that is, give meaning to— the text by reconstructing meaning in terms of *his* past experiences as a reader of similar texts and as a person who has experienced (even if in some limited way) the language of rustics. In short, Coleridge's estimation of Wordsworth's "experiment" further suggests that the way an evaluator finds meaning in a text is reflected in the method employed in evaluation. What's more, our literary history tells us that a common practice among poets is to write—or to have written for them—a document that reflects their understanding of what constitutes a poem. Even Wordsworth and Coleridge answered the question basic to my classroom-based research: What kinds of things would you take into consideration in evaluating a poem?

3

What if, as literary critics, teachers believe as Coleridge no doubt did, that meaning exists not in the text, but in the reader's reinvention of the text? There are certainly those in our ranks who carry such a belief but who evaluate student writing—literary and nonliterary both—as though meaning exists in the text. My classroom-based research, in attempting to determine if reader-response criticism might be profitably employed in evaluating student poetry writing, addressed two other related questions. First, what, exactly, do we ask students to do when we ask them to write poems? And, second, does a relationship exist between what students express as their current understanding of what constitutes poetry and what they ultimately write?

To explore these questions, I focused my attention not only on the texts produced during spring semester 1988 by the fifteen East Carolina University students in my Introduction to Poetry Writing class, but on changes they each made in a weekly assignment—that they answer, on the basis of their experiences as readers and writers of poems, the question Wordsworth seems to answer in his *Preface*: "What kinds of things would you take into consideration in evaluating a poem?"

Students were required to keep journals in which they wrote drafts of poems, reactions to poems read for class discussion, and an answer once each week to the above question. I would focus my energy on the answer and on a draft of a poem selected by the student, reading both texts and, in responding to the poem, applying criteria each student supplied in answering the question. Each week, I would attempt to influence what they believed constituted poetry by providing a brief reaction to their answer (that is, by interacting with them) and by referring to the poem they submitted with their answer.

The goal of this interactive procedure was to reach an agreement with students about what *their* poems should be. That an agreement between reader and writer must exist if meaning is to be made is amply demonstrated by Coleridge's reaction to Wordsworth's description of the language best suited to poetry. But more importantly, that agreement is the basis for a current theory for the generation of meaning, a theory still unexplored in its implications in evaluating student writing. If, in fact, meaning resides in such an interaction between writer, reader, and text, then we can reach several conclusions about what a system for evaluating student poetry writing should do and whether reader-response criticism would be useful in evaluating student writing.

First, any method of evaluation in poetry writing classes should acknowledge that each individual poem has its own integrity. It would be as much a mistake to use a single criterion to judge all poems as to apply a single criterion to the evaluation of all possible pieces of writing. If we think seriously about what we ask students to do when we ask them to write poems (and here I mean beginning poets of all ages), we must inevitably see that we are asking students to generate texts that represent their current understanding of what constitutes poetry. And that understanding may include a wide range of things.

Second, any method for evaluating poetry that hopes to guide students to the writing of a less random variety of texts (that is, that influences their understanding of what constitutes poetry) will be employed most successfully in conjunction with interactive techniques for in-process evaluation, such as workshops, conferences, and interactive journals. In the "workshop method," an interaction among peers especially popular in creative writing classes, student writings often conform to criteria imposed and agreed upon by the group, thereby limiting in some way the kinds of texts that might be acceptable. The workshop makes writing a social act and revision an attempt to accommodate the assumptions and expectations of the group.

Still, when the class acts upon a text, the teacher must first require the group to cite those criteria by which that particular community of readers identifies a text as a poem; only then will the teacher know the standards against which student texts are being measured. Instructors, of course, shape the criteria by assigning poems to be read and discussed in class. More effective, however, are conferences and interactive journals, since they provide the instructor with the opportunity to influence assumptions and expectations of readers *before* they assess a text during workshop. What's more, conferences and interactive journals permit instructors to approach each poem as a unique entity, with a life, a set of characteristics, and a direction not only different from all other kinds of texts, but different from all other poems as well.

This study focuses on the use of interactive journals as a means by which students' knowledge of what constitutes poetry can best be influenced and as a means of employing the principles of reader-response criticism.

4

What follows are my interactions with two students, Lisa and Chris, and the poems that resulted. I am including here a first attempt to answer the question "What kinds of things would you take into consideration in evaluating a poem?", my reaction to that statement, an answer written five weeks later, and one poem by each student. My goal was to determine if some relationship exists between what students describe as characteristics of poems, the poems they write, and the way a reader assesses the poems.

Lisa is a junior art major at East Carolina University, taking poetry writing as an elective. Lisa's first answer to the core question is as follows:

> I would consider a good poem one that expresses one's feelings. If I can read what someone has written and understand what they are trying to say, then they have done a good job in writing. I think a good poem should include abstract ideas that provide an image. Almost like a short story and a painting all rolled up into one.

I responded favorably to Lisa's description of a poem as "a short story and a painting all rolled up into one." Considering her major in art, I was not surprised to note her interest in the making of images. Still, I wanted her to explore the notion of what might result in a good poem; it was not enough, to my way of thinking, to say a poem is good simply because she can "understand what they [the writers] are trying to say." My response to her, written in the margins of her notebook, was an attempt to get her to think more specifically about language in poetry: "This week look at the way language is used—what kinds of words are most often employed in poems? What language makes poems like paintings?" My goal was to have her look at the poems assigned for class reading in a different, more discriminating way.

This interaction over four more exchanges resulted in a slight shift in the written record of Lisa's view of what a poem should be. A list of criteria nearer my view resulted, reflecting an interaction that respected the writer, the reader, and the text.

> Things I would take into consideration in evaluating a poem: imagery, imagination, the way the author expresses him/herself, if s/he's able to put a picture in my mind, free verse, an interesting arrangement of words and sentences, if the writer tries something new.

The biggest difference between this statement and Lisa's earlier statement is her focus on the kind of language that seems to be employed in the making of the poems we discussed in class. Lisa's view retains her natural preference as an art major for the visual scene. But by stressing "imagery" and "a picture," she has settled on the use of language best suited to making vivid, visual poems. This also became a view of poetry I easily accepted and used in evaluating "My Favorite Spot," the poem that follows:

My Favorite Spot

grass,
lots of it.
green space smothered with dandelions—
baseball field to right,
steeple to left,

bells chiming with the wind.
behind, the gravel road I travel.
in the middle, on a hill
me.

Evaluating this poem, as a result of the procedure followed thus far, was done in terms of what Lisa and I had agreed should be accomplished in writing a poem. "My Favorite Spot" is marked by imagery that is clear and visual. While this seems an imaginative piece, it is restricted in some ways by being, it seems, a remembered scene, one that may be truly and accurately represented in the poem. I felt, however, that Lisa did an excellent job of creating an attractive picture, relying chiefly on free verse, using the word "me" at the end to excellent effect. I enjoyed the way she arranged the poem on the page as well.

Chris, a junior chemistry major, also took the poetry writing course to fulfill elective credit requirements. He answered the core question as follows:

> To me, poetry provides a catharsis for those feelings that are inside of me and which I have difficulty expressing verbally. I would take the emotional meaning (my own interpretation) into consideration when evaluating a poem. How does it make me feel? What does it do for me? What problem or happiness is this poem solving? I also dislike poems that have a rigid rhyme.

Chris is more closely involved with his own reaction to a poem: How does the poem make him feel? What does it do for him? In a sense, Chris sees the writing of poems as an activity akin to the working out of problems that seem similar to problems worked out by the reader. In part, his reaction to the poem captures him first as writer and then as reader. I wanted to help him focus on "those feelings that are inside," which are difficult to express, since surely poetry contributes to the expression of emotions usually restrained in common discourse. I wrote: "Good start, Chris. Notice in this week's readings that writers often communicate inexpressible emotions by relying heavily on comparisons. A poet might recognize that the word 'love,' by itself, suggests a great many things to a reader. But if that emotion is compared to something tangible and specific, the writer can do a better job of limiting the reader's interpretations of what is meant."

Four weeks later, Chris wrote the following response to the question:

> The poem would have to have meaning for me. I guess that is just another way of saying the author presents a problem and solves it. The poem would have to have visual imagery so that I can picture the scene vividly—either in my brain or in my heart (as is the case with extended metaphors). I tend to like free verse and poems with plenty of metaphors, even surrealistic poetry. A poem that is stiff, pure rhyme and with no imagery, is dull to me.

The biggest change here is Chris's acknowledgment that comparisons can be employed to help the reader understand the writer's emotions. Not only does he want to "picture the scene vividly," Chris is an advocate of metaphor. The following poem adequately reflects this perspective on poetry:

Untitled

I am taking part in a great experiment
in which the only exit will be final.
The experimental procedure will be
    thrown by the wayside, in an attempt
to achieve the moon.
Indeed, the outcome will be fantastic
    and the effects irreversible,
for time is a power greater than any man
    and the travel across space will
be for all to watch, to ponder.
Those with me will never return,
as well,
but they know the cost, and the future is
    on our backs to ride to the end
only to get off and ride someone
else's later.
    We can't wait. We pass greatness so
others can reach new heights
    higher than time and ideas
of the mind.
    We have achieved much more than greatness.
We have drawn a CORRECT conclusion.

This poem seemed to satisfy much that Chris and I agreed upon in our interactions over the question, "What kinds of things would you take into consideration in evaluating a poem?" This poem, a versified analysis of the scientific method, certainly would have meaning for Chris and other scientists. He presents a problem, both in form and content, and solves it. And he expresses indirectly his exasperation over the details of the scientific method and its inherent limitations. His interest in surrealistic writing is evident throughout the poem. All in all, given the standard for measuring the success of Chris's poem as generated through our interactions, I judge this to be a fine poem, very different from Lisa's poem, but successful nonetheless.

5

This study leads me to conclude that reader-response criticism can be used in the classroom to help writers and readers construct the same text. By generating a set of criteria, reader response satisfies the two central concerns of most teachers who study and evaluate student poetry writing—first, that the method of evaluation acknowledge the integrity of each individual poem and, second, that it provide the opportunity for continued interaction between writer and reader and text. This study enabled me to see that students do, in fact, bring their personal experiences to bear upon their writing and reading. For instance, Lisa, an art major, made extensive use of imagery both in answering the question and in writing her poem. Chris, a chemistry major, explored the potential of metaphor and simile to explain unexplainable matters and, in the end, wrote best about the scientific method.

I reached several other conclusions that I hope to test further but present here as hypotheses that others might test. First, I believe that when we teach students to write poetry, we teach them to generate texts that represent their understanding of what constitutes poetry. This certainly seemed to hold true for Lisa and Chris, perhaps best in the poems selected for inclusion here. Second, this understanding of what constitutes poetry includes a wide range of things. While Lisa describes poetry as image-based writing and writes a poem that depends largely on her use of imagery, Chris thinks of poetry as an expression of emotions conveyed best through comparison. The resulting poems are very different; both, nonetheless, are poems. To evaluate them—as different as they are—by using a single criterion would violate their integrity as poems.

I also believe that the student's understandings of what constitutes poetry changes during the term, though it may never parallel the teacher's understanding (and needn't). In fact, I was able to influence the views of Lisa and Chris, but that, after all, is my responsibility as a teacher who has read more than they have and as a reader who is an active agent in the making of meaning in their poems.

No doubt a wide range of texts called poems is submitted to an instructor for evaluation during the term. That this range of texts is possible simply verifies what we find in examining volumes of poetry published by reputable presses. Still, in evaluating these poems, instructors need to recognize the influence on them of systems they employ in determining where meaning resides when they examine literature. If an instructor believes meaning resides in the text, New Critical methods can be profitably applied in evaluating the text. If, however, instructors perceive meaning to be something that exists in the reader's recreation of the text, then we need to consider new approaches to evaluation, interactions between reader/evaluator and writer not only to determine meaning but to determine worth as well.

THE WRITING TEACHER
AND AUTHORITY

20
Negotiating Authority in Peer Response

KATHLEEN GEISSLER

Increasingly, teachers of writing at all levels have come to use a workshop format that depends on students' response to each other's writing. Frequently they have adopted this model with some trepidation, concerned that their students will abandon their assigned task during small group discussions or that they will evaluate each other's writing by inappropriate standards. Teachers wonder whether students will be effective responders, offering substantive suggestions authors can use to improve their writing.[1] It is this last concern that arises most often during the weekly staff meetings I have with new teaching assistants.

Recently, one TA worried because four weeks into the term, students were still writing comments that began, "Nice paper. I really liked it." In a response prompted by what I have learned while examining students' comments, I asked whether what followed those opening sentences had changed. Did it seem that the rest of the response showed more willingness to address the specific features of the paper than had earlier comments that opened with similar plaudits? The TA agreed that such did seem to be the case. I went on to suggest that introductory expressions of praise like "Great paper" or "I really liked your paper" serve a ritual function within the speech event of responding to another student's paper. Though phrased as evaluation, I suggested, these statements are less an expression of critical judgment than a fulfillment of one's social obligation to be polite. As such, they have a role in the negotiation of role-related authority within the writing group.

Certainly, I have at times shared the teaching assistants' dismay at the persistence of these social niceties when I have asked students to respond to each other's writing. Before my close study of responders' comments, I might well have joined in the head-shaking. I would certainly have suggested ways to lead students away from such empty responses and toward the serious business of "really looking at the papers." Thus, one outcome of my work with students' written responses to their peers' writing has been a recognition

267

similar to one that emerges from Thia Wolf's study of peer group interaction. As Wolf points out, some features of students' work as peer responders that lead us to fear our students are straying from the task or not meeting its demands actually encourage the interaction on which the task depends. Without these features which enable the interaction, the task will never be completed. The fact is, as Jennifer Jackson and Barbara Lewis have argued in discussing the "Rhetoric of Negotiation" in peer evaluation, the task we expect our students to perform when we ask them to respond to each other's writing is a complex one, and is complex in ways that we only occasionally think about.

My own work addresses one of these complexities. Students are frequently uncomfortable exercising the authority implicit in the responding-to-writing role we thrust upon them. Their task, as they define it, is one of evaluation, and they assume at the outset that they lack the expertise requisite for the task. Lacking the expertise, they hesitate—understandably so—to claim the right that seems central to the responder role, the right, that is, to render definitive judgments. Will they, for their presumption, be made to suffer when it is their turn to be the vulnerable recipient of comments?

Despite their misgivings, students trust us enough—or are dutiful enough—to attempt what we ask of them. The written record of those attempts shows that students do indeed find ways to negotiate authority in their responder roles. They discover ways of surmounting the discomfort evident in their initial approaches to the task. What I have discovered is that the texts-upon-texts my students generated over the course of a ten-week term reveal an evolutionary pattern of responses; they also instruct us about the complexity of the task our students have accepted.

The student responses I am reporting on were written in a course titled Writing Workshop during the fall term of 1987 at Michigan State University. The university catalog describes this course as "sophomore level," but mainly third- and fourth-year students enrolled, along with a few sophomores and one first-year student. Although a number of students had not yet declared majors, those who had done so were in elementary education, journalism, communications, environmental studies, parks and recreation, and packaging. As this course was conducted, its central focus was on peer response to work in progress (and all work was in progress until exam week, when students presented portfolios of their work for a course grade). Students collaborated and responded to each other's work throughout the writing process. Within writing groups they talked through initial ideas and responded orally to early drafts. They distributed photocopies of "semifinal drafts" to their writing groups for out-of-class written response. (To emphasize the always-revisable character of writing for the class, the term "final draft" was reserved for the versions submitted in portfolios.) In addition, each time a semifinal draft was due, four students supplied photocopies for the entire class. After the class discussed the paper, each student wrote a response to the author and brought it to the next class. The written responses the authors received on their semifinal drafts took two forms—marginal notes and a final letter to the author. The directions I supplied for the letter were fairly simple. I asked students: (1) to tell the author what they liked, what worked for them, or what seemed effective, (2) to make suggestions for subsequent revisions, and (3) in each case, to refer to relevant points in the paper as they praised the author or made suggestions.

It is these written comments on semifinal drafts that I have studied, examining two groups of comments—those written by the entire class to one of each of the four papers written in the term; and those written by three students—members of one writing group—on all the semifinal drafts presented to the class. Letters in the first category—those written to an author by each member of the class—follow a path that suggests the students' evolving conceptions of their roles as responders-to-writing and their increasing willingness to exercise the authority implicit in the role. They also show, however, that responders must find warrants to exercise that authority.

The letters written in response to the first paper of the term, an account of how the author came to select her major, share a number of characteristics. As a rule, these letters are quite brief, and they tend to comment on the voice and personality of the author as conveyed by the paper. Thus, for example, they respond favorably to the writer's enthusiasm for her major and to her goals as a teacher, and they note their willingness to have her teach their children (if they had them, as most are careful to add). In short, in their compliments students respond to the writer as to a person they are getting to know at the beginning of a term. As expressions of approval, their comments have a place in the getting-acquainted rituals within the classroom group.

As they offer suggestions that the writer might use when she revises her paper, many students urge that she eliminate repetition of ideas. The general tendency of these remarks is summed up by one student's two-sentence letter: "The goals you have set for yourself in teaching are very good. You have a lot of repetition/redundancy in your paper." This responder also did extensive copyediting, combining attention to local matters with global evaluation.

Finally, these letters on the first papers of the term give evidence of students' discomfort in their role; they are unsure of the source of their authority, as the following examples illustrate.

> I really enjoyed your paper especially as an elementary education major myself. It seems somewhat repetitive though. You could possibly cut some of it out—I really enjoyed it though. Very personable.

In her discomfort, this responder hastens to reassure the author and to mitigate the criticism she offers: the problem she mentions did not, after all, interfere with her enjoyment of the paper. Another student, after commenting on repetition, adds, "I know it's hard, believe me, because I have the same problem." She does not, it appears, want to claim more expertise or skill than the author. She does not want to put herself on a pedestal by asserting an authority that would set her apart from her peers. Here, the mitigation functions as a defense against the responder's own vulnerability to criticism.

Another kind of disclaimer is made by a student who refers to marginal questions that asked for further development of several statements—one of the few students to make such a reference to marginal comments. Having mentioned those requests for clarification, she demurs: "Perhaps the information desired in those questions aren't [sic] relevant to your paper. They're only suggestions." Having simultaneously offered the disclaimer and acknowledged the writer's authority over the text, this reader proceeds to give encouragement: "The content is good. With some improvements, you'll have a very fine paper."

In responding to the second paper—a critical review—students found a way to alleviate some of this discomfort by grounding suggestions in their experience of the text. Both compliments and suggestions report on the reading process. Thus, in telling writers what they did well, students frequently make remarks like these: "I enjoyed your use of graphic detail to make a reader feel some of what you felt watching this movie in the theatre." Or, "I particularly like your opening with two questions; it made me wonder what the answers were." It is in their suggestions for revision, above all, that responders refer to their reading experience. They find in that experience the warrant for implicit injunctions to "fix it" as they alert writers to trouble spots. Thus, one reader reports, "I got rather confused in the detail, you seem to skip from one thought to another, especially in paragraph 2." A second reader informs the writer that "I had a lot of trouble with where you were going with your second paragraph." This sentence in the letter reiterates the responder's comment in the margin next to paragraph two: "I'm totally lost here. Are you talking about the movie?" A third student comments on her experience of the piece as a whole: "I didn't really know what your main point was until the conclusion. It was a bit jumbled and confusing at times for me."

With the third paper, which asked students to explain a technical concept in their discipline, responders adopted two new strategies which they continued to use for the remainder of the term. The first of these entailed adopting what I call the writing-coach role. This role builds on and extends the previously used reports of reading experience. In the reporting mode responders simply mention questions or problems that arose as they read. In the new role they also suggest possible revisions and discuss the revision's potential effect on readers. Thus, on a paper that discusses several approaches to elementary school discipline, one responder suggests that the author concentrate on a single method of discipline. She finds that because there are three being discussed, the author is vague—necessarily so, given the constraints of space. She has trouble, she says, with the arguments given and suggests that more elaboration on one method would allow for responses to likely counterarguments of the sort she herself has written in the margin.

The remarks of a second student illustrate both this writing-coach role and the way students begin to exercise this role even before they are fully comfortable claiming and exercising the authority the role implies. This student raises questions about points the author has mentioned only briefly, then adds: "If you were to elaborate on these parts it would be clearer about the room and it would answer the questions I asked and make it seem more full." The relative fullness with which the responder herself here discusses the impact a revision will have on the reading experience also helps establish her claim on the authority to make a suggestion. However, she still fears her warrant to suggest is shaky (or perhaps she fears the author will consider it so), for she follows her assumption of the writing-coach role with a disclaimer: "It was just my curiosity that made me ask those questions." Still, she refrains from conceding the point entirely and appeals instead to an interpretive community: "Maybe some other readers thought of those things too." In her supposition that she may not be the only reader experiencing difficulty we see evidence of the student's increasing, if hesitant, confidence in her perceptions as a reader and in her responder role. We also see her enacting the negotiation that the responder role requires.

The second trend that emerged as students responded to the third paper of the term involved their addressing issues raised by the paper. Students entered, as it were, into topic-based conversation with the author, indicating their own perspective on a position taken by the author. Something of this tendency is evident in the comment already cited in which the responder urges the author to anticipate counterarguments similar to those she has written in the margin. A further example of this trend appears as a second student reports her objection to a point made by the author: "I did have a problem with the kids that were neither good nor bad getting the special treat."

A third respondent refers more generally to the author's topic: "I find it quite interesting, the methods used to discipline in schools." She then advances her own evaluation of the methods described in the paper: "It seems like positive reinforcement would be the best method." In dialogic fashion, she then checks her perception of a portion of the paper before making a suggestion: "Is it true that the children that receive positive reinforcement get treated the same as the ones who don't get positive reinforcement? (movies, etc.) If this is true, I would expand your opinion about it in your paper."

With the third paper students seem to have found a comfortable way of negotiating the authority attendant on their role as peer responders, at least within this particular classroom community. When they responded to the fourth paper, which had asked authors to define a problem and propose a solution, they did not introduce any new roles or variations thereon. Instead, they relied on the three strategies they had already developed: (1) They reported on their experience as readers, a mode of response they had adopted for the second paper. Increasingly, however, they elaborated on their experience, instead of simply naming it. (2) As they had begun to do with the third paper, they continued to use the writing-coach role as they suggested changes and explained the effect the changes would have on the reader. (3) They raised objections to claims, offered writers additional information on the topic, and considered implications.

When, in my study, I turned to an examination of all the letters written by the three members of one writing group, I found one of the three to be a paradigmatic example of the evolutionary path followed by the class as a whole. A second observed the basic progression, with some variations which I shall describe shortly. The third member of the group, however, settled into a formulaic mode of responding that allowed her to write comments that might have been appended to almost any paper. On occasion, she did indeed write responses that addressed a paper more directly. Writing on one of the first set, she mentions an experience of confusion: "Great paper. I found the transition a little confusing because of the switch of majors, but very interesting. Super conclusion."

On one of the third set of papers, she refers to her lack of knowledge of the topic and uses that as her warrant for requesting clarification. "I thought your paper was very interesting. I just wanted to keep on reading more. Good job!" Somewhat uncharacteristically, she continues:

> You did a great job of covering what Gatekeeping is, but some of the words aren't defined and therefore unfamiliar to me being someone who doesn't know a lot about journalism. I made some comments in the margins—just suggestions that might help. [For the most part, these are questions about definitions of terms.]

As the letter proceeds, it offers this reader's invariant comment on conclusions: "Your introduction is very catchy and the conclusion does a great job of summing up your points." She then concludes her letter with more praise: "You did a good job too of taking the reader through the process step by step. Very easy to follow. Good job!"

In responding to another of the third set of papers, this student began to use the formula that with some minor variations served her for the rest of the term.

> This is a very interesting paper. It really kept my attention. It has great flow and I like the transitions. The paper is easy to follow. I made some suggestions in the margins that might help you out. Your conclusion really sums up the main points well. Good job.

This responder has, we might say, solved the authority problem by abdicating, by not taking the risk of making suggestions. Fully a third of all the comments she wrote praise authors in the stereotypical fashion reproduced here. Clearly, then, one way to negotiate authority is to fail to negotiate, and to retreat to formulas and the voice of "blanket" praise, relying almost exclusively on phrases and sentences that seem to have become obligatory rules of etiquette in the complex speech act of responding to another student's paper.

As I have already indicated, the third member of this writing group did adopt new roles as the term went on. However, he handled the authority of his role rather differently from most of his peers. In his responses to the first set of papers, he tends, as did many students, to give blanket favorable comments. His, however, are edict-like evaluations based on (perhaps) his gut response to the text. This student speaks authoritatively from the outset, displaying none of the role discomfort more typical of the responses to the first paper.

> Now *that* was a paper! I loved your use of light humor throughout the paper. It kept me quite interested in the material. Your flow was also excellent. With the exception of the spots I marked, don't change a thing (Really!).

This strong evaluative stance recurs with the second set of responses as he writes, for example: "Your strong message came through loud and clear. Good flow, energetic, and concise. With the few exceptions I have marked, this is great."

With the third set, this student's letters begin to change as he relies less on the "responding to writing" vocabulary he brought with him to the class. Instead, he refers to his reading process, and his comment on audience is based on his experience of the text:

> I like the way you took a concrete example and used it to explain your seven steps. That tactic gave your paper concreteness. I have one question, though. Who are you writing to? Who's your audience? I began slashing your first two paragraphs because of your use of terms that were unfamiliar to me, but then thought that perhaps your audience would already know them. It wasn't clear. You might also want to clarify your audience. Also, add a conclusion—tell me why all this is important. I feel sorta "dropped off."

As did other students at this point in the term, he begins to refer to his own knowledge of the author's subject as his warrant for raising questions. Thus he writes:

> I liked the subject matter of this piece. I've counselled at a few camps during my summers and I've either seen or used all of these methods several times. I would like to comment, however, on your three points. I was wondering what you thought about each of them. Do they work? Are they recommended? What do you think? I have my views on each method and was just wondering where you stood. Other minor comments are marked in text.

His own experience and his knowledge of the writer's subject provide a reference point for his suggestion, and he names the basis for his authority instead of simply asserting it.

In the fourth set of responses, he continues this engagement with the topic, as he enters into dialogue with the author about the piece, and he "owns" his position, his "beef" as he calls it. He begins by praising the author's clarity:

> I love your style. You write clearly and you define each part of your work (last sentence, paragraph one, for example). I wish my coursework were this clear! I am rather hard-pressed to find flaws.

He does find one, though, and hardly a minor one, as he goes on:

> However, (as I usually do) I have one beef—your solution doesn't hold water. Has a voluntary program worked before? Will it really work at all? Because your solution was weak, you may end up destroying your excellent work. If you can cite examples or give another alternative, you could put more validity into it. Granted, this *is* a tough subject and there may be no other route. . . . See what you can come up with.

As this and other comments indicate, students did change as readers. They adopted new roles as responders, and in so doing they negotiated the authority of the responder role in ways that allowed them to make suggestions. What factors contributed to bringing about these changes? I suggest that among the factors are at least three. First of all, a community has been built as students have negotiated their roles within the class. They have felt out the situation in the workshop and developed a trust that as responders they would not be offending other students by offering suggestions.

Second, the task has been renamed. What we are doing is making suggestions for revision. We are *not* "ripping the paper apart" or any of those other phrases that students often use to describe peer response at the outset of the term. Language *is* important—the terms shape perceptions of the activity. Moreover, the task has also been redefined. Contrary to their initial expectations, students are not required to deliver a definitive verdict on the quality of the paper, a task that seems to claim an authority and expertise, or a knowledge of preexisting standards, which students don't believe they possess. Instead, they are asked to give information on their interaction with the text, on their process of constructing meaning from it. To put their reading process at the center is empowering because it validates an authority they can feel comfortable in claiming. So it is not surprising, really, that students begin to use their experience as readers as the basis for their suggestions.

I will speculate further and propose as a subject for further study that this attention to their own reading may begin to change the way students approach texts in the literacy event of classroom response. I suggest that as their reading becomes less globally impressionistic, students become more attentive to the interplay between local and global levels. Such attention to this interplay offers an explanation for the writing-coach role in which students mention their experience of the text, offer suggestions, and explain the effect the proposed change will have on readers.

Finally, students have changed as readers because their task as responders is a significant one. The response is significant for the authors because all work is *in process* until the end of the term. Responses can be genuinely helpful as writers use them in subsequent versions of their papers. The task is also significant for the responders, and this significance increases for responders as they see authors acknowledge their authority by adopting (at least some of) their suggestions. The significance also increases as in their own writing responders use ideas they have received from their readers. I see evidence of this incremental progression most clearly in comments *within* writing groups, where talk about earlier versions has preceded the written comments I have discussed here. Comments from within the group regularly refer to the ways papers have evolved from earlier versions and to the way problems of those earlier versions have been solved.

I close with a representative anecdote recently told me by the instructor of a workshop in which students responded to each other's work in much the same manner as mine did. I cite the anecdote, on the one hand, because it offers a powerful demonstration of the difficulty students sometimes have understanding and exercising the authority they have as responders-to-writing and, on the other, because it underscores the significant role their own use of peers' responses plays in students' negotiation of authority. In this instructor's class was a student who rigidly restricted himself to complimenting the "interesting" topics his group members had chosen. He was, on religious grounds, unwilling to add to the negativity of the universe, and was further convinced that one neither could nor should force another person to do anything. Nonetheless, the student was receptive when the instructor noted that he had changed—and substantially improved—his own papers as a result of comments he had received from his writing group. The student subsequently rethought his position, revised his comments, and furnished each of his peers with a full page of insightful and helpful suggestions. One might well conclude from this story that a collaborative reading-writing-reading process empowering enough to prompt a reconsideration of one's convictions in this way is a powerful force indeed.[2]

NOTES

1. For further discussion of these concerns, see Anne Ruggles Gere and Robert D. Abbott, "Talking About Writing: The Language of Writing Groups," *Research in the Teaching of English* 19 (1985): 362–85; Thomas Newkirk, "Direction and Misdirection in Peer Response," *College Composition and Communication* 35 (1984): 301–11; and Martin Nystrand, "Learning to Write by Talking about Writing," in his *The Structure of Written Communication: Studies in Reciprocity between Writers and Readers* (New York: Academic Press, 1986), 179–211.

2. For a discussion of the reciprocity between writers and readers, see David Kaufer and Gary Waller, "To Write Is to Read Is to Write, Right?" in C. Douglas Atkins and Michael A. Johnson, eds., *Writing and Reading Differently: Deconstruction and the Teaching of Composition and Literature* (Lawrence: University Press of Kansas, 1985), 66–92.

21

The Teacher as Eavesdropper: Listening in on the Language of Collaboration

THIA WOLF

Because my position at California State University at Northridge included supervising graduate student teaching assistants, I spent large amounts of time in new teachers' classrooms. Originally, I arrived in these classrooms in order to observe and evaluate new teachers at work, but I found that most of the graduate students had followed my advice and made a practice of using group work extensively. Their use of sound pedagogy challenged me to observe and evaluate classroom practices in new ways, and I worked hard at listening to and understanding the clusters of students who engaged in group work around me. Eventually it dawned on me that I had a large body of notes about group activities and that these notes might be viewed as data about group behaviors.

Some of my observations of group work yielded nothing new. A comparison of my notes with the careful transcriptions made by Anne Ruggles Gere and Robert Abbott in their study of writing groups tallied perfectly. I found, as they did, that students in writing groups spent most of their time discussing writing content, context, and form. While this information cheered me, I believed my data yielded nothing new and, hence, could not develop into a real piece of research. Only after a year of eavesdropping on group conversations did I realize that another series of interactions was also taking place, a pattern of nonresponse to writing that seemed every bit as predictable and important as the discussions about written texts. For instance, I noticed that students in groups tended to complain about the same things in the same ways, tended to joke among themselves at the same regular intervals during draft workshops, and tended to disparage their own writing before anyone else in a group had the chance to do so. These observations led to my general hypothesis for this paper—that *all behavior in groups is purposeful.* By itself, this hypothesis conveys little information, but when paired with a system for understanding group interactions, it yields a wealth of insights into the ways groups work and what the language of collaboration really means.

Although I have an extensive background in clinical psychology, I had no theory, no frame of reference, for interpreting the behavior of groups. For this I turned to noted sociologist Erving Goffman and his studies of "focused gatherings." Goffman defines "focused gatherings" as those where small groups come together for a specific purpose (such as playing a game of bridge or performing surgery). Using Goffman's observations and interpretations, I scrutinized my records of collaborative behaviors that did *not* relate obviously or directly to writing. Originally I assumed that this language had to do mainly with furthering the groups' ability to remain on task and to develop and retain group identity. As it turned out, I discovered that I was both right and wrong in this assumption.

Let me begin with my simplest observation, a note on *group posture.* Students in groups will physically arrange themselves in a variety of ways within the space allotted to them. Several of the group postures I've observed are diagrammed in Figure 21–1.

Goffman calls small group activities "world building activities" (p. 27). In order for a group activity to be successfully tackled and accomplished, the participants must feel a sense of separateness from other demands and activities in their environment. "[A]n engaging activity," Goffman notes, "acts as a boundary around the participants, sealing them off from many potential worlds of meaning and action" (p. 25). The boundary, however, is not like a wall but more like a "membrane" or a "screen" (pp. 33, 65), allowing some

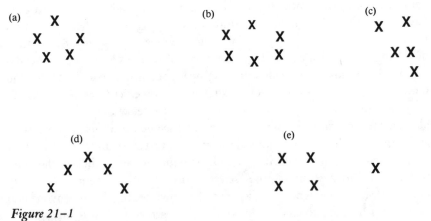

Figure 21–1
Group Posture

information from outside the group to make its way into the group interactions (such as a teacher's instructions about the group activity).

What I have come to think of as group posture aids or inhibits the development of this group membrane. Of the postures noted above, only *a* effectively helps groups to maintain concentration and stay on task. This arrangement of chairs and bodies allows all group members to maintain eye contact and to occupy roughly equivalent portions of the total space available for the group. The placement of every member with his or her back to the larger environment of the classroom helps to screen out all irrelevant sights and sounds that could interfere with the group's concentration.

Many groups do not opt for this effective posture; they manage to sit in a variety of ways that exclude certain members or that lead to a diminished sense of group engagement and responsibility. Posture *b* often results when groups become too large for the space allotted to them. I frequently visit classrooms where groups of six or more students try to form a true circle but wind up sitting in an oval shape instead. In this grouping, two or more students cannot make eye contact. Often, then, group activity centers at one end or the other of the oval, excluding two or more members almost completely. This elongated posture may be adopted by smaller groups, as in *c*; when this happens, one person may take over the work of the group, tackling a writing assignment on her own or doing the bulk of commenting on student texts. I can only guess that the elongated posture tends to confer status on some members over others, as if one or more persons were seated "at the head of the table." Postures *d* and *e* usually result in a kind of breakdown. Posture *d* leaves a large space open to the surrounding environment, destroying any chance that the necessary group membrane will form. Groups adopting this posture not only experience frequent distraction from the outside environment but also tend to disrupt the interactions of other groups. In group posture *e*, a student is either cast off by her group or chooses to remain separate from them. I have seen a surprising number of teachers allow this separation to occur, probably because a lone student is less easily spotted from the front of the classroom than from the middle or back (where I usually sit when I do observations). I recommend, therefore, that teachers stroll through their classrooms at the beginning of every group activity and make certain that students sit appropriately. The teachers I know who have followed this advice tell me that even "problem groups" work better when the members congregate in a true circle where eye contact and physical closeness maximize their chances for completing an activity successfully.

I have come to think of a less obvious, but frequent, group behavior in classrooms as *the litany of complaint*. Students in groups often complain the moment they come together in group configuration. Their complaints tend to center around school, homework, and family problems. Some groups I've observed wouldn't think of beginning a group activity without complaining first, a fact I found curious for a very long time. Initially, I thought the complaining monotonous and annoying, until I realized that some of the best groups in a class engaged in it almost ritualistically. In the end, I found myself believing that this ritual serves an important purpose.

Goffman explains that the group boundary or membrane, when successfully enacted, arises from the application of "transformation rules." These rules govern the transformation of disparate individuals into a team. In order to work together productively, group members must agree, explicitly or implicitly, on a reason for gathering, acceptable behaviors during a gathering, and interpersonal relationships or "deference patterns" within the membership of the group (p. 34). The litany of complaint, I believe, helps to establish the interpersonal relationships within a group.

The illustration provided below will help to clarify my meaning. Here is an example of a litany from a group composed of four students of similar ages and backgrounds. In this example, students were asked to work on an interpretive assignment in groups. They read an essay from an anthology and were asked to arrive at answers to a series of questions the teacher had posed.

EXAMPLE 1

CASEY: Do you understand this stuff? I didn't understand this stuff.

MARLENE: I've got too much other stuff to do. I can't keep up with all this reading.

MIKE: [Talking over Marlene] So did anybody do this reading?

CASEY: I did it, but I don't understand it. I don't understand anything that happens in this class. And my mother's yelling at me all the time about "did you do your homework? [spoken in imitation of his mother's voice]"

MIKE: What kills me are all the papers. Like when we had all those drafts and scratches and that due last week, then I had a chemistry test too.

JIM: So did *you* do this reading?

MIKE: Oh, yeah, I did it.

JIM: Me, too.

CASEY: Well, I don't even get this first question he asks. "How did the author portray her mother? Find and discuss some of the images and analogies the writer used."

MARLENE: What's *analogies*?

[Students begin work on the assigned task.]

In this sample interaction, we see group members establishing a common problem and common opinions about that problem. Most of them feel, or testify to feeling, overburdened in similar ways. In the space of less than three minutes, they have conveyed to one another that they belong together, that they share similar experiences and feelings, and that—given the limitations of their situation—they must rely on each other to complete yet another job that their taskmaster of an English teacher has devised.

The childishness of some of this group's complaints notwithstanding, we can see how quickly the litany of complaint passes into actual work on the task at hand. Students in this group have reestablished group identity in a very short period of time and have agreed to work together as compatriots in a difficult struggle. While their attitude toward school, parents, and learning may grate on us, we must recognize that their attitude toward group work is positive.

Often, a teacher standing on the outside of these groups may mistake the litany of complaint as a personal attack. I have observed teachers interjecting a comment in the same way that the teacher in the next example rushes to his own defense.

EXAMPLE 2 *

LISA:	—and everything else you have to do.
RITA:	Well, yeah. When you get all this work. Especially in this English class. [Speaks loudly] All this work.
KYLE:	For a 100-level class.
RITA:	For 155. And we have all of these papers and papers.
TEACHER:	[Overhears them and interjects] I have a harder level class.
RITA:	Every day there's something to do.

[*This transcript was taped. All other taped transcripts in this paper are asterisked.]

The justification by the teacher goes unacknowledged by the students in this group. He, after all, has missed the point; this group is not actually complaining about him or his class. Instead, the group uses its single shared experience of his classroom to establish a common bond. Interestingly, because this group contained students of varied ages (from nineteen to forty-something), two of them mothers, the usual subject of annoying parents never became part of their complaint ritual. If the younger students had complained about their parents, the litany could not have served its purpose. It might have put off two of the group's members rather than bringing all of the group members closer together.

Because writing groups require members to share so equally in the work at hand, group members must find a way to leave differences in intelligence, status, and style outside of the group boundary. The litany of complaint grants a kind of equality to all group participants, permitting them to develop a feeling of closeness and oneness of purpose. Writing teachers would benefit themselves and their groups, then, by not taking these "griping sessions" too seriously.

In fact, most group behaviors, even when they appear to the casual observer as a kind of "goofing off," actually serve to promote group integration. The single exception to this occurs when what Goffman calls "tension" overrides the focus of the group gathering. Tension arises when a participant's involvement in the group activity does not match his involvement in some other activity that would satisfy him more. As Goffman puts it, "The participant's two possible worlds—the one in which he is obliged to dwell and the one his spontaneous involvement actually does or could bring alive to him—may not coincide. . . . Under such circumstances, we can say that a *state of tension or dysphoria* exists for him in the encounter" (p. 42).

When students fail to become engaged in the task at hand, dysphoria often results. In the example provided below, students were given a collaborative writing assignment. This group wrote a paragraph explaining the fiscal deficit to an American farmer; before writing the paragraph, they were asked to brainstorm their topic and to list audience assumptions they should keep in mind while writing. The group below completed all parts of the assignment very quickly. When the teacher noticed they were finished, she called one of them to the front of the room so that she could check the paragraph. She told the student who brought her the paragraph that his group had not kept audience in mind while writing.

EXAMPLE 3

STEVE: [Returning from the teacher's desk] She says we haven't taken audience into account.

MAX: [Looking at Steve, then turning back to John, with whom he is having a conversation] The thing is, with this writer's strike, there hasn't been much available. Like, none of the agents are even taking new clients.

JOHN: But the strike ended.

MAX: Yeah, but it's still hard. There's like a backlog or something.

STEVE: She says we need to redo this [holding the paper up].

MAX: [Without turning around to face Steve; still speaking to John] But I got this part last year, just a small one, and I think this year I'll do better because my brother knows some people.

JOHN: So this is what you want to do? I mean, full-time?

MAX: Yeah. That'd be cool, wouldn't it?

STEVE: Hand me the brainstorming list, OK?

JOHN: What?

STEVE: Just hand me the brainstorming list. I want to see what we did wrong.

MAX: We didn't do anything wrong.

STEVE: She says we didn't take our audience into account enough.

MAX: Well, we've still got next time to do it in.

STEVE: Just hand me the list.

JOHN: So should we work on it today?

MAX: Nah. Let's work on it next time.

[John and Max resume their conversation while Steve reads the brainstorming list and compares it with the paragraph.]

This group has, of course, completely abandoned the assigned task and, in so doing, has disrupted its own internal identity. While dysphoria need not always result in a complete dismantling of group activity, it usually interferes with the group's ability to concentrate on the activity at hand. In this case, Steve's interest in the assigned task could not engage the rest of his group. Because he refused to become involved in the new topic of interest, the group fragmented, leaving Steve to tackle the assignment alone.

When I discussed this group's collapse with the teacher, she explained that the group ordinarily included a fourth member who tended to keep the participants focused on whatever task she assigns. We agreed that in future situations like this one, she would do well to address the group as a whole. While her instincts for checking the group's work were good, the fact that she singled one member out as a group representative may have added to the disintegration of group identity. This teacher's decision to address one group member finds precedent in the common practice of calling on a single group member to report on the accomplishments of her group. Group unity may be more effectively preserved if teachers can find ways to have all group members participate in synthesis sessions with the entire class.

If we must find ways to guard against dysphoria, then we must also find ways of encouraging its opposite, what Goffman terms "euphoria." Euphoria, as one might expect, occurs in the absence of tension. Group encounters may be described as euphoric when participants find that their world of spontaneous involvement and their world of obligation match (p. 44). The task at hand not only interests group members but enthralls them.

In my year and a half of observing group work closely, I have often seen euphoria at work. Students working in a state of ease rather than tension tend to talk simultaneously, express enthusiasm about other participants' contributions, and remain focused solely on the task the group is undertaking. A typical example of a euphoric interaction is given below. Students in this group have been given a collaborative writing exercise on audience: they must explain Michael Jackson to a member of a nomadic desert tribe.

EXAMPLE 4

SUE: We've got to, like, find what *he* sees as success. Ya know.

DAVE: How about camels? Camels are important. Probably the guy with the most camels is the best in the tribe. [Group laughs]

PHILLIP: —and harem girls.

TAMMY: [Speaking at the same time as Phillip] Blankets. How about blankets?

DAVE: They've got to have those hoods, you know, to keep out the sun. [General babble—too many people talking at once to make out what they're saying]

SUE: So Michael Jackson is this guy with the most camels and what—do those hoods have decorations? This would be easier if it were an Indian. We could say he has the most [feathers] in his headband.

DAVE: No, this guy wouldn't understand that.

PHILLIP: Well, what else?

TAMMY: I saw this show once where these desert guys had to sleep on their arms, propped up at the elbow, or the desert bugs would crawl in their ears.

SUE: Oh gross.

TAMMY: Oh yeah, it was—

DAVE: How could anyone sleep like that?

TAMMY: —bad because the bugs would lay eggs in your brain.

LESLIE: Oh stop.

DAVE: Maybe we can use that. Ya know, like this guy has so many servants that *they* hold his head up when he sleeps on the sand.

SUE: [To Leslie, who has been designated secretary] Did you get that?

LESLIE: [To the group] Do we want that?

SEVERAL
SPEAKERS: Yeah, yeah.

LESLIE: Ok, how do I put it down?

We see here an obvious spirit of enjoyment and cooperation. The group laughs, shouts, talks all at once, but also displays the ability to focus, to choose information that should be included in their written product. Group members are able to "play off" one another, as when Dave builds on Tammy's story about the people who lift their heads in order to sleep.

During a euphoric encounter, everything that happens within the group relates directly to the completion of the task. Although the group may seem chaotic from the outside, it functions with almost total efficiency at these peak moments. Group members get "caught up" in the group activity and work together to make connections between what is said and what should be written.

Such moments lie at the heart of group experiences. A group that never experiences itself as swept away during moments of concentrated activity will probably never *become* a group in the truest sense of that word. But a whole string of euphoric experiences in a row might easily leave an entire group exhausted. For this reason, groups develop what I have come to think of as a rhythm of responding to assigned tasks. Following euphoria, a period of joking or "irrelevant" chatter seems to relieve the tension of moving out of the euphoric mode into a new task or a new part of the same task. In draft workshops, for instance, students often take advantage of the shift from one paper to another to engage in "by-plays," Goffman's term for interactions between two or more group members who have an exchange that is not task-centered (p. 61). In my observation of groups, I have seen by-plays used to relieve tension, change the focus and pace of group activity, and promote camaraderie. (By-plays may also, according to Goffman, serve to exclude a member from group consideration, particularly if she has done something the group deems unacceptable.)

In the first example of a by-play given below, students address each other during a "lull" between discussing one paper in a draft workshop and reading another. The earlier discussion was quite lively and included two clear periods of euphoric interaction.

EXAMPLE 5*

KEVIN: Oh, do you speak French? I took French class for three years.

RITA: I don't speak a word of it. "Parlez-vous français?" Um, what else do I know? I can swear in seven different languages. I can proposition people in four.

LISA: [Loudly] Who is reading next? Which one?

This by-play, though short-lived, illustrates the exclusive properties of some by-plays (Kevin and Rita are flirtatiously engaged in front of, but not in relationship to, the rest of the group). Lisa objects to the by-play and puts an end to it, but for Kevin and Rita it has served its purpose as a brief distraction from an intense group activity. By-plays in successful groups do not take up much time, but they do occur periodically and of necessity. Without these moments of separation from the group task, it is unlikely that the group members could maintain their overall concentration on their work. As Goffman points out, we see this principle in many settings, including the "work place," where gossip and storytelling provide welcome relief from each person's immersion in her daily obligations (p. 61).

The next example of a by-play may occur only in classroom settings. Students sometimes try to entice their teacher into engaging in a by-play, hoping, perhaps, that the distraction from the task at hand will become extended. I believe the reasoning behind such by-plays goes something like this: if the *teacher* will talk to us about irrelevant matters, it *must* be OK not to do the group work she's assigned. The teacher, then, is used as a kind of sanction for avoiding or leaving the task at hand. As you will see in the sample provided, such by-plays seem particularly attractive to students when a task confuses or frightens them because it seems too complicated or because it is new. In this example, students have been asked to write collaboratively about their experience of writing individual in-class assignments. This is the first time they have been asked to write about writing in a group.

EXAMPLE 6

JUDY: It's hard to know where to start with this.

MITCH: [Looking up at the teacher, whose desk is near the group] Let's start with describing *her* when she gave us the assignment. You know, what she looks like. What she's wearing. How she sounds.

TEACHER: I told you earlier this semester that I don't want you writing about me.

MITCH: Just this once.

TEACHER: Nope, nothing doin'.

The teacher in the conversation above allowed herself to get pulled into a by-play that might have transformed itself into a litany of complaint if she had simply let it alone. Students display remarkable savvy about how to pull teachers into by-plays and how to keep them there once they've taken the bait. Such teacher-student interactions during group time effectively destroy group unity and keep group members from the task at hand. No matter what the provocation, teachers are better off steering clear of involvement in such interactions.

Among themselves, students may employ by-plays constructively, in order to support each other and to promote a sense of group identity. In the next example, we see students gathered in a group formation but forbidden to talk to each other. Instead, they are expected to write comments on each other's drafts.

EXAMPLE 7

SANDY: [Whispering loudly to the writer] This is really good.

LYNETTE: Thanks.

SANDY: [Still affecting a loud whisper] This happened to me when I was fifteen, too.

LYNETTE: Really?

TEACHER: There shouldn't be any talking right now.

[Sandy pokes Lynette on the shoulder conspiratorially. Lynette laughs and smiles.]

Because I have seen many such by-plays during silent group activities, I have come to think of the "silent group" as an oxymoron. Students communicate through touch and talk during these silent meetings in order to provide themselves and each other with a sense of security and group membership. It seems unfair, even a "setup," when we ask students to adopt a group posture and then deprive them of group contact. The by-plays we see in these situations as a form of misbehaving are really instances of solid group identity.

Closely related to by-plays are moments of "role distance." Goffman explains that all of us chafe a bit under the restrictions a single role places on us. No matter how serious or important the role, we yearn to show more of ourselves, and we need to communicate to those around us that there is more to us than the role permits them to see. Moments of role distance allow individuals to express identity, keep harmony among group members, convince group members to cooperate, and relieve individual tension. In the example provided below, students are sharing drafts in a draft workshop. Rita has given the writer, Cindy, a very hard time about not having enough clear information in her paper.

EXAMPLE 8 *

RITA: I mean, do they relate with one of the characters, or—? I mean, when we used to watch TV, we used to pretend that we were on the TV shows. Me and my friends were like bionic people.

KEVIN: Really?

RITA: Yeah. We used to after school.

KYLE: My mom had these, these flute wineglasses and we used to stick them up like— [general laughter]

In this instance, Kyle relieves growing tension in the group after Rita's rather forceful critique of Cindy's paper. What begins as a comparison between Cindy's children and Rita's own childhood ends with Kyle showing the group his imitation of a Martian, wineglass horns and all. The entire group laughs, dispelling some building ill-feeling, and the participants quickly return to a further reading of Cindy's draft. Kyle willingly leaves the role of student reader to reveal some other part of his identity to the group. This makes him the center of attention momentarily, but he almost certainly uses role distance here for a much different purpose—to deflect attention away from Rita and Cindy. The "willingness to express" role distance, according to Goffman, is enhanced in groups where individuals feel they belong; the greater the sense of belonging, the less terrible the risk of expressing more of oneself than meets the eye (pp. 111–12). Kyle's clowning around, then, indicates *not* that his group functions poorly but just the opposite. What may look to the uninformed observer like childishness is really a tactful and effective ploy for establishing group harmony.

A different sort of role distance comes into play when an individual in a group feels uncomfortable in or ill-suited to her group role. In the instances cited below, students are asked to move from the role of reader to writer. This shift causes tension in most of the students I have observed. Students moving from reader to writer roles usually allow their texts to be read only after disclaiming those texts' worth.

EXAMPLE 9 *

1. Mine isn't very good. It didn't come out the way I wanted it to.

2. Well, I'm not very impressed with it, so—

3. I didn't have time to finish this, really. It doesn't have as much in it as I wanted to say.

4. I don't know if you can follow this or not. I tried something new. I think it might be kind of confusing, but I wanted to try it out.

5. You won't like this.

This mild shirking of the writer's role should not be viewed by the teacher with worry or annoyance. Good writers and troubled writers alike employ role distance when faced with a group of peers who will read and critique their work. Here role distance functions as a kind of preparation for the experience that lies ahead, allowing the writer to distance herself slightly both from her work and from the demands that her group of readers will make on her.

In reviewing my observations as a classroom eavesdropper, I am reminded of James Britton's oft-repeated plea that we "take care that we don't cut the writer out of the writing; or to put that another way, cut the writer off from his resources at the spoken level" (p. 110). Britton championed the cause of informed teaching; he expected teachers of writing to understand the whole range of linguistic behaviors available to students and to make connections between natural linguistic behaviors and classroom language activities. As teachers in collaborative classrooms, we need to understand not only the linguistic behaviors of our students but also their natural group behaviors. We must know how to identify a group that has become dysphoric, and we must distinguish such a group from one where by-plays or euphoria occur. If we want our students to learn from each other, we must not only tolerate but encourage enthusiastic (even noisy) participation. And we must accept those digressions away from writing and reading tasks that make group functioning possible.

All teachers of writing should, to some extent, become eavesdroppers. We must familiarize ourselves with group behaviors and learn the signs of healthy and unhealthy group interactions. In order to do this, a teacher needs few tools: only pen and paper, keen observational skills, and another teacher's classroom to visit. (For obvious reasons, students in your own classrooms will be overly aware of and worried about your taking notes on their group interactions.) Teachers who spend a semester visiting another classroom regularly, recording dialogue and group interactions, will find themselves the possessors of a wealth of important information. To make sense of these collected observations, teachers use whatever resources are available: sociology and psychology texts, the experience and observations of other teachers, and common sense.

The reward of this effort comes when one applies what one has learned to one's own classroom. Careful observation of groups allows teachers to support students in all of their normal group behaviors, not just those behaviors that apparently move the lesson plan forward. Groups of writers, like individual writers, must discover and develop a process of thinking, questioning, drafting, revising, and coming to know. And groups, like individuals, must be granted time to wander off the track, think of something else, enjoy an unexpected memory or insight, before returning to the task at hand.

22

Subverting the Electronic Workbook: Teaching Writing Using Networked Computers

Lester Faigley

Below is part of an interview conducted for an assignment in a freshman English class that I taught at the University of Texas. The student, Arturo Rodriguez, interviewed Elia Barrientes, a thirty-year-old counselor in the Learning Skills Center at the University of Texas. Barrientes reflects about her former job as a secondary language teacher:

> I enjoy this work more than teaching junior high and high school students. After teaching in public schools, I really got burned out and frustrated. I really couldn't do a lot. My hands were tied. That's the way I felt. I feel that the way the public school system is set up the administrators don't have a lot of power to do things because of the new education laws that have come about and are coming about. It's very difficult to follow through with the laws and to do what you think is best for the school. You find a lot of principals, administrators, and teachers that are overworked, not because of teaching but because of paperwork. There is a lot of apathy. There is very little teaching going on in the schools now. A lot of it is preparing the students for tests. There is no real growth in thinking processes.

Elia Barrientes sums up the feelings of many teachers in Texas and elsewhere in the nation. Increasingly, teachers are being denied a role in planning the curriculum they teach. Instead the curriculum is reduced to a set of objectives or skills that can be measured on achievement tests and delivered to the students in prepackaged modules.

For those who believe that students learn best if they are given bite-sized chunks of knowledge one at a time, the computer becomes what Frank Smith calls "the ultimate weapon" (pp. xi–xii). The computer replaces the weak link in the curriculum-by-objectives—the teacher. The architects of the curriculum-by-objectives see computers as electronic workbooks, possessing nearly infinite patience until the student gets the right answer. In their view computers are "teacher proof." As long as the electricity is on and the students are in front of the screen, they will receive exactly the same lesson, no matter if they are in Harlem or on the Hopi reservation. The publishers promise that the software they sell will teach, test, correct, reteach, and retest. The potential market is enormous. In 1986 over 95 percent of junior high schools, over 98 percent of high schools, and nearly all colleges and universities in the United States used computers for instruction (U.S. Department of Commerce, p. 134).

Of course, many teachers at all levels have resisted the computerized version of the "skills-and-drills" curriculum, turning instead to word-processing programs that facilitate the composing and revising of multiple drafts. Some teachers have made innovative uses of individual computers. For example, teachers have asked students to submit their diskettes and then inserted suggestions for revising within the students' files, and they have encouraged students to collaborate while working on one computer. These kinds of activities, however, do not alter the nature of a writing class because the computers remain individualized.

Using networked computers to teach writing changes the nature of a writing class. That reading and writing are inherently social rather than individual activities is demonstrated when a class communicates electronically. Instead of being tools of repression in the skills-and-drills curriculum, computers joined in a network can be a means of liberation, particularly for those students who are often marginalized in American classrooms. In this chapter I am going to discuss a particular class that I taught at the University of Texas using networked microcomputers. This class demonstrates some of the ways communicating on networked computers affects possibilities for collaboration, relationships of power, and our understanding of language and knowledge. This technology encourages teachers to be researchers in their own classrooms because, since they can no longer control class discussion, they see their students setting their own topics and analyzing them. Because students quickly realize they have the same access to discussions as their teachers, they too become researchers, often at a sophisticated level.

A CLASS DISCUSSION
ON A COMPUTER NETWORK

Networked computers are now used to allow students to communicate with each other in two ways. The first approach is to use some version of electronic mail (e.g., Jennings; Selfe, "Computer-Based Conferences"). Electronic mail makes communication possible outside of scheduled class times and across great distances, allowing students at remote locations to participate in a class discussion. This approach does not require computers for every student nor does it require that computers even be located in the writing classroom. The second approach is far more computer-intensive. It requires that each student in a class have access to a computer configured in a network so that class discussions can be conducted in writing during class time. Two conferencing software programs have been written and tested extensively for such classes: the ENFI "CB" software (Batson) and the "InterChange" software developed by the Daedalus Group and tested at the University of Texas.[1]

The English department at Texas has offered both literature and writing classes taught either exclusively or in part in the computer classroom of the department's Computer Research Laboratory. The classroom is equipped with twenty-five IBM computers linked in a token ring network, which makes possible both approaches to networked communication as well as allowing students to use computers for more usual activities of composing and revising. The InterChange program, however, has drawn most attention. InterChange allows everybody to talk at the same time. A single key stroke introduces a split-screen "window" on which students compose messages. Another key stroke "sends" the message, which then appears as an addition to the list of messages on the screens of all the students in the class. The result is a truly hybrid form of discourse, something between oral and written, where the conventions of turn-taking and topical coherence are altered. Another difference from oral discussion is that students can move back and forth in the emerging transcript to check what was written earlier. Students as well as teachers can obtain a printed copy of the transcript at the end of class, which gives everyone an opportunity to reread and interpret what was written.

At this point I want to introduce a transcript of an InterChange session from an elective writing class titled "Thinking and Writing," which I taught during spring semester 1988. Although the course has a lower-division number, nearly all of the students were sophomores, juniors, or seniors.[2] We met three days out of four in the computer classroom, holding an informal class in a nearby lounge every fourth day to keep in mind the faces that went with the names that flashed across the screen. We used InterChange half the time we were in the computer classroom. On the other days we conducted peer reviews using electronic mail and worked on the essays for the course. The class from which the transcript is taken occurred midway through the semester and was connected to an assignment that asked students to write a microethnography. For this class students read as an example of an ethnography James Spradley and Brenda Mann's *The Cocktail Waitress*. Earlier they had read and discussed Clifford Geertz's "Deep Play: Notes on the Balinese Cockfight" and chapters from Spradley's *Participant Observation*.

The transcript represents what appeared on the students' screens. Attending the class were twenty-one (seventeen women and four men) of the twenty-two students enrolled in the course. Also invited to the class was JoAnn Campbell, a graduate student who was teaching the same course using the same texts in a conventional classroom. The students used for the first time a pseudonym option available in the InterChange program. The first 87 messages of a 191-message transcript are reproduced below. This segment was produced in about twenty minutes.

The first message refers to a paragraph on page 23 of the *The Cocktail Waitress*. Here is the relevant section:

> *Holly*
> At times, some of the girls sensed it vaguely. But for Holly, the mixture of feelings was always there, sometimes clear and intense, other times beneath the surface. Working at Brady's made her feel more like a woman and less like a woman than anything she had ever experienced. And these conflicting emotions were often simultaneous, causing her to both question and accept the identity of "Brady Girl."
> Brady's Bar was a man's world and being part of it brought an excitement all its own. You dressed for the men, served drinks to the men, laughed at jokes told by men, got tips and compliments from men, ran errands for men. Men called you sweetie and honey and sexy. Men asked you out, and men made passes. . . . And as you left after work, Mark or another bartender would give you a loving pat—and tell you how much you were appreciated. It was a good feeling to be needed.

Before they entered the program, each student selected a pseudonym which she or he used for the session. Lester Faigley's and JoAnn Campbell's messages appear under their own names. One student, Greg Homan, also elected to use his own name rather than a pseudonym. The message numbers were added, but the errors remain uncorrected. By this point in the semester, most students valued speed over correctness.

1. LESTER FAIGLEY:

   I'd like you to take a look at a paragraph on p. 23 in the middle. It starts out "Brady's Bar was a man's world . . ."Who do you think wrote this paragraph? James Spradley or Brenda Mann?

2. JOANN:

   I'm concerned about the relationship among the waitresses. Spradley writes that there's only a thin veneer of solidarity. And of course the antagonism between them and the female customers is really evident. So how do women join together to work for change?

3. PRESIDENT REAGEN:

   Well, I guess you're all wondering why I called you here today! Well, I'm not real sure either so we'll have to see how it goes.

4. ART:

   This paragraph was definitely from a woman's point of view. I think that the paragraph has a lot of truths in it though.

5. A. HITLER:

   Brenda Mann must have said this, unless James Spradley likes getting called sweetie and honey by men.

6. LESTER FAIGLEY:

   Yeah, JoAnn, I just read an article about how female bartenders in Britain don't like to serve female customers. Why is this? Is it just because women don't tip well, as is mentioned on p. 142? Or is there more to it?

7. KAREN:

   I think James Spradley probably wrote this paragraph. I can't see that a woman could possibly have written that about "feeling needed" in that way.

8. T.C.:

   Probably, Brenda wrote the paragraph because only the cocktail waitress herself knows how much the men are a part of her world.

9. JoANN:

   I would guess Spradley wrote it, just because he's talking about the excitement, and I would think Mann (ironic sort of name isn't it?) wouldn't have written the last line in the paragraph: it was a good feeling to be needed. What about the sentence saying she felt more like a woman and less like one? Are men doing the defining here?

10. ANGEL:

    I don't think that Brenda Mann wrote the paragraph. I don't think that the waitresses felt that the bartenders gave them "loving pats". Also I think that the paragraph might have been a little more negative and a little less about the role of men.

11. MICKEY:

    Truthfully, it is hard to tell. I can see points for either side.

12. JIMMY:

    Brenda Mann probably wrote the paragraph because it seems like it's from a woman's point of view.

13. KENNY G:

> Most women usually need a common interest to get things started. In the outside world they come together by common desire for equal wages, credit in the job market, and all other issues that affect all women. I became involved in a ERA argument. I am not even a avid supporter. But, I joined the fight w/another girl because we were both being attacked.

14. XERXES:

> I agree Karen. The statement about "feeling needed" bothered me, too. I mean feeling needed is one thing, but feeling used is quite another.

15. JANE DOE:

> I think that Spradley wrote this with a bit of a sarcastic tone.

16. LSP:

> I think Brenda Mann wrote it, or at least said it in an interview.

17. RAE:

> Brenda Mann probably wrote this paragraph because there is constant reference to "you" which makes it seem in this context from a woman.

18. GORDON SUMNER:

> I think it was written by Spradley, he makes it sound like the waitresses liked being treated in that manner.

19. LESTER FAIGLEY:

> I really don't know who wrote it. This is the third time I read COCKTAIL WAITRESS, and I started thinking more this time about how it was written. I had assumed that Brenda Mann probably wrote this part since she knew these women, but that last line is something else.

20. PRESIDENT REAGAN:

> Well, I think that Brenda Mann would have written this paragraph because it seems to be from a womans point of view. I think that some women who work as cocktail waitresses like the way that all of the customers make them feel needed in a sense. I think this paragraph is simply stating how some waitresses like to be appreciated, as does everyone.

21. GEORGE STRAIT:

> I think Brenda wrote the paragraph because it describes what men

do to waitresses in bars. I doubt these men were doing this to other men.

22. JoANN:

Does anybody blame the waitresses for their condition? Why didn't they protest more? Seems to me some things just wouldn't be said today, but I may be optimistic or naive. Has the accepted kind of discourse changed significantly in fifteen years?

23. KAREN:

JoAnn, I think that a man is defining this. Maybe it's just me but I can't see a woman placing herself in such a subordinant and demeaning way. Just the way he describes about the things they do makes it sound like they absolutely live for the male approval. Yuck!

24. MICKEY:

Good point Rae. But then I can also see a male saying something about bringing "an excitement all its own." Then again only a woman would know that she has been called sweetie, honey, and sexy. But yet, the loving pat part seems to come from a man because a woman would not look at it this way.

25. LESTER FAIGLEY:

We talked about how much things had changed in the last class, and several people said not that much.

26. T.C.:

It really depends on your state of mind. Some women would not find this type of behavior offensive. I think that some women really do feel needed in this type of situation.

27. KENNY G:

I believe that Spradley wrote it because it offers stereotyp[ical] feelings about how a women would feel being harassed. I think most women would react stronger than the author portrayed.

28. ART:

I think that it probably could have been written by either. The point of view that they are expressing is fairly common in a way. I think in a sarcastic way the author is saying that girls like to be thought of as attractive and needed, but the tone here expresses that in a bar scene it is an exaggeration of what happens in real life.

29. A. HITLER:

I agree with Ron Reagan—even though the "loving" pats and

nicknames "sweetie and honey" are very sexist, it is attention nevertheless.

30. JANE DOE:

In reference to the sentence about feeling more like a woman and less like a woman is a very strong sentence. It relays two different ideas about working in a bar. When you feel like a woman it's probably because of all the attention you get, but at the same time all this attention may seem confusing. The woman may begin to feel like an object.

31. LSP:

Maybe these women like the way the men treat them. There are people out there who have to find other ways of being needed. It does sound as if women are putting themselves in demeaning positions, but maybe it's true. I don't know.

32. MEGAN:

I blame the waitresses at least in part for their condition because they were far too passive if they didn't like the way they were treated. I guess perhaps they didn't protest more because they didn't want to lose their jobs, but I don't think that very many women today would work under those conditions.

33. PRESIDENT REAGEN:

Well, Karen, I think that I will have to disagree on the statement that you made about women dressing to please the male population. I don't believe the waitresses dress the way they do to please men, but to simply get better tips by looking good.

34. JOANN:

The notion of the object seems important, and I think is a real part of the antagonism between waitress and female customer. If these women are treated this way because they are women, and not because they are Holly and Sharon, then it's real threatening when other women enter the domain. After all, you can be exchanged just like that.

35. LESTER FAIGLEY:

I like the point you make, jane doe, that women become like objects. Spradley and Mann talk about this briefly on page 10.

36. ANGEL:

I think that things have changed. Certainly no one or not many people react to someone being a cocktail waitress in the same manner that the women in this piece said that their friends and relatives reacted.

37. JoANN:

Hey, Pres. Reagan, who is giving the tips?

38. GORDON SUMNER:

Things have changed. Women don't like being called "girls" anymore. Just as you wouldn't call a man "boy". Of course it still happens. You still get jerks in bars that want more than a drink and end up making complete asses of themselves.

39. KAREN:

I was just referring to the paragraph. Whoever wrote it is the one who said that they dressed for the men.

40. A. HITLER:

I think the women, divided for some reason, were afraid to protest their conditions individually for fear of being fired.

41. FRED:

I think the waitress is partially at blame in her situation. She could protest this environment if the waitresses banded together. It seems that the waitresses acted this way to define their femininity, just as the men wanted to show their masculinity. The women work at the bar because they cannot express their feminity in their situations such as school and other jobs.

42. JIMMY:

I agree with what t.c. said about some women actually enjoying this kind of male behavior. There are probably some women who are cocktail waitresses as well as hundreds of other jobs that have never gotten so much attention in their life. These women may be fewer, but who really knows? I see it as running along the same lines as this situation: a girl jogging gets whistled at four times. She feels complemented and flattered. The same thing happens to another girl and she is repulsed and embarrassed.

43. KENNY G:

Megan, you need to go to a convention sometime. Watch how alot of the men grope their waitresses after a few drinks. Women are not much better.

44. MICKEY MOUSE:

I agree with Megan on it being their fault. If they could change their attitude and were not afraid to stray from the norn, I think they could get a little more respect.

45. LSP:

I agree with Old Pres. I think the waitresses probably make themselves to look good to get better tips. That's different from dressing up to impress your boyfriend or girlfriend.

46. XERXES:

I think the waitresses dress the way they do because the person in charge gives them certain dress codes. Also, if they complain too much to the men they serve they are in danger of losing their tips and possibly their jobs.

47. ART:

The waitress is not just putting up with a situation, she is working to make money. I don't think the bar scene is much different now than it used to be. People just don't always see the things that happen to a cocktail waitress when she is working.

48. T.C.:

Megan, the waitress has to put up with a lot. If she protested each time that she was called "sweetie" or "honey", she would quickly lose money and maybe her job. Sometimes, the waitress doesn't like her treatment, but she seldom complains if she is a good waitress.

49. PRESIDENT REAGAN:

Well, as the real President Reagan would say, I am not able to answer that question at this time.

50. FRED:

Why do men achieve male solidarity in the bar, while the waitresses remain divided?

51. JoANN:

Mickey Mouse, you say they could change their attitude and get more respect, but how is that done? If this is the norm, if this is the way we see women respond on tv, in movies and books, where do we get a new norm? how do we adopt a new attitude when the power is in the hands of men?

52. GORDON SUMNER:

You have to remember that it is a job requirement to dress in a certain fashion, and an occupational hazard to be bothered by drunken men. They can always quit if they don't want to put up with it.

53. LESTER FAIGLEY:

Good point, fred.

54. KENNY G:

xerxes has a good point. IF the waitress says anything to her customer or her boss she/he runs the risk of loosing money. The reason most people are in this line of work is for the money.

55. GEORGE STRAIT:

Mr. President, do you not know the answer or are you just covering up?

56. MICKEY:

I agree Pres. I'm sure the waitresses do dress for the men because that is where they get their tips. Part of the responsibility of being a "good" waitress is that you have to put up with these snide remarks. Maybe if women were the patrons then the male waiters would have to put up with them.

57. MICKEY MOUSE:

Waitresses are not the only ones who have to put up with being called things such as "sweetie" and "honey." I work in an office where the women secretaries are called these sorts of names by the older (and higher status) men. They have to put up with it also, because if they don't they will get on these people's bad side real fast.

58. LESTER FAIGLEY:

Mickey, you get at what Spradley and Mann call the asymmetrical relationship. Men can get away with referring to women's bodies as "two fried eggs thrown against the wall," but women can't come back at the men.

59. GORDON SUMNER:

Good point JoAnn, things can't change overnight.

60. RAE:

Maybe the cocktail waitress could change her behavior, dress etc . . . and maybe she couldn't. It is almost impossible for us to determine this unless we were actually there or have had sufficient experience in this area. A comment was made somewhere in this ethnography that the waitresses had to learn to take the bartenders and mens' jokes and comments or it would be very difficult for them. I don't think this meant they would be fired, but it would just make their job a little easier. This is true today. Everyone at some time or another has to put up with something that they would rather not, but most of the time it is easier to cope with if you go along with it rather than fight it. Perhaps this is what the cocktail waitresses were doing.

61. XERXES:

> JoAnn, yes! The role of women in this society is laid out on t.v. in magazines—everywhere, and the role that is prescribed is not a good one. But, if enough women realize that to look like a fashion model and to please men is not where it's at eventually some radical changes will happen.

62. KAREN:

> Women see themselves as objects (some women anyway) and then society keeps assuring them that this is true. Advertisments are the worst. Commercials either portray women as housewives with rollers in their hair and screaming kids or as glamour type fashion models that very few people could actually look like with the products they try to sell.

63. DOLLY WOLLY:

> I think that some waitresses feel flattered by these type of compliments while others feel insulted. It all depends on your self concept of yourself in relationship to others. Some women are afraid to give a guy a dirty look when they don't like something he said because they don't want to appear cold and unfriendly.

64. JIMMY:

> There is no easy answer to how women should become more equal to men, it is going to happen gradually. Change doesn't happen overnight.

65. ANGEL:

> Gordon, it's easy to say "just quit" but it's not easy to do when you need the money.

66. LSP:

> I think that if the women don't want to put up with the men they should find another line of work or wait tables in a different setting. I know alot of women don't like the way the men treat them, but what about the men who get tormented by a bunch of drunk women and strip joints. They could be dancing and taking their clothes off just for the money too, yet you never hear much about them complaining about the harassment because they are getting tips put into their G-strings.

67. JoANN:

Gordon, I'm a little troubled by your comment, for I don't think my point was that things can't change overnight, although that seems to often be the case. But why is it just up to the women to risk their employment and earning power to get change? When will men join them and work toward this?

68. KENNY G:

What about a group of girls who go to a bar and sit their eyeing every guy who walks in. Isn't this the same treatment. Men do it. But, I think that it doesn't stand out as much because it is normal to see them do it. this same group of girls, is likely to get some unfavorable propositions from the male patrons because of their aggressive behavior.

69. MICKEY:

Basically, I think it is just who ever is at the bottom end of the totem pole has to put up with everyone else. It just so happens that the waitresses are below the customers and the waitresses are female while the customers are male. Can anyone come up with an example of where women are above men on the totem pole?

70. T.C.:

Fred, actually, the cocktail waitresses band together. When a certain customer walks in that has been a problem in the past, all the waitresses sypathize with the one whose section he ends up in. There is some solidarity among the waitresses themselves.

71. GREG HOMAN:

I think as far as calling women's bodies names and patting their butts, that it seems to be the way we have been educated in our society to act and ERA or not that social conditioning will take a long time to change.

72. GORDON SUMNER:

JoAnn, what man do you know that will help in giving away some of his power?

73. PRESIDENT REAGEN:

Well, I myself being a waiter, the type of waiter who serves in banquets and parties where alcohol is served alot, I can turn this point around to show my view. When I said the waitresses dress as they do for more money, I think all of us can see how that is true. But as far as the remarks go, I have recieved a few remarks myself from women at parties who had had a few too many drinks. So I don't feel that only women are the only ones who feel this way some times.

74. XERXES:

LSP, there will always be small instances where reverse descrimination occurs, but really can we justify everything by saying it happens to a few men as well?

75. ART:

I think a lot of waitresses band together because they can all relate to the same types of experiences. tc is right, they do sympathize with each other and help each other out in a bad situation.

76. KAREN:

Good point, xerxes!

77. LESTER FAIGLEY:

Yes, pres, but isn't it a lot more institutionalized for men to grab women and make remarks about their bodies? Isn't it always a little surprising when it happens the other way around?

78. KAREN:

The waitresses may band together but there is still that division between the waitresses and the female customer.

79. JoANN:

Gordon, good question, and so power is the issue. What we need is a structure that doesn't make power so appealing, that brings responsibility with it, that mandates the sharing of it.

80. LSP:

There are more than a few places. Pres. Reagan said that he gets remarks from women who have had a few drinks and he's a waiter that works banquets and stuff like that. I'm not saying that male discrimination is more prevalent than female discrimination, but it does exist and you don't hear about it as much. What about the things male nurses go through, or male secretaries. It's out there.

81. JANE DOE:

It is very doubtful that a man will put aside his pride or shall I call it a "macho ego" to help women gain any power because men like where they have women: right under the palm of thier hand.

82. LESTER FAIGLEY:

Yeah, Karen, take a look at p. 81. A waitress says, "I hate every one of them [the women]."

83. ART:

The point being that when men make comments about women, and grab at them it is almost accepted by most people as normal, but when a woman makes comments to a man she is considered loose.

84. A. HITLER:

Correct, Lester. It is socially accepted for a man to grab a woman's butt or make a remark towards her, but if the roles are reversed people think the woman is drunk or crazy or a whore.

85. PRESIDENT REAGEN:

Yes I guess it is a little surprising, and nice I might add! But I just wanted everyone to realize that women are not so morally above men that they are not capable of doing the same thing!!!!!

86. T.C.:

Dr. Faigley, the difference in men behaving like jerks and women doing it is that men can get away with it and are even encouraged by their friends. However, when women behave this way, they are brazen and too forward and often labled as sluts.

87. MICKEY:

Wait a minute Hitler! Who said it was socially acceptable to grab a woman's butt? It may be socially acceptable for men but it's not for women.

At first glance this transcript may seem fragmented, but given the disruption of usual conversational sequence, it shows a remarkable coherence. It begins with two bids for topics by Lester and JoAnn, and most of messages 4 through 20 come in response to Lester's question about the paragraph from *The Cocktail Waitress* in message 1. JoAnn's focus in 9 on a sentence from the same paragraph ("she felt more like a woman and less like one") also draws comments in the early going, especially from Karen (23) and jane doe (30). JoAnn's questions in 22 direct the discussion more specifically to the waitresses' responsibility for their working conditions ("Does anybody blame the waitresses for their condition? Why didn't they protest more? . . . Has the accepted kind of discourse changed significantly in fifteen years?"). These questions initiate a series of responses beginning with Lester (25), t.c. (26), LSP (31), Megan (32), angel (36), Gordon Sumner (38), A. Hitler (40), and fred (41). Megan's complaint in 32 that the waitresses "were far too passive" leads to another series beginning with Kenny g (43), Mickey Mouse (44), Art (47), t.c. (48), and fred (50). Mickey Mouse's agreement with Megan in 44 is questioned by JoAnn in 51, who then is supported by xerxes in 61, which in turn leads to additional responses. (See Figure 22–1.)

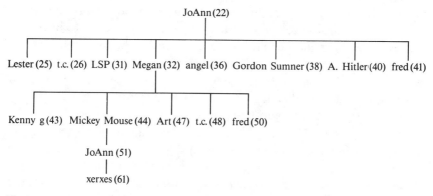

Figure 22–1
Comments in Response to JoAnn's Message 22

While students can move back and forth in the transcript while messages are being added, most stay at the end, reading messages as they are sent and then jumping in with a contribution when a particular message provokes a response. Messages that initiate several responses I will refer to as "hot" messages. JoAnn's message 22 is a "hot" message since it initiates seven or eight direct responses which then foster other sets of responses.

CHANGES IN THE NETWORK OF POWER

Several studies of classroom discourse in the United States, Britain, France, and Australia have described a three-part sequence of initiation, reply, and evaluation (see Mehan, "The Structure of Classroom Discourse"). In this sequence a teacher initiates a topic ("What is the capital of Canada?"), a student replies ("Ottawa"), and the teacher evaluates that reply ("That's correct"). Unlike ordinary conversation where when one speaker concludes a turn, another speaker can take over (Sacks, Schegloff, and Jefferson), class-room discourse is usually tightly controlled. The teacher begins by choosing the topic, then selects which student will speak, and concludes the sequence by taking back the floor when the student finishes. These steps typically are bounded by verbal and nonverbal markers. For example, teachers often slow the cadence of their speech and lower their voices in evaluations, then speak more rapidly and give nonverbal cues when they introduce a new topic (Mehan, *Learning Lessons*).

The InterChange session begins like usual classroom discourse with the teacher asking a question of the class. But unlike a usual classroom teacher, Lester cannot recognize one student to answer his question. Because most of the class respond quickly to his question, there is no opportunity for a conventional evaluation response. When Lester replies to his students in 19, he does not evaluate the students' responses, nor does he supply the answer, nor does he introduce a new topic. By this time he has lost control of the floor. JoAnn's "hot" message 22 initiates a string of responses, but she too loses control quickly. While the students respond to JoAnn in messages 31, 32, 36, 38, 40, 41, and 42, JoAnn and Lester have jumped ahead to comment on jane doe's message 30 which examines social definitions of women.

Lester and JoAnn's advantage in faster reading and writing becomes a disadvantage when they run ahead of the class. The next hot messages are Megan's message 32 and President Reagen's (*sic*) message 33, which together initiate most of the messages from 43 through 56. JoAnn gets drawn away into a conversation with Gordon Sumner beginning in 59, effectively taking her out of a topic-initiator role. Lester has hardly been a force in the discussion since message 1, in part because of his continual direct references to the text (which the others do only indirectly). By the end of this section we see a reversal of roles with the teacher replying and students making evaluative comments. Lester's response in 77 to President Reagen is in turn evaluated by A. Hitler in 84 ("Correct, Lester"). In terms of discourse structure, Lester has become a student in his own class. The paradox, of course, is that the class discussion has gone much farther and much faster than it ever could have with Lester standing at the front.

Not only is the discourse structure radically different from what goes on in a typical classroom, but so too is the level of participation. Even though I had no way of knowing who participated and who didn't, fifteen students joined in by message 21 and five others by the end of the transcript. (The one student not represented came late and sat for most of the class waiting for the old messages to load.) Students were well aware that their participation made the class work. Michael Allen, a student in the class, commented at the end of the semester:

> In my freshman English class, two or three people dominated class discussions every class meeting. But that was not the case in this class. Everyone was allowed an equal chance to participate and ask questions to anyone in the room. . . . Without the interaction of the students, this class would not have gone anywhere.

Furthermore, several students told me that they never would have talked so much in a conventional class. One woman told me outside of class that she had never said anything in a classroom since the tenth grade.

Cynthia Selfe ("Technology in the English Classroom") at Michigan Technological University and Jerome Bump at Texas also report greatly increased participation of women in classes using computer-assisted conferences. This participation runs counter to frequent accusations of sexism in computer software and in stereotypes associated with computers (e.g., Marcus). I'm not suggesting that patriarchal social structures vanish when students join an InterChange. One indication that constraints of gender are still very much present is that several of the women chose male pseudonyms for the Inter-Change session. But InterChange does more than disrupt the turn-taking structure of classroom discourse; it also disrupts the subject positions assumed by classroom discourse. InterChange releases students from some of the socially defined limits of being a student as well as those of gender. It offers a degree of anonymity, even if names are attached to the responses. Michelle Davis, a student in the "Thinking and Writing" class, put it this way:

> Clearly, the main advantage of using InterChange discussions is that it allows you to be both anonymous and public at the same time. By this I mean that your opinions and comments come across the screen for everyone to read and interpret. However, you are not put on the spot by having everyone look at you when you speak. Furthermore, you have no idea when the people are reading your comments or if they are reading them at all. All comments were treated with the same respect and courtesy. All comments were based on their own merits. The students' comments were just as important as the professor's. However, this would not have been the case had the professor's comments been highlighted.

Davis's observations support the findings of psychological studies that compare oral conferences with computer-assisted conferences. Sara Kiesler, Jane Siegel, and Timothy McGuire found that communication is more equitable and less inhibited when such factors as appearance, paralinguistic behavior, and the gaze of others are removed in computer-assisted conferences. In each of the four college classes I have taught using a computer network, at least one student has objected early in the semester to using InterChange. In an InterChange session they have asked: "Why can't we just meet in a regular room and talk?" Each time they have found no support from the other members of the class. And each time the complaining student has been a man.

Women are not the only marginalized group who see benefits in using this technology. A student from Sri Lanka in a graduate course noted that the computer removed his foreign accent, giving him greater license to speak. Another remark came from the only Hispanic student in the "Thinking and Writing" class who later told me he had used the pseudonym "President Reagan." He wrote of the experience using InterChange: "Something that the InterChange did do that is sometimes not done in conversation is that it made everyone equal. One comment had no more impact than another because the computer has only one color and the same print."

The equity of communication produced subtle changes over the semester, which the students saw more clearly than I did. Michelle Davis analyzed the development of the InterChange sessions:

> In the beginning I found myself constantly checking over everything that I typed for mistakes. However, at the end of the semester my mistakes did not seem to bother me as much. Instead I found myself just trying to get my ideas across. I believe that this was the case with most people. In the early InterChange sessions the students did not seem to be as open as they did towards the end. This had to do with the fact that people sensed that they were not being singled out for their specific comments. For example, I can remember a lot of what was said throughout this class. However, I cannot tell you who specifically said what.

Again, Davis's analysis echoes the conclusions of scholars who have studied classroom conferences on computer networks. Both Cynthia Selfe ("Computer-Based Conferences") and Michael Spitzer note a shift in importance from *who* says what to *what* is said in computer-assisted discussions.

RESISTING CLOSURE

Reading an InterChange transcript has for me become like reading a "found" poem. In oral class discussions I tend to remember the remarks that neatly state positions, the ones that seem to tie up segments of knowledge. In InterChange transcripts, however, there are no such crescendos followed by nods of agreement. The movement of discourse in InterChange is more wave-like, with topics ebbing and flowing intermingled with many crosscurrents. Not only do the many voices act out Bakhtin's principle of dialogism, but the movement recalls the opposition he described between the monologic centripetal forces of unity, authority, and truth and the dialogic centrifugal forces of multiplicity, equality, and uncertainty.

The responses of the student who chose the pseudonym President Reagen are important for charting this movement. I suspect that most of the class guessed Reagen's identity because of this student's characteristic humor in InterChange sessions. He was older than most of the other students, the only Hispanic (as I mentioned earlier), the only business major, and more politically and socially conservative than most, if not all, of the others. Even though I frequently disagreed with his views, I admired his rhetorical skills in fast exchanges and his willingness to enter the fray when the odds were against him. In this InterChange session he was heavily outgunned. Seventeen of the other twenty students in the room were women, several of whom had expressed feminist opinions in previous InterChanges, and his two teachers tip their hand in this direction early in the session. After announcing himself in 3 (the only student to do so), in 20 he treats Lester's question as unproblematic: "Some waitresses like to be appreciated, as does everyone." His next comment in 33 challenges Karen, who in 23 claims that the waitresses live for male approval. Reagen says, "I don't believe the waitresses dress the way they do to please men, but to simply get better tips by looking good." JoAnn comes back quickly in 37, "Hey, Pres. Reagan, who is giving the tips?" but Reagen succeeds in getting Karen to qualify her comment in 39, "I was just referring to the paragraph," and in drawing support from LSP in 45.

Reagen then begins to display his rhetorical shrewdness. In 49 he deflects JoAnn's question with humor: "Well, as the real President Reagan would say, I am not able to answer that question at this time." He then waits for an opportunity. He picks up on the discussion of sexist remarks initiated by t.c. in 48 ("If [a waitress] protested each time that she was called 'sweetie' or 'honey,' she would quickly lose money and maybe her job") and continued by Mickey Mouse in 57 ("Waitresses are not the only ones who have to put up with being called things such as 'sweetie' and 'honey'"). In 73 Reagen continues his denial of a patriarchally organized society by arguing that people are just people. He begins by establishing his credibility: "I myself being a waiter, the type of waiter who serves in banquets and parties where alcohol is served alot [*sic*], I can turn this point around to show my view." He then makes a power move, claiming the consensus of the class for his earlier point even though only one other student supported him: "When I said the waitresses dress as they do for more money, I think all of us can see how that is true." Then he disposes of sexist remarks in similar fashion on the basis of his having received similar remarks from drunken women: "So I don't feel that only women are the only ones who feel this way some times." Reagen tries to restructure the debate in moral terms. By arguing that women can make sexist remarks, the remarks become simply immoral and not a manifestation of a male-dominated society. Reagen's claims of unvarying human nature, however, are quickly deconstructed when other students point out that sexual harassment is socially constructed. t.c. writes that the difference between men harassing women and women harassing men is "that men can get away with it" (86).

Another example of how simple dichotomies are deconstructed comes in response to JoAnn's question, "Why didn't [the waitresses] protest more?" After the class goes back and forth, Rae enters a long response at 60: "Maybe the cocktail waitress could change her behavior, dress etc . . . and maybe she couldn't. It is almost impossible for us to determine this unless we were actually there." The idea of resistance itself turns out not to be a simple concept. Essences dissolve into local knowledge on InterChange. InterChange sessions have taught me that the tidy closures we like to achieve in our classrooms and in our scholarship are always an illusion. The InterChange sessions have been the first time in my twenty years of teaching that students have refused to leave the classroom when I tell them it's time to go. When discussion is lively, a few students always linger to get in the last word, attempting to bring the session to a definitive end. But it never happens. Each comment always raises one more response until students become tired and stop or another class evicts us.

When I tried to explain InterChange to a visitor from another campus, he surmised, "So you use it for invention." I replied, "Yes, that's one way of looking at it." My sense is that InterChange demonstrates something more important about how writing works. A written message in InterChange is not an isolated container of meaning but part of a constantly moving stream of communication. Each message both reflects previous responses and anticipates future responses. When we began bringing copies of articles from the library to the class on a specified topic which we summarized and discussed, one student wrote that the scholarly community was like a big InterChange. The categories of professional research and student research became less distinct. Because students had access to each other's essays as well as the InterChange sessions, they began citing the examples and conclusions of other students as well as published research in their essays.

Too often we know little about the potential of students as researchers because we have been deaf to the possibilities of student dialogue. When we create space for students, we allow them to discover that meaning is not fixed but socially reconstituted each time language is used. The skills-and-drills curriculum and standardized testing of language abilities is possible only in authoritarian discourse that assumes meaning is fixed and there can only be one right answer. The play of language in InterChange subverts authoritarian discourse by showing human discourse is composed of many voices. A student in another InterChange said it better: "When I first came to this class, it seemed abnormal to participate all the time. Now it seems abnormal to sit still and listen to a lecture for an hour and a half."

NOTES

1. See Bump for a comparison of the ENFI "CB" and InterChange. Other software has been developed for face-to-face business meetings that may have classroom applications (see Stefik et al.). Information on InterChange can be obtained from Paul Taylor, The Daedalus Group, Inc., 2118 Guadalupe Street, #133, Austin, Texas 78705.

2. Since most of these students had minimal typing skills, I wondered what would happen if students lacked such skills. Would they become frustrated with the technology? To answer this question I volunteered to teach a course in the University of Texas' Youth Opportunities Unlimited program during summer 1988. The Y.O.U. program is designed for disadvantaged fourteen- and fifteen-year-olds. The students I taught were predominantly black and Hispanic, and only one was a proficient typist. Nonetheless, their communicative skills more than made up for their lack of keyboard skills. They produced shorter messages but were even more active and enthusiastic than my college students.

23

The Struggle
with Empowerment:
Hearing the Voices of Dissent
in a Content-Area Course

DIANA GEORGE

We speak much of empowerment these days. I, in fact, use the term often because it has meant to me a way of returning control to students without giving up the business of teaching. Under the early influence of such scholars as Ken Macrorie, Peter Elbow, and Donald Murray, many teachers of composition have struggled to turn the business of learning back to the students, to give them a voice and an opportunity to use that voice. Some of the most recent scholarship in this field (for example, of Patricia Bizzell, James Berlin, and Henry Giroux) reminds us that the struggle for empowerment is not a struggle between the single teacher and the single student but a struggle that occurs within a political, social, and historical context.

Informed by the past and the present, some of us even believe that we have achieved the goal of empowerment by creating classes that turn on dialectic, that resist closure, that force critique. What I will suggest, however, is that the goal of empowerment is a more distant one than we might have imagined. In fact, for many of our students, the attempt to give them a voice can easily seem just another kind of control. Let me explain.

Over the past three years, I have been involved in a project that examined the work of engineering students in an elective course—Art Appreciation. Influenced by the work of James Britton and by the writing-across-the-disciplines movement, I designed the study in order to discover whether or not the writing in the course made any difference in what or how the students were learning.[1]

For the first two years of the study I worked to set course assignments, specifically designing them with writing-as-a-learning-tool in mind. During the third year, we trained four undergraduates to serve as an observation team, we collected all student writing during the term, then we contracted an external reader of the student writing to supplement the team's and my readings. When that initial work was completed, I formed a collaborative partnership with my colleague Art Young to make meaning from the written data, which included interview transcripts, classroom observations, and all student writing (class notes, notebooks, exams).

As Art and I worked through the piles of data and met with the outside reader, we were eventually able to write about the connection between what students had written and what they seemed to have learned in the class.[2] We were able to come to at least four statements about the role writing played in this course:

1. All students in the course were more willing and able to make claims and try their own interpretations by the conclusion of their notebook.

2. The sequence of writing assignments in the notebook necessitated that move.

3. Some students actually used the notebook to narrate their process of decision making—trying an idea, revising that idea, using the revised version to present to the instructor for evaluation.

4. Many students wrote clearer, more lively prose in the notebook than they did when they were restricted by exam questions—even though questions were broad and were given to students well in advance of the actual exam.

The study seemed to indicate that any given class must allow for a number of kinds of learning opportunities—since learning and personality differences seemed to play a key role in how students demonstrated what they had learned. The study, thus, reinforced our sense that we cannot measure students' progress in only one way. As well, the study suggested that we can never know, for certain, what our students are thinking about a course, an assignment, or an idea. The best talker was not the best student; the most quiet student was not the alienated student; the most polite student was not the student happiest with the course. And so empowerment too must not be judged by the loudest voice but by a multiplicity of voices and ways of speaking, listening, and writing.

TALKING ABOUT TROUBLES:
READING AGAINST THE GRAIN

I am always happy to talk about success. It is like putting out the good linen for company. The linen is real enough, I am proud of it, and I like to share it. Perhaps, though, it is time that I begin to think and talk about that which remains troublesome, time that I read my own study against the grain—time (if you will) that I opened up my sock drawer. The sock drawer is also real, but I don't usually open it in front of strangers. When I open the sock drawer of this particular course, I am struck by student comments (in interviews and in notebooks) that make me wonder if empowerment is ever entirely possible in a system that is, on the whole, disempowering.

Although students interviewed did express confidence that they had been given the freedom to think and write what they felt, several statements made early in the quarter and a few made later indicate that freedom is a confusing, though much valued, goal in this system. One student characterized learning in this way:

> I'm a student. I'm this sponge. I don't really form opinions about art until after the class, after I hear all sides of it.

Others talked about their general fear of volunteering to speak in class, even though they acknowledged that this particular class did not seem threatening to them (that is, they did not think that I—as the teacher—would embarrass them):

> It's strange because I'm afraid of being wrong. I shouldn't really care. They're just students. But it matters.

Comments like this one come in many forms: "I don't want to look like a fool"; "I don't know what I'm supposed to say"; "I don't know what she wants." They are familiar to us because we have frequently heard them from our students. We do not, however, often pause to examine what they might mean. Instead, most of us understand that students go through some difficulties adjusting to any given course; we trust or hope that by the end of the course those fears will be dispelled.

Certainly, the students' writing told me a great deal about their learning, but their reluctance and resistance in class, their fears, and their frustrations can potentially tell us even more about education as an institution and our attempts to change within that institution. Within that context I began to explore two issues that may be at the center of student reluctance, fear, and anger. The first might be categorized under the general heading "Freedom of Thought"; the second I would call "the Terror of Ambiguity."

FREEDOM OF THOUGHT

Those student remarks, common enough in most classes, carry with them a central theme: the deep divide students sense between what the teacher wants them to know (her opinions) and what they are really thinking (their opinions). Even in a class in which their opinions were encouraged, students felt the tension.

Freedom of thought, the freedom to hold and express opinions, is integral to the development of independent thinking. Certainly, in William Perry's scheme, it holds the top position—a goal to be worked toward. Freire's pedagogy aims for the same—independent thinkers capable of critique. All students interviewed in our study indicated that they had been encouraged during the course of the quarter to form their own opinions about the material. Furthermore, if we look at course evaluations for the quarter preceding the study and the two quarters following the study, we note that when students did make a comment at all (they were under no direction or obligation to write anything; these were computer-scored evaluations), they often took the time to write about freedom of thought. While most mentioned that they had been encouraged, even forced to think for themselves, a small percentage (less than 7 percent) said the opposite. One even said, "In retrospect, I feel I was more programmed to like these paintings than to make decisions for myself."

Seven percent might not appear significant in a course that seemed, for most students, a real success. In all evaluations, my ratings were well above the university average, scoring, for example, 4.85 (on a five-point system) on the question that asks students if they were treated with respect. Still, if we look through interview transcripts, we might discover the real importance of those dissenting voices. One of the students interviewed was extremely concerned about this matter of opinion. It became a central theme throughout all of his interviews and, even though he said in the last interview that he liked the course because he thought I encouraged students to express their own opinions, his fear of being graded down for those opinions became the driving force when he felt he had to choose between writing what he thought I wanted and writing what he said he wanted to write.

From the very beginning of the course, Don was concerned about grading policies and freedom of thought. In fact, his suggestion, mentioned at least twice, was that the course should be graded only on effort. He said, in the first interview:

> I'll get a B. I might get an A, too, but I'll surely get a B, 'cause I know what's expected of me. But I think . . . the class should be more graded on like how much effort you put forth. You know, I put forth a lot of effort. And . . . if you could form your own opinion . . . and even if it doesn't agree with someone else's, it's all right.

When he was asked about the first exam, Don was confident that he would do fine:

> I'm just gonna write down my opinion. You know, I've a feeling that my opinion is a lot like hers anyway, 'cause . . . I've read the same material and . . . everything.

That first interview ended in the way it began, with Don concerned about how his opinions would be graded:

> You can't grade a person on their opinion. I mean that's basically what we're getting graded on.

In his second interview, which took place in the middle of the term, Don had decided that I did care about people's opinions. In response to the interviewer's question on how he would describe me to another student, Don immediately mentioned opinion:

> She doesn't seem like some instructors, like you know like that don't care about your opinion . . .

So, it is clear that freedom of thought is important to this student. He mentioned it in every interview, came back to it repeatedly no matter what the interviewer was asking about, and linked his desire for freedom of thought to his desire for a good grade.

In his final interview, Don again mentioned opinion, again saying that he liked it that I allowed him to hold his opinion and that, in some way, the course grade did reflect effort. However, when the interviewer asked Don whose opinion he would use on an exam for a grade, he said he would use mine, not his own:

> We had a difference of opinion and she said the painting [Manet's *Olympia*] looked kind of sleazy. I thought it looked kinda nice. I kinda liked it. . . . I still like that painting. . . . I think that it doesn't look that sleazy. You know? On the exam I wrote that it was.
>
> INTERVIEWER: WHY?
> DON: Because that's the way she thinks.

In fact, I *don't* think Olympia looks sleazy. That, of course, isn't the point. The point is that somehow, in my dialogue with Don (playing devil's advocate or engaging in dialectic or whatever we want to call it), Don decided that he liked the painting and that I didn't really like it. To get a good grade, Don decided he had better say on the exam that the painting was sleazy, something he identified as my opinion and thus likely to get him a good grade. He wasn't going to take any chances, freedom of thought or no, on ruining his grade. Early in the course, he had made the interesting distinction that "the notebooks are for my opinion. The tests are for her opinion."

In his first term at Michigan Tech, Don got a 4.0. He knew how to succeed.

THE TERROR OF AMBIGUITY

Which leads me to my next point—the Terror of Ambiguity. During the term we examined, we noticed that students were particularly upset when questions or assignments went beyond the textbook and when generalizations were difficult or impossible to form. One way of explaining this (a way that is often used at Michigan Tech) is that these are primarily engineering students. Engineers, we are told, are uncomfortable with ambiguity. Humanities majors, many of us like to believe, just think differently.

This was not an adequate explanation for me since I had had long-term experience with engineering students in a number of different kinds of courses, both required and elective. While it is true that one initial reaction among many Tech students is a frustration with ambiguities, it is also true that these same students *do* allow themselves to be caught up in the questions (the ambiguities, if you will) of a course. In fact, all of the students interviewed mentioned that the problem with humanities courses was that they took too much time. They did not all indicate that the time was due to overwork. In fact, many mentioned that the course took too much time because they liked it, they got caught up in the reading or writing, and they couldn't afford to "get caught up in" any course that took time away from coursework in their major.

My colleague Steve Loughrin-Sacco and his research partner Wendy Sweet have offered one way of understanding why these students seem so worried over spending time outside their majors. In an ethnographic study of students learning in a French class, Steve and Wendy looked at Michigan Tech's self-study to learn that many of our students carry as many as seventeen hours of coursework per ten-week term in a curriculum that requires as many as 202 hours to graduate: "Only 30 percent of Tech students complete their education in four years. The average GPA ranges from 2.28 for future chemists and chemical engineers to 2.79 for future civil engineers. Because of the demanding course load," Steve and Wendy argue, "students prioritized their courses according to perceived importance and difficulty" (Loughrin-Sacco and Sweet, p. 6).

Don, who had just transferred from a college downstate, characterized Tech in this way:

> Everyone's too busy. And everyone's got a lot of pressure on 'em. Like, you know, you see people's faces as you walk through campus and, like, everyone looks like . . . they're just gonna explode or something.

Don's friends in the dorm thought he was foolish for sticking with a course that took time away from other classes. In the second interview, he mentioned that:

> A lot of my friends, they told me to drop this class. 'Cause they'd seen how much work I had to do for it and stuff. They're goin', "Don, drop that

humanities class."—"I don't know, guys, I don't know."—'Cause I kinda think it's interesting but it does require a lot of work, but you know, 'cause I like art a lot. 'Cause I used to wanna be an artist, you know, so it's kinda neat.

Another student interviewed mentioned the same phenomenon. She said she would sign up for humanities courses every term:

> Almost every term I have one and I'll be like overloaded with credits, I'll have like 18, and I'll say like oh my God, I can't do this, and so boom, there goes my HU class. Isn't that terrible? I like them, though. They're interesting.

Ambiguity just slows these students down in a fast-paced, no-looking-back curriculum. The frustration these students felt when answers were problematic was usually expressed in terms of grades or examination questions. In other words, students did not typically dismiss the material of the course. Instead, they worried about how they might answer questions on a test. As the material of the course became more complex and answers less straightforward, the students responded, most typically with anger. Nancy, for example, became extremely frustrated when the course turned to questions of realism in the context of the textbook discussion of Goya and realism:

> To me, realism is dealing with real things, emotions, feelings—etc.—in a realistic way. I'm still very unclear on what realism is actually supposed to be or how it is represented. Goya confuses me. Daumier does too.

Nancy was a high achiever, a senior who had won the mathematics department's student achievement award that term. When I asked her what bothered her most about that section on realism, she admitted that she was worried about a future exam. "How am I supposed to give a definition?" she asked. She was worried about her grade.

One of her classmates, Tim, was worried about much more than the next test. Characteristically, he spent much time in my office and in front of the display case in which I had posted images the class was studying. By the end of the term, he had an A in the course, and I thought he had gotten over his initial worry, expressed after our first conference. How, he had asked, could I grade the class on essay exams? Some students write faster than others. He wrote very slowly. He did not want to be penalized. Tim showed up at my office one week after the term ended. Instead of being pleased with his A, he was sure it was just my quirky teaching. What he wanted was a place in *any* course I was teaching, as long as that course counted toward graduation. It took three hours of listening and talking and convincing to get him into another colleague's course. He did not want to risk his grade point on another teacher.

WHERE DO WE GO FROM HERE?

I'm not the type to leave you here with no hope. I don't want to work toward empowerment, discover that the system mitigates against it, then give up the struggle. That would be foolish and cynical.

What I would like to suggest is that writing across the disciplines, though an important first step in reforming the institution, is only a first step. We must continue to work toward a Connected Curriculum, one that takes into account a student's entire university career. Those of us who work within the confines of the engineering curriculum are perhaps most keenly aware of how students are forced into a particular kind of learning—literally pushing away from themselves any course that gets them too interested. They are least comfortable with ambiguity because ambiguity makes tests difficult to predict. Yet, they want and need to express their opinions. They want freedom of thought—something the university curriculum, as a whole, has yet to offer.

NOTES

1. I wish to acknowledge the work of those colleagues who assisted in this research project: Stephen Jukuri, Elise Morano, Wendy Sweet, and Marci Wichtowski, undergraduates in Michigan Technological University's Scientific and Technical Communication program, who served as the observation and interview team. Wendy Sweet, whose interviews are referred to in this chapter, read over the text to check for accuracy. Ellen Bommarito, a former English instructor at MTU, trained the undergraduate team in ethnographic observation techniques and interviewing skills. Pauline Moore served as the outside reader for the project. She is a graduate student in MTU's Rhetoric and Technical Communication program. Her contributions provided invaluable insight and checked my own enthusiasm as I read transcripts.

2. This article, written with Art Young of Clemson University, will appear in *Nothing Begins with N*, Peter Elbow, Pat Belanof, and Sheryl Fountaine, eds., to be published by Southern Illinois University Press.

THE WRITING TEACHER
AND LITERACY

24
Language and Literacy from the Student Perspective: What We Can Learn from the Long-term Case Study

RUTH RAY

Before I became a teacher-researcher, I taught as if my students, including non-native (NN) English-speaking students, shared my perspective on language and literacy. Through my research on NN speakers, however, I have discovered that students have their own perspective on language and literacy that is sometimes quite different from that of their teachers. This discovery shouldn't have been a surprise: Shirley Brice Heath has vividly described the contrasting "ways with words" used in school and community; Richard Hoggart and Richard Rodriguez have given poignant accounts of their own struggles to reconcile the differences between life at home and life at school; and Patricia Bizzell and David Bartholomae have argued that college teachers must address the fact that students bring to school dialects, discourse conventions, and worldviews that conflict in significant ways with those of their teachers. But this research was not real to me in a way that affected my teaching. My growth and change as both scholar and teacher occurred when I conducted my own research and discovered for myself the differences between me and my students—between my perspective and theirs—and the considerable effect these differences had on their learning.

My perspective on language and literacy is one I think I share with many other college English teachers. It guides both what we do in the classroom and how we gauge students' progress as writers. According to this perspective, written language is intrinsically valuable; it is, in Berthoff's words, a "philosophical enterprise," a method of thinking and learning. Development of language is crucial to development of mind. Thus, we teach students to use language for thinking in ways academics value: to examine and identify; to question and clarify; to make comparisons; to see relationships between concrete and abstract, specific and general; to define, classify, and differentiate. These uses of language are what many of us refer to when we talk about "academic literacy."

In this chapter I present a four-year case study of one NN writer whose perspective on language and literacy conflicts with the English-teacher perspective described above. I will describe the situation that led to my research, the assumptions underlying the study, the data collected, and the conclusions I have come to as a result of analyzing the data. Finally, I discuss how the study changed my thinking about both teaching and research.

BACKGROUND

My study began with the need to address a very real problem at Wayne State University: NN students in large numbers were failing the university's English Proficiency Exam, an impromptu essay written sometime after the sophomore year as a graduation requirement. Three times as many NN speakers as native speakers failed. The word around campus was that if English wasn't your native language, you were surely going to fail the exam.

There were many research approaches I might have taken, all of which would have addressed different aspects of the problem: an analysis of the exam itself to determine its validity; a review of the grading procedures to determine their reliability; interviews with NN students to find possible explanations for success or failure; or a discourse analysis to find textual explanations for successful and unsuccessful NN writing. I had tried text-oriented methods before. The results of these analyses helped explain why failing exams were unsuccessful, but they did not explain why NN students wrote failing exams. I wanted further insight into the context of NN students' writing—the thinking, learning, and living that students bring to the task. I believed a richer way to study the development of language and literacy was to do so in "real time," in terms of an ongoing process over a period of years, rather than in terms of one piece of writing produced solely to meet a university requirement. As far as I knew, no long-term studies of the kind I had in mind had ever been done on NN college writers.

Thus, I began my study in the fall of 1983 with a basic writing class of fifteen NN speakers. This was the first semester at the university for most students. For some, it was their first year in the United States. I followed as many students as possible from this first semester, through their sequence of required writing courses, to the semester in which they wrote the English Proficiency Exam. My data base consisted of weekly interviews with each student during the first semester; periodic interviews with students and their English teachers during subsequent semesters; copies of all the writing students did during the first semester; as many writing samples as possible from subsequent semesters; transcripts of students' classes and grade point averages; and a teaching journal in which I noted students' progress, raised questions, and considered changes in students' perspectives as they moved through their college coursework. In my analysis of the data, I looked for patterns in writing and in students' talk about writing. I tried to find connections among what the students said about their writing, what teachers said about the students' writing, and what the writing itself demonstrated.

In the process of collecting and analyzing this data, I came to see and articulate three key assumptions underlying my own teaching and that of my colleagues in the English department:

1. Student writers will steadily improve as they move through the required sequence of composition courses.
2. What teachers do in class and say in response to student writing motivates and facilitates this improvement.
3. Success on the English Proficiency Exam depends on student improvement in English classes.

It became clear that my colleagues and I taught as if student writers developed in stages that directly correspond to the semester system: When students finished one English class, they went on to the next class, performing at higher and higher levels of competence, until they reached the final stage—the ability to pass the English Proficiency Exam.

The case of Fida challenges these assumptions about NN students' progress toward proficiency. In four years of undergraduate study, Fida and her writing remained essentially unchanged.

CASE STUDY

Fida is a premed major who was a first-semester freshman when she took my basic writing class for NN speakers. She is a shy girl who looks and acts much younger than her years. She and her mother, a retired chemistry professor, moved from Iraq to the United States after Fida's father died. The two depend mostly on each other in this new country. When they are together, which is often, they speak Arabic, their native language. Fida has little social life; nearly all of her time outside of school is spent studying. When she does "take a rest," as she calls it, it is between semesters. Fida has always been a good science student, but admits that she has never been a good writer, even in Arabic. She studies hard and gets good grades in all areas but English. In her four years at the university, Fida has had two terms of intensive English language instruction, a basic writing course, two composition courses, and a literature course.

Fida's perspective on language and literacy is considerably different from her English teachers' perspective. She thinks of language solely in terms of correctness; if her language is grammatical and understandable, she is satisfied. She thinks of writing as a school requirement to be completed for teachers; it is something that she neither understands nor controls. In order to meet this requirement, she needs a teacher to tell her exactly what to do and how to do it. This is the perspective she has had on college writing since her first semester at the university.

From the beginning, Fida was highly dependent on teachers. During her first semester, she was quiet and reluctant to talk unless she was repeating what had been taught in class. She sought explicit directions for her writing and dutifully followed what I said, even when it did not make sense to her. For example, in an essay she wrote comparing apartment life with dorm life, she had organized a paragraph around the following sentence:

> The advantages of living in the apartment are that you're on your own and you can have guests over any time.

Since the paragraph talked about many issues unrelated to this sentence, I suggested during our conference that she divide the paragraph into several new paragraphs, each beginning with a sentence even more specific than the one she had originally written. I wrote the following sentence on the bottom of her paper to demonstrate the level of specificity I had in mind:

> Living in a dorm is convenient.

In her revised essay, submitted the next week, Fida began every paragraph with a new sentence that included an embedded version of the structure I had given as an example:

> The advantages of living in the apartment are [very convenient] that you're on your own. . . . The disadvantages of an apartment [are uncomfortable] that you have to be independent.
> The advantages of living in the dorm [are amusing] that you will not be lonely and you can have guests over any time.

The revised sentences illustrate that writing for Fida involved repeating what the teacher said, even when she had no idea why the teacher said it or how it was supposed to make her writing better. The revision also illustrates Fida's concept of writing and rewriting as manipulation of language at the sentence level.

Though I recognized that Fida approached the study of writing in a very rigid and controlled way, I felt unable and even unwilling to change this behavior at the time. I wrote in my journal at the end of the semester:

> Fida suffers from a fear of failure in writing. She is so afraid to take chances that she adheres to the same simple formula for every essay. . . . Yet reluctantly I passed her because on the final exam she got everything right: she had a clear essay format, paragraphing was good, thesis was clear, paragraphs followed through on thesis with some details, transitions made for coherence and there were few grammatical errors. I also considered that a failure would devastate this sensitive creature and destroy the small amount of confidence she does possess. I am hoping her next teacher will demand that she take chances, think hard about large subjects, and for a while at least, forget about what her writing is supposed to look like in an effort to make it more than just a display of what she has been taught.

These comments illustrate my own uneasiness about Fida's perspective on language and literacy. On the one hand, she needed to produce an essay that would pass the final exam and get her into the next level of writing class. Indeed, passing my class and going on to the next stage was Fida's only concern. On the other hand, she needed to be challenged in her writing, to be pushed beyond her current limits in order to develop both her thinking and her writing. I knew that kind of challenge would mean her writing would suffer in terms of structure and correctness. At the time, these two goals seemed mutually exclusive, at least in terms of the outcomes I could realistically expect from a NN speaker in a one-semester course. I chose to focus on the first goal, hoping to build students' confidence by teaching them about language in terms of correctness and control. The use of written language to think and learn, I decided, was the domain of higher-level English classes.

I could not know that Fida would never achieve the second goal I had set for her writing, partly because she avoided new learning experiences that would challenge her abilites, and partly because her other teachers took the same approach I had taken, focusing on correctness and form, and supporting Fida, rather than challenging her. Fida's avoidance behavior is evident in her selection of classes. She dropped the freshman composition class she enrolled in during her second semester because it was "too hard"; the teacher wanted her to think and write in ways that were unfamiliar. She took the class again the following semester, after shopping around for an "easier" teacher. This one assigned essay topics similar to the ones Fida had written on before, met with students individually, and provided support and assistance in revising every paper. This teacher's assessment of Fida's work at the end of the term sounds very much like my own earlier assessment in its focus on correctness and its shifting of responsibility to another level:

> Fida works hard and will complete any task assigned. However, she is uncomfortable if things are not precisely spelled out. These include matters of content and word choice as well as general requirements of the assignment. She is so afraid to make mistakes that content and development [of thought in her papers] suffer greatly. . . . Because her papers are usually organized—albeit rigidly and mechanically—and because of the significant improvement in grammatical English, I gave her a C. I feel now I should have probably failed her. Better yet, she should have had more preparation before entering [my class].

Fida's teachers in other subjects approached her writing in much the same way, thus reinforcing Fida's perspective on language and literacy. For example, Fida says her philosophy teacher helped teach her how to "think about the questions and the right way to answer the questions, to make a good sentence to let my professor understand what I mean."

"How did philosophy teach you the right way to answer a question, how to think about a question?" I asked. From my teacher perspective, I anticipated a reference to the ways philosophy encourages inquiry into the relationships between language and thought.

"OK. . . . First of all I answered the questions at home, and I went to her [the professor's] office. She read it and if there were any mistakes she said, 'Here you have a mistake' . . . like, 'this sentence, you can make it like this.' So I take it back home and I change it."

From Fida's perspective, the study of philosophy consisted of answering homework questions according to teacher specifications and correcting whatever the teacher found wrong in her answers.

Fida's perspective on language and literacy remained unchanged as she moved through the required sequence of composition courses at the university. A journal entry she wrote during her third English composition class demonstrates her continued dependence on teachers and her concept of writing as a display of knowledge generated by others:

> Although I am improving my composition, I am still having troubles in some areas such as supporting examples or specifics, completing sentences and full paragraph development. The thing that might help me is to deal [with] each of my compositions with my instructor. Also, my instructor can give me some ideas about some subjects, and can give me a good way to know how to develop a full paragraph.

The ways in which Fida's teachers have responded to her writing actually encourage this perspective. Bereiter and Scardamalia have argued, on the basis of their research on the development of young writers, that "teachers play into and support the 'knowledge telling' strategy, striving through suggestions, criticisms and examples, to get students to refine the strategy. Through prewriting activities, conferences, and through encouraging procedures of topic outlining and freewriting, they help students avoid the mental burden of considering several aspects of the writing task simultaneously" (p. 32). This teacher response, particularly to NN writing, is understandable. Teachers want students to succeed in school; they want them to write in ways that other teachers will value. When teachers read a NN writer's text, they tend to focus on correctness, for it is the non-native-like language that is most immediately noticeable. Further, English teachers, believing that writing ability progresses in stages, often assume that correct language is a prerequisite for other, "higher" uses of language for thinking and learning. The problem with this perspective, as is apparent in Fida's case, is that NN writers can spend all of their time in college learning to produce correct English and never come to see writing as anything more.

Fida's lack of change as a writer is most apparent, however, in the writing itself. The essays she produced over the years reveal a strategy she developed and refined through her interaction with teachers: she made every new writing task an old task. Rather than trying new approaches, thinking new thoughts, using new language, she used the same approaches she had always used and wrote about the same things using exactly the same language. That way, there were no surprises ahead in the writing. This strategy became obvious only when I looked at Fida's writing over a period of several semesters. (See Figures 24–1 through 24–3.)

The excerpts in Figure 24–1 are good examples of knowledge-telling. Fida repeats the same ideas across different essays written for the same class. Further, she uses the same language in constructing these ideas, all the while trying to make her "pre-fabricated patterns" (Hakuta) fit the task at hand. In the case of the second essay, the fact that getting good grades and being accepted at Wayne State (ideas from her previous essay) have more to do with hard work than luck (the topic of the current essay) seems irrelevant to Fida. She is not concerned about constructing new meanings or understandings in her writing; she is concerned about using language correctly.

The examples in Figure 24–2 illustrate that, in her second composition course, Fida relied on the same strategy of repeating phrases and sections from previous papers. "A Comparison Between the Way of Life of My Parent's Generation Fifty Years Ago and Today" is essentially the same essay as "A

Fida

English 101, Fall 1983

In-class assignment:
>Write about a significant event or occasion from your past or present.

Excerpt from essay: "When I was eighteen years old, I finished the last year from high school. Then I decieded to come to the United States to study medicine. So, I sent a letter to Wayen State University to apply. Therefore, I completed all my documents. Then, I got a student visa, and I came to the United States. At last, my second visiting to the United States with my mother was to study medicine.

Out-of-class assignment given one week later:
>Write about a time in which you had very good or very bad luck.

Excerpt from essay: "When I was eighteen years old I had a good luck. I was in high school and I decided to get a good scour. So, when I had a test, I studied very well and I could get a high scour. In the summer vacation, my mother and I got a ticket to Japan, Thailand, Hong Gong, and India. So, we traveled for one month and we enjoyed so much. Also, after we came back from our trip, I decided to learn driving a car. After I learned driving, I got a driver license, and my mother bought a new car for me. In addition, when I became nineteen years old, I decieded to come to the United States to study medicine. So, I sent a letter to Wayen State University to apply. Therefore, I completed all my documents, and I came to the United States to study."

Figure 24–1

Fida

English 102, Summer, 1984

Excerpts from an out-of-class comparison/contrast paper:

A Comparison Between Iraquian Women
Forty Years Ago and Today

The lives of women forty years ago in my country, Iraq, were very different from those of women today in terms of having freedom, receiving an education and getting a job.

Until forty years ago, a woman could not go out of her home unless accompanied by a member of her family. She did not have the freedom to go out alone or with her friends to see movies or go shopping. She had to stay at home to help her mother by doing housework. Also, she did not have freedom to say whatever she wanted or to express her opinion at home. She could not make friends with men or choose her husband; instead, her parents chose a husband for her. In the home, a married woman's jobs were to coock, to clean the house and to care for the children. The man took care of all other responsibilities such as arranging their monthly bodget, taking his wife and children to the doctor and buying whatever they needed. Whenever the husband had his friends as visitores, his wife was not allowed by her husband to sit with them; rather, her duty was just to prepare dinner and whatever her husband and his friends needed....

In the last forty years, the life of woman in Iraq has changed, and her life now is developed and better. Nowadays, a woman has an important position in society. She has freedom to go wherever she likes either alone or with her friends....She can continue her study at the university, and graduate as a doctor, a nurse, a lawyer or an engineer...."

Impromptu exam written in class two weeks later:

"Discuss how the interests and concerns of your generation are different from those of your parents' generation."

A Comparison Between the Way of Life of My Parent's Generation
Fifty Years Ago and Today

The way of life of my parents' generation fifty years ago was very different from that of the generation today in terms of having freedom, getting a job and spending free time.

Until fifty years ago, my parents' generations, either men or women, did not have freedom to do whatever they wanted such as going out of home, expressing their opinions or making friends with each other. According to women, they should stay at home to help their mothers by doing housework. On the other hand, if the women wanted to go out, they should be accompanied by a member of their families. The men also did not have freedom to go out of their homes because they should help their fathers in their works either at home or outside. Both men and women were not respected for expressing their opinions to their parents. Also, the men and women could not make friends with each other and

Figure 24–2   *(continued)*

choose their wives or husbands, instead, their parents chose either husbands for women or wives for men. The married women could not have a job and work outside. The women's jobs, in contrast, were just to coock, to clean the house, to care for the children and to prepare whatever the husbands needed when they had visitors. The men took care of all other responsibilities such as arranging their monthly bodget, taking their wives and children to the doctor and buying whatever they needed. . .

In the last fifty years, the way of life of generations has changed, and their life now is developed and better. Nowadays, the women have the freedom to go out either alone or with their friends to see movies or to go somewhere else. . .They can also work outside, and become whatever they want such as doctors, nurses, lawyers, engineers and other employees. . .

Figure 24–2   *(continued)*

Fida

English 102, Summer, 1984

Out-of-class assignment: "What is your concept of education?"

My Concept of Education

The education is what we study and learn about many things in our life, and become educated people after many years of studying. It is also increasing our information and knowing the things that we do not have any ideas about them. My concept of education is that every person should be educated so he can be an active person, and become whatever he likes in his future such as a doctor, a lawyer, and engineer and a teacher, and helps other people.

Fida

English 108, Fall, 1984

Assignment: Read selected essays on education in the textbook, brainstorm, and write an essay defining a "good" education.

Good Education

A good education is studying and learning about many things in our life. I think that people could be educated by studying after many years. Education is also increasing our information and learning about things that we do not have any ideas about. I think that every person should be educated so he can be an active member of society, and become whatever he want such as a doctor, a lawyer, an engineer and a teacher, and help other people.

Figure 24–3

Comparison Between Iraquian Women Forty Years Ago and Today," even though the topics to which they respond are different. To make her old essay fit the new topic, Fida merely inserts language from the new topic into the second essay: she adds "parents' generation" in the first and second lines and replaces "a woman" in the second line with "either men or women." The fact that "A Comparison Between the Way of Life" was written in class as an impromptu essay suggests that Fida had *memorized* enough of "A Comparison Between Iraquian Women" to reproduce it verbatim later in the semester.

Figure 24–3 shows how Fida took sections from essays she wrote in previous classes and repeated them in essays for subsequent classes. Though both topics are designed to elicit some philosophical thinking on the part of students, Fida treats them as requests for a display of knowledge—again, for a demonstration of language correctness.

In submitting the same writing with only slight variations, Fida was confident that she would always get a passing grade. After all, each of these essays had already been "teacher-tested and approved." Teacher responses to the essays were always the same: develop ideas more and rewrite the essay. Though Fida's "revisions" were usually "recopies," with only the grammatical errors corrected, teachers always passed them, sometimes assigning split grades (one for correctness and one for content) or giving her extra credit for effort. Shaughnessy has noted that this encouraging response to basic writing is common among college faculty. Beginning adult writers such as Fida appear "so open and vulnerable" in their writing that "teachers often turn sentimental in their response to it, urging them into the lion's den of academic disputation with no more than an honest face for protection" (p. 101).

The lion's den, for Fida, took the form of the English Proficiency Exam, administered and evaluated by the English department. The purpose of the exam is to assure that students have achieved the level of academic literacy appropriate for college graduates. Fida failed the exam four times over a period of two and a half years. When I spoke to her after her fourth try, she was totally baffled: she had passed all her English classes, she thought she could write. She had no idea why she kept failing the exam:

"After I wrote it [the fourth exam], I think I am writing very well, but when I get my grade, I don't know. . . . I don't know what the problem is, really."

"Do you have any ideas at all?" I ask.

"No."

"Did you know after the first time you failed the exam, and then [we discussed it], did you know why you failed the first time?"

"Yes."

"Why was that?"

"It was not developed very well, and I need to talk about, to talk more about some things. . . ."

"So do you think maybe you still have those problems?" I ask.

"I think so."

"So you think maybe that's why you failed this [last] time, for the same reasons?"

"I don't know."

At the end of this conversation, I asked Fida what she planned to do in order to pass the English Proficiency Exam. She said she did not know what to do and looked to me, asking hopefully, "Do *you* have any ideas? Can I do something before I take the exam, like maybe to refresh my ideas or to make it better?" These questions show Fida's continuing reliance on teachers and her concept of writing as knowledge-telling, even during her senior year in college. She speaks as if she could "refresh" her memory for writing an essay the way she does when preparing for a biology test.

Fida failed the English Proficiency Exam repeatedly because she had failed to think and write in the way English teachers value. Readers' responses to her exams indicate that her writing is underdeveloped, "superficial," and unrelated to the topic, and that her language is "simplistic." An analysis of Fida's failing exams reveals that she used some of the same key phrases and ideas she had used in previous English papers. In writing the exam, she had merely done what she had always done for English classes. Yet English teachers were now telling her she was doing something wrong.

This story has a happy ending for Fida, but it raises many issues for me and for teacher research in general. On her fifth try, during the second semester of her senior year, Fida passed the English Proficiency Exam. The passing grade, however, in no way reflects improvement in Fida's writing; instead, it reflects a change in the test. The exam format changed that semester, and Fida was asked to summarize a two-page article, rather than write an impromptu essay. The summary task, as the examples in Figure 24–4 illustrate, allowed Fida to use the strategy she had perfected. She repeats in her summary the key phrases from the original text, piecing them together to create the "new" text. It is a writing exam, finally, that Fida is prepared for.

CONCLUSIONS

For Fida, written language is an object to be memorized and duplicated, and literacy is the proper adherence to rules of language set forth by teachers. This is the perspective she entered the university with, and it is the perspective she

Fida

English Proficiency Exam, Winter, 1988

Assignment: Read the attached essay. Then in your own words, without quoting, provide a summary of the essay that is complete, concise, coherent, and objective.

From the last paragraph of "The Advent of Printing,"
by James Burke:

The advent of printing, whether due to a German or a Dutchman—or even, as has been suggested, to an Englishman—was one of the most critical events in the history of mankind. Printing first and foremost made it easy to transmit information without personal contact, and in this sense it revolutionized the spread of knowledge, and craft technique in particular. 'How to do it' books were among the first off the press, written about almost every field of human activity from metallurgy, to botony, to linguistics, to good manners. Printing also made texts consistent, by ending the copying errors with which manuscripts were rife. In doing so it placed on the author the responsibility for accuracy and definitive statement, since many more people were not likely to read his material who might know at least as much about it as he did himself. . . .

From the first paragraph of Fida's summary of
"The Advent of Printing"

The advent of printing, was one of the most critical events in the history of mankind during the fourteenth and fifteenth centuries. The first advantage of printing was to transmit information without personal contact. It also helped in spreading the knowledge, and crafting technique in particular. Printing made texts consistent, by placing on the authors the responsibility for accuracy and definitive statement, that many people like to read. . . .

Figure 24–4

leaves with. It is in direct conflict with the English teacher's perspective on language and literacy as a philosophical enterprise.

Fida's case offers insights into the nature of one NN student's learning (or failure to learn) and the effect teachers have had on that learning. It challenges teachers' assumptions about NN students' development in English, and it raises important questions about the teaching and testing of language and literacy at the university. Fida's case also demonstrates the usefulness of teacher research and of the case-study method in particular.

In the process of collecting and interpreting the data for this study, I was forced to question and ultimately abandon the assumptions that had guided my teaching. Fida was a student who did *not* significantly improve as she moved through her required English courses; what teachers did and said in response to her writing did *not* always facilitate improvement and, in fact, may have discouraged any real improvement; and Fida's success on the English Proficiency Exam, ultimately, was *not* related to her improvement in English. These results suggest that my colleagues and I need to rethink the way we respond to NN writers, and the university needs to question the validity and appropriateness of its literacy test.

Fida's case also opens up many new areas of inquiry. The issues raised are far more specific than the ones that originally motivated the study. The following questions provide direction for future teacher research on NN learners:

- What perspective on language and literacy do other NN writers bring to the university? Does this perspective conflict with the English teacher's perspective? If so, what strategies do other writers develop to overcome this conflict?

- What effect does a NN writer's first culture have on his/her perspective on language and literacy in a second culture?[1]

- How do NN students' experiences writing in their first language affect their learning to write in a second language? (The fact that Fida had been unsuccessful as a writer in Arabic surely affected her attitude toward writing in English.)

- How do NN students' concepts of self within a new culture affect their desire and ability to write in that culture? (Fida, who did not socialize with Americans, had little sense of herself as part of the American culture outside the university. Her goals for writing reflect her goals for life: to please teachers, get good grades, and get into medical school.)

- Do NN women, particularly those from highly patriarchal societies that privilege the educational goals of the male child, have a different perspective on literacy in a second language than NN men? Is their perspective different from that of native-speaking women? If so, how do these different perspectives affect learning?

Finally, Fida's case convinced me of the importance of teacher research. Through an extensive long-term study of Fida, I came to understand that not all students share my perspective on language and literacy. I was also forced to acknowledge my own and other faculty members' ambivalence about teaching NN writers and evaluating their work. Fida's case is a study in contrasts: English teachers believe "academic literacy" requires the ability to use language for thinking and learning, but their teaching of NN students suggests that academic literacy means the use of correct language; English teachers believe that students should use language to become independent, creative thinkers, but their teaching of NN students encourages dependence.

The case also demonstrates a crucial conflict I felt between my role as teacher and my role as researcher. As Fida's teacher, I felt responsible for her learning. As researcher, I did not feel that same responsibility. In fact, I believed I had to maintain some sort of distanced, observer status, even after I had identified the strategies Fida used that hindered her growth as a writer. I was uncomfortable with my findings and unwilling to confront Fida with what I saw as one source of her failure—a dependency on teachers that I, as one of her teachers, had helped create.

Though all of these issues have been raised in others' research, they did not affect my own thinking or teaching until I made the issues "mine"—until I became a researcher myself. That may be the most compelling reason of all to become learners in our own classrooms.

NOTES

1. In a study of reading strategies among Arabic speakers, Dudley-Evans and Swales conclude that students in Arab countries rely heavily on memorization and copy techniques. Educators in these countries encourage the accumulation of knowledge and are ambivalent about the place of critical discussion and comment in the learning process. Fida's strategy for writing may have been developed and encouraged in Iraq.

25
Tutoring Dyslexic College Students: What These Students Teach Us About Literacy Development

Nancy Grimm

A dyslexic student struggles to get his interpretation of an assigned reading into print:

> *Achevement of disire by Richard Rodigoues*
>
> Rodagiuous speakes of eduaction as if it were something that one vontory chose to have, this is not the case, even in primiteve place one must learn to surive, and gain knolge in one way or antorer. he speake s as if this chose was something he might have made diferently if he had known more about the conqucees but I donnt belive anyone would shose to remain ingornate. Eduaction he claims is a chose but in any socity it is nessary to learn. the idia that schooling alone is responsiblie for much of his changed nature is rubish, any experince changes a person no one is the same person they were yesterday.

When college professors confront such difficult writing (and they do so with increasing frequency), their response is often "Make an appointment as soon as possible at the Writing Center." What happens when these students arrive at a writing center? About seven years ago, when our writing center first began dealing with students whose difficulties with language resisted our best efforts, we turned to reports of traditional research. This research was often laboratory-based and focused mostly on elementary-aged children. It told us what these students couldn't do—something we already knew firsthand. They couldn't spell, they couldn't hold ideas in their short-term memory long enough to get them on paper, they had difficulty remembering what they had read, they had trouble putting ideas in sequence, they couldn't copy words correctly, they were frequently late for appointments or missed appointments altogether, and they were close to despair under the weight of a college reading load. They laughed at themselves; they apologized; sometimes they cried. Yet the simple fact of their enrollment at our competitive scientific and technical university reminded us that they were smart enough to compensate for their differences during the previous twelve years of their education. The increased pace and pressure of college plus the absence of parental support often brings their disability into focus for the first time.

To explain dyslexia, much of the laboratory research uses a medical model, implicating the student's memory as a static diseased entity. The instruction that results from this model is decontextualized rote training. When we first started working with these students, we found ourselves turning to these decontextualized methods. We tried phonics drills, penmanship practice, organizing exercises. Meanwhile the students fell further behind in their coursework and became more frustrated. The exercises were not only inappropriate and impractical, they also focused on the students' weaknesses and prevented them from using their strengths. In our concern about dealing with students who were different, we forgot to do what writing centers do best— that is, work within contextual constraints, capitalizing on what an individual student does best. The turning point came when we stopped viewing these students as disabled and instead saw them as *students who learn differently.* Our acronym for them (SLD) corresponds to the acronym now preferred by the experts—SLD students, or students with a specific *language* deficit.

After working closely with about ten SLD students, our writing center began tentatively calling our methods the SLD coping model. We are beginning to find theoretical support for our approach. In "Psychological Theory and the Study of Learning Disabilities," Brown and Campione do a thorough job of defining the problems with the static, medical model that focuses on intellectual weakness. They argue instead for a dynamic, domain-specific model of assessment and contextual instruction emphasizing metacognitive strategies. We can be encouraged by this call for redirection of research, but we can't wait for results. Researchers have been arguing about dyslexia since 1883 when the term was first used. Constance Weaver has suggested that we not focus on the victim, but instead look at instructional and environmental factors. She says that dyslexia might be more appropriately called dyspedagogia or failure on the educator's part to find appropriate strategies. Others have agreed. Gerald Coles says that the source of dyslexia may even be the school's erroneous expectations and methods.

The student whose writing begins this chapter scored high enough (above 27) on the ACT to be placed in honors English, yet giving him the standard advice to buy and use a dictionary will not help him deal with his serious spelling difficulties. Let me now list the central features of our model, then define them with reference to four of the SLD students we have worked with.

The components of our coping model are:

1. Determine the SLD student's cognitive strengths and teach them to him/her.

2. Emphasize metacognitive skills in the context of real situations and employ multisensory techniques.

3. Understand the ecological variables of SLD.

Component 1: Determine the SLD student's cognitive strengths and teach them to him/her.
This is not as simple as asking, "What are you good at?" Susan Vogel, who has worked extensively with SLD students, notes that they are well aware of their weaknesses, but rarely know or remember their strengths. Our tutors use ethnographic interviewing techniques to discover how the SLD student's mind works. For example, in the context of a completed writing assignment, the tutor notes strong features and asks the SLD tutee to explain how he wrote it. This responsibility of explaining forces the SLD to articulate strategies that worked for him. The tutor must take careful notes as the tutee explains because many SLD students will have difficulty recalling what they said.

Three aspects of ethnographic interviews are especially important here: (1) the tutor must establish a trusting relationship with the tutee before collecting data, (2) the tutor must show respect for deviant information (yes, some SLD students read better holding the book to the side of their head), and (3) the tutor must permit impressions to emerge rather than forcing paradigms on the information. The situation must be reciprocal, with tutee teaching tutor how his/her mind processes information. Many SLD students can be ideal informants for a couple of reasons. Because they have been relatively unsuccessful in playing the game of school, they are untainted with artifice; and because they are accustomed to opposition to and frustration with their way of knowing, they are disarmed by someone's genuine interest.

Our most valuable experience with this component involved working with Will, an adult learner, enrolled in an electrical engineering technology program. Will has serious difficulty with perception of symbols, which affects his reading comprehension, spelling, syntax, and computation. His strength is his oral fluency. This, plus his maturity and willingness to be introspective, make him an ideal person to teach others how the mind of one SLD student works. Will told us that he was passed through high school on social promotions. He didn't learn to read until he was 27, when a friend of his wife's convinced him that she could teach him. Paulo Friere might say that Will's movement into literacy was socially and politically rooted. He had experienced a spiritual conversion and his desire to have access to scripture was his motivating influence. His teacher capitalized on his auditory strength and his motivation by having him read the Bible aloud along with her. The teaching was contextual, the motivation was personal, the social support was strong, and Will was learning to read from a book already familiar to him.

My questions about this success caused some introspection for Will. He returned to the writing center the next day to explain that what most of us think of as our mind's eye or mind's ear is inoperative for him. He explained that he can't see or hear a word in his head but the sense of feeling the words in his throat and tongue helps. (When I hesitate on the spelling of a word, I write several versions, choosing the one that "looks" right. When Will questions a spelling, his only resource is thinking how the word feels in his throat.) Will further illustrated the importance of the kinesthetic sense to him when he explained that when he tries to remember his Navy submarine experience, he can't picture what the ship looked like or see the faces of his close friends. He can, however, recall the sensation of the ship's movement, the feel of the bow coming out of the water, the clammy, close air.

Will's reading comprehension improves greatly if he can read aloud. Finding him a place on a college campus where he can feel comfortable doing this isn't easy. Since beginning his work with us, Will has changed programs and is now working towards a teaching degree which will eventually enable him to work with young people with SLD. Interestingly enough, Will is having some difficulty in this program for different reasons. Because he is mostly self-taught, he has difficulty playing the game of school. His consuming interest motivates him to read the entire text early in the term. Consequently, when the teacher gets to chapter 5 in the eighth week, he is often unprepared for class discussion and quizzes. Learning to "read" the teacher's syllabus and assignment sheets and to follow the teacher's agenda is a new challenge for Will.

Component 2: Emphasize metacognitive skills in the context of real situations and employ multisensory techniques.
According to Vygotsky, learning involves internalization of procedures practiced in cooperative social settings. A writing center tutor can provide the social support as well as the expert guidance that are important components of the Vygotskian scaffolding method (see Greenfield). The practice of reciprocal teaching works especially well with SLD students in writing centers. The tutor begins by modeling a strategy within the context of a course the student is currently enrolled in. To model the reading of a scientific text, for example,

the tutor thinks aloud the questioning, the clarifying, the summarizing, and the predicting that occurs as she reads. The tutor must explain the purpose of these metacognitive strategies so that the tutee is a fully informed participant. It is especially important that the SLD tutee understand why the strategy will work for them and when it can be applied. Gradually, responsibility is transferred to the student so that the student begins teaching the tutor (see Dansereau or Brown and Campione for discussion of reciprocal teaching).

The aim of this guided practice is not to strengthen the memory muscle but to teach and model tactics for acquiring, retaining, and applying knowledge. Because SLD students have specific deficits in these areas, it becomes especially important that they know how to use search strategies, rehearsal strategies, advance organizers, semantic maps, and self-monitoring or self-questioning strategies. One SLD tutee was amazed when his tutor explained how she gave herself pep talks and talked through problems and procedures in her head. No one had ever taught him the metacognitive strategy of inner speech.

The goal in teaching these strategies is to enhance conceptual understanding of procedures, not to improve accuracy or speed. The challenge for the tutor is learning to specify procedures used by expert readers and writers and to model these procedures in a modality that capitalizes on the SLD student's strengths. Keith was a student whose auditory and visual senses were strongest. His weaknesses were in reading comprehension and organization. Keith's tutor capitalized on his strong auditory sense by talking to him about his course reading—both in terms of the content and on ways to approach it. For instance, when Keith was working on a research paper for his first-year English class, she asked him to bring in an article that he thought would be useful for his research. While Keith listened, she modeled the reading process aloud for him. She began with the title, reading it and asking, "What do you suppose this is about?" Keith and she discussed their guesses and some of the information they thought they already knew about the subject. Because Keith has trouble organizing his own ideas or recognizing the organizational patterns used by others, the tutor pointed to and read aloud each of the subheadings, discussing the organizational pattern of the article, reminding Keith that he should do this when he read independently.

To capitalize on Keith's strong visual ability, his tutor taught him how to structure information visually in order to understand and remember it. They made study charts of information in his textbooks, arranging material in neat boxes according to meaningful patterns. They rewrote his class notes so that they were visually pleasing and uncluttered, making use of white space, color, underlining, and hierarchical form. Taking notes on cards was especially helpful for Keith because it gave him something physical to manipulate; he could spread them out on a large, empty table so he could see all of his information at once and gradually rearrange and group the cards into meaningful order. His tutor noted his progress in understanding how to use his visual strength when, on his own, he began drawing dark boxes around paragraphs on his papers and labeling them with numbers prior to reorganizing.

A second student, Ann, was similar to Keith in that she learned well through visual and auditory senses. She was stronger verbally than Keith but had serious difficulty storing and retrieving information. Ann's tutor recognized the value of recitation for Ann and required her to do most of the talking during each session. She also had her record study questions on tape so that she could play them back and answer aloud. Ann worked well with a study partner, especially one that allowed her to do most of the talking. Although Ann recognized that she remembered better when she recited, she had to be taught to use her visual strength. She learned to cluster her study notes, drawing circles around the main ideas, adding color, branching off supporting ideas. After successfully taking a test, she reported to her tutor, "I could just see those blue balloons!"

Component 3: Understand the ecological variables of SLD.
Exhorting SLD students to use the technology that might help them cope, such as tape recorders with variable speeds, word-processing programs with spelling checkers, and talking books, may have either no results or disastrous results depending on the tutor's sensitivity to how memory, comprehension, and organizational problems extend beyond reading and writing into daily life. SLD students often need help understanding when and how to make best use of the support systems and technology. Don, for example, is an adult learner enrolled in a mechanical design program. He has a strong mechanical aptitude and also learns well visually. His weaknesses are his short-term memory, organization, spelling, and penmanship. His penmanship in fact is so poor that he often can't read his own writing. A well-equipped word-processing laboratory sits across the hall from our writing center, but part of Don's disability affects his ability to understand social sequences. It takes most students less than a few minutes to understand the procedure of signing up to use the facility. With Don, it took two half-hour sessions to help him understand whom to see about signing up, which terminals he could use, and when the machines were available. Once he made the arrangements, he learned the word-processing program faster than most adults. It solved a number of problems for him. By typing on the computer, he can proceed quickly without worrying about error. This way, he can get his ideas recorded before they overwhelm his memory. He can reorganize by pressing a few keys, solve

his penmanship problem, and use the spelling checker. The more we work with SLD students, the more we find ourselves helping them organize study schedules, unclutter their work environment, rehearse conversations with professors, prepare for interviews, manage their time, and explain their differences to roommates and friends.

Working with students like Don, Keith, Will, Ann, and others has taught us to value other ways of knowing. It has forced us to question some of the developmental models of literacy that used to so conveniently explain language problems. All the SLD students that I've worked with have functioned comfortably at a Piagetian formal operations level in spite of the barriers we print-disposed people have created. Adult learners such as Don and Will have moved into Perry's third mode as a result of life experience, not book experience. They are rooted in an oral culture yet engage in Ongian abstraction. The technology of print that was supposed to have increased memory by giving us a way to store information has only created problems for these students. I'm not suggesting that these developmental models are no longer useful, but as my SLD tutees have taught me, print can make thought rigid rather than fluent. In an article in *College Composition and Communication*, Mike Rose offered an excellent synthesis and critique of the limitations of these models. His conceptual touchstone is this: "Human cognition—even at its most stymied, bungled moments—is rich and varied" (p. 297). We still have much to learn about language development, and our work with SLD students must be tentative and experimental. Writing centers are ideal places for naturalistic observation and research, and SLD students, by confronting us with what we take for granted when we compose and comprehend, can throw refreshing new light on the processes of reading and writing. This chapter is an invitation to the professors who send us their most alarming cases. We need much more research on SLD students in college. Follow those students into the writing center, and help us discover how to help them learn.

Works Cited

Altick, Richard D., and Andrea A. Lunsford. *Preface to Critical Reading*, 6th ed. New York: Holt, 1984.

Anderson, Paul, Carolyn Miller, and R. John Brockmann, eds. *New Essays in Technical and Scientific Communication*. Farmingdale, NY: Baywood, 1983.

Applebee, Arthur. "Balancing the Demand for Practical Outcomes." *Research in the Teaching of English* 20 (October 1986): 221–23.

———. "Musings. . . . Teachers and the Process of Research." *Research in the Teaching of English* 21 (1987): 5–7.

———. *Writing in the Secondary School*. Urbana, IL: NCTE, 1981.

Aronowitz, Stanley, and Henry A. Giroux. *Education under Siege: The Conservative, Liberal and Radical Debate over Schooling*. Granby, MA: Bergin and Garvey, 1985.

Atwell, Nancie. "Class-based Writing Research: Teachers Learning from Students." In *Reclaiming the Classroom: Teacher Research as an Agency for Change*, edited by Goswami and Stillman, 87–94.

———. "Everyone Sits at a Big Desk: Discovering Topics for Writing." In *Reclaiming the Classroom*, edited by Goswami and Stillman, 178–86.

———. *In the Middle: Writing, Reading, and Learning with Adolescents*. Portsmouth, NH: Boynton/Cook, 1987.

Bakhtin, M. M. "Discourse in the Novel." In *The Dialogic Imagination*, edited by Michael Holquist, translated by Caryl Emerson and Michael Holquist, 259–404. Austin, TX: University of Texas Press, 1981.

Baldwin, T. W. *William Shakespeare's Small Latine & Lesse Greeke*. 2 vols. Urbana, IL: University of Illinois Press, 1944.

Bales, Robert. *Interaction Process Analyses*. Chicago: University of Chicago Press, 1981.

Bartholomae, David. "Inventing the University." In *When a Writer Can't Write*, edited by Mike Rose, 134–65. New York: Guilford, 1986.

Batker, Carol, and Charles Moran. "The Reader in the Writing Class." In *Only Connect: Uniting Reading and Writing*, edited by Thomas Newkirk. Portsmouth, NH: Boynton/Cook, 1986.

Batson, Trent. "The ENFI Project: A Networked Classroom Approach to Writing Instruction." *Academic Computing* 2.5 (February 1988): 32–33, 55–56.

Bazerman, Charles. *Shaping Written Knowledge: The Genre and Activity of the Experimental Article in Science*. Madison: University of Wisconsin Press, 1988.

Beach, Richard, and Linda Wendler. "Developmental Differences in Response to a Story." *Research in the Teaching of English* 21 (October 1987): 286–97.

Bereiter, Carl, and Marlene Scardamalia. "Does Learning Have to be So Difficult?" In *Learning to Write: First Language/Second Language*, edited by Aviva Freedman, Ian Pringle, and Janice Yalden, 20–33. London: Longman, 1983.

———. "From Conversation to Composition: The Role of Instruction in a Development Process." In Vol. 2, *Advances in Educational Psychology*, edited by Robert Glaser, 1–64. Hillsdale, NJ: Lawrence Erlbaum, 1982.

Berkenkotter, Carol. "Understanding a Writer's Awareness of Audience." *College Composition and Communication* 32 (December 1981): 388–99.

Berthoff, Ann E. "Abstraction as a Speculative Instrument." In *The Territory of Language*, edited by Donald McQuade, 227–37. Carbondale, IL: Southern Illinois University Press, 1986.

———. "Dialectical Notebooks and the Audit of Meaning." In *The Journal Book*, edited by Toby Fulwiler. Portsmouth, NH: Boynton/Cook, 1987.

———. "From Dialogue to Dialectic to Dialogue." In *Reclaiming the Classroom*, edited by Goswami and Stillman, 75–86.

———. "The Teacher as REsearcher." In *Reclaiming the Classroom*, edited by Goswami and Stillman, 28–39.

Bissex, Glenda L. *GNYS AT WRK: A Child Learns to Write and Read.* Cambridge: Harvard University Press, 1980.

Bizzaro, Patrick. "Publishing Poetry in *Teaching English in the Two-Year College*." Paper presented at the Southeastern Conference on English in the Two-Year College, Jackson, Mississippi, February 1987.

———. "Teacher as Writer and Researcher: The Poetry Dilemma." *Language Arts* (1983): 851–59.

Bizzell, Patricia. "What Happens when Basic Writers Come to College?" *College Composition and Communication* 37 (1986): 294–301.

Blau, Sheridan. "Invisible Writing." *College Composition and Communication* 34 (October 1983): 297–312.

Bloom, Benjamin S. *Human Characteristics and School Learning.* New York: McGraw-Hill, 1976.

Bolster, Arthur S. "Toward a More Effective Model of Research on Teaching." *Harvard Educational Review* 53 (August 1983): 294–308.

Boomer, Garth. "Addressing the Problem of Elsewhereness: A Case for Action Research in Schools." In *Reclaiming the Classroom*, edited by Goswami and Stillman, 4–13.

Bortoft, Henri. *Goethe's Scientific Consciousness.* Tunbridge Wells, UK: The Institute for Cultural Research, 1986.

Bowles, Samuel, and Herbert Gintis. *Schooling in Capitalist America: Education Reform and the Contradictions of Economic Life.* New York: Basic Books, 1976.

Brinsley, John. *Ludus Literarius: or, The Grammar Schoole* (1612). Edited by E. T. Campagnac. Liverpool: Liverpool University Press, 1917.

Britton, James. "The Composing Processes and the Function of Writing." In *Children and Writing in the Elementary School: Theories and Techniques*, edited by Richard L. Larson. New York: Oxford University Press, 1975.

————. *Prospect and Retrospect: Selected Essays of James Britton*. Edited by Gordon M. Pradl. Portsmouth, NH: Boynton/Cook, 1982.

————. "A Quiet Form of Research." In *Reclaiming the Classroom*, edited by Goswami and Stillman, 13–19.

Britton, James, and Tony Burgess, Nancy Martin, Alex McLeod, and Harold Rosen. *The Development of Writing Abilities (11–18)*. Urbana, IL: NCTE, 1978.

Broadhead, Glenn, and Richard Freed. *The Variables of Composition*. Carbondale, IL: Southern Illinois University Press, 1986.

Brown, Ann L., and Joseph C. Campione. "Psychological Theory and the Study of Learning Disabilities." *American Psychologist* 41 (October 1986): 1059–86.

Bruffee, Kenneth. "Collaborative Learning and the 'Conversation of Mankind.'" *College English* 46 (1984): 635–52.

Bruner, Jerome. *Actual Minds, Possible Worlds*. Cambridge: Harvard University Press, 1986.

————. *Toward a Theory of Instruction*. New York: Norton, 1968.

Bryant, Paul T. "A Brand New World Every Morning." *College Composition and Communication* 25 (February 1974): 30–33.

Bump, Jerome. "Radical Changes in Class Discussion Using Networked Computers." Typescript, 1988.

Calkins, Lucy. *The Art of Teaching Writing*. Portsmouth, NH: Heinemann, 1986.

————. "Forming Research Communities among Naturalistic Researchers." In *Perspectives on Research and Scholarship in Composition*, edited by Ben W. McClelland land and Timothy R. Donovan, 125–44. New York: MLA, 1985.

Cazden, Courtney. "Classroom Discourse." In Vol. 3, *Handbook of Research on Teaching*, edited by Merlin E. Wittrock, 432–63. New York: Macmillan, 1986.

Clark, Donald Lemen. *John Milton at St. Paul's School: A Study of Ancient Rhetoric in English Renaissance Education*. New York: Columbia University Press, 1948.

————. *Rhetoric in Greco-Roman Education*. New York: Columbia University Press, 1957.

Coe, Richard M. "If Not to Narrow, then How to Focus: Two Techniques for Focusing." *College Composition and Communication* 32 (1981):272–77.

Coleridge, Samuel Taylor. *Biographia Literaria*. In *English Romantic Writers*, edited by David Perkins. New York: Harcourt, Brace and World, 1967.

Coles, Gerald. *The Learning Mystique*. New York: Pantheon, 1987.

Connelly, F. Michael, and D. Jean Clandinin. "Personal Practical Knowledge and the Modes of Knowing." In *Learning and Teaching the Ways of Knowing*, edited by Elliot W. Eisner, 174–98. Chicago: University of Chicago Press, 1985.

Connors, Robert C. "The Rise of Technical Writing Instruction in America." *Journal of Technical Writing and Communication* 12 (1982): 329–51.

Connors, Robert J., and Andrea A. Lunsford. "Frequency of Formal Errors in Current College Writing, or Ma and Pa Kettle Do Research." *College Composition and Communication* 39 (1988): 395–409.

Council-Grams: Professional Information for Leaders of NCTE and Its Affiliates 50.5 (May 1988).

Council-Grams: Professional Information for Leaders of NCTE and Its Affiliates 51.1 (September 1988).

Dansereau, D. "Transfer from Cooperative to Individual Studying." *Journal of Teaching Reading* 30 (1987): 614–19.

Davis, Murray S. "That's Interesting! Towards a Phenomenology of Sociology and a Sociology of Phenomenology." *Philosophy of Social Science* 1 (1971): 309–44.

Dewey, John. *Experience and Education.* New York: Macmillan, 1963.

Dobrin, David. "What's Technical about Technical Writing?" In *New Essays in Technical and Scientific Communication,* edited by Anderson, Miller, and Brockmann, 227–50.

Duckworth, Eleanor. "Teaching as Research." *Harvard Educational Review* 56 (November 1986): 481–95.

Dudley-Evans, T., and John Swales. "Study Modes and Students from the Middle East." The British Council: *English Language Teaching Documents* 109 (1983): 91–100.

Dunlap, Louise. "The 'Deskilling' of Writing in the Professional Workplace." Paper presented at the Penn State Conference on Rhetoric and Composition, University Park, Pennsylvania, 1985.

Elbow, Peter. "Embracing Contraries in the Teaching Process." *College English* 45 (April 1983): 327–39.

———. *Embracing Contraries.* New York: Oxford University Press, 1986.

———. *Writing without Teachers.* New York: Oxford University Press, 1975.

Emig, Janet A. "From 'Non-Magical Thinking: Presenting Writing Developmentally in Schools.'" In *Reclaiming the Classroom,* edited by Goswami and Stillman, 62–67.

———. "Hand, Eye, Brain: Some 'Basics' in the Writing Process." In *Research on Composing,* edited by Charles Cooper and Lee Odell, 59–71. Urbana, IL: NCTE, 1978.

———. "Writing as a Mode of Learning." In *The Web of Meaning: Essays on Writing, Teaching, Learning and Thinking,* edited by Janet Emig. Portsmouth, NH: Boynton/Cook, 1983.

Faigley, Lester. "Nonacademic Writing: The Social Perspective." In *Writing in Nonacademic Settings,* edited by Odell and Goswami, 231–48.

Festinger, Leon. *Toward a Theory of Cognitive Dissonance.* Stanford, CA: Stanford University Press, 1957.

Flower, Linda, and John Hayes. "A Cognitive Process Theory of Writing." *College Composition and Communication* 32 (December 1981): 365–87.

Freedman, Sarah, and A. M. Katz. "Pedagogical Interaction during the Composing Process: The Writing Conference." In *Writing in Real Time,* edited by Ann Matsuhashi, 58–80. Norwood, NJ: Alex, 1987.

Freire, Paulo. "Letter to North-American Teachers." In *Freire for the Classroom: A Sourcebook for Liberatory Teaching,* edited by Ira Shor, 211–14. Portsmouth, NH: Boynton/Cook, 1987.

———. *Pedagogy of the Oppressed.* New York: Seabury Press, 1970.

Gebhardt, Richard C. "Initial Plans and Spontaneous Composition: Toward a Comprehensive Theory of the Writing Process." *College English* 44 (October 1982): 620–27.

———. "Review of *Country Cousins* by Michael Brownstein." *Choice* 12 (March 1975): 68.

Gebhardt, Richard C., and Dawn Rodrigues. *Writing: Processes and Intentions.* Lexington, MA: D. C. Heath, 1989.

Geertz, Clifford. *Works and Lives: The Anthropologist as Author.* Palo Alto, CA: Stanford University Press, 1988.

Gerber, John. "Suggestions for a Commonsense Reform of the English Curriculum." *College Composition and Communication* 28 (December 1977): 312–16.

Gere, Anne Ruggles, and Robert D. Abbott. "Talking about Writing: The Language of Writing Groups." *Research in the Teaching of English* 19 (1985): 362–85.

Goethals, Ann. "Strategies for Teaching Poetry in High School: A Case Study." Master's thesis, University of Chicago, 1987.

Goffman, Erving. *Encounters: Two Studies in the Sociology of Interaction.* Indianapolis, IN: Bobbs-Merrill, 1961.

Goswami, Dixie, and Peter R. Stillman, eds. *Reclaiming the Classroom: Teacher Research as an Agency for Change.* Portsmouth, NH: Boynton/Cook, 1987.

Goswami, Dixie, et al. *Writing in the Professions: A Course Guide and Instructional Materials for an Advanced Composition Course.* Washington, DC: American Institute for Research, 1981.

Gould, Stephen J. *The Mismeasure of Man.* New York: Norton, 1981.

———. *Time's Arrow, Time's Cycle: Myth and Metaphor in the Discovery of Geological Time.* Cambridge: Harvard University Press, 1987.

Graves, Donald. *Writing: Teachers and Children at Work.* Portsmouth, NH: Heinemann, 1983.

Green, Hannah. "Mister Nabokov." *The New Yorker* 52 (February 14, 1977): 32–35.

Greenfield, Patricia Marks. "A Theory of the Teacher in the Learning Activities of Everyday Life." In *Everyday Cognition: Its Development in Social Context,* edited by Barbara Rogoff and Jean Lave. Cambridge: Harvard University Press, 1984.

Grego, Rhonda C. "Science, Late Nineteenth-Century Rhetoric, and the Beginnings of Technical Writing Instruction in America." *Journal of Technical Writing and Communication* 17 (1987): 63–79.

Hakuta, Kenji. "Prefabricated Patterns and the Emergence of Structure in Second Language Acquisition." *Language Learning* 24 (1974): 287–98.

Heath, Shirley Brice. "A Lot of Talk about Nothing." In *Reclaiming the Classroom,* edited by Goswami and Stillman, 39–48.

———. *Ways with Words.* Cambridge: Cambridge University Press, 1983.

Hillocks, George, Jr. *Observing and Writing.* Urbana, IL: NCTE, 1975.

———. *Research on Written Composition.* Urbana, IL: NCTE and ERIC/RCS, 1986.

Hirsch, E. D., Jr. *Cultural Literacy: What Every American Needs to Know.* Boston: Houghton Mifflin, 1987.

Hoggart, Richard. *The Uses of Literacy.* Fairlawn, NJ: Essential Books, 1957.

Hoole, Charles. *A New Discovery of the Old Art of Teaching Schoole* (1660). Edited by E. T. Campagnac. Liverpool: Liverpool University Press, 1913.

Jackson, Jennifer A., and Barbara Lewis. "A Rhetoric of Negotiation: Researching Discourse Performance in Peer Evaluation Groups." Paper presented at the Miami University Conference on the Teaching of Writing, October 1988.

Jaeger, Werner. *Paideia: The Ideals of Greek Culture.* 3 vols. New York: Oxford University Press, 1943.

Jencks, Christopher, et al. *Inequality: A Reassessment of the Effects of Family and Schooling in America.* New York: Basic Books, 1972.

Jennings, Edward M. "Paperless Writing: Boundary Conditions and their Implications." In *Writing at Century's End,* edited by Lisa Gerrard, 11–20. New York: Random House, 1987.

Jensen, Julie M. "Commentary." In *The Dynamics of Language Learning: Research in Reading and English,* edited by James R. Squire, 55–60. Urbana, IL: ERIC Clearinghouse on Reading and Communication Skills, 1987.

Johnson, Roy Ivan. "The Persistence of Error in English Composition." *School Review* 25 (October 1917): 555–80.

John-Steiner, Vera. *Notebooks of the Mind: Explorations of Thinking.* New York: Harper and Row, 1985.

Johnston, Peter H. "Understanding Reading Disability: A Case Study Approach." *Harvard Educational Review* 55 (1985): 153–77.

Kantor, Kenneth J. "Classroom Contexts and the Development of Writing Intuitions: An Ethnographic Case Study." In *New Directions in Composition Research,* edited by Richard Beach and Lillian S. Bridwell, 72–94. New York: Guilford, 1984.

———. "Questions, Explorations, and Discoveries." *English Journal* 74 (October 1985): 90–92.

———. "Research in Composition: What It Means for Teachers." *English Journal* 70 (February 1981): 64–67.

Kantor, Kenneth J., Dan R. Kirby, and Judith P. Goetz. "Research in Context: Ethnographic Studies in English Education." *Research in the Teaching of English* 15 (December 1981): 293–309.

Kiesler, Sara, Jane Siegel, and Timothy W. McGuire. "Social Psychological Aspects of Computer-Mediated Communication." *American Psychologist* 39 (1984): 123–34.

Koeller, Shirley. "Review of Beach and Bridwell, *New Directions in Composition Research.*" *Journal of Research and Development in Education* 18 (1985): 68–73.

Koretz, Daniel. "Arriving in Lake Woebegon: Are Standardized Tests Exaggerating Achievement and Distorting Instruction?" *American Educator* 12.2 (Summer 1988): 8–16, 44–52.

Lampert, Magdalene. "How Do Teachers Manage to Teach? Perspectives on Problems in Practice." *Harvard Educational Review* 55 (May 1985): 178–94.

Langer, Judith, and Arthur Applebee. *How Writing Shapes Thinking.* Urbana, IL: NCTE, 1987.

Larson, Richard L. "The 'Research Paper' in the Writing Course: A Non-Form of Writing." *College English* 44 (December 1982): 811–16.

Latour, Bruno, and Steve Woogar. *Laboratory Life: The Construction of Scientific Facts.* 2d ed. Princeton: Princeton University Press, 1986.

Leff, Michael. "In Search of Ariadne's Thread: A Review of the Recent Literature on Rhetorical Theory." *Central States Speech Journal* 29 (1978): 73–91

Lindberg, Gary. "Coming to Words: Writing as Process and the Reading of Literature." In *Only Connect: Uniting Reading and Writing*, edited by Thomas Newkirk. Portsmouth, NH: Boynton/Cook, 1986.

Loughring-Sacco, Steven J., and Wendy Sweet. "Anatomy of an Elementary French Class." Paper presented at the Conference on Research Perspectives in Adult Language Learning and Acquisitions, Columbus, Ohio, October 1988.

Luke, Carmen, Suzanne De Castell, and Allen Luke. "Beyond Criticism: The Authority of the School Text." *Curriculum Inquiry* 13.2 (1983): 111–27.

Lunsford, Andrea. "Cognitive Development and the Basic Writer." *College English* 41 (September 1979): 39–46.

———. "Cognitive Development and the Basic Writer." In *The Writing Teacher's Sourcebook*, edited by Gary Tate and Edward P. J. Corbett, 257–67. New York: Oxford University Press, 1981.

Marcus, Stephen. "Computers in Thinking, Writing, and Literature." In *Writing at Century's End*, edited by Lisa Gerrard, 131–40. New York: Random House, 1987.

Marrou, H. I. *A History of Education in Antiquity*. Translated by George Lamb. New York: New American Library, 1964.

Martin, Gail. "From 'A Letter to Bread Loaf.'" In *Reclaiming the Classroom*, edited by Goswami and Stillman, 165–70.

Martin, Nancy. *Mostly about Writing: Selected Essays of Nancy Martin*. Portsmouth, NH: Boynton/Cook, 1983.

———. "On the Move: Teacher-Researchers." In *Reclaiming the Classroom*, edited by Goswami and Stillman, 20–27.

Martin, Nancy, Pat D'Arcy, Bryan Newton, and Robert Parker. *Writing and Learning Across the Curriculum (11–16)*. Portsmouth, NH: Boynton/Cook, 1976.

Mathes, J. C., and Dwight Stevenson. *Designing Technical Reports*. Indianapolis, IN: Bobbs-Merrill, 1976.

McCloskey, Donald. *The Rhetoric of Economics*. Madison: University of Wisconsin Press, 1985.

McKerrow, R. B. "Form and Matter in the Publication of Research." *Review of English Studies* 16 (January 1940): 116–21.

Mehan, Hugh. *Learning Lessons*. Cambridge: Harvard University Press, 1979.

———. "The Structure of Classroom Discourse." In *Handbook of Discourse Analysis*, edited by Teun A. van Dijk. Vol. 3, *Discourse and Dialogue*, 119–31. London: Academic, 1975.

Miller, Carolyn. "Technical Writing as a Form of Consciousness: A Study in Contemporary Ethos." *Central States Speech Journal* 29 (1978): 228–36.

Murray, Donald M. *Write to Learn*. New York: Holt, Rinehart and Winston, 1984.

———. *A Writer Teaches Writing*. 2d ed. Boston: Houghton Mifflin, 1985.

Newkirk, Thomas. "Looking for Trouble: A Way to Unmask Our Readings." *College English* 46 (December 1984).

——— "Looking for Trouble: A Way to Unmask Our Readings." In *To Compose:*

Teaching Writing in the High School, edited by Thomas Newkirk, 147–59. Portsmouth, NH: Heinemann, 1986.

North, Stephen M. *The Making of Knowledge in Composition: Portrait of an Emerging Field*. Portsmouth, NH: Boynton/Cook, 1987.

Odell, Lee. "Planning Classroom Research." In *Reclaiming the Classroom*, edited by Goswami and Stillman, 128–60.

Odell, Lee, and Dixie Goswami, eds. *Writing in Nonacademic Settings*. New York: Guilford, 1985.

Perl, Sondra. "Understanding Composing." *College Composition and Communication* 31 (December 1980): 363–69.

Perl, Sondra, and Nancy Wilson. *Through Teachers' Eyes: Portraits of Writing Teachers at Work*. Portsmouth, NH: Heinemann, 1986.

Perry, William. *Forms of Intellectual and Ethical Development in the College Years*. New York: Holt, Rinehart and Winston, 1970.

Peters, Roger J. "Working Smarter: The Business of Practical Intelligence." *National Forum* 68 (Spring 1980): 12–15.

Piaget, Jean. *Six Psychological Studies*. New York: Vintage Books, 1968.

Pianko, Sharon. "Reflection: A Critical Component in the Writing Process." *College Composition and Communication* 30 (October 1979): 275–78.

Pradl, Gordon. "Editorial." *English Education* 20 (October 1988): 127–33.

Rawlings, Marjorie Kinnan. *Cross Creek*. New York: Charles Scribner's, 1942.

Reither, James A. "Writing and Knowing: Toward Redefining the Writing Process." *College English* 47 (October 1985): 620–28.

———. "Writing and Knowing: Toward Redefining the Writing Process." In *The Writing Teacher's Sourcebook*, edited by Gary Tate and Edward P. J. Corbett, 140–48. 2d ed. New York: Oxford University Press, 1988.

Reither, James A., and Douglas Vipond. "Writing as Collaboration." *College English* 51 (December 1989): 855–67.

Rodriguez, Richard. *Hunger of Memory*. Boston: David R. Godine, 1982.

Roen, Duane, and R. J. Wiley. "The Effects of Audience Awareness on Drafting and Revising." *Research in the Teaching of English* 22 (February 1988): 75–88.

Romano, Tom. *Clearing the Way: Working with Teenage Writers*. Portsmouth, NH: Heinemann, 1987.

Ronald, Kate. "On the Outside Looking In: Students' Analyses of Professional Discourse Communities." *Rhetoric Review* 7 (1988): 130–47.

Rose, Mike. "Narrowing the Mind and Page: Remedial Writers and Cognitive Reductionism." *College Composition and Communication* 39 (1988): 267–302.

———. "Rigid Rules, Inflexible Plans, and the Stifling of Language." *College Composition and Communication* 31 (December 1980): 389–441.

Rosen, Harold. Postscript to *And None of It Was Nonsense* by Betty Rosen. Portsmouth, NH: Heinemann, 1988.

Rosenblatt, Louise M. *The Reader, the Text, and the Poem: The Transactional Theory of Literary Work*. Carbondale, IL: Southern Illinois University Press, 1978.

Sacks, Harvey, Emanuel Schegloff, and Gail Jefferson. "A Simplist Systematics for the Organization of Turn-Taking in Conversation." *Language* 50 (1974): 696–735.

Scholes, Robert, Nancy R. Comley, and Gregory L. Ulmer. *Text Book: An Introduction to Literary Language*. New York: St. Martin's, 1988.

Schön, Donald A. *Educating the Reflective Practitioner*. San Francisco: Jossey-Bass, 1987.

————. *The Reflective Practitioner: How Professionals Think in Action*. New York: Basic Books, 1983.

"School Reform Takes Another Twist," *Lafayette Journal and Courier*, 4 September 1988, sec. E, p. 1.

Schumacher, E. F. *Small Is Beautiful: Economics as if People Mattered*. New York: Harper and Row, 1973.

Schwartz, Jeffrey. "The Drudgery and the Discovery: Students as Research Partners." *English Journal* (1988): 37–40.

Selfe, Cynthia L. "Computer-based Conferences and the Politics of Resistance: Expanding the Space for Academic Discourse." Typescript, 1988.

————. "Technology in the English Classroom: Computers through the Lens of Feminist Theory." Typescript, 1988.

Shaughnessy, Mina. *Errors and Expectations*. New York: Oxford University Press, 1977.

————. "Some Needed Research on Writing." *Journal of Basic Writing* 3 (1980): 98–103.

Shor, Ira. *Culture Wars: School and Society in the Conservative Restoration 1969–1984*. Boston: Routledge and Kegan Paul, 1986.

————. "Educating the Educators: A Freirean Approach to the Crisis in Teacher Education." In *Freire for the Classroom: A Sourcebook for Liberatory Teaching*, edited by Ira Shor, 7–32. Portsmouth, NH: Boynton/Cook, 1987.

Shulman, Lee S. "Knowledge and Teaching: Foundations of the New Reform." *Harvard Educational Review* 57 (February 1987): 1–22.

Sizer, Theodore. *Horace's Compromise: The Dilemma of the American School*. Boston: Houghton Mifflin, 1984.

Sloan, Gary. "The Subversive Effects of an Oral Culture on Student Writing." *College Composition and Communication* 30 (1979): 156–60.

Smith, Frank. *Insult to Intelligence: The Bureaucratic Invasion of Our Classrooms*. New York: Arbor, 1986. Portsmouth, NH: Heinemann paperback, 1988.

Smith, Michael W., and George Hillocks, Jr. "What Inquiring Writers Need to Know." *English Journal* 78.2 (1989): 58–62.

Sommers, Nancy. "Revision Strategies of Student Writers and Experienced Adult Writers." *College Composition and Communication* 31 (December 1980): 378–88.

Spitzer, Michael. "Computer Conferencing: An Emerging Technology." In *Critical Perspectives on Computers and Composition Instruction*, edited by Gail Hawisher and Cynthia L. Selfe, 187–200. New York: Teachers College Press, 1989.

Spring, Joel. *The American School, 1642–1985*. New York: Longman, 1986.

Stefik, Mark, Gregg Foster, Daniel G. Bobrow, Kenneth Kahn, Stan Lanning, and Lucy Suchman. "Beyond the Chalkboard: Computer Support for Collaboration and Problem Solving in Meetings." *Communications of the ACM* 30.1 (1987): 32–47.

Sternberg, Robert. "Critical Thinking: Its Nature and Measurement." In *Essays on the Intellect*, edited by F. R. Link. Alexandria, VA: Association for Supervision and Curriculum Development, 1985.

Sternberg, Robert, and Marie Martin. "When Teaching Thinking Does Not Work, What Goes Wrong?" Typescript, n.d.

"Teachers Feel They Lack Influence," *Lafayette Journal and Courier*, 11 September 1988, sec. A, p. 2.

"Tests Becoming the End, Not the Means, Professor Says," *Lafayette Journal and Courier*, 11 September 1988, sec. E, p. 1.

Tomlinson, Barbara. "Characters Are Coauthors." *Written Communication* 3 (1986): 421–48.

U.S. Department of Commerce, Bureau of the Census. *Statistical Abstract of the United States, 1988*. Washington, DC: Government Printing Office, 1987.

VanDeWeghe, Richard. "Research in Composition and the Design of Writing Programs." *ADE Bulletin* 6 (May 1979): 28–31.

Vogel, Susan A. "On Developing LD College Programs." *Journal of Learning Disabilities* 15 (1982): 518–28.

Vygotsky, Lev S. *Thought and Language*. Cambridge: MIT Press, 1962.

Wallerstein, Immanuel. "The Bourgeois(ie) as Concept and Reality." *New Left Review* 167 (1988): 91–106.

Weaver, Constance. *Reading Process and Practice: From Socio-Psycholinguistics to Whole Language*. Portsmouth, NH: Heinemann, 1988.

White, James Boyd. *Heracles' Bow: Essays on the Rhetoric and Poetics of the Law*. Madison: University of Wisconsin Press, 1986.

White, Robert W. *Lives in Progress*. New York: Dryden Press, 1952.

Wigginton, Eliot, ed. *Foxfire 2: Ghost Stories, Wild Plant Foods, Spinning and Weaving, Midwifing, Burial Customs, Corn Shuckin's, Wagon Making, and More Affairs of Plain Living*. Garden City, NY: Anchor Press/Doubleday, 1973.

———. *Foxfire 3: Animal Care, Banjos and Dulcimers, Hide Tanning, Summer and Fall Wild Plant Foods, Butter Churns, Ginseng, and Still More Affairs of Plain Living. Living*. Garden City, NY: Anchor Press/Doubleday, 1975.

Witte, Stephen. "Some Contents for Understanding Written Literacy." Typescript, 1988.

Witty, Paul A., and Roberta LaBrant Green. "Composition Errors of College Students." *English Journal* 19 (May 1930): 388–93.

Wolcott, Harry F. "On Ethnographic Intent." In *Interpretive Ethnography of Education: At Home and Abroad*, edited by George Spindler and Louise Spindler, 37–57. Hillsdale, NJ: Lawrence Erlbaum, 1987.

Wolf, Thia. "The Teacher as Eavesdropper: Listening in on the Language of Collaboration." In *The Writing Teacher as Researcher*, edited by Donald A. Daiker and Max Morenberg, 277–89. Portsmouth, NH: Heinemann, 1990.

Wordsworth, William. *Preface to the Second Edition of Lyrical Ballads (1800). Selected Poems and Prefaces*. Edited by Jack Stillinger. Boston: Houghton Mifflin, 1965.

Contributors

Joan E. Alofs and **Janet Gray-McKennis** are in their fifth year of naturalistic research in the elementary classroom, and they are continuing to investigate young children's writing. Janet teaches at Ancona Montessori School on Chicago's South Side. She has taught writing at both the primary and preprimary levels. Joan holds a B.A. and M.A. from Michigan State University and a Certificate of Advanced Study from the University of Chicago. She recently opened a Montessori day-care facility.

James A. Berlin, Professor of English at Purdue University, spent his first years of teaching in public elementary schools in Detroit and Flint, Michigan. After earning a Ph.D. in English at the University of Michigan, he taught composition at Wichita State University, where he was also director of the Kansas Writing Project. He went on to serve as Director of Freshman English at the University of Cincinnati before going on to Purdue. He is the author of *Writing Instruction in Nineteenth-Century American Colleges* and *Rhetoric and Reality: Writing Instruction in American Colleges, 1900–1985.*

Glenda L. Bissex's first book, *GNYS AT WRK: A Child Learns to Write and Read*, was a case study growing out of her research as a parent. A classroom teacher for more than ten years, she returned to classrooms as Researcher with the Vermont Writing Program. For the past five years she has taught the case study course in Northeastern University's Institute on Writing and Teaching, working with teachers of writing from elementary through university levels. Out of that experience came her second book, coedited with Richard H. Bullock, *Seeing For Ourselves: Case Study Research by Teachers of Writing* (Heinemann, 1987).

Patrick Bizzaro is Associate Professor of English and Director of Writing Across the Curriculum at East Carolina University in Greenville, North Carolina. He teaches courses in composition theory and practice, poetry writing, and English Romanticism, in addition to composition and technical writing. He is the author of six chapbooks of poetry, most recently *Undressing the Mannequin*, as well as a pair of textbooks, most recently *Writing with Confidence*. His articles have appeared in *College Composition and Communication, Language Arts*, and *Teaching English in the Two-Year College*, among others. His poems have won the Madeline Sadin Award from the *New York Quarterly* and the Poetry Prize from *Four Quarters*. He is currently poetry editor of *A Carolina Literary Companion* and codirector of the Coastal Plains Writing Project.

Edward P. J. Corbett is Professor of English at Ohio State University. He has served as Director of Freshman English at Creighton University in Omaha, Nebraska, and at Ohio State University. He was the Chair of the CCCC in 1970 and the Editor of *College Composition and Communication* from 1974 to 1979. He is the author of *Classical Rhetoric for the Modern Student* and of *The Little English Handbook*, and the coeditor, along with Gary Tate, of *The Writing Teacher's Sourcebook*. In 1986 he won a Distinguished Scholar Award at his university and a Distinguished Service Award from NCTE.

Donald A. Daiker is Professor of English at Miami University and Secretary-Treasurer of the Council of Writing Program Administrators. With Andrew Kerek and Max Morenberg, he coauthored *The Writer's Options* and coedited *Sentence Combining: A Rhetorical Perspective*. His work appears in *College Composition and Communication, Freshman English News, WPA*, and *Research in the Teaching of English* as well as in *The Territory of Language* (SIU), *New Methods in College Writing Programs* (MLA), *What Makes Writing Good* (Holt), and *Writing and Response* (NCTE).

Lester Faigley teaches in the English Department at the University of Texas at Austin. In 1986–1987 he was a senior fellow at the National University of Singapore, where he worked with M. A. K. Halliday and other linguists interested in the study of language from a social perspective. He is currently finishing a book on writing and politics.

Richard C. Gebhardt, English Department Chair at Bowling Green State University, is editor of *College Composition and Communication* and coauthor of *Writing: Processes and Intentions*. His essays on composition and its teaching have appeared in such journals as *College Composition and Communication, College English*, and *Rhetoric Review*, and in several collections, such as *Sentence Combining: A Rhetorical Perspective* (Southern Illinois University Press, 1985) and *Training the New Teacher of College Composition* (NCTE, 1986).

Kathleen Geissler is Assistant Professor of English and American Thought and Language at Michigan State University. In ATL she teaches a three-term course for first-year students that combines composition instruction with women's studies. In the English department, she supervises graduate teaching assistants, conducts sophomore-level and advanced writing workshops, and teaches courses in the history of rhetoric and in composition theory and pedagogy. Her research interests include literacy studies, gender and writing, and women's autobiography. She is currently working on the abolitionist and feminist writings of Jane Grey Swisshelm, nineteenth-century newspaper editor and publisher.

Diana George directs the First-year Writing Program at Michigan Technological University. She has been on the Executive Board of the National Writing Centers Association, and is currently serving on the Editorial Board of *The Journal of Writing Program Administration*. Her work in composition studies has appeared in *College Composition and Communication, English Journal*, and *The Journal of Teaching Writing*.

Nancy Grimm is the coordinator of Michigan Technological University's Reading/Writing Center. Her teaching includes experience at junior and senior high school, community college, and university levels. For the last ten years, she has taught first-year English, scientific and technical writing, journalism, literature, and content-area reading at Michigan Tech. She has also served as director of the local site of the National Writing Project. She has published articles about pedagogy in *College Composition and Communication*, the *Journal of Teaching Writing*, and *Academe*.

Sharon Hamilton-Wieler began her teaching career in a one-room eighth-grade school on the Canadian prairies. Seventeen years later, inspired by the work of James Britton and Harold Rosen, she resigned as chair of the English department in a suburban high school in Winnipeg, Manitoba, to undertake cross-curricular research of the writing of British secondary students through the University of London Institute of Education. This research provided the basis for her chapter in this collection of essays. An assistant professor of rhetoric and composition at Indiana University at Indianapolis, she is currently directing a research project that explores speaking-writing relationships in freshman composition classrooms set up as collaborative writing studios.

George Hillocks, Jr., is Professor in the Departments of Education and English at the University of Chicago. He taught junior high and high school English for eight years before moving to Bowling Green State University, where he taught English and served as director of freshman English. His articles have appeared in *Research in the Teaching of English, English Journal, American Journal of Education, American Educational Research Journal*, and *Educational Leadership*. His books include *Dynamics of English Instruction, Alternatives in English, Observing and Writing*, and *Research in Written Composition: New Directions for Teaching*. His current research is funded by grants from the Ford Foundation and the Benton Center for Curriculum and Instruction.

Ken Kantor is Professor in the Graduate School of the National College of Education. He directs the doctoral program in Instructional Leadership and teaches courses in writing, linguistics, and qualitative research. His publications include articles in *English Education, Research in the Teaching of English, Language Arts, English Journal*, and *Theory into Practice*. He also has chapters in several book collections. His current research interests are in the areas of curriculum theory, writing contexts, and teachers' practical knowledge.

Barry M. Kroll teaches composition and literature courses in the English Department at Indiana University. In his research, he has explored various aspects of writing development and the psychology of composition. He has coedited several collections of essays on writing, most recently, with Eugene Kintgen and Mike Rose, *Perspectives on Literacy*. Currently, he is working on a book about the students in his courses on the literature of the Vietnam War.

Andrea A. Lunsford is Professor of English and Vice-Chair of Rhetoric and Composition at Ohio State University. She has coauthored *The St. Martin's Handbook, Four Worlds of Writing*, and *Preface to Critical Reading*, and has coedited *Essays on Classical Rhetoric and Modern Discourse*. A past winner of the Richard Braddock Award (1984) for the best article published in *College Composition and Communication* and the MLA Mina Shaughnessy Award for the best book on the teaching of language and literature (1985), she is currently coauthor of *Singular Texts/Plural Authors: The Theory and Practice of Collaborative Writing* (with Lisa Ede), and *The 1987 English Coalition Conference: Democracy through Language* (with Richard Lloyd-Jones), and editor of *Alexander Bain's English Composition and Rhetoric*.

Max Morenberg teaches linguistics and directs the composition program at Miami University. He codirects the Ohio Writing Project and, with Mary Fuller, coedits the *English Language Arts Bulletin*. Along with Don Daiker and Andrew Kerek, he has written a sentence-combining text, *The Writer's Options*, a research monograph, and a series of journal articles. His research interests include developmental syntax and literary style. His introductory college-level grammar text, *Doing Grammar*, will be published by Oxford University Press.

Donald M. Murray, who received the Pulitzer Prize for editorial writing, is Professor Emeritus of English at the University of New Hampshire. He is a *Boston Globe* columnist, the paper's writing coach, and writes fiction and poetry as well as books on the writing process. His books include *A Writer Teaches Writing* (2nd edition), *Learning by Teaching, Expecting the Unexpected, Write to Learn* (2nd edition), and *Read to Write* (2nd edition).

Lee Odell is Professor of Composition Theory and Research at Rensselaer Polytechnic Institute, where he is also Director of Graduate Studies for the Department of Language, Literature, and Communication. He has edited three books: *Evaluating Writing, Research on Composing*, and *Writing in Non-Academic Settings*. He has served as Chair of the Conference on College Composition and Communication and as a member of the Executive Committee of the National Council of Teachers of English. He has consulted widely on writing-across-the-curriculum programs in colleges and universities and is presently completing a three-year study of the writing and thinking of public school students in mathematics, science, social studies, and English.

Ruth Ray is an Assistant Professor in the Department of English at Wayne State University, Detroit. Her research interests are in composition theory and applied linguistics. She is currently working on two major projects that have grown out of her own teaching. One is a study of women from various language backgrounds whose expectations for themselves as learners conflict with faculty expectations in American universities. The other is an examination of the meaning of "academic literacy" for non-native English speakers.

James A. Reither teaches courses in writing, rhetorical theory, and dramatic literature at St. Thomas University, Fredericton, New Brunswick, Canada. He has presented papers at CCCC, the Wyoming Conference on English, MLA, and CCTE. As well, he has given workshops on writing and knowing as social-collaborative processes at various colleges and universities and at several conferences, including CCCC. Founder and longtime editor of *Inkshed*, the newsletter of the Canadian Association for the Study of Writing and Reading, he has published articles in *College English, PRE/TEXT*, and elsewhere.

Tom Romano has taught high school students for seventeen years, all but one of those at Edgewood High School in Trenton, Ohio. Throughout that time he has been informed and instructed by the adolescents who have written, read, and talked in his classroom. His poems and articles have appeared in *Language Arts* and *English Journal*. His book, *Clearing the Way: Working with Teenage Writers*, was published by Heinemann in 1987.

Jeffrey Schwartz is currently Head of the English Department at Greenwich Academy in Greenwich, Connecticut. He formerly taught at Sewickley Academy in Pittsburgh, where the research in his article took place. For the past five summers with his wife he has codirected the computer room at the Bread Loaf School of English in Vermont. He is coauthor of *Word Processing in a Community of Writers* (Garland, 1989). His poems have appeared in many magazines and in a book published by alice james books in 1978.

Jack Selzer has been teaching graduate and undergraduate courses in composition and rhetoric, scientific and technical writing, and belletristic literature at Penn State since 1978. A cofounder of the Penn State Conference on Rhetoric and Composition and currently Director of Composition Programs, he has written about everything from *The Wanderer* and *Piers Plowman* to Faulkner and Cather (and baseball); but most of his published efforts have been attempts to make sense of technical and scientific writing. In 1990 he will become president of the Association of Teachers of Technical Writing.

Thia Wolf is Coordinator of Writing Across the Disciplines at California State University, Chico. She had previously been Director of Composition and a Mentor/Teacher for graduate students at California State University Northridge, where she also directed the University Writing Lab and the Writing-Across-the-Curriculum Program. She has published on writing anxiety, and her article on responding to student writing appears in a UCLA volume titled *Teaching Analytic Writing*. She was the first student to earn a doctorate from Miami University's graduate program in composition and rhetoric.

Robert P. Yagelski brings to the teaching of writing several years of experience as a freelance writer: his nonfiction articles and essays have appeared in such publications as the *Boston Globe*, the *Philadelphia Inquirer*, *New England Monthly*, and *Country Journal*; his first children's book, *The Lifting Bridge*, is scheduled for publication in 1990 by Bradbury Press. He has taught writing at the University of New Hampshire, at Vermont Academy, where he chaired the Department of English, and at Ohio State University, where he is currently a doctoral candidate in composition and rhetoric. He has published on the teaching of writing in *Radical Teacher* and the *Journal of Teaching Writing*.

Art Young is Campbell Chair in Technical Communication and Professor of English and Professor of Engineering at Clemson University in South Carolina. Previously (1976–87), he was Professor and Department Head of Humanities at Michigan Technological University at Houghton. He is the author of *Shelley and Nonviolence* (Mouton, 1975) and coeditor of *Language Connections: Writing and Reading Across the Curriculum* (NCTE, 1982), *Writing Across the Disciplines: Research into Practice* (Boynton/Cook, 1986), and *Writing Across the Curriculum: Programs, Practices, and Problems* (Heinemann, 1989). He currently serves on the College Section Committee of the National Council of Teachers of English.